Praise for *The Who Helped Win the War*

'She was a shining example of how to find a distinctive yet loyal role as a political spouse; in her case, of such an eminent but egocentric politician.'

Rachel Smith and Vince Cable

'It is often forgotten how voluntary action on the home front added to and supported Britain's armed forces during the First World War. Richard O'Brien's new book adds significantly to the scholarship on this subject as well as demonstrating how significant individuals, many of them women, were at the forefront of this vital addition to wartime solidarity and social capital.'

Dr Peter Grant, City St George's University of London, and author of *Philanthropy and Voluntary Action in the First World War*

'This exciting volume is an admirable companion study to the same author's *The Campaigns of Margaret Lloyd George* (Y Lolfa, 2022) which brought to the fore her active political campaigning during Lloyd George's peacetime Premiership from 1916 to 1922. This present work focuses on her key role as the dedicated wife of the wartime Prime Minister, considering mainly her work in relation to several welfare campaigns, the National Fund for Welsh Troops, sailors, food and economy, temperance and society, and hospitals and healthcare. It casts much valuable light on many aspects of the Great War and contains many striking illustrations.'

Dr J. Graham Jones

'Based on wide-ranging research and with fascinating detail, this book reveals the immense contribution to charities and the welfare of the British people during the demanding period of the First World War undertaken by Dame Margaret Lloyd George, once fittingly described as "the uncrowned Queen of Wales".'

Gwyn Jenkins, author of *A Welsh County at War*

'A long overdue look at the woman behind the great man.'

Dan Snow

The Woman Who Helped Win the War

THE WELFARE CAMPAIGNS OF MARGARET LLOYD GEORGE, 1914–1918

to Neal with thanks for all his encouragement.

Richard.

The Woman Who Helped Win the War

THE WELFARE CAMPAIGNS OF MARGARET LLOYD GEORGE, 1914–1918

RICHARD RHYS O'BRIEN

To my Cardi cousins, Yvonne and Eifion Davies

First impression: 2025

© Copyright Richard Rhys O'Brien and Y Lolfa Cyf., 2025

The contents of this book are subject to copyright, and may not be reproduced by any means, mechanical or electronic, without the prior, written consent of the publishers.

Cover photograph: © National Portrait Gallery, NPG x82383
Cover design: Y Lolfa

ISBN: 978 1 80099 640 3

Published and printed in Wales
on paper from well-maintained forests by
Y Lolfa Cyf., Talybont, Ceredigion SY24 5HE
website www.ylolfa.com
e-mail ylolfa@ylolfa.com
tel 01970 832 304

Contents

Acknowledgements 9

Introduction 11

Chapter 1 – Peacetime Prelude 18
(December 1913 to July 1914)

The Wartime Diary, 1914–1918

Chapter 2 – 1914: Onto a War Footing 30
(August to December 1914)

Chapter 3 – 1915: Campaigns Get Underway 33
(January to December 1915)

Chapter 4 – 1916: Last Year at No. 11 53
(January to December 1916)

Chapter 5 – 1917: First Lady, with Celtic Commitments 73
(January to May 1917)

Chapter 6 – 1917: The Uncrowned Queen of Wales 87
(June to August 1917)

Chapter 7 – 1917: Keeping Going 101
(September to December 1917)

Chapter 8 – 1918: Saving Money, Saving Lives 114
(January to April 1918)

Chapter 9 – 1918: Sustaining the Effort 123
(May to July 1918)

Chapter 10 – 1918: War Begins to Turn 133
(August to October 1918)

Chapter 11 – 1918: Peace at Last 145
(November to December 1918)

The National Fund for Welsh Troops

Chapter 12 – Establishing the Fund and Reactions (December 1914 to February 1915) — 156

Chapter 13 – The Fund Settles In (February to May 1915) — 173

Chapter 14 – Parcels for Prisoners, Flags for the French (June to September 1915) — 183

Chapter 15 – The War Office Steps In (October to December 1915) — 193

Chapter 16 – Coordinating with Wales (January to December 1916) — 207

Chapter 17 – Olwen Flies the Flag (January to March 1917) — 230

Chapter 18 – Treatment and Retraining (March to December 1917) — 239

Chapter 19 – From Comforts to Care and Children (January to December 1918) — 253

Recruitment, Sailors, Food & Economy, Hospitals & Healthcare, Temperance & Wartime Sobriety

Chapter 20 – Recruitment (1914 to 1916) — 266

Chapter 21 – Safe Havens for Sailors (1917 to 1918) — 287

Chapter 22 – Food and Economy (1917) — 293

Chapter 23 – Food and Economy (1918) — 315

Chapter 24 – Hospitals and Healthcare (1914 to 1918) — 336

Chapter 25 – Temperance and Wartime Sobriety (1914 to 1918) — 359

Endnotes — 380
Bibliography — 400
Index — 403

Acknowledgements

As with my first book on Margaret Lloyd George, for which this is the prequel, it would not have seen the light of day if my grandfather, the Rev. J. T. Rhys, had not left behind his treasure trove of papers. In making sense of it all, once again I am indebted to Dr J. Graham Jones, Emeritus Director of the National Library of Wales, who again has painstakingly reviewed and expertly critiqued my research, and also to Rob Phillips, Archivist of the Welsh Political Archive, and all the staff at the NLW for their enthusiastic assistance. I am also very grateful for the support of the Lloyd George family, notably to David Lloyd George, 4th Earl Lloyd-George of Dwyfor, for his review and encouragement of my work, to Angela V. John for her friendly and professional advice, to Annie Cottingham and Julie Green for their generous help, and to Peter Grant and Pete Alcock for their insights and encouragement as I investigated the complex world of welfare. Thank you also to all the team at Y Lolfa: to my editors Eirian Jones and Carolyn Hodges, to Alan Thomas for his design, and to Lefi Gruffudd for backing me, and most of all a big thank you to my wife Christine for her critiques and support.

'I felt proud at that moment that I had been able to help him even a little in bringing the war to a successful end and the country out of its darkest hour.'

Margaret Lloyd George

'Of the wives of Prime Ministers the noblest of them, in his opinion, were Lady Russell, Mrs Gladstone, and Mrs Lloyd George, and of these the greatest was Mrs Lloyd George. She was one of the greatest women Wales had produced and for all time the nation would be proud of her.'

The Rev. J. T. Rhys, lecturing in Tylorstown / Pendyrus, May 1923

Introduction

The Inspiration

THIS BOOK IS the 'prequel' to *The Campaigns of Margaret Lloyd George: Wife of the Prime Minister, 1916–1922* which brought to the fore her unprecedented political campaigning during the Lloyd George-led Coalition Government after the First World War. The inspiration for these books originates from my good fortune to inherit a unique archive of papers that my grandfather, the Rev. J. T. Rhys (JTR), accumulated during his time as the private secretary of Margaret Lloyd George at No. 10 Downing Street.

During the 1914–18 war, party politics were largely off the agenda but there were troops on land and sailors at sea to be supported, the injured to be cared for, and a country to be fed and economies to be made when shipping lanes were being blocked. Campaigning for social progress, health and welfare, women's rights and temperance remained as important as ever, albeit sensitive to the conditions of a country dealing with existential threat. War was devastating, yet it accelerated some social progress, not least in launching women into the workplace.

This book focuses on the continuous wartime efforts of Margaret Lloyd George in supporting these multiple campaigns when her husband was, successively, Chancellor of the Exchequer, Minister for Munitions, Minister for War, and from December 1916, Prime Minister.

Her story is one of someone who successfully used her position and visibility to encourage and comfort the thousands of people striving to win a long war at home and abroad. Illustrated with the perspectives of contemporary newspapers, letter writers, sketch writers and critics, and drawing on the correspondence and papers in the JTR Collection and key archives at the National Library of Wales, I hope it provides an accessible vignette on the ways in which the challenges of the war were tackled. The boom in volunteerism during the war was unprecedented and made a lasting impact on the country's development of welfare.

The Wartime Diary and Six Campaigns

This story is told in three main parts. After this introduction to wartime welfare and to her major campaigns, and an opening chapter (Chapter 1) on her pre-war undertakings, the first main part, her 'Wartime Diary', Chapters 2 to 11, provides a chronological review of her public work against the timeline of the ongoing challenges of war, cross-referenced with her major campaigns which are covered in detail, campaign by campaign, in the second and third parts of the book.[1]

The second part of the book, Chapters 12 to 19, follows the progress of her most distinctive campaign, the National Fund for Welsh Troops, which she established in late 1914 to provide 'comforts' for the Welsh troops at home and abroad, a campaign that owed much to the work of the Fund's Hon. Secretary, William Lewis, whose detailed minute-taking survives as a valuable archive at the National Library of Wales. (illustration 37)

The third and final part, Chapters 20 to 25, reviews five further campaigns. Chapter 20 records her strong support for the recruitment of a new Welsh Army, possibly seeming out of character for the humanitarian chapel-going Margaret Lloyd George, but very much in line with Nonconformist support for the 'just' war. Her campaigning, on which William Lewis also spoke with passion, would ease off when conscription was imposed in 1916.

Chapter 21 reviews her fund-raising for the Nonconformist British and Foreign Sailors' Society (BFSS), as the country's seafarers sought to keep supplies coming despite Germany's U-boat submarine attacks. By chance her appeal for funds began in December 1916 just as she entered No. 10 Downing Street. In this she was supported by my grandfather, JTR, who just as coincidentally had left his Swansea ministry to join the BFSS 'to do more for the war effort'. He became her private secretary at No. 10 in the spring of 1917, serving until 1922.

Chapters 22 and 23 cover her campaign to help the country feed itself and economise, ranging from the provision of communal kitchens and restaurants, and helping people make the most from scarce supplies through good housekeeping and improved domestic science training for women. A particular ally in this campaign was

The Inspiration

Lady (Sybil) Rhondda, the latter also supported by JTR. The recent research of Dr Bryce Evans in *Feeding the People in Wartime Britain*, on the National Kitchen phenomenon, draws out the economic, social, political and cultural choices that have to be made in times of crisis.[2]

Chapter 24, Hospitals & Healthcare, details her support of new hospital facilities, both for treatment of the wounded as well as against prevalent diseases such as tuberculosis, and championing child and maternity care. Reducing child mortality became even more urgent as the 'flower of Britain's manhood' was slaughtered on the battlefields. Here she supported the primary work of others, not least the surgeon Dr John Lynn-Thomas, and the health campaigner Lady Violet Mond.

The final Chapter 25, Temperance & Wartime Sobriety, continues her lifelong 'war against the drink', which in wartime also needed to ensure the Forces were sober, the workers were sober, and that barley and other grains were available for critical foods, so that the 'brewer's dray should not block the way of the ammunition waggon and the baker's cart'. Here she had the support of JTR, himself a noted temperance campaigner.

Running through all her activities was the support of all things Welsh (its people, jobs, music, culture, language, education), and advancing the interests of women and children.

Of course the 'campaigns of Margaret Lloyd George' were not the campaigns of some superwoman, singlehandedly fighting foes on all fronts. The detailed literature now available, not least Sally White's aptly titled *Ordinary Heroes: the Story of Civilian Volunteers in the First World War*, on the contributions of individuals and organisations, rich and poor, paid and unpaid, from all walks of life, throughout the war, is inspiring.[3] Vivien Newman's *We Also Served, The Forgotten Women of the First World War* also underscores to great effect the contribution of the many women who helped to win the war, at home and on the Front.[4] Margaret Lloyd George's contribution was to inspire and cajole, orchestrating meetings and smoothing rough edges, exploiting her prestigious vantage point of Downing Street and the Lloyd George name. In a period where there was an explosion of charitable organisations, it was important that people's generosity at times of austerity and stress was not squandered. In addition to the aforementioned William Lewis, and JTR, she was supported by an army of (mainly) well-networked women in a position to fly the flag, who on many occasions would plant the flag onto people's lapels in return for the change in their pockets, tapping into the deep well of generosity, however inspired. As Mrs Lloyd George was quoted as saying in mid August 1918, when victory in the field was looking more and more hopeful: 'My experience of social warwork teaches me that if charity is still a rarity, vanity is certainly not.'[5]

Wartime Welfare

> 'Masses of rather inarticulate people quickly got together and committees seemed to exude from the mass and to coagulate more or less at random.'[6]
> Mrs C. S. Peel, director of the women's service,
> Ministry of Food

The post-war reflection of Constance Peel on the population's instant response to meeting the welfare of others is as apt as it is inelegant. While the Liberal Party, under PM Herbert Asquith and Chancellor Lloyd George, had been building the foundations of public welfare, charitable provision and volunteering were still dominant. Two reports for the Royal Commission on the Poor Laws and Relief of Distress had recently been published, a 'Majority Report' arguing that charitable provision should continue to play a central role in the future development of welfare, challenged by a 'Minority Report' calling for the public provision of welfare, the approach championed by the Labour Party.[7]

As soon as war was declared, the people at large got to work, knitting comforts, raising money, volunteering in healthcare. *The Daily Chronicle* estimated that by February 1916, after nineteen months of war, people had donated £29 million to causes linked to the war.[8]

In addition, on the day war was declared, a cabinet committee was charged 'to advise on the measures necessary to deal with any distress that may arise in consequence of the war'. Two days later local government boards circularised all mayors and local authorities to set up local committees to oversee relief work – more than 300 were established.[9]

The very next day an emergency meeting of the Labour Party established its 'War Emergency: Workers' National Committee', producing a 'war manifesto' to protect working-class interests, listing

twelve demands for state aid and action – a clear exposition of the challenges ahead:
1. War relief should be merged and administered by the Government.
2. Labour representation (both male and female) on all national and local committees established in connection with the war.
3. Full provision out of public funds both for dependant allowances and comforts for soldiers and sailors.
4. Rates of allowances and war pensions should be adequate.
5. Establishment of cooperative canteens in all camps and barracks.
6. Provision of public works for the unemployed displaced by the war.
7. Active government encouragement to increase home-grown food supplies.
8. Protection against exorbitant price increases, especially for food.
9. A comprehensive programme of municipal housing.
10. The establishment of maternity and infant centres for workers.
11. Provision of free school meals.
12. A continuation of state control of the railways, docks etc. after the war.[10]

The speed of reaction reflects that this conflict was not a great surprise.

In his extensive study *Philanthropy and Voluntary Action in the First World War: Mobilizing Charity*, Peter Grant points out that while 'depending upon one's political persuasion, these demands were either utopian or a dangerous socialist threat ... by 1918, virtually all of them had been achieved and most had happened without direct popular action and many with the support of those entirely opposed to socialism.'[11] Demand number nine, on public housing, not war-related, remained a challenge for post-war governments, Lloyd George's 'Homes for Heroes' being only the start. More housing was started in 1924 by Ramsay MacDonald's short-lived first minority Labour Government. Demand number twelve, state control of key sectors, was another post-war issue, and remained contentious, not least with respect to the status of the coal mines, nationalised temporarily during the war.

Mrs Lloyd George's Liberalism was probably comfortable with most of these demands. From this manifesto her campaigns focused on comforts for troops, support for sailors, pensions, canteens, domestic food production, and maternity and infant centres for workers.

As to where responsibility lay, we may assume that she had no problem with increasing state support – her husband David Lloyd George, after all, was pioneering the welfare state. At the same time she was all for tapping into the available pool of donor funds and volunteer time. After the war, when wife of the Prime Minister, and appealing for donations for hospitals – still largely dependent upon private support – she would not shy from carefully expressing the need for more state support.

She began her wartime campaigning activities almost immediately, on home soil in north Wales and from 11 Downing Street, where she had been resident since 1908. She made the most of her prestigious address, living at the heart of government, but not being of the government, and was an effective networker, chair of committees, a popular and well-known figure, and skilful in avoiding the pitfalls inherent in being the wife of a powerful politician.

She championed causes in which she believed, playing to her strengths, seizing the opportunities open to her. Her campaigns adapted as needs changed. While she actively supported others' organisations and movements, one campaign, the National Fund for Welsh Troops, was largely her 'fiefdom', albeit one of many such funds around the country. When the explosion in voluntary and charitable activities had to be brought under greater government control, led by a new Director General of Voluntary Organizations, she was able to maintain the Fund's independence, not least a reflection of the efficiency by which it was run and the sense that she was someone who could be trusted and not cause embarrassment.

The volunteer-led charity sector, comprising some 18,000 organisations, raised around £150 million.[12] It is estimated that more than one million women knitted 15.5 million garments.[13] Many charities familiar to us today were born at this time, such as Save the Children, St Dunstan's for the Blind (now Blind Veterans UK), and the British Legion. Some activities ended as quickly as they had begun: a third of the 363 wartime communal kitchens closed within six months after the Armistice. However, many hospitals set up at the time (the State was slowly moving into healthcare provision) still operate today. The British and Foreign Sailors' Society (now the Sailors' Society) celebrated its second century in 2018. The Women's Institute celebrated its centenary in 2015. The work of welfare is never finished. As Peter Grant has put it:

> The First World War saw the greatest act of volunteering ever in Britain. Two-and-a-half million men volunteered to fight in a conflict that cost more than 700,000 of them their lives. There was, however, another act of volunteering between 1914 and 1918 on at least the same scale, though without the same life-and-death consequences. This was the voluntary effort at home especially to support the men at the front, in health and in sickness, but also to aid numerous other causes.[14]

The various campaigns of Margaret Lloyd George provide a further illustration of what it took to deliver the ambition of helping those in need.

CHAPTER 1

Peacetime Prelude

(December 1913 to July 1914)

'There yet remained a so-called "inevitable war",
the Franco-German War, or the Anglo-German war,
or the Russo-German war, or all three at once.'

M. le Baron d'Estournelles de Constant, July 1914

WE START OUR story just before the last peaceful Christmas, in 1913, before running through the last months of peacetime when Europe experienced one of the hottest summers on record and lurched towards one of the darkest periods in its history.

On 4 December 1913, Mrs Lloyd George was in Swansea, accompanying Lady (Violet) Mond, wife of local MP Sir Alfred Mond, at the foundation stone laying ceremony of the Rhyddings Congregational Church, the second that the Rev. J. T. Rhys (JTR) had rebuilt in south Wales.[1] As his parishioners put it: 'It is the lot of some ministers to go from place to place cleaning old chapels, Mr Rhys goes about building new ones!'[2]

Three years earlier, Lloyd George, who JTR had got to know since the early 1890s, had sent a supporting telegram when JTR had been inducted into this, his third parish: 'Parliament-street 3pm. To the Rev. J. T. Rhys, 19 Finsbury Terrace, Swansea. Success in your new sphere of activity. Congratulate your church on having received ministry of such an earnest and capable worker. Lloyd George.'[3]

Mrs Lloyd George also would have been aware of JTR's temperance campaigning. In 1912 he had dedicated, with permission, his research book, *Wales and its Drink Problem*, to her husband.

At the December 1913 ceremony, after several brief speeches, she confided to him that 'she wished the speeches were equally as short in the House of Commons, because then they would be able to do their work with greater expedition than at present.'[4]

The persistent fund-raiser JTR had one regret:

> In expressing his gratification at the consummation of their labours, he said that the only thing he felt sorry for was that it was a fine day. (Laughter) He had been praying most earnestly for the stormiest day that year to happen, as nothing would so appeal to their hearts and pockets as to experience for themselves under what distressing conditions the church had had to work in the old building. If they had warm weather in the summer the building got intolerably hot; in winter the roof rattled horribly, and if it rained they had almost to put up their umbrellas. (Laughter) It was the first unkindness the chairman had ever done him, to bring fine weather with him from London. (Loud applause)[5]

The Chancellor's wife used the opportunity to deliver a favourite homily, on a little debt being a stimulation for further effort:

> Mrs Lloyd George, received with loud applause, said she had come there merely as a spectator, but she was very glad to see that they in that church were in the same spirit as David, King of Israel, in not being satisfied themselves to dwell in comfortable houses and worship God in a tin tabernacle. (Applause) She reminded them that the Temple of David, that was built by his son, was built silently. All the wood and stone was brought there ready dressed so that there should be no hammering, and she hoped that the church would be built in the same way, quietly, without strife, and with plenty of brotherly love. (Applause)
>
> They would have a debt of about £1,500 in the beginning, and when they went on to build a schoolroom they would have a debt of between five and six thousand. A debt was a good thing for a church to have as long as it was not too heavy, and a small debt stimulated a church to activity and to work. (Applause)
>
> She was a member of the Welsh Calvinistic Methodist Church, and in London they had about 15 or 18 churches, some of them in the poorest parts of London. They had had a crushing debt, and some two years ago they decided to have a national collection to put the churches on a proper footing for doing national work. They collected £6,000, and they wanted

£10,000, so they had a big bazaar, and got £4,000. (Applause) It was the greatest blessing. People got to know each other better, and many talents were discovered through it. (Applause)[6]

The organiser of the 1912 London Welsh National Bazaar was the Welsh Calvinistic Methodist shipowner William Lewis, who had served on a Board of Trade committee in Lloyd George's time. In 1915 he would join Mrs Lloyd George in Downing Street to run her Welsh Troops Fund. Perhaps he was one of her 'discovered talents'.

JTR's Swansea chapel would be opened on 3 September 1914, a month into wartime, at a cost of £3,600 but with £2,000 already paid.[7]

Lady Mond had invited Mrs Lloyd George late in the day to support JTR's event, quite possibly as Swansea MP Sir Alfred Mond had been unable to attend. It is likely that Mrs Lloyd George was in town to present awards to the elder girls of the Swansea elementary schools on the subject of mothercraft, which she did the following day, at Lady Mond's 'Mothers and Babies Welcome' at the Mond Buildings. *The Cambria Daily Leader* reported: 'Mothercraft is one of the subjects which is taught at the Mothers and Babies Welcome, and the work has been so successful that it has been taken up by the Educational Authorities, and been carried into other districts.'[8] Mrs Lloyd George would often visit on future occasions.

Lady Mond, an active child and health campaigner, was well known to JTR: a *Lady Mond Recipe Book*, published in aid of his church's funding, survives in the JTR archive, with recipes from local women, including three from my grandmother Jane Annie Jones, her mother Margaret, and adopted sister Violet.

These Swansea events, supporting churches, education, and childcare, were typical of Mrs Lloyd George's peacetime causes. They also introduce three important participants in her work: William Lewis, Troops Fund Hon. Secretary; J. T. Rhys, working with the sailors, campaigning on temperance and food, and as her private secretary; and Lady Mond on healthcare and education.

Three years after her visit to Swansea, almost to the day, Margaret Lloyd George would become wife of the Prime Minister, while JTR in November had left his Swansea parish and moved to London.

The last sweltering summer of peacetime

We now fast-forward towards the sweltering summer of 1914, via Berlin. Mrs Lloyd George was not only well known at home, but was also becoming a target for European April Fool humour:

> On April 1st the *Berlin Illustrated Gazette* printed a photograph of Mlle. Polaire, the French actress, who has a great shock of hair, with the words, 'New suffragette tactics: Mrs Lloyd George has sworn not to comb her hair while her husband declines to grant women the vote.'[9]

Perhaps the closest Mrs Lloyd George came to being the poster girl of suffragism. Though opposed to violent suffrage action, and by her own admission a slow starter in the cause of women's suffrage, she was very active in the advancement of opportunities for women and girls, in health, employment, and education, noting in 1917: 'Every girl, like every boy, should have a profession.'[10] With very clear principles with respect to her responsibilities as a mother, a wife, and housekeeper, her more moderate approach meant she could fall short in the eyes of the women's movement. Her position was undoubtedly influenced by frequent suffragette attacks on her husband. During the war, however, the suffrage movement desisted from further violence, and by 1918 many women over 30 finally won the right to vote in parliamentary elections.

The merry month of May 1914 kicked off with a May Day Ball in London for one thousand guests, hosted by Sir Alfred and Lady Mond in honour of their debutante daughter Eva, and well attended by the London Welsh.[11]

On 11 May Mrs Lloyd George and Mrs Asquith (unaccompanied by their husbands), attended the Covent Garden Royal Gala, in the presence of the King and Queen, and 'more than 30 royalties'. Perhaps the Chancellor and PM had an inkling that a suffragette would harangue the Royal Box during the interval: the occupants reportedly paid no attention.[12]

Four days later Lloyd George did accompany his wife to a Palace banquet for the King and Queen of Denmark.

The month continued with a visit to Salisbury to support the local Nonconformists who were raising funds for their Sunday schools. Noting that 'the object of the bazaar was to wipe out one debt and to plunge them into another in order to rebuild their schools', she underlined the importance of child welfare, of having 'sanitary and well-ventilated rooms for the sake of the children and young people', and expounded on the importance of Sunday schools, reminding her audience that attendance in Wales was lifelong.

She concluded with a word in favour of voluntary aid as opposed to the State's, and a closing call for women's suffrage:

> Commenting upon a remark by the Rev. T. Collins that they could not go to the Chancellor of the Exchequer for a grant, Mrs Lloyd George said she thought the Voluntary system was much better. She noticed a great many chancellors of homes in attendance, and she hoped they had so arranged the finances of their households that something could be spared to make purchases from the stalls. Women rendered valuable help at bazaars, although they were voteless. Some looked forward to the time when they would find themselves on more equal terms with the men. (Applause)[13]

A week later, in Camberwell, south London, she revealed who had denominational bragging rights in the Lloyd George household, while helping her husband's Baptists pay their ministers:

> Mrs Lloyd George opened at the Surrey Masonic Hall, Camberwell, yesterday afternoon, a bazaar organised by the south London churches in aid of the Baptist Union Sustenation Fund ... Her husband, she added, was a great Baptist, and although she herself was a member of the Calvinistic Methodist Church, she was very regardful of the Baptists. It was a feather in the cap of her husband that only one of their children had followed her, the other three being Baptists.[14]

Her next engagement, on Saturday 23 May, was pure politics, accompanying Lloyd George to the Ipswich by-election, gaining more electioneering experience, a skill she exploited after the war. On their return to Cricieth for the Whitsun Bank Holiday, suffragettes disrupted an outdoor address by Lloyd George, an unexpected consequence being she was unable to travel that afternoon to Ruabon for another bazaar.

Shortly afterwards, she addressed a baby show near Caernarfon, at Rhostryfan, promoted by the Llanwnda District Nursing Association, combining child welfare campaigning and temperance.

It was, she said, the first gathering of the kind she had ever attended. Such competitions were capable of rendering valuable help in producing a healthy and sturdy race. There was nothing she detested more than the unwholesome 'dummy' and if she had her way she would destroy every one of them.[15]

Another departure for which she pleaded was the enrolment of all children under seven years of age in the temperance society called the White Ribbon Army. Mothers should know that it was wrong to dose their children with gin or other forms of alcohol.

Relating an incident from her own domestic circle, Mrs Lloyd George said that when rearing her first-born she was, according to a frequent practice among the country nurses of those days, offered some bread and beer. This she resolutely refused. Crestfallen and disappointed, the nurse left the room and confided to others in the house her fears that she (Mrs Lloyd George) would never recover to rear the child. (Laughter) She, however, reared that boy and four other children without the aid of either gin or bread and beer. (Hear, hear)[16]

JTR's wife, my grandmother, secretary of her local women's temperance association, and member of the White Ribbon Army, had also declined her doctor's advice to drink Guinness. (illustration 85)

Whitsun over, it was time to return to London for the hot 'summer season', beginning by hosting an 'At Home' at No. 11 for the Women's Liberal Federation, with representatives from all over the country, following the federation's earlier council meeting at the Portman Rooms, Baker St.[17] The women's suffrage paper, *The Common Cause*, was less enthusiastic about the Liberal women's commitment to the cause, who failed, 400 to 465 votes, to pass a motion that would have pledged them not to support anti-suffragist candidates: *viz*. 'That in order to ensure that the next Parliament shall contain a majority of members pledged to vote for the enfranchisement of women, this Council urges all Liberal women to help only those candidates who fulfil this condition.'[18] How Mrs Lloyd George voted is not recorded.

On 28 June, a car took a wrong turning in faraway Sarajevo, bullets were fired, and the world turned on its head within a month.

On 30 June, Mrs Lloyd George was on the guest list for a very Welsh reception given by Mrs Ellis Griffith (wife of the Home Office Under-Secretary) at Radnor-place, Hyde Park, London, where 'the rooms were cooled by large blocks of ice concealed by shrubs'.[19] Ice was in great demand that summer, cooling drinks, rooms and theatres.

The same evening, she deputised for her husband at a Savoy dinner with French and Belgian journalists who were visiting Britain's watering holes. Also attending were mayors of several seaside resorts including Bangor, Caernarfon, Conwy, Pwllheli and Tenby. The tourism business would be enjoying its last summer for a while.

Other attendees whose names still resonate today included J. L. Garvin, then editing both *The Pall Mall Gazette* and *The Observer*, Gordon Selfridge, the American founder of the eponymous store, and the explorer Ernest Shackleton and his wife. The distinguished French diplomat Baron d'Estournelles de Constant, senator and Nobel Peace Laureate (for keeping the peace between rival colonial powers), spoke of the *entente cordiale* and the hope for peace. M. le Baron was clearly concerned:

> The *Entente* had served as a means of education unequalled in the whole world. It had put an end to the legend of so-called inevitable wars, but it had not yet limited the expenses of armed peace, which had increased paradoxically with the progress of general security, so that they had become to-day the great menace of international peace and of social peace.
>
> There yet remained a so-called 'inevitable war', the Franco-German war, or the Anglo-German war, or the Russo-German war, or all three at once. France and England reconciled must act with Russia, with the United States, with the large majority of the truly peace-loving states, so as to be in a position to demonstrate to Germany, in her turn, that her interest was to do away by mutual concessions with the legend of inevitable war.[20]

Ernest Shackleton would avoid the first years of war: on 1 August his ship *Endurance* left the Thames *en route* for the South Atlantic, only to be trapped in the winter ice and finally abandoned in October 1915. He would return to Britain in May 1917. Margaret's daughter Olwen later related that, while her father had not responded positively to Shackleton's request for Treasury money, in 1912 he gave the explorer City contacts who might help, asking Shackleton to let him know how he got on. When Shackleton returned to report his funding success, he quipped: 'They said if I were to take you with me and leave you in the Antarctic they would treble it!'[21]

The social round continued with a First of July ball given by Lady Julia Henry, at 5 Carlton Gardens, in honour of the coming of age of her son Cyril.

> A temporary ballroom was erected in the garden and kept beautifully cool, for the sides of the marquee were open, and the terrace, together with Lady Dudley's terrace, which she kindly lent, was covered with delightfully cool sitting-out places. Supper was served at little tables dotted about the garden, and in one of the big rooms at the Automobile Club, which adjoins, and the dance was a brilliant success in every way.[22]

Lieutenant Cyril Henry would be killed at the age of 22 at the Battle of Loos in September 1915. Lady Henry would later set up a day and night crèche for the munitionettes' children at the Woolwich munitions factory. (illustration 27)

The next week Mrs Lloyd George was off to the Central Hackney Liberal Radical Association's annual garden party in the grounds of the Hackney Reform Club.[23]

And then to Nottingham for a Liberal assembly hosted by Lady Boot and her husband Sir Jesse Boot, who had transformed his father's pharmacy business into that well-known national retailer, his wife Florence, daughter of a Jersey bookseller, playing a significant role in developing the company's retail business, notably cosmetics and books, and promoting employee welfare. She became a company director in 1917.[24]

The press described the summery scene:

> The tree-girt lawns of 'Plaisance', the charming Trent-side pleasure grounds of Sir Jesse and Lady Boot, were gay with colour yesterday afternoon, when, in glorious summer weather, some 1,000 members of the Nottingham Women's Liberal Union assembled to greet, with the utmost enthusiasm, Mrs Lloyd George, the wife of the Chancellor of the Exchequer.
>
> They were all more than delighted to have Mrs Lloyd George with them, for they had expected her on two or three previous occasions, and that was why they made a determined effort to secure her presence that day. Unfortunately, their guest was not quite well and was afraid it would

be impossible for her to make a speech; but through the telephone that morning the speaker had informed her that the Liberals of Nottingham would be satisfied if they only saw her (laughter and applause) so that she had pleasure in asking Mrs Lloyd George to say, 'How do you do.'[25]

Their visitor did manage a short speech, encouraging her 'fellow women workers', hoping that:

> ... the men of Nottingham were in as good spirits as the women. At present women could help the men to send Liberal members to Parliament, but she hoped soon they would have the vote themselves – (applause) – and when they had the suffrage extended to them she felt quite sure three Liberal members would be returned for Nottingham. (Applause)[26]

At times Mrs Lloyd George would not be able to fulfil all her promises – in February her daughter Olwen had stepped in for her at a Liberal Social Council 'At Home' at the Municipal Hall, Tottenham,[27] but the next day the Liberal women of south London had been less forgiving when she sent a late apology for not being able to attend, as president, the annual meeting of the Croydon Women's Liberal Association. She had already missed the summer garden party, 'due to an indisposition', but this time honesty wasn't the best policy when she said she had to be in Cricieth for 'a property transaction'. The chairman stopped short of calling for a vote of censure, but proposed 'they would do better to elect a president in a less exalted position instead of one whose face they, as an association, had not yet seen'.[28] *The Nottingham Evening Post* headlined its coverage scathingly: 'Property before Duty.'[29] Perhaps that had been an added spur not to disappoint Lady Boot's Nottingham gathering in June.

On 14 July, there was another 'brilliant' reception, given by Lady Reading at 82 Curzon Street, attended by the Asquiths, Lloyd Georges, Winston Churchill, Monds, and many others.[30] Lord Reading, Rufus Isaacs, had a long association with Lloyd George, not least both surviving the 1912 Marconi insider trading share scandal. In 1921, when Viceroy of India, Reading would appoint Olwen's husband Tom Carey Evans as his personal physician. The Monds' daughter Mary would marry the Readings' son Gerald.

By now Margaret Lloyd George had spent more than six years in Downing Street, at No. 11. An active contributor to the Liberal

Women's Association (*pace* Croydon), she spoke on the multiple issues in the Liberal Party's active reform programme and often stood in for her husband, later observing, 'I am in effect my husband's second in command.'[31] In January *The Daily Mirror* had observed that Mrs Lloyd George 'is considered now such an attractive platform speaker that she is in requisition almost as much as her husband, though, of course, she only accepts a tithe of the invitations she receives. Her speeches are always interesting enough to be generally reported.'[32]

She even outranked Prime Minister Herbert Asquith, if you believe the powerful liquor lobby, expressed in a mocking comment at the annual meeting of the Chester-le-Street and District Licensed Victuallers' Association: 'In the future they had been promised by Mr Asquith, and by even greater authority, Mrs Lloyd George, that a new Licensing Bill would be sprung upon them.'[33]

Temperance was a lifelong campaign for Margaret Lloyd George, as it was for my grandfather.

On 16 July, she attended a reception for Norman Angell, the lecturer, journalist, and writer who had been riding high on the success of his book *The Great Illusion*, positing that war was no longer possible, as it no longer paid. That illusion was about to be shattered. Other familiar names at that reception, hosted by Lady Barlow at her 19 Carlton Terrace home, included the Monds and George Bernard Shaw, his play *Pygmalion* having just been launched – possibly a source of gossip was the word 'b****y' uttered by the flower-girl.

But the metaphorical clouds were gathering, less than three weeks after the Sarajevo assassination of Archduke Franz Ferdinand, heir presumptive to the throne of Austria-Hungary, and of his wife Sophie.

The next evening, 17 July, Mrs Lloyd George accompanied her husband to the annual Mansion House banquet for bankers and City merchants. As Lord Grey's 'lights' were about to start flickering before they 'went out all over Europe', the Chancellor, while warning of labour challenges at home and the perils of the Irish question, tried to put a calm face on things: 'In a reference to the international situation, he said there were always clouds in the international sky, that there were clouds even now, but his view was that common sense, patience, and forbearance would pull us through.'[34]

A week later, on 23 July, Mrs Lloyd George and her daughters Olwen and Megan were among the many invitees for Mrs Asquith's garden party at No. 10, guests including the German ambassador,

Prince Lichnowsky, and the Serbian minister, where 'a number of small tea tables were dotted about on the lawn, and a string orchestra played during the afternoon. Mrs Lloyd George, in a black and gold cloak and white feathered hat, had Miss Lloyd George, in powder blue, and her little daughter Megan with her.'[35]

Prince Lichnowsky was doing all he could to avert war, afterwards generally regarded as a 'good German' for his efforts. Foreseeing catastrophe for the world and defeat for Germany, he argued his case in a series of cables to Berlin, including one sent two days after the Asquith garden party, urging Germany to accept King George's V's offer to mediate between Serbia and Austria-Hungary. Ultimately he was ignored, if indeed the offer was ever shown to the Kaiser.

On 28 July, precisely one month after Gavrilo Princip fired his fatal shots, Austria-Hungary shelled Belgrade, beginning hostilities. On 4 August, after Germany invaded Belgium, Britain declared war. Supposedly 'over by Christmas', the conflict lasted four years, three months and two weeks. Not 'the war to end all war', but many things changed for ever.

It was time to get prepared. Out would go parties on the lawn, party politics, and suffragette attacks, as the country sought a degree of unity to meet an external threat which had now become reality.

THE WARTIME DIARY
1914–1918

CHAPTER 2

1914: Onto a War Footing

(August to December 1914)

*'The Liberals of Cricieth united with the
Conservatives in holding a bazaar in aid of the
National Relief Fund and the Red Cross Society.'*
Lincolnshire Echo, August 1914

ON BANK HOLIDAY Monday, 3 August, the day before Britain declared war on Germany, gunboats arrived in Caernarfon Bay 'arranged as a result of the Town Council's request to the naval authorities and through the influence of Mrs Lloyd George, who sent a letter to the Admiralty.'[1]

The next day, with daughter Olwen, and sister-in-law Mrs William George, she attended a Cricieth meeting setting up a local Voluntary Aid Detachment (VAD), where Olwen signed up to nurse. (see p.336)

In addition to the recruitment of nurses, Mrs Lloyd George threw her support into the recruitment of volunteers for the army, especially the newly proposed Welsh Army, an effort that would last until compulsory conscription was introduced in early 1916, the war by then in its second year.

With party politics sidelined, the focus of fund-raising was changing:

> The Liberals of Cricieth, who contemplated holding a bazaar in aid of a new Liberal Club, postponed the project, and on Wednesday united with the Conservatives in holding a bazaar in aid of the National Relief Fund and the Red Cross Society. The opening ceremony was performed by Mrs Lloyd George, who said it would be a help, inspiration, and comfort to our

brave soldiers and sailors to know that those at home were looking after the dear ones they had left behind and were doing all they could to soothe and help their wounded comrades.[2]

The bazaar was held at her home, Brynawelon, on 26 August.[3]

The National Relief Fund (NRF) had been set up two days after war was declared (the Prince of Wales as Treasurer) to aid servicemen and their dependants. Almost simultaneously Queen Alexandra announced an appeal for the existing Soldiers' and Sailors' Families Association (SSFA). Both funding projects were soon amalgamated under an Executive Committee.[4]

Though the NRF raised funds quickly – £2 million in the first two months, eventually reaching £7 million – the challenge lay in the distribution of the money, with 'confusion between entitlements and charitable gifts'. It eventually came under state control. The large amounts raised showed how much social spending was possible, arguably bringing 'the potential of a welfare state a step closer'.[5] The need to add greater coherence to the booming charity work prompted Mrs Lloyd George's setting up of her Troops Fund later in the year.

Refugees to house

By October, with Belgium overrun by Germany's troops, there were refugees to succour. Mrs Lloyd George made available a house inherited from her parents: 'Mrs Lloyd George has placed Llys-Owen, Criccieth, at the service of a committee for use as a home for 12 Belgian refugees. The house, which occupies a delightful situation overlooking Cardigan Bay, is being furnished in readiness to receive the Belgians, who are expected to arrive on Saturday.'[6] (illustration 6)

These refugees were from Dinant, which had already suffered badly, many civilians being executed – and a Lieutenant Charles de Gaulle being wounded. In the more peaceful 1840s it was the home of Adolphe Sax, the creator of the saxophone.

Perhaps it was the Belgians' arrival that prompted her to take French lessons, becoming quite proficient after six months. Dinant residents were most likely French rather than Flemish speaking.[7]

Germany's invasion of Belgium had triggered Britain's entry into the war, bolstering the case that this was a 'just' war.[8] (see p.270) Considerable solidarity was felt in Wales towards the suffering of small nations such as Belgium and Serbia, the first to be caught up in the 'Great Power' conflict. By June 1915 there were 265,000 Belgian refugees in Britain, 'the largest refugee movement in British history'.[9] In January the *Carnarvon and Denbigh Herald* filled almost two columns with over 400 names (including that of Mrs Lloyd George), addresses, and amounts donated, as weekly subscriptions or gifts in kind, to the Carnarvon Belgian Relief Fund, as wartime giving surged.[10]

Newspapers later would be filling their columns with battlefield casualties.

On Monday, 9 November, she accompanied her husband to the annual Lord Mayor's Banquet at the Mansion House in the City, preceded by a more military parade than usual:

> The Invitation Card in this historic year marks a departure from what is customary. The design is essentially symbolical of the present European War, embodying as its principal features the flags and coats-of-arms of the Allied Nations – Great Britain, France, Russia, Belgium, Japan, and Servia [*sic*]...[11]

The next week they joined their son Gwilym in Northampton, where he was billeted with his regiment. (see p.271)

Mrs Lloyd George was now getting close to establishing her most significant independently-run war campaign, her Troops Fund. The inaugural Fund meeting took place at No. 10 on 11 December. (see p.157)

The Lloyd Georges celebrated Christmas and New Year in Cricieth, attending a Boxing Night patriotic concert given by the children of the local council schools,[12] and perhaps visiting their Dinant guests.

In France, some German and British troops declared their own Christmas truce, sang carols, exchanged gifts, and kicked a football.

CHAPTER 3

1915: Campaigns Get Underway

(January to December 1915)

> 'Do not let us forget that there are hundreds
> of thousands of women who want to serve,
> but who can do nothing else except help their own
> homes, suffering and waiting patiently.'
> Margaret Lloyd George, November 1915

THE CHANCELLOR'S WIFE stayed in Cricieth until mid January, leaving the first two Troops Fund committee meetings, held at No. 11, to be chaired by Lady Glanusk. Mrs Lloyd George chaired the third and fourth meetings, on 18 and 25 January. (see p.163) Establishing a firm foundation for the Fund would be a primary task in 1915, not least when the charity boom faced new regulations. As war intensified Mrs Lloyd George continued her familiar campaigns: temperance, healthcare, supporting the churches, supporting her husband as his responsibilities moved from managing the country's money to equipping the forces with much needed munitions, and furthering the opportunities for women.

A family announcement

In late January the Lloyd Georges had news concerning one of their own soldier sons:

The engagement is announced of Captain Richard Lloyd George, eldest son of the Chancellor of the Exchequer, and Miss Roberts, daughter of Sir John Roberts, solicitor, Carnarvon, who received a knighthood in 1911. Captain R. Lloyd George is now at Llandudno, on the staff of Brigadier-General Owen Thomas, who is in command of the First Brigade of the Welsh Army Corps.[1]

Richard's engagement was later called off. In April 1917 he married Roberta McAlpine, the daughter of Robert, the founder of the eponymous construction and engineering company. In 1921 Gwilym, Richard's younger brother, married Edna Gwenfron Jones, the sister of a Mayoress of Caernarfon.

Death in the darkened streets of London

On 23 January, Margaret Lloyd George would undoubtedly have been shaken by the death of an old friend, knocked down by a bus in a darkened Whitehall, shortly after leaving No. 11:

SWANSEA LADY'S DEATH: KNOCKED DOWN BY MOTOR BUS: An inquest was held in London on Saturday on Mrs Emma Kate Freeman, of St Leonard's terrace, Chelsea, widow of the late Mr Thos. Freeman, tinplate manufacturer, Swansea, and sister-in-law of Mr Llewelyn Williams K.C., M.P. Mrs Freeman was killed by a collision with a motor-bus on Friday evening when leaving Downing street after making a call on Mrs Lloyd George.

Mr Llewelyn Williams K.C., M.P. identified the body as that of his sister-in-law. Mrs Freeman was rather short-sighted and wore glasses. Miss Uline Barbier, Kensington, said on Friday afternoon she met Mrs Freeman at 11 Downing street. They left together about 6 and started to cross Whitehall. They had reached the first refuge and the witness had her head turned momentarily from the deceased, and when she looked round again she saw Mrs Freeman lying on the ground in front of the motorbus, which had pushed her along. The night was very dark. The jury returned a verdict of 'Accidental death', and exonerated the driver from blame.[2]

She had long been a prominent worker and speaker with the Liberal party, and was always a leading figure in the great party gatherings. A charming and vivacious personality, she was very popular in Wales and in London-Welsh circles, and enjoyed the close friendship of Mr and Mrs Lloyd George.[3]

1915: Campaigns Get Underway

Kate's late husband had been Mayor of Swansea.

Miss Uline Barbier was the 26-year-old, Cardiff-born, youngest daughter of a French-born professor at the University of South Wales in Cardiff. Her sister Marie, Madame Raoul Vaillant de Guélis, would run the 14 July French Flag Day in Cardiff. Perhaps it was in that connection that Uline was in Downing Street.

In 1895, Lloyd George had written an encouraging letter to his wife: 'You have more brains than you give yourself credit for. Mrs Freeman was telling Towyn Jones on Monday that you were the very essence of commonsense. She never met anyone so thoroughly sensible. That is exactly my opinion.'[4]

Kate Freeman's brother-in-law, W. Llewelyn Williams, was a long-time ally of Lloyd George, but they fell out over conscription. On Monday 25 January the Lloyd Georges attended Kate's funeral at Highgate Cemetery.

The *Bolton Evening News* voiced concerns that the accident reflected the dangers of blackout. The first Zeppelin bombing raid on Britain had occurred on the night of 19 January, with two casualties in Yarmouth. *En route*, bombs were dropped on King's Lynn, causing three casualties – the Chief Constable said to have been slow to switch off the street lighting.[5]

> London's Darkened Streets. The fatal accident which happened last evening in Whitehall to one of two lady friends who had been calling upon Mrs Lloyd George is another instance of the peril we are suffering from the darkening of the streets and of the way it takes its toll. If the existing state of things had to be maintained many months, some scheme would probably be devised whereby more light would be available, subject to a provision whereby it could all be switched off on a warning from the outer watchers. The airships move fast, but the action of a well-regulated mechanism should be speedier, and most nights it should be possible for observers to give information of the approach of an airship. There need be no fear of excitement in such cases. The British public decline to be alarmed, despite all the efforts of the Germans to frighten them.[6]

Funding negotiations with the Allies

In the first week of February the Chancellor of the Exchequer left for Paris for an emergency conference with Britain's 'Triple Entente' Allies, France and Russia, to strengthen their financial arrangements, not least to increase the supply of munitions. His special wartime passport, 'not valid for the zone of the armies', is one of the more special articles in JTR's archive.

Welsh funds from America

In his absence Mrs Lloyd George retired to Wales to chair a meeting in Caernarfon called to discuss the best way of making the most of a gift of £1,500 (a somewhat smaller amount than the sums being discussed in Paris) that had been sent direct to her husband from Welsh donors in America.

> DISTRESS FUNDS FROM AMERICA: SYMPATHY OF OVERSEAS COMPATRIOTS: The conference decided that Mrs Lloyd George, Messrs. Joseph Davies, Cardiff, R. Silyn Roberts, and J. Owain Evans should act as an executive to administer the funds; that district or parish committees should appeal for assistance through their secretaries to the executive, and that Mr J. Owain Evans should act as secretary. It was resolved that this fund should be reserved for cases which cannot be dealt with under the regulations of the Prince of Wales Fund.[7]
>
> It was explained that there was no distress anywhere in Wales, except Carnarvonshire and Merionethshire, and the conference resolved to use the money to alleviate the suffering in these two counties.[8]

While the suggestion of limited distress might seem surprising, it was not exceptional. At the outset of war there was much concern with regard to the potential for great hardship, while the reverse was the reality: the increasing numbers of men joining the army led to low unemployment, the greater problem being shortages of labour and skills, and generous state payments helped avoid great distress. By October 1915 London decided to reduce staffing for its Unemployment and Distress office to a small staff.[9] That said, under the patronage of HRH Princess Christian, a National Guild of Housecraft was established to help educated women rendered distressed by the war, giving them free training in housekeeping, and for those who intended to emigrate, providing them with 'the skills needed to apply for highly paid posts in America and the Colonies'.[10]

The executive appointed to run the 'Lloyd George American Relief Fund' were well placed. Joseph Davies, a country magistrate living in Cardiff, and Liberal parliamentary candidate for Crewe, was appointed chairman and he and Owain Evans, secretary, had both been appointed to the Cabinet Committee to deal with Unemployment and Distress. Mrs Lloyd George was appointed treasurer. Subscriptions to the Fund eventually reached £8,750. When Lloyd George became Prime Minister, Joseph Davies became a member of Lloyd George's inner circle, joining his five-member No. 10 'Garden Suburb' secretariat. Knighted in 1918, Sir Joseph was elected MP for Wrexham, Mrs Lloyd George giving him support on the election hustings.

Owain Evans was the National Health Insurance Commissioner for north Wales. To aid those needing support after the wartime collapse in demand for slate, he sought to persuade the War Office that slate would be better than timber in roofing military huts.[11] Well known to the Lloyd George family, later known to Richard Lloyd George's son Owen as Uncle Jack, his barrister son David Eifion Evans (Uncle David) would marry Roberta (after her 1933 divorce from Richard Lloyd George).[12]

R. Silyn Roberts, a former slate-quarryman, Crown bard at the 1902 National Eisteddfod, and Welsh Calvinistic Methodist minister, was active in seeking commissions for Welshmen in the armed forces. A Labour member of the Merioneth County Council, he also campaigned against tuberculosis. After the war he was appointed commissioner for Wales to organise training for disabled ex-servicemen.[13]

The Lloyd George American Fund trustees would keep a close eye on progress, together visiting the projects and the people that the monies would support during the war. They also co-opted two textile industry experts, Ralph Green and Philip Williams, to the committee. Philip Williams also advised Mrs Lloyd George's own Troops Fund in sourcing comforts for the army. In the first two years of war, the socks made at wool workrooms were distributed to the Troops Fund, but as output increased they were sold under contract to the military at market prices.[14]

Toy-makers in the Vale of Clwyd, Denbighshire, were also recipients of the American benevolence. In February, Mrs Lloyd George joined a British Toy Association committee, along with children's writer Edith Nesbit, writer Pett Ridge, and illustrator John Hassall (who would design a poster for the 1916 St David's Day Flag Day), in a toy-making promotion project. (illustration 9) Many toys had been imported from Germany, and already with an eye on the next Christmas, it was realised that toy-making in homes could enable people to earn money in straightened times.¹⁵ Production increased rapidly – wooden toys, dolls, trains, dolls' houses – and alongside furniture-making proved an occupation for which war-disabled men could train. A Miss Mary Heaton had founded the Vale of Clwyd Toy Company in May 1914.

The Welsh toy-makers were not the only people eyeing a new opportunity, as the *Stratford-upon-Avon Herald* would warn in August:

> THE TOY-MAKING INDUSTRY. The Chinese are adopting German business methods in order to capture the world-wide German toy-making trade. This will be a fresh blow to the Huns, who are beginning to see that they will be ruined even if they were to win the war. The Chinese Government is sending experts to America and other countries to collect samples and study the markets, and is subsidising this new industry at home.
>
> As regards cheap labour, China will easily beat the Black Forest, but elaborate and expensive machinery plays an important part in the toy-making industry, and in this section Germany leads the world. We, too, are establishing toy factories, and many private and organised efforts are being made to promote village small-ware industries. We have made great progress in recent years in establishing technical schools, but our educational system is more concerned for training the mind than the hand, and if every child had to learn some trade or handicraft it might go far to revive countryside prosperity.¹⁶

On 11 August 1916, they visited the wool workrooms:

> WELSH WOOL FOR THE FRONT. The workrooms set up by the Lloyd George American Fund Committee at Penygroes, Bethesda, and Blaenau Ffestiniog for the purpose of making socks, etc. were on Friday visited by Mrs Lloyd George, Mr and Mrs Joseph Davies (Cardiff), and J. Owain Evans, secretary. No fewer than 15,000 pairs of socks have been ordered by the various units to be sent direct to the Front. Welsh wool is being used in this undertaking, an industry which, it is hoped, will be encouraged after the war with a view to providing employment in districts which have suffered by the depression in the slate trade.¹⁷

In February 1918, after their visit, it was reported: 'Sock-making for Welsh Troops Creates Jobs in north Wales: The three towns are turning out an aggregate of between four and five thousand socks weekly, while the circulation of about £4,000 annually in wages alone in the hard-hit quarrying centres is a veritable boon.'[18]

In July 1918, a bride and groom in Blaenau Ffestiniog were given a guard of honour by the local knitting centre workers, who wore their new uniform given to them by Mrs Lloyd George and Sir Joseph Davies.[19]

When the Lloyd George Fund was wound up, in 1925, the workrooms and equipment were sold to others prepared to continue the industry. Overall, 500,000 pairs of socks were sold, and £7,000 paid in wages to the women employed.[20]

A political wedding

On St David's Day, 1 March, while Welsh women were selling flags for the Troops Fund in London and in Wales, the Lloyd Georges reviewed the nascent Welsh Army in Llandudno on a bitterly cold day that would confine the Chancellor's wife to bed for much of the month. (see p.277 and illustration 5) Her next reported public engagement was shortly after Easter, on 8 April, at St Margaret's, Westminster, the church of choice for politicians to tie the knot. Mrs Lloyd George, in shot-blue silk, and her husband joined Queen Alexandra, two princesses and the political world at the wedding of Neil Primrose, Liberal MP for Wisbech, second son of former Prime Minister Lord Rosebery, to Lady Victoria Stanley, daughter of the 17th Earl of Derby and great-granddaughter of the 14th Earl of Derby, Prime Minister (1866–1868). The groom would serve in Lloyd George's government, before dying of his wounds in Palestine in 1917.[21]

Mrs Lloyd George missed the two April Fund meetings, before chairing the three meetings held in May and June.

MAY 1915

On 4 May, she listened to her husband deliver what would be his last budget speech in the House of Commons, where he dropped his plans for beer and wine duties – defeated by Irish Nationalist and Conservative opposition.[22]

The Right to Kill

That evening the *Daily Mirror* gossip columnist thought the Chancellor's wife was a 'little shocked' at the theatre:

> After the Budget Speech. Dressed in pale grey satin, Mrs Lloyd George was in a box at His Majesty's Theatre on Tuesday night. She sat in the corner nearest the stage, and I fancy was just a little shocked by some of the rather brutal situations in *The Right to Kill*, which Sir Herbert Tree has correctly described as 'a play for grown-up people'. The Chancellor of the Exchequer was also there. He came in a little late.[23]

The play, translated from the French, and a melodrama set in Constantinople, posed the question: 'If a woman is being tortured by a man, has a third party the right to intervene and kill the torturer?'[24]

The wartime diarist Samuell Pepys Junior, writing in the style of the seventeenth-century diarist, explained in his 'Diary' entry for 5 May:

> To His Majesty's playhouse, being bidden of Sir H. Tree, who would know my mind concerning a new play called *The Right to Kill*. He plays a French count, a Quixotish fellow, that loves secretly another's wife, and kills her husband to get from him a writing that confesses her adultery with another man, which I doubt any man should do outside a play or a novel. What pleased me most was A. Bourchier's playing of a sly Turque, chief of the Sultaun's police, the scene being laid in Constantinople, which they do call Stamboul, after the Turques' fashion.[25]

Throughout the war the self-styled Samuell Pepys Junior ran his quirky commentary in the campaigning paper *Truth*, founded by the late anti-feminist Liberal politician Henry Labouchère, his diary entries later published in three books, in 1915, 1917 and 1919.

On 7 May, a German submarine torpedoed the liner *Lusitania* off Ireland. One thousand, one hundred and ninety-nine lives were lost, including 128 American civilians. D. A. Thomas, later Lord Rhondda, and his daughter Margaret were among the survivors, the latter being picked up from the sea, fortuitously kept afloat by a wicker chair, her rescuers initially thinking her to be a fatality.[26]

On Thursday, 13 May, the Lloyd Georges attended the Welsh Calvinistic Church, Charing Cross, for a memorial service for

William Jones, the Welsh Ministerial Whip, Liberal MP for Arfon in Caernarfonshire since 1895, and Junior Lord of the Treasury since 1911.

The following afternoon they were at the Kingsway Hall, Holborn, where Lloyd George unveiled a portrait of the late Rev. Hugh Price Hughes, Wesleyan Methodist social campaigner, founder of the West London Mission and of the *Methodist Times*. Hughes had led the campaign to persuade Methodists, traditionally Conservative, to support the Liberals. JTR would perform a similar role in 1922, interviewing Nonconformists who were wavering in their support for his Coalition government.[27] The Rev. Hughes is still remembered in a series of lectures.

A fortnight later, on 25 May, Lloyd George left the Treasury to become the first Minister of Munitions, as the country moved into Coalition government under Prime Minister Herbert Asquith. It is thought neither Uncle Lloyd nor his wife were in favour, Lloyd George writing in response: 'Judging by your & Uncle Lloyd's letters you will disapprove of my action in taking this new job. I am quite convinced that I have done the right thing & that you will agree with me when I have time to put the matter before you.'[28]

In his filial memoir Richard Lloyd George's recollection was that his mother steered clear of the subject, in his words, 'adhering to a lifelong policy of non-interference'.

However, the Lloyd Georges remained at No. 11, the deal being that Lloyd George would return to the Treasury later, Reginald McKenna taking on the Chancellorship in the interim.[29] Richard recalled his mother facing the immediate possibility that Lloyd George would sequester the three rooms at No. 11 used by the Troops Fund for his new job, only for him to acquire the Government-commandeered Metropôle Hotel for the new ministry.[30]

Methodist debts

On Wednesday, 26 May, the wife of the Minister of Munitions continued to support debt-burdened churches, this time helping her own 'galvanised' Methodists in Bangor. Conscious of the many calls being made on people's generosity, her comments in praise of volunteering were a model of her style of remarks on these occasions:

MRS LLOYD GEORGE AT BANGOR: CHAPELS AND THEIR DEBTS: A sale of work with the object of liquidating the debt on the New English Wesleyan Schoolroom, Bangor, was held on Wednesday at the Schoolroom. Mr J. R. Davies (Ceris), who presided, said he understood that if they raised £100 that day they would be entitled to an equal sum from a Wesleyan fund established for that purpose.

He said they were all glad to help each other in this woeful matter of paying debts, which was one of the most terrible calamities that afflicted our country, for there was not a single denomination (except the Church of England, which insisted on having the money before beginning to build) which did not begin to build before they got the money. The Calvinistic Methodists, or the 'galvanised Methodists' as they had been called, had a bad habit of building their churches first and then thinking how they were to get the money to pay for them, but he hoped that in the good days to come these troubles would be solved.

Mrs Lloyd George said she thought the Wesleyans of Bangor were very enterprising to have a bazaar now, when there were so many calls upon the public. We had volunteered to look after the Serbian wounded, and in this matter Wales had done very well, and also to do our best for the French and Russians and all who were fighting with us, and especially the Belgians. There was a Welsh church in London which spent £10 a week in keeping Belgians, and there was another Welsh church there of only 200 members, not one of whom was a rich man, which spent £3 a week in keeping a house and a family of Belgians.

It was difficult for congregations to keep up their chapels and to subscribe to these charitable objects as well. But everything was voluntary in this country, and they were proud of the fact. All their young men were coming forward voluntarily in a really wonderful manner. No other country could equal that. (applause) All Nonconformists had to rely on voluntary contributions to keep their chapels going, and the sacred edifices dotted about the hills and valleys of Wales were monuments of the voluntary system. Mr Davies had expressed the hope that they would get the money to pay off their debt that day but she had been told it was a bad thing to pay off the debt altogether, as a little deficiency was an incentive to work, so she hoped there would be a small deficiency that day. (laughter) She had pleasure in declaring the bazaar open. (applause)[31]

Her Troops Fund had already been seeking money from the chapels.

At the end of May she had her own anxieties when seeing Olwen, albeit 'a little under age', off to France to serve with the Red Cross.[32] Not front-line nursing but 'over there':

> Miss Lloyd George, daughter of the Minister of Munitions, left Victoria yesterday afternoon for Folkestone en route for France, where she will take up duty as a Red Cross nurse. Other Red Cross nurses – including Miss Dorothy Hudson, daughter of Sir Robert Hudson [the head of the British Red Cross Society] and members of the St John Ambulance Association made up a party of a half-dozen. After leaving Downing Street Miss Lloyd George made a hurried visit to her father at the Munitions Department, and then drove with her mother and sister to the station. Mrs Lloyd George stated that the services of her daughter – who was particularly keen to 'do her bit' – would probably be utilised at one of the rest camps.[33] (illustration 67)

Olwen, in fact, soon found herself scrubbing the platform of Boulogne railway station, ready for the arrival of the hospital trains. (see p.339)

That evening London experienced its first Zeppelin raid.

JUNE TO JULY 1915

Temperance for the troops, the Palace and the nurses

On 3 June, Mrs Lloyd George continued her war against drink at a temperance military concert in Cricieth, encouraging the soldiers, and Parliament, to follow the Royal example (King George having been persuaded by Lloyd George to ban alcohol in the Royal Household). (see p.360) She then returned to London to entertain Welsh Methodists, who were hosting their annual assembly.[34] On 7 June, she chaired the one Fund committee meeting held that month, reviewing plans to get comforts to Welsh prisoners of war. (see p.183) On 10 June, she encouraged nurses to be abstemious (see p.362) and later that month presented her daughter Megan (and others) with book prizes at the Clapham Welsh Calvinistic Methodist Church (her London spiritual home).[35]

Looking after Megan

She then took a short break at the Llandrindod Wells spa with Megan, but could not keep a wholly low profile when attending the anniversary of the Sunday school at the local Congregational church where:

> ... the new minister [the Rev. D. Arthur Davies] thought he saw Mrs Lloyd George, together with her daughter, Miss Megan, enter the church. During the service he ventured to welcome them on behalf of the church, and to assure the lady of the good wishes of the whole congregation for herself and husband. The minister took some risk in making his statement, for he had never seen Mrs Lloyd George before. A conversation with her at the close of the service, however, confirmed her identity.[36]

The 13-year-old Megan was the Lloyd Georges' only child yet to have flown the nest, their two sons and eldest daughter now in war service. Mrs Lloyd George's own commitment still included looking after Megan in the school holidays when the latter was not at boarding school.

While in Radnorshire, on 18 June she made her last army recruitment rally appearance (before compulsory conscription came in). (see p.278)

Megan had been unwell, causing her mother to miss a meeting regarding the Belgian Repatriation Fund, in Hampstead, London.[37] Mrs Lloyd George also excused herself from a meeting of the Women's Auxiliary of the National Council of Free Churches held at the Welsh church, in Charing Cross Road, London, where it was noted that 'she had been obliged to go into the country to her little girl, who was now happily better'.[38] Under discussion were plans for a new maternity and training home in Wiltshire for unmarried mothers.[39]

Child mortality was much higher then, and in 1907 the Lloyd Georges had suffered the very sudden loss of their eldest daughter, Mair, after an operation for appendicitis. The apple of her parents' eyes, her brother Richard later wrote, 'She would have outshone us all in her accomplishments as well as her saintliness.'[40] To some extent their affection and hopes transferred to Megan.

The two July Troops Fund meetings, on 5 and 12 June, were chaired by Lady Glanusk in Mrs Lloyd George's absence.

On 11 July, Mrs Lloyd George and Megan were joined in Llandrindod Wells by Lloyd George, just returned from the Front. He could never get away from it all, not least because of a threatened Welsh coal miners' strike over pay. It was a critical moment in the effort to keep everything on an even keel at home.

> GALLANT MINERS: LLOYD GEORGE'S SPEECH AT A CONCERT: Mr Lloyd George said he had really come to Llandrindod Wells for rest, quietness, and recuperation, but the invitation of the chairman to attend the concert was simply irresistible.
>
> The Army needed coal quite as much as the Navy did, as without an abundant supply they could not manufacture the explosives which were to give their brave men a chance in this terrific struggle. The colliers had shown great patriotism. Over 200,000 had already enlisted. If anything, the colliers had been too patriotic, for they were really wanted more at the coalfields where they could help their comrades at the Front in more effective manner. On the battlefield the miners had shown immense bravery. Their conduct had equalled the very best. He had heard of them from the Front; they were most tenacious soldiers – almost too reckless. (cheers) He made a strong appeal to the miners who were left behind to work harder than ever and concluded his brief impromptu speech by moving in complimentary terms a vote of thanks to the chairman, the performers and the choir.[41]

A week later the Minister of Munitions would visit Cardiff and, to his credit, after meeting miners and coal owners, the latter were persuaded to concede ground under certain conditions and a strike was averted. Diarist Samuell Pepys Junior offered his own take on the transaction:

> News this morning that Ll. George hath got around the cole-men, being to that end despatched into Wales by the Ministers, who did think, it seems, to set a Welchman to catch a Welchman. But whether his getting round them be but another word for giving way to them, of this I do greatly doubt.[42]

Flags for the French

On Monday, 12 July, after 'a very hearty send-off outside Gwalia Hotel' the Lloyd Georges motored to Stratford-upon-Avon for a short stay and thence to Leamington, taking tea at the Regent Hotel before Lloyd George and Megan took the train for London, Mrs Lloyd

George preparing to travel to Cardiff to attend the French Flag Day.[43] (see p.186)

AUGUST 1915

One year into hostilities, Mrs Lloyd George represented the Minister of Munitions at the 5 August St Paul's Cathedral service, marking a day across the British Empire of 'solemn intercession for the success of the Allied arms in the war', attended by the King and Queen. Practically all the Cabinet were present.[44] She then left for a north Wales summer break.

The Land of My Fathers

On 7 August, after participating in the Bangor National Eisteddfod, the first since 1913, the Lloyd Georges and Megan visited Bangor's university, meeting Sir John Morris-Jones and Professor Lewis Jones, two professors compiling a new book for the Troops Fund, *Gwlad fy Nhadau, Rhodd Cymru i'w Byddin, The Land of My Fathers, Wales' Gift to its Army*. (illustration 12) Sir John was another ardent proponent that men should enlist to fight the 'just' war. They were joined by Sir Vincent Evans and Llewelyn Williams MP. Also present was the draper Sir John Prichard-Jones, of the Dickins & Jones London store, a generous university benefactor.[45]

Llewelyn Williams would shortly be helping the Minister of Munitions at Whitehall Gardens, even though a fracture in their relationship was imminent:

> On Monday Mr W. Llewelyn Williams, K.C., M.P., takes up a position as a sort of law officer of the Crown, unpaid. There are, it appears, some 30 to 40 Acts of Parliament, emergency and otherwise, which affect the Ministry of Munitions, and, of course, that Ministry being of such recent creation, many questions of a legal character, as yet unsolved, have arisen and are likely to arise. Last week, Mr Williams offered his services to Mr Lloyd George, and the latter gladly accepted them with a view to elucidating from the legal points of view these points. The hon. member commences his honorary task to-day, and will continue, as far as is at present arranged, at the Ministry of Munitions during the long vacation, thus placing his holidays at the service of the country. He returned yesterday from north Wales, where, since the National Eisteddfod, he has been the guest of Mr

and Mrs Lloyd George. The Minister of Munitions, who has spent the week-end at Criciteh, is also expected back at Whitehall Gardens to-day.[46]

Like Lloyd George, Llewelyn Williams had opposed the Boer War but supported this war, in support of Belgium – but he would draw the line at conscription.

On 29 August, at Westbourne Park Chapel, London, Mr and Mrs Lloyd George and daughter Megan attended the retirement service of the Baptist preacher Dr John Clifford, who Mahatma Gandhi would later cite as one of the early models of passive resistance.[47] Dr Clifford campaigned against the Boer War, though his reputation for passive resistance was born primarily from his opposition to the 1902 Education Act, which he regarded as an exercise in imposing denominational teaching in schools. Though he had condemned the press for its hostility to the Germans in the run-up to the 1914 war, he supported British participation as a response to German violation of Belgian neutrality.

With summertime news scarce, there was room for gossip, whether on Mrs Lloyd George's early search for a cup of tea in London, or on a wife's place in the world.

> Mrs Lloyd George, wife of the brilliant Minister of Munitions, is a native of Wales. Speaking of her first visit to town, Mrs Lloyd George once made this confession: 'I remember coming to London. It was one Sunday afternoon. One of the things which struck me most about it was that we could not find any place where we could get a cup of tea. The public-houses seemed the only places open.'[48]
>
> Mrs Lloyd George, despite all the influences of London and position, still retains a simple, natural, womanly charm. 'It used to be thought, years ago, that women should do nothing outside their homes, or beyond the kitchen and the nursery,' she told an audience on one occasion. 'That time has long passed, of course, but still the home should be her first consideration.' Mrs Lloyd George's home and her children have always been her first consideration, and even now that her husband is earning as many thousands a year as he formerly earned hundreds, she still keeps up but a comparatively modest establishment. Two or three maidservants, generally from Wales, and a boy for the rougher work, is her usual domestic staff.[49]

She did have three homes to look after, in Cricieth, in Surrey, and in Downing Street. Wales, Walton, Whitehall.

While in north Wales she called in at her old school, Dr Williams', Dolgellau.[50]

SEPTEMBER 1915

On 1 September, Olwen returned to France after a leave of absence, seen off on the boat train at Victoria Station by her mother, sister and some lady friends. This was her final Red Cross assignment abroad, serving at Hesdigneul-lès-Boulogne rest station until November.[51] She would then work at Devonshire House, Piccadilly, the Red Cross HQ, until June 1916.

On 17 September, her mother and sister accompanied Lady Mond to Netley, near Southampton, where a moveable Welsh hospital had been built in short order in October 1914. (see p.341)

The Troops Fund committee met on 6 and 27 September, Mrs Lloyd George in the chair, and some fresh faces were also recruited to the committee. In the last three months of 1915 the Fund committee met 12 times, Mrs Lloyd George chairing all but two sessions, as it carefully negotiated a new arrangement with the new War Office regulator Sir Edward Ward, retaining its independence while keeping a strong focus on delivering those comforts deemed necessary to the troops in the field. (see p.192)

Supplying Christmas puddings was deemed out of scope. On this decision, not all their 'customers' might have agreed, as one Welsh soldier, Sapper Dewi David of the 53rd (Welsh) Infantry Division wrote home from Salonika: 'At the base we were at last, I had a square inch of pudding allotted to me – that was another gift. But just wait till your parcel with that Xmas Pudding in it arrives for me – By Gum, I won't half give it socks.'[52]

'Socks', in this case, being schoolboy slang for a treat, as opposed to knitted comforts.

Serbian flag day in London

On 22 September, the day after Chancellor Reginald McKenna's first budget, Cabinet ministers arriving in Downing Street ran a gauntlet of ladies 'in the Welsh national costume out of compliment to Mrs Lloyd George' selling Serbian flags.

Mrs Lloyd George was in charge of the Westminster depot and Mrs H. Samuel occupied a similar position at Paddington. Well-known actresses, among them Miss Louie Pounds [mezzo-soprano, D'Oyly Carte Opera], Miss Iris Hoey [stage actress, later in films], Miss Phyllis Bedells [ballerina], Miss Dorothy Minto [actress], and Mlle Delysia [French musical theatre] were helping.[53]

Like the flag of France, the red, white and blue Serbian flag at the time was known as the Tricolor (as it is today).

OCTOBER / DECEMBER 1915

In October, in Swansea, Mrs Lloyd George's future private secretary, the Rev. J. T. Rhys, had been 'enlisted' by the War Office, in that he was appointed officiating minister to the Swansea garrison.[54] He had also been busy criticising the liquor trade for objecting to the wartime curbs on drinking.

On 9 November, it was Cinema Day, with most of the country's cinemas donating all or part of their takings to the Red Cross.[55]

On women in the war

On 5 November, a long interview with Mrs Lloyd George, conducted by MP and social campaigner Percy Alden, was published, focusing on the role of women in the war. In addition to praising the nurses at home and abroad (see p.337), she applauded the Women's Emergency Corps, even if not all employers were sufficiently enlightened to take them on:

> MLG: You will remember that the Women's Emergency Corps was started only two days after the declaration of war. It was not then known in what direction help could be most effectively given, but in a time of national danger and emergency it was thought that such an organisation would be able to co-operate with the authorities without loss of time, and if necessary be adapted to any contingency that might arise. This work originated with the Women's Suffrage societies, and naturally it has swept into its ranks large numbers of women of independent means. I believe in the first fortnight it received and classified 10,000 candidates, doctors, nurses, interpreters, motorists, and the untrained

who desired training and were willing to do anything that was offered to them.

The result of their enterprise can now be seen everywhere in the country, for apart from what one may call the main service of war, thousands of women have been placed in situations in connection with trams, buses, and railways, thousands more are taken on by the big commercial undertakings, and a very large number are engaged in munitions works. In that connection perhaps I ought to add that the Munition Workers' Auxiliary Committee fulfils a useful function in relieving the ordinary women workers at arsenals and munition factories. For the most part they are engaged on Sundays. There is, you are probably aware, a hostel at Woolwich which they use for the time being while engaged at Woolwich Arsenal.

PA: I imagine that the Women's Emergency Corps is really a kind of clearing house for women's labour. I know that they have a good many departments, for I have frequently recommended people to apply to their organisation for assistance.

MLG: Yes. I think it is true to say that they would be able to supply almost anyone you required. You yourself have hinted that they have assisted in Holland with the Belgian refugees, but they have also done a very great deal for the Belgians in this country. They met them at the stations and saw them safely to their various destinations, supplying them with clothes and food. There is a Hospitality Department which looks after both refugees and stranded Englishwomen.

At one time they had a section of women engaged in toy making. These are now for the most part on munitions work. Some 20,000 applied for this kind of work, but I am not able to give figures as to how many of them were actually engaged. Many thousands applied for agricultural employment and where the farmers are sufficiently enlightened they have been taken on. Unfortunately, it frequently happens that the farmers are rather conservative in outlook, and, not being in the habit of employing women, refuse to engage them.

I am perfectly certain there is room for the tens of thousands of women in munitions. A great deal of the labour is necessarily unskilled, requiring alertness and dexterity, but nothing much more. If men are to be released for service with the Colours, it is certain that women must continue to take their places.

Perhaps, however, some the most useful work has been accomplished by women in connection with the canteens. I believe canteens are run not only at Woolwich and Enfield by Lady Lawrence, but also at Euston,

Victoria, and other stations connected with the YMCA. Labour has been supplied through the Labour Exchange for the making of tents, respirators, and clothing, and a large number of clerks have been sent to Government offices.

PA: What about the future of women when the war is over, Mrs Lloyd George?

MLG: I do not think there is very much doubt that they will play a larger part in the life of the country, and they deserve to. Think of what they have suffered, and what they have achieved. I trust that men will not misjudge them, and will repay their services after this time of conflict has passed by fair and due recognition. Meanwhile, those who are working for wages must be well paid, and must see to it that the standard of living is not lowered. Above all things, we must care for their health, for if we undermine the health of these women, many of whom are comparatively young, we are destroying the possibilities of the future. May I add one more word if you have space?

Do not let us forget that there are hundreds of thousands of women who want to serve, but who can do nothing else except help their own homes, suffering and waiting patiently. We are apt to forget, in the midst of all the rush and turmoil of this war, that women give their sons and their husbands. Every shell that bursts in a British trench tears a wound in some woman's heart.[56]

Women were not missing the opportunity to demonstrate their value in the workplace, for those who needed convincing.

Asquith / Bonham Carter wedding

November closed with a strong Liberal turnout (including the Lloyd Georges) at St Margaret's, Westminster, for the wedding of Violet Asquith, daughter of the Prime Minister, and of Maurice Bonham Carter, his private secretary.[57] Violet Bonham Carter would prove to be a notable campaign opponent for Mrs Lloyd George in 1921, their 'Battle of the Amazons' enlivening the Cardiganshire by-election, a contest that hardened the Liberal Party divide.[58]

Virtual and non-appearances

Just before Christmas there was even a rumour that the busy Mrs Lloyd George had been sighted across the Atlantic:

The following is from the *Welsh-American* (Pittsburg, Pa): Mrs David Lloyd George was in Lorain (Ohio) today. Now wait a minute, don't get excited, and we will tell you all about it. You see, the students of Lowell school had a big exhibit at their institution this afternoon. Each child was asked to exhibit some of its work – the boys training and the girls sewing. So one girl, Elisabeth Williams, of No. 177 East Thirty-first street, daughter of W. H. Williams, a member of the school board, dressed a doll in the same style of clothes worn by Mrs Lloyd George, wife of the great English statesman. That's how 'Mrs David Lloyd George' came to be in Lorain today.[59]

In truth, a customary winter cold was curtailing her engagements, and a visit to the Welsh community in Bethnal Green (let alone Pennsylvania) was missed.[60] She was also attracting the attention of younger observers nearer home – in Bangor a 15-year-old student, Miss Mem Williams, delivering a paper on Mrs Lloyd George at the local literary society, at the Ebenezer Schoolroom. Another paper was presented on Florence Nightingale.[61]

Christmas was spent in Cricieth with Lloyd George and their two daughters, their 'two soldier sons [being] abroad with their regiments'.[62] She closed her year at a Cricieth temperance demonstration with the campaigner Agnes Slack, on 29 December. (see p.362 and illustration 82)

CHAPTER 4

1916: Last Year at No. 11

(January to December 1916)

'The change of hostesses at No. 10 is one of the *coups d'état* of these epoch-making days in which we're fashioning the new England.'

'Blanche' of *The Bystander*, December 1916

JANUARY / FEBRUARY 1916

ON 12 JANUARY 1916, a little history was made when Mrs Lloyd George chaired and spoke at a meeting of the Agricultural Organisation Society (AOS) that set up the Cricieth Women's Institute (WI), the fifth in the UK. The WI was taking off, north Wales its launching pad (on 25 September 1915, in Anglesey), building on ideas from Canada. One of the WI's Canadian founders, Mrs Madge Watt (who emigrated to Britain), attended the Cricieth meeting. The AOS supported the WI's development with funds. WI members would play their part in feeding the country in a time of shortage.[1]

Two days later, on 14 January, Mrs Lloyd George chaired the Troops Fund committee, preparing for William Lewis to travel to Swansea to persuade the borough to work with the Fund. (see p.207) On the 24th she was personally handing cigarettes and chocolates to recruits training on London's Hampstead Heath. (illustration 17)

On 4 February, the Minister for Munitions joined the distaff side of the Liberal Party leadership when Mrs Lloyd George and the newly-married Violet Bonham Carter, Asquith's daughter, visited a YMCA dining room for munitions workers, run by Clementine, Mrs Winston Churchill, 'the fairy godmother of the enterprise', who organised and worked at several dining rooms across north-east London.[2]

On 9 February, the Lloyd Georges attended the St Margaret's, Westminster, funeral service for the Rt Hon. Russell Rea, former MP for South Shields, Junior Lord of the Treasury, a ship-owner with businesses in Cardiff and elsewhere.[3]

On 23 February, she attended an auction in Wrexham in aid of the Troops Fund (see p.211), and visited the Croesnewydd Military Hospital, formally opening a new X-ray installation, funded by a private donor.

MARCH 1916

The first of March 1916 witnessed the second St David's Day Flag Day in London in aid of the Troops Fund, the scale growing each year. Nursing a cold, Mrs Lloyd George directed operations from No. 11. She had missed the London Welsh Stage Society's matinée performance, 'under the fund's patronage', at the Haymarket Theatre on 29 February,[4] but did attend the London Opera House celebration on St David's Day. (see p.218)

On 14 March, at the British Women's Hospital Star and Garter Fund matinée at the Criterion Theatre, Piccadilly, run by actress and theatre manager Mary Moore, she was seated in the dress circle rather than the stalls, it becoming 'a more popular spot especially for charity shows, where there was less coming and going, sometimes a chance of hearing what the stage had to say over the chatter of programme girls.'[5]

At the end of April diarist Samuell Pepys Junior reportedly gave his six pen'orth to the cause:

> Up, and going abroad, was on all sides beset with women that would sell flaggs, and to get money for the Starr and Garter Tavern in Richmond, being to make of it an hospice for broaken soldiers, and to be done, they profess, by the women of England. Whom I did resist a long while, conceiving it an impudent thing that, if women would do this, they beg men to pay for it. But, in fine, a pretty wench has 6d. of me in Piccadilly.[6]

On Saturday, 25 March, the Lloyd Georges' visit to the Welsh military hospital at Netley was cancelled as the Minister of Munitions had to meet M. Thomas, his French opposite number.[7] She also missed back-to-back temperance meetings in south Wales on 28 and 29 March. (see p.364)

APRIL 1916

On 12 April, at the Catford Hill Baptist Church in south London, observing again that it was a bold venture to be holding bazaars in wartime, she noted that debt tended to paralyse church work and they had to keep the lights burning, a slight revision of her standard homily that a little debt sustained the incentive to improve.[8]

Since January, Mrs Lloyd George had been chairing twice-monthly the Troops Fund committee. On 13 April, she chaired two sub-committees, the first on prisoners-of-war parcels, and the second preparing for a fund-raising auction of paintings to be held in May at the Mendoza Gallery, Old Bond Street. (see p.223) Lady Glanusk would chair the final July meeting, and Violet Douglas-Pennant the only other summertime meeting, in September.

On 17 April, the Lloyd Georges reviewed a demonstration of trench warfare with the visiting Prime Minister of Australia, the Welsh-born William 'Billy' Hughes (known as the 'Little Digger') and his wife Mary. On the global stage Lloyd George would be merely the second premier of Welsh heritage. (illustration 49) The Lloyd Georges and Billy Hughes would also attend a recruitment rally in Conwy in May.

That month Mrs Lloyd George also became one of the numerous patronesses of the French Wounded Emergency Fund.[9] While in Wales she opened a new TB hospital in Caernarfon. (see p.345)

MAY TO JUNE 1916

Some gifts being donated for fund-raisers were thought of as being sub-par, as *The Cambria Daily Leader* reported: 'A satirical London publication asks if Mrs Lloyd George was not a bit disappointed at the quality of some of the jewellery that was sent her for the sale in which she has taken such an active interest?'[10]

Perhaps such criticisms encouraged the establishment of the Jewel Fund for children's welfare, of which she would be vice-president, set up on New Year's Day 1918 and led by noble ladies, monitoring and upgrading the quality of jewellery on offer?

Being on the road had its own challenges, the *North Wales Chronicle* reporting: 'ACCIDENT TO MRS LLOYD GEORGE: Mrs Lloyd George is suffering from a sprained wrist. She was motoring with her daughter Olwen, and in starting the car it backfired. She was able to attend the war fair at Caledonian-road, London, on Tuesday.'[11]

The occasion was the Great Fair held at the Cattle Market, Caledonian Road, for the Wounded Allies Relief Committee.[12] She was not billed as a distinguished attendee, the first day (Tuesday) being opened by Queen Alexandra and the Princess Royal. A wounded attendee for wounded allies?

This may be the same event, reported 30 years later by her son Richard, albeit replacing Islington with Hampstead:

> With Olwen at the wheel my mother was on her way to open a charity bazaar in Hampstead. Half-way something went wrong with the engine and the car came to a stop. When Olwen had finished all she knew how to do to the various gadgets under the bonnet – and still could not make the wonky motor come to life – my mother decided it was up to her to put matters right. Although she knew nothing about a car, or anything mechanical for that matter, she did know from observation that the one way to make the engine 'turn over' was to 'wind it up' with the crank-handle. So, with Olwen in the driver's seat with her foot on the accelerator and her hand on the choke, my mother took up her place in front of the radiator and took a firm grip on the hand-starter.
>
> The engine back-fired as my mother 'wound it up' – and the next instant came the crack of a broken bone and the crank-handle dealt her a crashing blow. Of course, Olwen was almost overcome with alarm, but my mother was quite calm. Disguising the pain as well as she could, she got back in the car and directed Olwen to drive to the home of a doctor in the neighbourhood whom, fortunately, she knew. (In spite of the back-fire the engine was still running.) So off they went again, and presently the fracture had been set, and my mother's arm put in splints. Naturally the physician and Olwen took it for granted that my mother would call off the engagement and go home to bed. But my mother was having none of that. She insisted on going to the bazaar.
>
> And she presided at the opening ceremonies, delivering her gracious little address quite as if nothing had happened to her! With her one good arm she held the inevitable gift bouquet of flowers and brought them home with her.
>
> How many women could duplicate that performance, I wonder?[13]

The 'wonky motor' was Richard's 'Vulcan of very ancient vintage', lent to Olwen when he went to France in 1915.[14] A similar story is also related by Ffion Hague, albeit citing north Wales.[15] It may have happened more than once.

On 5 June, the armed cruiser carrying Lord Kitchener to a meeting with the Tsar of Russia was mined off Orkney. The Secretary of State for War, military hero, the face of the First World War poster 'Your Country Needs YOU!', died with 737 others. Mrs Lloyd George attended his memorial service at St Paul's with her husband, who succeeded Kitchener as War Minister.[16]

On 15 June, she was unable to join Lady Mond in Swansea when the latter opened a new crèche at Trinity Place, part of her 'mothers and babies welcome' project which Mrs Lloyd George had visited in December 1913.[17] She would, however, present prizes in February 1917, by then being the wife of the Prime Minister.[18]

On Sunday, 18 June, the Lloyd Georges attended a major date in the London Welsh calendar that they rarely missed, the midsummer flower festival at the Baptist Welsh Chapel on Castle Street (now Eastcastle St), close to Oxford Circus, Lloyd George taking the chair. This year Lloyd George had not been expected to attend, and when he did it could have been a little awkward, as the chairman was Llewelyn Williams, with whom he was now at odds over conscription. The newly-appointed Secretary of State prefaced his remarks with some light-hearted jousting:

> He thanked Mr Llewelyn Williams for taking the chair, adding that, although Mr Williams had that day supplanted him, he had the pleasure in moving a vote of thanks to him in order to show what Christian spirit they as Baptists possessed. On some questions he and Mr Williams had not seen eye to eye – (laughter) – but there was one thing that held them inseparably together: that was their love of Wales and its language. (Applause)

He followed up with a short oration on the theme of the Creation:

> When the dawn will come I do not know, but we have to-day a period when the dawn is in sight – (applause) – and when the dawn comes you will find a new era. The old world will be changed, and from the sound of battle and the tribulations of war there will be a new earth, a Heaven for us all. For when the night is gone the sun will rise. (Applause)[19]

JULY 1916

July began with good news on the home front:

> An engagement is announced between Captain T. G. Carey Evans, I.M.S., F.R.C.S., eldest son of Dr Evans, Ffestiniog, north Wales, and Miss Olwen Elizabeth, elder daughter of Mr and Mrs Lloyd George, 11, Downing Street, London.[20]

And help for waifs and strays:

> Mrs Lloyd George was at home at 11, Downing Street, on Tuesday, to a gathering of those interested in the Waifs and Strays Society and the New Cripples' Home. 'We must look after the children,' she said. 'Babies were ever precious; but in war time they are more precious than ever, and we should do all we can to keep those little children and to bring them up healthy and strong.'[21]

Founded in 1881, the 'Church of England Incorporated Society for Providing Homes for Waifs and Strays' is today known as the Children's Society.[22]

On 14 July, Mrs Lloyd George was back on 'military' duty, standing in for the Premier, opening the Percy Illingworth Soldiers' Institute at Aldershot, established by the Baptist Union. The late Yorkshire-born Percy Illingworth, Liberal MP and Chief Whip, Parliamentary Secretary to the Treasury, and prominent Baptist, who had served in the Boer War, had died suddenly in January 1915 of typhoid.

That Bastille Day she carried 'good news from France' for her audience, saying that her husband had told her, just before she left London, that 'the army had just captured three more villages and two woods, and that our troops were going on'.[23]

It was village by village, wood by wood in that awful conflict. The 1916 Battle of the Somme, which had started on 1 July, would last until 18 November. On 7 July, his second day as War Minister, Lloyd George had written to his wife from the War Office: 'The Welsh Division has just captured Mametz Woods, taking four guns and 400 prisoners.'[24] In the same letter he indicated that the General (Ivor Philipps) had returned home with ill-health, accompanied by his ADC Gwilym Lloyd George, and that Lloyd George had appointed David Davies MP, of Llandinam, as his Parliamentary Secretary. In

1917 the latter would play an important role when the Troops Fund began its transition from sending comforts to providing long-term care for the casualties of war.

The battle of Mametz Wood, one of several woods listed on the battle roll-call that week, had finished two days earlier, having been eventually captured by the 38th, the Welsh Army, but at great human cost, with almost 4,000 men wounded and some 600 killed in a week's fighting. The attack, in reality a terrible baptism of fire, is today commemorated by a dramatic red Welsh dragon, grappling with barbed wire, erected in 1987.

The 38th Division, like other new army battalions untrained for this form of combat, was not expected to be sent into battle until 1917, but the 1916 Somme offensive had been called in the light of the German attack on Verdun. It would be a year before the 38th would be involved in another major engagement, when they would be praised for their valour at the commencement of the Battle of Passchendaele in Flanders.

Summertime was no longer party time, but fund-raising entertainments continued. On 21 July, Mrs Lloyd George, Mrs Churchill and Queen Alexandra attended a matinée for the Anglo-Russian Hospital supporting the Allies.[25] Also in July she, Lady Plymouth and Lady Mond arranged a concert for the Fund, hosted by Lady Cowdray. (see p.225) Olwen was also getting noticed, one gossip columnist attending that concert remarking that:

> Miss Lloyd George ... is charming, with a manner as natural as it is fascinating. I should think her fiancé a very happy man, but that he is in Mesopotamia, and therefore a victim of Government muddle.[26]

Almost a year later, in May 1917, when Tom Carey Evans was granted permission to come home from India to marry Olwen, a Miss Mela Brown Constable wrote to her own fiancé:

> I see that Miss Olwen Lloyd George's fiancé has been given permission to come home in June from Mesopotamia, in order that their marriage may take place. He is Captain Evans RAMC. When I read this in yesterday's paper I was mad with jealousy! I should have thought Mr Lloyd George would not have favoured one man more than another and would not like a special favour granted to his future son-in-law. If you get the opportunity

you might ask if you might come home too – only the difference is I am not a Prime Minister's daughter![27]

Six weeks later Miss Brown would write, perhaps feeling a little differently:

> The boat on which Miss Lloyd George's fiancé, Captain Evans RAMC, was coming home on has been torpedoed. Captain Evans is safe but cannot say when he will reach England.[28]

AUGUST 1916

On 7 August, the wife of the War Minister was in Pwllheli in support of a concert promoted by Brigadier General Owen Thomas in aid of the Belgian Wounded Fund. (see p.226) They also celebrated Mother's Day, when 'mothers of all the soldiers and sailors in the borough numbering about 120 were entertained at an open-air tea by the Mayoress, Mrs Cornelius Roberts … [Mrs Lloyd George] congratulated the town on the large number of heroes' mothers it contained. Welsh mothers had good reason to be proud of their sons, for on no battlefield had there been more valiant or courageous soldiers. (Applause)'[29]

In January, the prospect of Mrs Lloyd George and Mrs Roberts becoming mothers-in-law had ended when the engagement of Richard Lloyd George and Dilys Roberts had been broken off, though 'a close friendship between the two families remains unimpaired by the ending of the young couple's engagement'.[30]

To Aberystwyth

Another annual event in the Lloyd George, and Welsh, calendar was the National Eisteddfod in 1916 in Aberystwyth (which had been due to host the 1915 festival). 'The successful bard was invested with the prize by Mrs Lloyd George, installed in the chair by Dyfed according to ancient rites, the sword being returned to its sheath to the cries of "Heddwch" Bardic effusions.'

The chair ceremony at Birkenhead in 1917 would prove more sombre.

The Aberystwyth National Eisteddfod was particularly notable for Lloyd George's speech – 'Why should we not sing during this war?'

– responding to those who thought that such festivals should not continue during wartime. JTR's brothers were among those opposed to the event, their *Welsh Gazette* arguing that 'to hold a National Festival during the present terrible struggle is as impolitic as it is unseemly ... Indulgence in every form of costly and ostentatious pleasure should disappear in the face of a common task and a common danger.'[31]

As the war entered a third year there were calls for peace, perhaps with American mediation, but in 1916 Lloyd George was calling the war to be fought 'to a knockout'.

Almost a year later some of the Aberystwyth profits would be donated to wartime causes:

> DIVISION OF EISTEDDFOD PROFITS. The Executive Committee of last year's National Eisteddfod has decided to divide £500 of the surplus among war funds, and made the following allocations: National Fund for Welsh Troops, raised by Mrs Lloyd George, £80; YMCA War Fund, £50; Aberystwyth Surgical Requisites Association, £75; Aberystwyth Comforts for Soldiers Committee, £75; Sergeant-Major Fear's Fund, £25; National Institute for Blind Soldiers, £25; Wounded Breton Soldiers Fund, £25; Netley Hospital (Aberystwyth bed), £70; local Red Cross Hospital for Wounded Soldiers, £50; local YMCA hut for wounded soldiers, £25. The committee are reserving £300 for future claims.[32]

The Aberystwyth bed would be one of the sponsored beds at the Netley Hospital for the military near Southampton, and the cultural festival clearly was recognising its fellowship with the Bretons.

While in the seaside resort and university town, on 17 August, as the guests of surgeon Dr John Lynn-Thomas (the driving force behind the Prince of Wales Hospital for the limbless and disabled in Cardiff), Mrs Lloyd George and the Premier had a private visit to the National Library of Wales which had opened its reading rooms that year.

The family party then had a special train home to Cricieth:

> The War Minister was given a rousing reception at Cricieth last night. Accompanied by Mrs Lloyd George, Miss Megan, David Davies M.P., the Rev. John Williams, Brynsiencyn, and Mr and Mrs William George, he arrived home at six o'clock by special train from Aberystwyth. The local special constables lined up on the station platform. The distinguished party walked to Brynawelon, where Mr Lloyd George will stay over the

weekend. They were escorted by a large crowd, who raised enthusiastic cheers.³³

During their Criccieth stay there were some night-time goings-on involving the constables:

SWANSEA CHAUFFEUR AND MR LLOYD GEORGE'S CAR: Mr Lloyd George recently arranged for his motor car to be taken from Criccieth to Swansea for repairs. The chauffeur sent by the repairers, on arrival at Criccieth by the evening train, found the town full of visitors. Being unable to get a vacant bedroom he telephoned Mrs Lloyd George, and got her consent to leave with the car that night for Swansea. Four special constables, suspecting an adventure at Brynawelon, followed him to the War Minister's residence. They watched closely. Presently they saw the stranger bring out the car, and with commendable zeal pounced on their man and detained him. Not until they had awakened Mrs Lloyd George and been satisfied with regard to the Swansea man's bona-fides would they let him go. They parted, however, the best of friends, although the 'specials' were closely [*sic*] disappointed.³⁴

The *South Wales Post* entertained its readers a little further, with a few factual differences (including who owned the car), and not without a sly reference to the early-to-bed habits of the seaside town and its 'police force':

COMEDY AT CRICCIETH. SWANSEA MOTOR MANAGER'S ADVENTURE. An adventure of a particularly thrilling kind befell on Monday evening. Having occasion to proceed to the pretty town of Criccieth, in North Wales, famed as being the home of Britain's great War Minister, to bring back a car purchased from Mr Lloyd George by Messrs. R. E. Jones, Ltd., of Swansea, Mr Day arrived by the last train in the evening, and being desirous of returning to Swansea as quickly as possible, telephoned to Mrs Lloyd George and secured her permission to bring the car back that night to Swansea. After supper that evening, therefore, Mr Day strolled across to the residence – situated in a commanding position about half a mile from the town – and arrived there about 10 o'clock – rather a late hour for Criccieth.

Finding that the family had all retired for the night, with the exception of one servant, who had been instructed to show Messrs.

Jones's representative the garage, Mr Day commenced to get the car ready for the journey. Everything was in darkness, and he had been in the electrically lighted garage some time when the local police sergeant made his appearance. He wore an appearance of great determination and seemed anxious to protect the War Minister's property to his last drop of blood. Viewing Mr Day's preparations with great distrust, he prepared to instantly arraign him, and it was only after considerable difficulty that the representative was able to satisfy him as to his identity, and then only after the production of cards, papers, etc.

At any rate, Mr Day is not likely to forget the vigilance of the Cricieth 'police force' in a hurry.[35]

While in Cricieth Mrs Lloyd George was also helping to nurse Lloyd George's beloved uncle, Richard Lloyd, suffering from cancer.

In August, she and her daughters spent one afternoon in Llanwnda, south of Caernarfon, with William Lewis and his wife, a rare record of their meeting in a private capacity: 'Last week Mrs Lloyd George, accompanied by Miss Olwen Lloyd George, and Miss Megan Lloyd George, spent the afternoon at Cefn Coch, with Mr and Mrs W. Lewis, of Brondesbury Park, London. Mr and Mrs Lewis and his family are currently staying with Mr W. Roberts, at Cefn Coch.'[36]

Her presence in Cricieth also allowed her to host, at Brynawelon, the annual September conference of the Lleyn and Eifionydd Temperance Society.[37]

SEPTEMBER 1916

Elsewhere a little more north/south Welsh rivalry surfaced, in *Llais Llafur* (Labour Voice):

Mr Morgan Hopkin appeared before the committee and urged that they should take immediate steps to see that Labour was represented on the Welsh Soldiers' and Sailors' Farm Colony Committee. It was observed that practically all the members on the committee were North Walians, the only South Wales representative being a Bridgend gentleman. The movement had been inaugurated by Mrs Lloyd George, and it was not difficult to see that there was partisanship in the appointment. The executive recommended that the committee be written to, demanding that there should be more general representation, and that Labour should also be represented.[38]

On 10 October, Mrs Lloyd George was back on the temperance platform, in Swansea, with 'Merched y De', the south Wales women's temperance association, JTR no doubt also present. (see p.365)

Two days later she chaired, at No. 11, a sub-committee focused on the strategic choices facing the Troops Fund. (see p.226)

The Welsh hostess of Downing Street was always keen to promote Welsh artistes, this time featuring Welsh violinist Miss Laura Evans, a protégée of the highly popular writer Marie Corelli.

> Miss Laura Evans, who it will be remembered played at the Judges Hall about two years since, just prior to returning to Germany, had the honour of giving an exhibition of her talent at an 'At Home' given by Mrs Lloyd George at 11 Downing Street, last week. It was specially arranged on the suggestion of Miss Marie Corelli in order that the War Minister and a few personal friends might hear her protégée, Miss Laura Evans, of Pentyrch, Cardiff, play the violin.
>
> The young lady was discovered at a Cymmrodorion reception at Cardiff three years ago, during the late Sir Marchant Williams's presidency, when Miss Corelli was the guest of the evening. With her sister, Miss Constance Evans, she was in Berlin when war broke out, having just made her debut in some of the leading concerts there. They escaped, after some exciting experiences, to Denmark, where they have been until quite recently. Miss Corelli is charmed with the progress the young virtuoso has made, and suggested the introduction to Mr Lloyd George. Among those present, in addition to Mr and Mrs Lloyd George and their daughter, were Sir George and Lady Riddell, Sir Vincent Evans, Mr and Mrs Emsley Carr, Colonel David Davies M.P., Mr D. Oliver Evans (the violinist's father), Mr William Davies, Mr Oswald Stoll, Mr Merlin Morgan and, of course, Miss Corelli herself.
>
> A delightful programme was given. The whole company was charmed with the performance, Miss Evans proving herself an artiste of fine temperament, with an unusual brilliance in technique and a delightful purity of intonation. Mr Lloyd George congratulated her, and from Mr Merlin Morgan, who is the musical director of Daly's [a Leicester Square theatre], came the high tribute that he had never heard the Mendelssohn concerto played more beautifully. Miss Corelli was very enthusiastic.[39]

Guest Sir George Riddell, managing editor of *The News of the World*, was Lloyd George's great benefactor, and a neighbour at Walton

Heath (having provided Lloyd George with his house, that which the suffragettes had attacked). William Emsley Carr, also a Walton Heath resident, also edited the paper, working with Riddell.

Relations between Miss Evans and her mentor didn't last. In May 1919, Miss Evans, then performing as Nanette Evans, was no longer acknowledging the support of Miss Corelli, instead suggesting she was a Lloyd George protégée when playing at No. 10.[40]

On 15 October, getting from Surrey to north London proved impossible, prompting an apologetic telegram from Walton Heath to those expecting her to open their event in Muswell Hill: 'I am stranded here. Car failed me. Bad train service. Unable to come.' Stepping into the breach to open the War Hospital Supply Exhibition was Mrs Asquith's niece, Violet Tennant, who remarked to her audience that Mrs Lloyd George had a pretty stiff job keeping pace with the late Chancellor of the Exchequer, late Minister of Munitions, and now Secretary of State for War.[41]

On 17 October, the Lloyd Georges were presented with a portrait of Olwen, by Welsh artist Ellis Roberts, for the Welsh Division, in a ceremony at No. 11 attended by many Welsh MPs and other compatriots, including a number who actively worked on Mrs Lloyd George's projects: David Davies (also at the No. 11 concert), Lord Justice Bankes, Sir Vincent Evans, draper Philip Williams, surgeon Dr John Lynn-Thomas, and the Hon. Violet Douglas-Pennant, who made the presentation. Lloyd George, in accepting, paid tribute to the heroes of Mametz Wood. The Troops Fund at the same time was making a grant of £460 to the Division.[42]

NOVEMBER / DECEMBER 1916

For Mrs Lloyd George, November was relatively quiet, albeit chairing two Fund meetings. (see p.227) Richard came home from the Front with dysentery, but the day he arrived, 18 November, Mrs Lloyd George did visit the VAD (Voluntary Aid Detachment) Hospital at Northwood, Middlesex.

However, life was about to get busier.

Support for Prime Minister Herbert Asquith was collapsing, and on 6 December David Lloyd George concluded his short five months tenure as War Minister, taking up the prime ministerial reins of one of the world's largest empires. Uncle Richard Lloyd sent his congratulations, as in this extract from his unpublished four-page letter in the JTR Collection:

> My dear Children
> ... hardly ever I felt more pleased with my boy's achievements during the great historic week than I did that evening ... Congrats my dearest boy – with God speed bound to be given you as to the course of events and to carry Barn fuddugoliaeth [Judgment victory] as certain as the noon sun shines brightly on my paper when writing this to you.
>
> Bound to succeed to establish peace all the world over in due course by Right divine help and over ruling of the most High. Ymlaen machgen annwyl, annwyl i [Forward dear boy, dear to me].
>
> Very proud of Dick and Gwil's news of both getting on well in every sense, with a month rest in view too. Hope the Labour, coal, parties may come to some settlement for a while at most of course...
>
> Best love dearest children and xxxx for pets all. Byth Uncle Lloyd [43]

The spotlight now would turn on Margaret Lloyd George a great deal more, though eight years of residence in Downing Street, at No. 11, meant she was as well prepared as anyone for the attention.

Support for the sailors

By coincidence, on 5 December, the day before becoming wife of the Prime Minister, Mrs Lloyd George launched an appeal for the British and Foreign Sailors' Society (BFSS), to assist the mothers, widows and orphans of sailors. Born in a seaside town, Mrs Lloyd George had long supported seafarers in their funding appeals, including the BFSS and the Royal National Lifeboat Institution, the RNLI. Supporting an established hundred-year-old organisation would not require a great deal of time, but the military and merchant shipping community were battling intense submarine warfare and trying to maintain supplies. (see p.287)

She would soon resume her acquaintance with JTR, who had just joined the BFSS as one of its two London Metropolitan Superintendents.[44] (illustration 79)

One of the first public outings for the Prime Minister's wife was on familiar Nonconformist territory, opening a sale of work on 7 December at the Congregational Union Chapel in Islington, accompanied by Olwen:

Mrs Lloyd George, accompanied by Miss Olwen Lloyd George, visited the Union Chapel, Islington, yesterday afternoon, and opened a sale of work in aid of two branch churches. She said that it was very difficult even for a strong church to keep going in a time of war, and it was much more difficult for small and weak ones. They were naturally anxious to keep the work going until the return of the young men from the Front.[45]

It would also be one of the many Congregational chapels where JTR would later preach on the London circuit.

The following week, on a foggy 14 December, she and Olwen were running a stall at a sale on behalf of the Italian Red Cross at the Hotel Cecil.[46] [47]

It was decidedly rough on the promoters of the Italian Flag Day that London should have been mantled in a thick yellow fog yesterday morning. The contrast between London and southern Europe is always pretty great in December, and yesterday it was particularly so. In fact, one's first impression on emerging from the Underground Railway into the mist and being asked to 'Remember Italy' was one of irritation. But the appeal is a very strong one, and I think the Red Cross Fund of our Allies will be found to have received a considerable augmentation. Mrs and Miss Lloyd George have been assisting Lady Primrose at the Hotel Cecil, and there has been the usual company of ladies of note selling the flags, commemorative of different parts of 'Italia Irredenta'.[48]

Irridentism was an association started in 1878 that sought to bring some neighbouring regions with a predominantly Italian population back from foreign control. (illustration 75)

The social revolution in Downing Street

It would take until late January to move next door, but the media had a field day appraising the new hostess of No. 10, a complete contrast to the departing Margot Asquith.

The *Daily Mirror* 'Gossip' column ran a picture of Mrs Lloyd George with Megan, with a note on the BFSS appeal, commenting: 'Many politicians, including the late W. Gladstone, have been largely helped in their duties by their wives. We may be sure that Mr Lloyd George is having this sympathetic support at the present trying hour. I well remember Mrs Lloyd George staying in the Ladies' Gallery throughout an all-night sitting during the Budget.'[49]

She would shortly be in the House of Commons Ladies' Gallery again, joined by Lady Mond, as Lloyd George announced his government's policy as Prime Minister.[50]

She was also still more familiar to the Welsh than the English:

> About mid-day on Saturday a middle-aged lady, accompanied by her beautiful daughter, asked a railway official at Charing Cross from what platform her train left. 'Next one to this, ma'am,' he replied, 'and you'd better 'urry up or it will go without you.' The lady was Mrs Lloyd George, who was accompanied by her daughter Olwen. They were unrecognised. Before she reached the door of the next platform a Welshman recognised her, rushed forward, and raising his hat, said in the vernacular: 'Llwyddiant i'r achos Mr Lloyd George' ('Success to the cause of Mr Lloyd George'). The Premier's wife turned round and replied: 'Diolch yn fawr i chwi' ('Thank you very much'). The beautiful Miss Olwen smiled serenely, and the Welshman departed in a glow of Cymric rapture.[51]

The ladies' correspondent for the *Belfast News-Letter* Metropolitan Gossip column was quite swift with a pen-portrait.

> From a woman's point of view the wife of the new Prime Minister is of interest. I cannot say that I know Mrs Lloyd George, but I have spoken with her on several occasions. Save on the last, I thought her as the wife of a chief member of a Ministry I hated and despised, for it was in pre-war and bitterly party days.
>
> For the life of me I could not help liking her, and one doesn't want to like the wives of those accounted enemies. Her manner is kind and absolutely natural. There are, in American parlance, no frills about Mrs Lloyd George. She has a sunny, cheery, charming face, and I think it beams most when she has just done someone a real kindness, and she does a great many, I am told, in a very quiet way. She is neither brilliant nor brainy, but she is good and true and kind.
>
> I believe she will be quite a success in her new position. She will not seek to shine, but there will be a wholesome radiant aura round her that will be the antithesis of artificiality, excitement, and neurotic brain display. Her household is, I believe, modest and absolutely British. Her elder daughter also I have spoken with, and thought her a delightful girl. The boys I

heard nothing of, save that they are in the army, and the little girl, who is so much with her father, seems clever and precocious a child that she may be in some danger of paying the price of precocity necessarily in the public eye. I imagine, however, that her mother's good sense will save her from that.[52]

Whatever one's views on gossip, it would seem to offer pretty good likenesses.

The Sketch pictured her with Olwen, with the caption: 'Aides to the Popular Premier, On the Distaff Side.' The Scottish *Daily Record* opined, reporting her BFSS appeal, that Mrs Lloyd George…

… has never aspired to be a Society leader, such as most ladies who have occupied the exalted position she is now called upon to fill, have proved themselves. She has, however, associated herself with many of the philanthropic schemes which have been instituted during the war, and has particularly interested herself in the cause of the sailors.[53]

The *Sunday Mirror* had design changes in mind:

It seems that some of the private rooms at 10, Downing-street are decorated in futurist styles. Mrs Lloyd George has simple tastes, and is, according to her friends, sure to have these modes 'strafed'.[54]

Perhaps not a word Mrs Lloyd George would have used.

The Bystander, for all its flippancy, saw a sign of the times in the 'social revolution in Downing Street', with a new 'First Lady' very different from her predecessor, Margot Asquith:

IN ENGLAND NOW (A WEEKLY LETTER FROM 'BLANCHE')
Dear Cousin
NOW things have settled down again and there's a little time to think it over, I'm not at all sure that the biggest happening of all these last momentous weeks hasn't been the terrific social change. We've been laying the foundation for the future of the Empire, and the great tidal wave of democracy that's been gathering strength so long has burst the gates at last and poured over the country with an overwhelming rush.

AND in its passing, I wonder, will it sweep away all the tired old fetishes and wash the slate clean of injustice? What will go first, the feudal system and all the privileges of rank and the omnipotence of riches and the degradation of extreme poverty? For I suppose if there is one thing more certain than another it is that under the new force wealth, sooner or later, will be conscripted. It'll be very dull, of course – things always are that are really good for us. All roast beef and rice pudding and prunes, instead of supreme de sole Ritz and faisan rôti and pêche Melba.

PICTURE to yourself, cousin, the social revolution that's happened in Downing Street alone. Why, it's a complete upsetting of all the traditions and conditions we've clung to like limpets for centuries. The change of hostesses at No. 10 is one of the coups d'état of these epoch-making days in which we're fashioning the new England. The late chatelaine, all that there is of last-wordism, strongly flavoured with the exclusiveness of blue-blood and the conscious superiority of landed proprietors. The new one the domestic woman.

FOR all these war and pre-war years, 'Margot,' who even in childhood conversed with scholars, argued with statesmen and had views on everything that mattered in the world; who was always in the movement and mostly a little bit ahead of it; who had no slavish respect for conventions or persons; who was a devotee of the intellectual, great on cults and culture, on clothes, and on all new things, in art, in books, in the theatre. Restless, nervous, autocratic, full of energy, a critic on the hearth. Above all, a personality utterly independent, having opinions of her own, sufficient unto herself, modernism rampant.

AND NOW, Mrs Lloyd George. 'Mrs Lloyd George,' one reads, 'has no ambition to be a political force. She does not care to influence appointments. She is concerned only about her husband's health' – in fact, everything Britain expects of a British wife and mother. Quiet, retiring, a devoted helpmate with absolutely no wish to shine except in the reflected glory of her brilliant husband's radiance. You have only to look at her to see she is untouched by the hectic restlessness that is one of the hallmarks of the newer woman.

EVEN the modern extravagance in clothes has passed her by; indeed, one does not associate extravagance in any form with England's new 'First Lady,' and you simply can't imagine her wearing herself to shreds in the throes of Russian ballet and opera, or running a new 'ism,' or a parade of mannequins from Paris. The Pauline type, you know – 'submit yourselves to your husbands,' etc. But for all her womanliness Mrs Lloyd George is not womanly in the sense that she takes no interest in anything outside her house and home. Social reform finds her always a keen disciple, and the common sense of her class is a boon on committees.

SO there we are, you see – instead of complexity, simplicity; instead of the Smart Set, the Social Democrats. No more of those impromptu-ish lunches, with bishops and actresses and peers and poets passing each other the port; no more meetings of souls wonderfully arrayed and dancers wonderfully disarrayed. Instead a purely political household with only one person that matters in it, and that its master. Delicious antediluvian idea, isn't it. But the simplicities that's what they say we've got to get back to, you know, so perhaps, after all, the new order in Downing Street is really a sign of the times.[55]

Closing off the busy year, the *Sheffield Daily Telegraph* devoted a column (extracted here) to the new mistress of Downing Street.

When I had the privilege some time ago of having a long chat with Mrs Lloyd George in one of the cosy reception rooms at No. 11. Downing Street, it was easy to see from a hundred little things what great delight and interest she still took in everything pertaining to her 'home'.

Mrs Lloyd George still retains here and there that slight Welsh lisp or accent – or whatever it may be called – which proves her nationality beyond doubt to one who has ever lived in Wales. Moreover, there are about No. 11 other traces of the fact that here a bit of Cricieth, or at least of Wales, has been transplanted into the middle of London. For the maids also speak with a similar lisp or accent, which shows you that they did not come to No. 11 by way of Kent or Lancashire, nor from Cornwall or Norfolk.

The Ship's Tiller
As I sat the other side of the bright fire I felt more than ever how the woman before me was the real presiding genius of that home, how much more the nation owes her than it actually recognises. David Lloyd George may be the great captain to whom the whole nation looks for success, says *The Mother's Magazine*, but the hand that guides the tiller of his ship is the hand of his wife. The nation's immense debt to her will some day be recognised, perhaps, but it can never be paid.

I have so far said hardly anything about Mrs Lloyd George's philanthropic work, though she is never idle in that direction also. She is continually helping forward schemes for the needy, for the sick and afflicted. She is a devoted worker for temperance reform, and on behalf of young women and girls. To speak of half her enthusiasms in these directions would require a whole article to itself. In reply to a question, she told me what were her two real hobbies. In the first place she puts gardening. Mrs Lloyd George's other chief recreation is reading, of which she is very fond. But her regret is that her time for this is so curtailed.[56]

The reading and much of the gardening may have had to wait a while.

The evening paper, *The Pall Mall Gazette*, under the heading 'The Prime Ministress,' asked 'How will Mrs Lloyd George fulfil her new role of a Prime Minister's wife?':

> She has had, to my knowledge, troops of friends since the entrance of her husband upon his public career, and in her wider social sphere of action her simplicity and charm, combined with her natural tact, will win her many more.[57]

The reviews reflect not only that she was already well known in town but that she was very much a breath of fresh air. To posit one major achievement of the next six years it would be that the level-headed Welsh woman fulfilled those expectations, let nothing go to her head, and devoted herself to her duties, as she saw them. That she didn't spend all her time in the Westminster 'bubble' – as we now term it – may well have been a real advantage in being able to take a broad view, making her popular and welcome.

CHAPTER 5

1917: First Lady, with Celtic Commitments

(January to May 1917)

'The righteous aims for which the Allies were fighting must make a mighty appeal to the Scottish people. Their whole history was one of determined struggle where high principles were involved.'
Margaret Lloyd George, Edinburgh Fèill, March 1917

JANUARY 1917

THE NEW PRIME Minister's wife returned from Cricieth to London with Megan on 9 January. During Christmas, Olwen had been nursing at the nearby Wern Military Hospital, Porthmadog.[1] (illustrations 65, 66) Lloyd George had stayed in London, meeting the French Armaments Minister, M. Albert Thomas.

It took until 29 January to move into No. 10.[2] It is noted in Margot Asquith's diaries that Mrs Lloyd George had said there was no need to hurry in moving out, while Frances Stevenson noted in her diary that Margot thought it wouldn't be long before she was back in again.[3]

The *Liverpool Daily Post* column, 'A Diary in War-time', noted a glass ceiling being tested:

Women in Clubs: The London papers have gossiped a good deal about the fact that Mr Lloyd George dined with Mrs Lloyd George at the National Liberal Club the other day, and it has been pointed out that some clubs do not permit women to dine or have a meal within their precincts.

This rule is no doubt a very proper one so long as it is proved by reasonable exceptions. But many clubmen are very jealous of women. Recently a Liverpool club had a dinner at which women were present, and some of the men seemed quite depressed about it. And yet it seems to me that if men's clubs are to retain their popularity – or recover their prosperity – they must open their doors more often to women than they have hitherto done. The club habit of the old type is dying out, and I fancy that men, if they are to keep their clubs going, must make them a little more useful or double the subscriptions.[4]

At the movies

On 15 January, Mrs Lloyd George and her future No. 11 neighbour Isabel Bonar Law (daughter of the new Chancellor, Bonar Law), were among the 250,000 watching *The Battle for the Ancre and the Advance of the Tanks*, a new official film on the war, released in 112 venues in London and the boroughs.[5] It followed the 1916 propaganda film *The Battle of the Somme*, possibly the highest grossing film of the silent-film era. Box office takings for *The Battle of the Ancre* were even higher in the first three months of release than for its predecessor, and it has been considered as the better film cinematically, with its haunting images of trench warfare, the mud of the battlefields, the waves of troops advancing into no-man's-land, the use of horses and the first views of the 'Tank' – first demonstrated to British military leaders in September 1915, touted as the secret weapon to break the deadlock on the Western Front.[6] These box office records would not be surpassed for 60 years until the arrival of *Star Wars*, fortunately fiction. (illustration 21)

On 17 January, she was at a Mansion House meeting hosted by the Lord Mayor, planning the next March Flag Day.

The reality of war was brought closer to home two days later by the 'Silvertown Explosion' at the Brunner-Mond chemicals factory, now producing munitions, on the north bank of the Thames, part-owned by Alfred Mond (who went on to establish Imperial Chemical Industries (ICI), once the largest British manufacturing company) and his family. Seventy-three people died and more than 400 were injured. Windows were shattered in Muswell Hill to the north-west and Lewisham to the south, and the explosion was heard in Hampton Court.

On Sunday, 21 January, the Premier, Mrs Lloyd George and some family members visited the East End for a cup of tea at the Woolwich home of Will Crooks, the local Labour MP, before visiting the infirmary where a number of those injured in the explosion had been taken. A long-time supporter of many of Lloyd George's social policies, Will Crooks was recovering from an operation. Mrs Lloyd George would visit him several times.[7]

Her increasing visibility was noticed, the *Dundee Evening Telegraph* observing: 'No-one could accuse Mrs Lloyd George of pushfulness but she has come out of her shell quite a good deal since her husband became Premier and she is quite an admirable speaker.'[8]

On 26 January, *The Times* reported that Gwilym had been promoted to captain, while Richard had arrived in Bath for convalescence.[9]

During the month there was some reaction in the press to her Christmas article on drink, where she supported Lloyd George's line that drink was the country's worst enemy. (see p.369)

FEBRUARY 1917

Once in possession of No. 10, Mrs Lloyd George and her husband left for north Wales, arriving at 1.30 on 2 February by train at Bangor before going on to Cricieth. It was generally a nine-hour train journey, via Birmingham and Crewe.[10] They were accompanied by the Hon. Neil Primrose (Joint Parliamentary Secretary to the Treasury) and Ellis Griffith, MP for Anglesey. The new Prime Minister would be making a speech in Caernarfon, an early oration on his plans for government, which would be attended by some 5,000 electors. Tickets were hard to come by, and not everyone was welcome:

> A remarkable and, in all probability, unprecedented feature of the meeting which the Prime Minister is to address in Carnarvon to-morrow afternoon is the extraordinary interest which has been evinced by the foreign Press in the proceedings. A very considerable application for tickets of admission was made by the London representatives of a number of foreign and local journals, and special accommodation is being provided for them at the meetings.
>
> Extraordinary precautions are being taken with the issue of tickets. With very few exceptions, women will not be admitted. Only Carnarvon Boroughs electors will receive tickets, which must bear the name and

address of the holder, whose bona fides must be guaranteed by the endorsement of the agent issuing the ticket.[11]

The speaker's wife and daughter Olwen may well have been among the very few women in the audience, joined by Richard.

The move to No. 10 was increasing the demands for her time, which included chairing another war funding committee:

> At a representative conference of London women, held at the offices of the National War Savings' Committee, a resolution was passed stating that the meeting desired to give its whole-hearted support to the War Loan, and would do all in its power to assist the Lord Mayor's Committee. A committee was appointed to make further arrangements as to the details of the co-operation with the Lord Mayor's Committee, and of this Mrs Lloyd George was appointed chairman and Miss Beatrice Chamberlain, sister of Mr Austen Chamberlain, vice-chairman.[12]

Beatrice Chamberlain, educationalist and active campaigner, helped organise the French Wounded Emergency Fund (she was fluent in French) supporting French hospitals.[13] She died in the 1918 flu pandemic, ten days after the Armistice was declared.

On 5 March, Mrs Lloyd George would speak at a major London conference organised by the sub-committee, as the women's food and economy campaigns took shape. (see p.294)

After two February meetings in west London's Ealing, preparing with the local community for St David's Day, Mrs Lloyd George left for Cricieth. She would not return for the Flag Day as, no sooner had Lloyd George arrived at No. 10, his uncle Richard Lloyd became gravely ill. They would not meet again. He was being cared for at Lloyd George's younger brother William George's house, Garthcelyn, Cricieth, supported by Mrs Lloyd George.

Richard Lloyd gave his last sermon on 11 February. On 17 February, *The Times* Court page reported his serious illness and that the PM was leaving for Cricieth. Lloyd George, however, had to go to Paris and the Front (where he visited the Welsh Division and met Richard and Gwilym) and was kept up to date on Uncle Lloyd's progress by telephone and by many short notes, as was then so common. The JTR Collection conserves five notes Lloyd George sent to his wife, expressing concern and offering advice.

1917: First Lady, with Celtic Commitments

20th February 1917

Dearest hen gariad [old love], I earnestly pray you will find an improvement when you arrive… a nice letter from W [William George]. I know that they are all doing their best for Uncle Lloyd but sometimes you can persuade him to do things when the rest of us fail. Wire or phone first thing in the morning. I am very anxious & worried about it, Love D[14]

22nd February 1917

My dearest hen gariad, So very very pleased to get your letter & to hear how bright Uncle Lloyd is. I am especially delighted to hear that he is taking nourishment. I have been twice on the phone today & was overjoyed to hear from Dr Davies that his patient had taken nourishment today.

I phoned this morning to Dr D reminding him of Brocklebank's advice to give him 'solids'. They enable the weak bowel to act. There is nothing the matter with the digestion. It is all in the lower bowel so Brocklebank said & Uncle Lloyd has been ever so much better since he took his advice. Why not try bread and butter? Lots of butter.

Prysur ofnadwy [extremely busy], French Ministers here today. Going to France Sunday. Much love to you all, D[15]

Lloyd George was preparing for the forthcoming Anglo-French Conference to be held on Monday/Tuesday 26–27 February, trying to create a more unified line of command for the Allies.

23rd February 1917

Hen gariad, So pleased to get your letter this morning; & the one just arrived. I am especially pleased to learn that Uncle Lloyd has taken nourishment well. I today made my pronouncement on the shipping trouble. Spoke for an hour & 40 minutes… beer & spirits down to nearly 1/4th what it was before war. A long successful speech I ever delivered in the House. Balfour yn wylo [is crying] over my peroration. Gone amazingly well.

Cariad lawer at bawb [much love to all]. Give it especially to the dear old boy who is fighting his way back to health. D [16]

Lloyd George had been making a major speech on the shipping crisis, shortages, and measures he proposed to take.

77

Undated
Hen gariad, Cychwyn i Ffrainc [Leaving for France]. Byddaf yn ôl dydd Mawrth rwyn disgwyl [I expect to be back Tuesday].

I enclose a letter for you in the event of the worst happening. Don't open it otherwise. Love to you all, D

Megan A1. She was very sweet (?). We had long walks.

I am very very unhappy and sad about poor Uncle Lloyd.[17]

Undated (most probably Tuesday 27th)
Hen gariad, Only just returned. Well well, what an anxious time you are having. It has been a terrible time for me here but what it must have been for you watching at the dear old boy's bedside.

Although I had one of the most difficult and trying tasks of the war to put through, events at Cricieth haunted me right through. He is in God's keeping whatever happens. Love to you all, D

The Conference was a great success.[18]

Richard Lloyd died on 28 February, the day Lloyd George returned from Calais.

While Lloyd George achieved his aim of putting the Allies under the command of French General Nivelle (fresh from success at Verdun), he greatly angered Field Marshal Haig. The failure of the next offensive under Nivelle in April/May resulted in mutinies in the French ranks and Nivelle's replacement by Marshal Pétain.

MARCH 1917

With the funeral of Richard Lloyd on 3 March, Olwen took the lead for the London Flag Day. (see p.233) Mid-March was an anxious time for Mrs Lloyd George as Megan fell ill with the measles, then more dangerous than today, a vaccine still almost 40 years away. They spent some time in Brighton together,[19] which meant she missed a meeting of Welsh temperance societies in London,[20] and on 24 March Lady Rhondda stepped in to open a Fancy Fair in aid of wounded soldiers and sailors, where 'Tommy' had a go at the lucky dip.[21]

Scotland the brave

Megan recovered in time for her mother to support Celtic warriors north of the border, the first of three visits to Scotland in the coming months. Before awarding medals, at 'a port on the East Coast', to those working on the minesweepers and submarines, and inaugurating a new hut for the men, on 29 March, in Edinburgh, she opened a Highland bazaar, or fèill, helping the Scots to raise funds for comforts for their own Highland regiments, as reported by *The Leeds Mercury*:

> In the course of her address Mrs Lloyd George said Scotland had performed a noble part in the war. Scottish troops had a reputation before this war, but they had surpassed all previous records. It was a well-known fact that the enemy had a wholesome fear and respect for Scottish troops.
>
> The righteous aims for which the Allies were fighting must make a mighty appeal to the Scottish people. Their whole history was one of determined struggle where high principles were involved. We were called upon now to suffer privations and undergo sacrifices. We knew what the people of Scotland had already done and what they had to do in the future, and we felt sure they would go on with all their strength until victory was secured.
>
> The Highland regiments had a proud and peculiar place of their own, and their splendid prowess and daring achievements had earned the praises of everyone. She herself claimed kinship with the men and women of the Highlands. Those who were born near the mountains never forget them.
>
> We might have had our grievances in times of peace, but we put them on one side and forgot them when we were called to fight for our country. In some of the Highland villages there was not a man left, and they had kept up the name and traditions of the Celtic regiments both in Scotland and in Wales. They came as a voluntary army, before they heard of the Military Service Act.
>
> At the close of the ceremony a bouquet of daffodils and red roses was presented to Mrs Lloyd George. Psalm 46 was sung in Gaelic by a choir in the old style, the precentor reciting each line before it was sung by the choir.[22]

The Southern Reporter, a more local paper, from Falkirk, observed:

CELTS AND THE WAR: Mrs Lloyd George referred to the very significant position which the Celts of Scotland and of Wales hold in relation to the war.

In times past, when we have heard the boast that the English were the first of the Teutonic races, we wondered to what extent people would be led by their mad obsession to Germanism. Perhaps those who were foremost in boasting of their Teutonic origin would now be glad to forget all that they had said. Certainly the Celtic population of Scotland have been able to enter into this conflict without any taunt of 'civil war', and as far we know, not one Saxon corps has hailed the men of a Highland regiment as 'Kamerades'. We should regard it as very deep disgrace if they did.

The Celts in times of peace, as Mrs Lloyd George remarked, have their grievances, but the Celts of Scotland have a wonderful way of sinking their personal interests when it comes to a question of country and race.[23]

The Courier from Dundee added:

Mrs Lloyd George said that any appeal for the benefit of soldiers and sailors was bound to have a very great response. The Germans held Scottish troops in wholesome fear and respect... There was no rivalry between Highland and Lowland regiments except in zeal and anxiety for the best service of their country... They must bear in mind the many men who would be broken in body and in spirit, and they must do what they could to help them to start again in the Old Country.[24]

Three reports combining verbatim quotes with selected paraphrasing and emphasis. It was then off to the secrecy of the unidentified 'port on the East Coast':

PREMIER'S WIFE AND NAVAL SECRETS: GALLANT SAILORS AND OFFICERS DECORATED:
Mrs Lloyd George yesterday performed the opening ceremony of a hut which has been erected at a port on the East Coast, under the auspices of the Edinburgh Citizens' Prohibition Committee, at a cost of £1,400, for the benefit of the men employed on the minesweepers.

Mrs Lloyd George presented decorations for gallantry in minesweeping submarine work to the following officers and men: Lieut. A. Robinson, R.N.R.; Lieut. C. Stewart Burgon, R.N.R.; Lieut. W. Highton,

R.N.R.; Skipper D. Wallace; Second Hand Horace Taylor; Deck Hands John Inglis, Norman L. Carlton, James M. Thain; Leading Seaman J. E. Worseley; and Skipper Samuel Jenkins (for long and faithful service).

At the conclusion of the ceremony Mrs Lloyd George was presented by Admiral Startin with a memento of the occasion, and in returning thanks said she would always value the gift very highly. 'I am very glad,' she added, 'to get into the inner secrets of the navy for once. I think I shall be able to keep them. But will you allow me to tell the Prime Minister?' (Laughter)[25]

We are not told what the memento was, but other newspapers cited the 'unidentified location' as Granton, on the outskirts of Edinburgh, on the Firth of Forth.[26]

The PM's wife would be privy to further naval secrets four months later, courtesy of Winston Churchill returning to the fold, as we shall see.

APRIL 1917

The well-organised Troops Fund's committee was now meeting less frequently, six times before the summer break and four times in the autumn/winter months. William Lewis was engaged in a passionate and lively correspondence with MP David Davies on future Fund strategy. (see p.239) With William Lewis no longer based in Downing Street and focused on the Fund, JTR was close to moving to No. 10 to work for Mrs Lloyd George. In April he renewed his acquaintance with Lloyd George, as he later recalled when lecturing on his time there:

> During World War I, I attended a deputation to urge temperance – Rival Deputations – Heard both sides at once. Sagacity. Room full. Had not met him for years. I did not expect him to recognise me. As soon as I was in the room he nodded genially and as soon as meeting was over he came up and greeted me cordially by name. One of his most marked traits and most valuable assets. Shortly after this I entered Downing Street as Secretary to Dame Margaret.[27]

While recuperating in Bath from trench fever, Richard Lloyd George not only regained his health but met Roberta McAlpine, the youngest daughter of Robert McAlpine.[28] After a whirlwind romance, they married at Bath Abbey on the weekend of 6–7 April, the Lloyd Georges in attendance. The *Sheffield Daily Telegraph* headlined its story: 'To be Mrs Lloyd George Junior.'[29]

On 12 April, the PM's wife returned to Scotland, leading a large delegation of Welsh dignitaries to Glasgow, hosted by Alexander Gracie, Chairman of the Fairfield Shipbuilding and Engineering Company. The City Chambers were also visited by the Lord Mayor and Deputy Lord Mayor of Cardiff and the Lord High Sheriff of Glamorgan.[30] Although the papers covered the visit, down to the detail that Mrs Lloyd George shared a train compartment on the journey south with soap manufacturer Sir John McCallum, MP for Paisley, and his wife, the purpose of the visit itself was not mentioned.[31] Post-war newspapers revealed that the mission was to launch HMS *Cardiff* at the Fairfield shipyards, on 12 April.[32] The light cruiser, assigned to the Grand Fleet, participated in the Second Battle of Heligoland Bight in late 1917 and was briefly deployed to the Baltic in late 1918, supporting anti-Bolshevik forces during the British Baltic campaign during the Russian Civil War.

It was time for some Celtic relaxation: 'PREMIER'S WIFE RESTING: Few women have worked harder lately than Mrs Lloyd George. Not only London but various parts of the provinces have witnessed her activities, while her two daughters have been almost equally busy. The three are now resting at their house, Brynawelon.'[33]

The Somme Front was now particularly intense, Canadian troops successfully capturing the Vimy Ridge, the French using tanks for the first time, but neither side achieving a real breakthrough. American troops would arrive on French soil in June.

Duty soon called in London, where on 27 April Mrs Lloyd George, Olwen and Megan accompanied the PM to the London Guildhall where he was presented with the Freedom of the City of London.[34]

MAY 1917

May Day 1917, appropriately perhaps, was Lifeboat Day (though the call sign, after the French *m'aidez*, would first be used in the 1920s). Mrs Lloyd George was busy selling lifeboat badges on the Underground. A favourite cause.[35]

As always, not all invitations, even commands, could be accepted, as reported on 3 May: 'The Right Hon. D. Lloyd George (Prime Minister) and Mrs Lloyd George had the honour of being invited to the Castle both this week and also last week, but were unavoidably prevented from obeying their Majesties' commands.'[36]

The food economy and housekeeping campaign was now well underway, including the opening of more food kitchens in the East End of London, on 4 May, with Lady Rhondda, and on 18 May in south London, in Camberwell, with Megan, Lady Rhondda and by local MP and Parliamentary Secretary to the Admiralty, Tom Macnamara. (see p.297)

If you thought the celebration of every day being a special day for something or other was a more modern fashion, think again.

> LAMP DAY: Every day seems be a 'day' in the now acceptation of the word, and the London suburbanites come into town each morning in the sure confidence that they will be asked to help some deserving cause or other. This has been Lamp day – the festival organised to commemorate the birth of Florence Nightingale, the Crimean heroine, and to benefit the wounded in the Scottish Women's Hospitals at the various battle fronts. People everywhere wore the little silk flags or the imitation lamps which were the symbols of their contributions to the Funds, and a large number of ladies, headed by Mrs Lloyd George, who was in charge of the depot at the Florence Nightingale statue [in Waterloo Place], assisted in the sale of the souvenirs.[37] (illustration 51)

On 16 May, Mrs Lloyd George disappointed Ealing's Latymer Road Mission by not being there as planned to receive the 'purses of money collected by some of the younger friends of the mission on behalf of the day nursery'.[38]

On 17 May, she opened a sale of work at the Kensington War Supply Depot.[39] It was the first War Hospital Supply Depot to be set up, in 1915, by four people with just £15 in capital, first in two houses, then extending to five. Such depots were invaluable for storing much-needed hospital supplies, often finding space in people's houses.[40]

That afternoon she and Olwen attended a concert for the Welsh wounded:

> A concert arranged by the Committee for the Care of the Welsh Wounded Soldiers in London hospitals, organised by the London Welsh Churches, was held at Queen's Hall last night, among those present being Mrs Lloyd

George and Miss Olwen Lloyd George and Lord Harlech, commanding the Welsh Guards. The band of the Welsh Guards, together with a number of Welsh vocalists and instrumentalists, contributed to the programme.[41]

The popular Queen's Hall in Langham Place, adjacent to All Souls' Church, was blitzed in the next war and never rebuilt.

The North Wales Heroes' Memorial

Alongside supporting the troops at the Front, the sailors at sea, and caring for the wounded at home, there was the task of commemorating the fallen – 'Lest we Forget'. The North Wales Heroes' Memorial project was a good example of wanting to fund something useful, in this case education, not *just* a carved memorial. Another project benefiting from Robert Thomas's generosity, the debate concerning north-south Wales coordination continued:

> North Wales Heroes' Memorial: Mrs Lloyd George presided to-day at a meeting held at 10 Downing-street, with the object of interesting Welsh people in London in the North Wales Heroes' Memorial. The scheme was explained by Mr R. J. Thomas, himself a beneficent donor to the Fund. It includes the erection and equipment of science buildings in connection with University College, Bangor, and the establishment of a subsistence fund which would enable the children of fallen soldiers to obtain free university education. The Welsh communities in London, Liverpool, and Manchester, and the United States, are expected to contribute liberally, and Mr Thomas hopes the amount raised may be sufficient to provide free university training for every poor child in north Wales whose attainments warrant such advancement. The meeting heartily approved the memorial, and formed an organisation to assist in its realisation.
>
> It appears that south Wales is undertaking a similar movement, and both General Sir Francis Lloyd and General Sir Owen Thomas suggested that it would have been better if one national scheme had been adopted. It was stated by Miss Douglas-Pennant and others that there was no conflict or misunderstanding in the matter, and that the two projects would proceed without overlapping. They were not antagonistic, and, indeed, each could help the other. Mrs Lloyd George, who was appointed chairman of an influential Executive Committee, mentioned that the Prime Minister was in complete sympathy with the movement.[42]

1917: First Lady, with Celtic Commitments

The building still stands today, with rebuilt science blocks behind. While a Welsh National War Memorial was first mooted in 1917, formal proposals were not put forward until 1919 – a number of towns declining on the grounds they already had their own memorials. A fund was started by the *Western Mail* in December 1919 and the Welsh National War Memorial in Cardiff was finally unveiled in 1928, on which Second World War casualties are now also commemorated.

On 22 May, Mrs Lloyd George was the principal guest at an 'At Home' hosted by the ladies of the Overseas Club, in London, in connection with Empire celebrations.

OUR FIRM KNIT EMPIRE: MRS LLOYD GEORGE AND GERMANY'S BLUNDER: Mrs Lloyd George said she was sure the old country would never forget the loyalty of the Dominions in the hour of her trial. The Germans had counted on the old country having to stand quite alone, but the Germans had been disappointed to find that the Empire was firmly knitted together. (applause)[43]

The Overseas Club (today the Royal Over-Seas League) was founded in 1910 by Sir Evelyn Wrench to embrace the British Empire, not just as a political and economic network but as a 'far-flung brotherhood of individual men and women of diverse creed and races living widely apart under differing conditions in different latitudes'. The club was to be non-sectarian, non-party, open to women and non-jingoist. Sir Evelyn, author and journalist, founded the English Speaking Union in 1918.

The following day she supported another small nation caught up in the Great War:

ARMENIA'S FLAG DAY. Mrs Lloyd George, who is taking the keenest interest in Armenia's Flag Day to be held on Wednesday, June 13, is announced to be present at an inaugural meeting at the Holborn Restaurant this afternoon, when the plan of campaign is to be discussed. Many other prominent ladies will be present, including Viscountess Bryce, whose labours, as well as those of Viscount Bryce, on behalf of the scattered remnant of Armenians who have escaped the vengeance of the Turk, have been unwearying.

The Armenian Refugees' (Lord Mayor's) Fund, 96, Victoria-street, has done valiantly. Nearly £70,000 has been collected. Armenia's Flag Day is the first great popular appeal on behalf of this stricken people.[44]

She then travelled to south Wales to visit Dr John Lynn-Thomas's new hospital in Cardiff, Lady Mond's Swansea crèche, the Mothers' and Babies Welcome, and the Victoria Red Cross Hospital at Mumbles.[45]

The approachable wife of the Prime Minister, always willing to support a good cause and to reward initiative, got the attention of some local Scouts:

Three Mumbles Boy Scouts, anxious to participate in the Empire celebrations and unable to obtain leave to absent themselves from school, hit on the idea of enlisting the support of the Premier's wife. Consequently they waited on Mrs Lloyd George, who was staying with a friend, put their case before her, and obtained not only her sympathy, but support, and departed happy boys with a letter to their schoolmaster, and an orange apiece.[46]

In Cardiff she also visited a food exhibition at the City Hall, before 'motoring' the final leg of her journey to Cricieth.[47] On 30 May, she opened a large War Economy Exhibition in Bangor, as well as a fund-raising event for the Bangor Women's Patriotic Guild. (see p.302)

At the end of the month the *Hampstead News* noted her social rank:

Mrs Lloyd George is kept pretty busy, for a Prime Minister's wife is socially a very important personage. With the exception of Royalty and the wives of the Lord Chancellor and the Archbishops of Canterbury and York, she takes precedence over all other ladies in the land. She is constantly sought after for opening bazaars and for other similar charitable functions, and as regards these, Mrs Lloyd George gladly and willingly does her best.[48]

CHAPTER 6

1917: The Uncrowned Queen of Wales

(June to August 1917)

'I cannot help feeling anxious – not on my own account – about this bold stroke, and you know how profusely I hope he will not have cause to regret it.'
Winston Churchill, July 1917

JUNE 1917

THE SIXTH OF June was time for a 'coronation', thanks to the girls of west London:

> MRS LLOYD GEORGE AND WOMEN'S WORK: A great reception was given to Mrs Lloyd George on Wednesday evening at the annual display by the 1st Hanwell Company (Elthorne Park Presbyterian Church) of the Girls' Guildry, in St Ann's School. Mrs Lloyd George, after distributing the prizes, referred to the value of such physical training for young girls as that carried on by the Guildry and heartily congratulated all who had taken part, especially those who are responsible for instructing the young performers.[1]

Their guest was rewarded with eggs:

> They honoured her for her own sake and for the sake of her distinguished husband, on whose shoulders rested the heaviest burden that had ever been imposed upon a single citizen. We should never be able to repay

Mr Lloyd George for all he had done and was doing for our safety and the defence of our land. To Mrs Lloyd George it was proposed to hand a basket containing three eggs. Two parcels of 120 eggs had been gathered by the girls to give to Mrs Lloyd George in order that she might offer the gift to any hospital for wounded soldiers of which she had knowledge. There were new-laid eggs, there were fresh eggs, there were shop eggs, and there were eggs. These were not merely eggs, they were not shop eggs, they were even better than fresh eggs. They were new-laid eggs.

Eggs were prized during wartime. Civilians were mobilised to collect eggs, the National Egg Society provided 44 million eggs to hospitals over four years, and in 1914 a National Egg Collection Fund for the Wounded, with Queen Alexandra as patron, had been formed, aiming to send 20,000 newly-laid eggs a week to the wounded in hospital in Boulogne, and eventually it was collecting or purchasing 200,000 eggs a week.[2]

Mrs Lloyd George disclaimed any intention of giving a lengthy address, and added that she was sure the members of the company who had been working so hard were quite ready to go home. It was the first time she had attended a Girls' Guildry function; she understood that the movement was rather a new undertaking. She was very delighted with the way the girls had done their work and she congratulated them all. She thought the Guardian had rendered very able service in giving the necessary instruction.

The only two she was sorry for were the lady judges. She thought they must have had a very hard time and experienced great difficulty in selecting the best candidates. She was very glad to see so many little ones connected with the company and also to notice the support received from the big girls, who were about to take their place in the world. She was told on all hands that women worked very conscientiously, and she was very proud to hear that. She thought they were all very proud of their sex.

She wished the Guildry every success, and she was only sorry that her own little girl was not present that evening. Her daughter was very interested in affairs of that sort, but was just now at school. She remembered with pride the association of Wales with the song 'Keep the home fires burning' and she thought we who remained at home should endeavour to realise the necessity of 'carrying on', not only in the industrial world, till the boys came home once more.

Proposing a vote of thanks to Mrs Lloyd George, Mr Miller said they could not thank her sufficiently for her kindness. The day had been a red-letter one for all of them, and more especially for the girls of the Guildry. He was sure that when the latter considered that Mrs Lloyd George was the uncrowned Queen of Wales – because what was she if she was not that? – they would remember the function with the greatest pleasure.[3]

In 1922, Mrs Lloyd George would write from Genoa, to Thelma Cazalet, while attending a conference with the Premier, warning that, 'I was actually called the Queen of England one day. So be on your guard.'[4]

Despite the shared compliments, the uncrowned queen of Wales could disappoint too, a *Hanwell Gazette* columnist reporting:

I saw and heard Mrs Lloyd George at St Ann's School last week. Mrs Lloyd George is very quiet, and her voice musical, but very soft. I went there to take down her speech, but being at the back of the room could not hear her. I was rather disappointed in the speech myself. The display was good, but the senior girls' Indian Club exercises impressed me most.[5]

Though microphones were in use, it is a bit mysterious as to how her voice carried to large audiences. Or perhaps it didn't carry, but as her hostess Mrs Jesse Boot in Nottingham might have said, just being there was the important thing.

The Girl Guides were founded in 1910.

In June a trip to Bournemouth was mooted in support of the local Free Church Council, where her publicity value was appreciated:

I understand (says Dr Jones in the *Richmond Hill Magazine*) that there is a great probability that Mrs Lloyd George will pay a visit to our town in connection with the work of the Women's Auxiliary of our Free Church Council towards the end of this month. Mrs Lloyd George is an extraordinarily busy person, and it is more than kind of her to help our Bournemouth ladies in this way. Of course, they well deserve the help. I sometimes think that the work the women do in connection with the Rescue Home and the Babies Home is the best bit of practical Christian work being done in Bournemouth. It only wants to be known to receive the practical help it so richly deserves. Mrs Lloyd George's visit will help it, I believe, to this wider publicity. The best of it is that Mrs Lloyd

George, if she comes, will come as one genuinely interested in every form of Christian work. We shall give the Prime Minister's wife a very cordial welcome.[6]

A third trip to Scotland meant this visit was delayed, but it did take place in early July.

June was the time for the second family marriage in relatively quick succession, when on Tuesday, 19 June, Olwen Lloyd George married Captain Tom Carey Evans at the Welsh Baptist Chapel in London. The King sent a congratulatory telegram.[7] Lloyd George's biographers recount how he slipped away from the Cabinet for the wedding, but was discussing politics until the moment he had to lead Olwen to the altar.[8]

Two days later it was tea and cake for the soldiers who had formed the guard of honour:

> The Prime Minister and Mrs Lloyd George yesterday entertained to tea the wounded soldiers from Millbank Hospital who formed the guard of honour at their daughter's wedding on Tuesday.
>
> Mrs Lloyd George personally received her guests, and the Prime Minister spent a few minutes chatting with the men. The soldiers viewed the large number of wedding presents, and each man was given a portion of the bride cake, which, it was observed, complied with the Food Controller's Orders, inasmuch as the customary icing and sugar decorations were absent.
>
> Taking their departure, the men gave hearty cheers for their host and hostess.[9]

Olwen recalled: 'One of my friends said to me, "What it is to be the daughter of the Prime Minister and having icing on your wedding cake!" I told her to go and try some – for all that beautiful icing was a sham, carefully modelled out of white card!'[10]

Roberta on the Red Cross roof

On 21 June, the Prime Minister's wife was also in attendance when the newest Mrs Lloyd George, Roberta, the new bride's sister-in-law, opened a Red Cross hut on the roof of the Ladies' Empress Club (a member-only ladies' club), at 35 Dover Street, off Piccadilly. The hut would serve the Emergency Voluntary Aid Committee and had been paid for by Roberta's brother, Thomas McAlpine, who worked at the Ministry of Munitions.[11] It was also close to Devonshire House, the Piccadilly wartime HQ of the Red Cross.

On Sunday, 24 June, those Lloyd George family members not on honeymoon nor at the Front – the PM, Mrs Lloyd George, Richard and Roberta, and Megan – were back at the Castle Street Welsh Baptist Chapel for the annual flower festival. Having framed his 1916 remarks in the context of The Creation, and 'the dark before the dawn', this year Lloyd George described the war as the worst catastrophe since The Deluge, and (presumably countering the increasing calls for a peace settlement) that if the dove was released now he feared it would not return.[12]

Mrs Lloyd George shortly had to make her peace in East London, having realised late in the day that the flower festival clashed with her promise to be at the Plashet Park Congregational Church for their Sunday school celebrations. She did however visit on the Monday for a further celebratory meeting.

> The training they gave was excellent for the young. They were showing the young the right way in which to start life. It was more important than ever that democracy should be united with religion. Their social salvation lay in that direction. (applause) They needed a clear vision to start with, and she did not know of any better way than the study of the Bible.[13]

JTR may have recalled this diary clash some six years later, in February 1924, when he gave his popular talk on 'No. 10 Downing Street' to the Young People's Guild at the church, not least as it may have fallen to him to proffer his mistress's apologies, or it may have been his oversight that resulted in the clash, not long after beginning his No. 10 service.[14]

Rulings from the palaces

The *Daily Mirror* page covering Olwen's wedding ran two stories from London palaces, reflecting the times. First, from Buckingham Palace, the King was discarding the German names of the Royal family members, so goodbye Saxony and Schleswig-Holstein. The House of Windsor had arrived.

At the Palace of Westminster, there was a futile, last-ditch attempt to prevent women getting the vote.

Sir Frederick Banbury moved an amendment urging the deletion of the clauses by which women on the Local Government register who have attained the age of thirty shall be entitled to a parliamentary vote. A division being taken, the figures were: Against the amendment 385; For the amendment 55; Majority in favour of woman suffrage 330.

Although the result was generally considered a foregone conclusion, the strongest supporters of women's suffrage had never expected such a thumping majority. Sir Frederick, in support of his amendment, stated that the measure would add some 12,000,000 voters to the list. He quite recognised the valuable service done by women in the war, but the women who wanted the vote were not the women who had done the work. Women who wanted the vote, wanted it before the war for reasons quite apart from the war. A vote was not reward given for some meritorious service. It was given to people who had shown they were fit and capable to exercise the duty thrust upon them.[15]

The *Birmingham Post* observed:

Sir Frederick Banbury... endeavoured to interest a drowsy audience in a dissertation on the nature of woman, accompanied by political reflections such as an experienced Parliamentarian who had always opposed woman suffrage could summon from recollection of past speeches. It was not an exhilarating performance. Woman, according to Sir Frederick Banbury, is a hysterical and sentimental creature, peculiarly liable to gusts and waves of feeling. She is therefore unfit to vote and take part in public affairs.[16]

Banbury was regarded as quite an institution in the House, a diligent backbencher, punctual and fond of formal attire. His remarks didn't win the day.

Welsh concert at Downing Street, for the depot

On Tuesday, 26 June, Downing Street hosted a charity concert with a Welsh programme in aid of the Welsh Industries Association (WIA) depot. The concert was presided over by Princess Mary, the first time she had been officially associated with a purely Welsh movement. The PM popped in from time to time, including when a Welsh Guards glee party sang the Welsh national anthem.[17] In 1919, JTR would organise another concert for the WIA, the first No. 10 concert open to the paying public.

On Thursday, 28 June, Mrs Lloyd George opened a sale of work on behalf of the Bromley Cripples' Parlour, but her impending trip to Scotland meant she had to disappoint those expecting her to open the bazaar in the rectory gardens of St George's, Stepney, in the East End. Lady Benn, wife of Sir John Benn who had been with Mrs Lloyd George when visiting the Mile End Road kitchen in April, did the honours.[18] Sir John had previously been the local MP, the seat now held by his son William Wedgwood Benn (beginning the Benn political dynasty). (see p.299)

Freedom in Scotland

On 29 June, accompanied by a large party of Scottish MPs, she returned to Glasgow, where the PM was granted the Freedom of the City. On arrival at the station the women of the local munitions workers choir gave a rousing rendition of 'Men of Harlech', warranting full front-page coverage in Christabel Pankhurst's WPSU journal, *Britannia* (incorporating *The Suffragette*).[19] Lloyd George was pushing hard to win the war in the face of calls to settle for peace, and such events with munitions workers were aimed at sustaining support for battling on.

On 30 June, the newspapers also covered an interview, on the challenges of drink, that Mrs Lloyd George had given to Judge Neil of Chicago (a US campaigner for 'Mother's Pensions'), during National Baby Week. Her realistic approach, that for temperance to be successful men working in hot conditions would need something other than beer to drink, gave the liquor lobby scope to suggest she had 'let the cat out of the bag'. (see p.372)

JULY 1917

While north of the border she made her own side trip, making five stops in the city of Dundee:

> Mrs Lloyd George made a round of visits in the city on Monday [2 July] before taking her departure for the south. In company with the Lord Provost Don and Mrs Don, she first called at the Red Cross Hospital, Lochee, and spoke some cheering words to the wounded soldiers.
> Next she visited King's Cross Works and Mid St Mill belonging to the firm of which the Lord Provost is senior partner, and was shown the

various processes of jute spinning and manufacture, in which she evinced much interest.

Thereafter the party proceeded to a shell factory and saw the girls at work, Mrs Lloyd George receiving as a memento of her visit the base of a shell to be used as a match-box.

The next call was at the yard of the Caledonian Shipbuilding and Engineering Company, where the party were received by Mrs Grant Barclay, the wife of the manager, and Miss Grant Barclay, and shown over the yard.

Finally, a visit was paid to the warehouse of Mr D. M. Brown, Mrs Lloyd George expressing her gratification at seeing such a handsome emporium in Dundee.

Among the wounded soldiers introduced to Mrs Lloyd George during her visit to Lochee Red Cross Hospital was one bearing the name of George Lloyd. It was explained that he was, however, generally called Lloyd George – a sort of compliment to the Premier.

The wife of the Premier took her departure from Dundee on the 4.18p.m. train, and met her husband at Edinburgh.[20]

It was then, as promised, off to Bournemouth on Thursday, 5 July, attending a reception held at the Richmond Hill lecture hall in connection with the Free Church Council Homes, and in the evening presenting the prizes at the annual speech day at the Bournemouth Collegiate School for Girls.[21] The next day, while on the south coast, she visited the Netley Welsh Hospital, staying the weekend with the Monds, at Melchet Court.

The National Economy Exhibition

On Tuesday, 10 July, Mrs Lloyd George was at the National Economy Exhibition at the New County Hall, on London's South Bank. The next day, after a Troops Fund meeting, she opened a YWCA canteen in Euston in the evening. (see p.306)

After another Fund sub-committee on 11 July, she chaired the full executive committee a week later.

On 12 July, it was down to Poplar to open a fete, along with Will Crooks (with whom she and the PM had had tea in January). *Pathé News* filmed the event.

1917: The Uncrowned Queen of Wales

Mrs Lloyd George, opening a fête at Poplar on Thursday in aid of local charities and the V.T.C. [Volunteer Training Corps], at which the Right Hon. Will Crooks was present, congratulated that gentleman on his recovery, and said she hoped he would live long to fight the battle of the people.[22]

Will Crooks' latest 'battle of the people' was in voicing their protests that promises to stem the frequent air raids were failing, there having being nine or ten Zeppelin raids over the East End. On 9 July, Lloyd George had called a meeting at No. 10 in connection with the latest raid, the crowds calling for reprisals.[23]

Naval comparisons... and a bold stroke

On 17 July, Lloyd George brought Winston Churchill back in from the cold, where he had languished since the Dardanelles disaster, appointing him as Minister of Munitions. This letter, in the JTR Collection, of 19 July from Churchill to Mrs Lloyd George, thus came at an interesting juncture.

> 33 Eccleston Square, SW1, 19.7.17
>
> My dear Mrs Lloyd George, I think you took away the copy I gave you of Naval Comparisons. This is to let you know that it has secret information in it, and that, if you have it, it should go into the fire or into one of the Prime Minister's boxes after you have read it.
>
> I cannot help feeling anxious – not on my own account – about this bold stroke, and you know how profusely I hope he will not have cause to regret it. I don't think he will.
>
> Very many thanks for all your kindness to me. Yours and mine, Winston Churchill[24]

Was the 'bold stroke' his appointment, or some other strategic move?

In his 1960 memoir of his father, Richard Lloyd George recalled what may well have been the same dinner:

> It was a turning point for Winston Churchill... He dined with father at No. 10. After the meal, father took him into another room. There, on the wall, was the framed placard brought out by the *Daily Express* at the time of the Marconi affair. It read 'Churchill defends Lloyd

George'. It must have been a great moment for the two battle-scarred friends.[25]

Clearly Mrs Lloyd George could be trusted with the naval secrets. Hopefully Churchill would be more careful about leaving papers lying around.

Music, Music, Music

On Friday, 20 July, the PM's wife was in south London, giving out prizes at the Royal Normal College and Academy of Music for the Blind, in Upper Norwood.[26]

The following day the Lloyd Georges attended the Belgian National Feast at Queen's Hall, London, in commemoration of Belgian Independence Day. After the singing of *'La Brabançonne'* (The Song of Brabant) by a choir of 400 Belgian refugee children, Lloyd George gave a speech in French.[27]

That afternoon, as the Baby Week month drew to its close, she was again welcomed to the strains of 'Men of Harlech' at a new nursery for 30 children in Hendon. The children all looked happy, notwithstanding that her visit (shortly after 3pm) interrupted their normal afternoon siesta. She urged the country to match the efforts made in her own county.

> Mrs Lloyd George, who was enthusiastically applauded on rising to speak, said she was sure they would forgive her for not making a speech. It was a pleasure, however, to be able to take part in that function. She had just been to see the day nursery, and was delighted to find the babies looking so happy and comfortable. The committee, she thought, were to be congratulated on finding such a nice airy place for the little ones.
>
> Children, she said, were getting a good show in these days, and it was to be hoped that much good would result from Baby Week. It was more important than ever that the lives of the children should be saved and that everything possible must be done to help mothers by giving them good nourishment so that their babies might grow to be strong men and women.
>
> She was pleased to see that much was being done in this way in all parts of the country. In her own county of Carmarthenshire [*sic*], education authorities had for two years at least looked after the children's tonsils,

teeth and eyes, and although 2,000 operations had taken place, only one child had died. (Applause) This spoke well for the work done in Wales, and she would like to see every country doing as much as her own.[28]

Carmarthenshire, Carnarvonshire… easily confused.

At the end of the month, a year on from Mametz Wood, the Welsh 38th redeemed its reputation in a successful attack at Pilckem Ridge, near Ypres in Flanders, which opened the Battle of Passchendaele, the appalling mud and bloodbath which would last until November, though not before claiming the life of that year's bard at the Birkenhead National Eisteddfod.

AUGUST 1917

Elected, in absentia

Mrs Lloyd George spent most of August in Wales. In absentia she was elected deputy president of the north Wales branch of the Welsh Housing and Development Association, another position accumulated as a public figure.[29]

The grilles come down, in absentia

Until now women had to observe House of Commons debates through the ladies' grille, behind which 'little can be heard and still less seen of proceedings in which they took a great interest'.[30]

> THE LADIES' GRILLE: Wednesday May Decide Its Fate: On the invitation of Sir Alfred Mond, First Commissioner of Works, the House of Commons on Wednesday will be asked to decide the fate of the grilles in front of the Ladies' Gallery. Not long ago, a petition headed by Mrs Lloyd George and signed by nearly 200 wives of Ministers and members was presented to the Government requesting the removal of the obstruction.
>
> The present House seems to be sympathetic to the idea. In the past this has not been the case. In 1869 a proposal to remove the grille was opposed by Mr Layard, the then First Commissioner of Works, who read a letter from a lady, pointing out the advantages of the grille conferred on all parties. One was that it enabled a lady to leave unobserved when a bore was speaking, even though the bore happened to be the friend who

had obtained her seat for her. He thought there was a good deal of truth in that letter, and that the House would take the ladies' view of the matter. The House did, and the motion was withdrawn. The subject arose again in 1885, but by 121 votes to 75 the House refused to sanction the alteration. This week's decision, however, will probably go in favour of the removal of the grille.[31]

On 15 August, the House voted to remove the grille, approving the sum of no more than £5 to defray costs. After a call that the grilles should not leave the House, they remain today in an inner window, marked by a plaque, with one in the Museum of London. Millicent Fawcett suggested they should be displayed in the House with wax dummies behind them. The Women's Freedom League requested one, and the Countess of Strafford suggested the grilles be melted down to produce Braille type for poor blind soldiers.

Mari Takayanagi, Senior Archivist at the Parliamentary Archives, wrote on the centenary of their removal:

> Although the decision to remove the grilles was collectively made by the House of Commons, Sir Alfred Mond clearly took care to find a new home for them and to put his name on this plaque. It is good to know that Mond must have taken pride in this, as he was also a great supporter of women's suffrage; he had spoken on the issue in Parliament, in particular seconding a Conciliation Bill in 1912, and been vice-president of the Men's League for Women's Suffrage.[32]

Mrs Lloyd George knew the ladies' grille well, not least from when Lloyd George was negotiating his ground-breaking 1909/10 Budget Bill, as recalled by Charles T. King in his history, *The Asquith Parliament*:

> One night I looked up at the ladies' grille about midnight. Quite a number of wives and relatives of MPs were there. At one o'clock most of them had gone... It was not until the Chancellor of the Exchequer some time towards the morning thrust his papers wearily into a red despatch box, snapped the fastening with a little click and vanished into the shadows behind the Speaker's chair that the silent watcher above broke her lonely vigil.[33]

The first Women's Institute hall

On Wednesday, 22 August, Mrs Lloyd George motored inland from Criccieth, with Megan and Mrs William George, to Penrhyndeudraeth, to open the UK's first Women's Institute hall. Much credit was due to local-born Alice Williams, a key founder of the movement, sister of Sir Osmond Williams, Lord-Lieutenant of Merionethshire. The hall survives today alongside Minffordd station on the Ffestiniog tourist railway of Snowdonia / Eryri National Park. (illustration 52)

> Mrs Lloyd George, who was received with cheers, congratulated the president on the Welsh atmosphere at the gathering. It was a pleasure to see young ladies dressed in Welsh costume and the troop of Welsh Boy Scouts. The Women's Institutes were becoming very popular in north Wales, thanks to the public spirit and patriotism of Welsh women, assisted by Mr Nugent Harris, secretary of A.O. Society.

Nugent Harris had been on the January 1916 Criccieth WI platform with Mrs Lloyd George.

> The object of these Institutes was to organise women to cultivate vegetables, fruit, etc., and to rear poultry, etc., and thus increase the food supply of the district in which they happened to reside. Cottagers and small-holders would find that in doing so they were not only serving their country by producing food, but that they were doing pleasant work, for there was great pleasure in gardening, farming, poultry rearing, and other profitable avenues of agriculture.
>
> French women had been working on the land for years, but until the outbreak of the war they rarely met with women workers on the farms of this country. Today it was quite a common sight to meet women engaged in the healthy work of cultivating land. (hear, hear) In this way they were bringing their country nearer to that period when they would be able to live entirely on their own resources. (cheers)
>
> They ought to be able to do much in the way of vegetable growing, and especially in the cultivation of fruit in that part of the country, for the climate was mild, while frosts were rare.
>
> Speaking in Welsh, Mrs Lloyd George hoped the women of that part would take up fruit growing, and following the example of French women go whole-heartedly into the work. In a short time they would find themselves in love with their fruit trees. That was why the women of

France were as indignant with the Germans over the wanton destruction of their fruit trees as they were over the shelling of their beautiful churches and cathedrals.

She hoped that in a very short time they would be able in that part to depend entirely on their own efforts to cultivate vegetables and fruit, and that all the jam they needed would be home-made, for there was nothing like jam made from home-grown fruit.[34]

There followed more speeches and a presentation to Alice Williams.

Mrs Lloyd George, a keen gardener, would at times open her own gardens at Brynawelon to the public.

Welsh wind and rain blows down the tent

The next week, things didn't go quite to plan. On Tuesday, 28 August, the weather intervened at a fete in aid of the Welsh Heroes Memorial Fund at Robert Thomas' Garreglwyd, Holyhead, estate. A huge marquee was blown down, and torrential rain made the entertainment from notable artists from around the country (including George Robey, perhaps the most famous music-hall performer of the era) nigh impossible, though some stayed on to do their bit in two local cinemas made available by their owners.[35] Mrs Lloyd George would return in September for a rescheduled Garreglwyd fete.

The next day, 29 August, the organisers of a sale at the Red Cross Hospital near Bangor were also concerned that bad weather might scupper their efforts, but the gods were kinder than at Holyhead, allowing her to do the honours, accompanied by Red Cross VAD Olwen. Works made by the soldiers were sold and Private Loud, Nurse Jones *et al* competed in the races. (see p.350)

That evening the Methodist Mrs Lloyd George was in Caernarfon celebrating the bicentenary of the birth of William Williams of Pantycelyn: 'the chief hymn-writer of the Methodist awakening in Wales, and much of the success of Welsh Methodism must be attributed to the popularity of his hymns.'[36] In Richard Lloyd George's view, 'his hymns will stand comparison with Luther's'.[37] We may assume a few hymns were sung.

CHAPTER 7

1917: Keeping Going

(September to December 1917)

'I hope that his tremendous load of responsibilities will not crush him. Upon him we lean, to him the Empire looks for guidance and aid. Cymru am byth.'

W. M. Hughes, September 1917

SEPTEMBER 1917

HOSTILITIES HAD ENTERED their fourth year in August, with an end still not in sight, though American troops had now entered into the field. At home, campaigns continued to feed the nation, to care for the increasing numbers of wounded, and cope with ongoing austerity.

On 1 September, Mrs Lloyd George wrote to the *Daily Telegraph* on domestic science training. Her letter gained attention, some reactionary voices suggesting women should abandon politics and return to their household duties. (see p.307)

Billy sends a cheque

She also received a £100 cheque for the Fund from Billy Hughes, the Welsh-born Prime Minister of Australia, the money coming from a similar Australian fund. He signed off his letter with his support (see above) for her husband, two prime ministers under pressure, working to win the war.[1]

On the silver screen: movie time for mothers

Mid-month, Mrs Lloyd George and friends hit the silver screen, appearing 'as themselves' in a new short silent film called *Motherhood*, part of the ongoing Baby Week campaigns. (illustration 29)

> MATINEE AT THE PALACE: On Thursday afternoon, by permission of Mr John Thornburn, a matinee was held at the Palace. The picture programme, which was of highly entertaining character, included the first-rate film, *Motherhood*, in which Mrs Lloyd George, the Duchess of Marlborough, Lady Rhondda, and the late Sir Richard Burbidge are seen. The Palace orchestra attended and played in pleasing style a capital selection of music.[2]

This particular 'Palace' was the Tamworth cinema, in the Midlands.

A recent (2019) synopsis of the film describes the plot as one where, 'A factory girl makes use of the National Baby Week Council while a slut's baby dies.' But Mrs Lloyd George is not visible. Perhaps at the beginning of the film there was a showing of the council's meeting, with her in the chair, and statements perhaps from some of those around the table. We get one clue from this snippet from *The Sunday Pictorial*:

> I think it's the Mascot Day organiser, who is also on the Baby Week Council, who tells that amusing story about the *Motherhood* film. Mrs Lloyd George was bidden to start speechifying while the operator operated and the lesser lights registered attention, as we've learnt to say in movie talk. 'That's enough,' said the operator after a while. 'Now applaud,' and the obedient Mrs Lloyd George was the first to applaud her own speech. And after that they started the film over again![3]

Freedom of Birkenhead and the 'Black Chair' Eisteddfod

The month's most significant public event was a visit to Birkenhead, the Prime Minister receiving the Freedom of the City and the Lloyd George family attending the National Eisteddfod on 6 September. The 'Black Chair' Birkenhead National Eisteddfod is long remembered for the poignant absence of the prize-winning bard 'Hedd Wyn', Private Ellis Evans, of the Royal Welch Fusiliers, who had sent his poem from the Front in Flanders, but who was killed in July, serving with the 38th on the first day of Passchendaele. After his name was read out, as per tradition for him to take his place, a black cloth was draped over the empty chair. The chair that year had been designed and carved by a Belgian refugee, resident in Birkenhead.

As poignant, though less remembered today, was the appearance on the stage of Lance Corporal Samuel Evans, himself crippled for life, the sole survivor of a choir from the 17th Battalion Royal Welch Fusiliers that had won a prize at the 1915 Bangor National Eisteddfod, but who had all made the supreme sacrifice. Lieutenant-General Sir Owen Thomas pinned a white and black rosette to the chest of the survivor, a tribute which had been sent by the family of two of the fallen choir members.

The tradition of singing at the Eisteddfod, at the National Psalmody Festival begun in Aberystwyth in 1916, was held again for the second time, attended by the Lloyd Georges.[4]

Llanystumdwy unveilings

After the Eisteddfod they drove to Criccieth, and were joined by Sir George Riddell and Lloyd George's secretary Philip Kerr, picnicking *en route*. Lloyd George fell ill on 8 September and stayed at Criccieth longer than planned.[5] Despite illness, the PM, accompanied by Mrs Lloyd George, their two daughters, his brother William Lloyd George, and many visitors (including Marie Corelli the novelist), unveiled two portraits at his Llanystumdwy boyhood home: one of his old schoolmaster David Evans, and one of Sir Hugh Ellis-Nanney, his opponent at his first election in Carnarvon Boroughs, in 1890, when Lloyd George won by 18 votes after a recount.[6]

Fete at Garreglwyd

Mrs Lloyd George returned to Holyhead on 12 September for the rescheduled Garreglwyd fete (blown away in August's wind and rain). She read out a signed message from the Prime Minister, which sold for £100.[7]

OCTOBER 1917

On 15 October, Miss Olive Edis FRPS came to Downing Street to photograph Mrs Lloyd George and the PM for the forthcoming biography of the Premier by Harold Spender. (illustration 2) In 1918, Olive Edis would be the first woman appointed as an official war artist, and was to visit France to photograph women's war work. The trip was delayed, in part due to opposition to a woman visiting a war zone. She did travel over in 1919 to chronicle the lives of women working on the front lines, and the devastation. Miss Edis was one of the first people in the country to use the Lumière brothers' autochrome colour process professionally.[8]

Welsh troops funds move towards merger

Lady Glanusk chaired the 11 October Fund committee, and on Friday, 19 October, Mrs Lloyd George and the Fund's sub-committee met representatives of Sir Owen Thomas' fund to finalise plans for a merger of their funds, to be reviewed and ratified at a Shrewsbury conference in November.[9]

That weekend she travelled to Wales, and on Monday, 22 October, received a noisy reception from drink prohibitionists in Carmarthen when calling on the temperance movement to unite. (see p.375)

Bazaar at Holywell, north Wales

While in Carmarthen, she joined the mayor and mayoress at the local YMCA, 'expressing admiration for the work done there'. On Wednesday, 24 October, on her first visit to Holywell, north Wales, she opened a four-day fund-raising bazaar for the Rehoboth Calvinistic Methodist and the English Presbyterian churches, later attending a Free Church singing festival at the nearby Bagillt Colliery district. An address of welcome, in album form, was presented to her.

> Mrs Lloyd George referred to the immense delight which Welsh people experienced in singing their hymns. She thanked the people for the collections which were made that day on behalf of the Welsh Troops Fund. The authorities in London were still sending out comforts for the Welsh soldiers, and that work would be continued during the winter. The Government was giving substantial aid, and the outside efforts were

to supplement that aid, which would also be used for assisting disabled soldiers who returned home after fighting.[10]

Breakfast for the clergy

The imaginative *Edinburgh Evening News* had other ideas for what she might have been doing that evening, their column on 26 October querying the PM's choice of breakfast companions, as he was being roundly criticized for being absent from Parliament.

> THE MORNING AFTER
> The 30 clergymen who breakfasted with Mr Lloyd George yesterday had an unexampled opportunity of discussing what manner of man he really is. Yesterday morning was, of course, 'the morning after the night before'. To be blithe and cheerful at breakfast is said to be a good indication of a sweet and wholesome nature. Mr Lloyd George's conversational sallies, following upon the defeat of his latest scheme to endow the landlords, must have been particularly interesting.
>
> Picture Mrs Lloyd George rushing round to the grocer's shop the previous evening for bacon and eggs to supply 30 clerics 'of all denominations' – and these commodities (the bacon and eggs, not the clergymen) so scarce and dear! We read that their visit lasted a couple of hours, and that the meal was followed by an informal talk on war conditions.
>
> Lucky clergymen to have privileges which the House of Commons can only command when the Government is in a hole – the fellowship and the views of the Premier.
>
> It is, of course, nobody's business but his own whom Mr Lloyd George invites to breakfast, but we find it a little difficult to trace any connection between a clerical breakfast party at Downing Street and 'the vigorous prosecution of the war'. Perhaps, however, the Premier has some new jobs to offer at the public expense and was unselfishly devoting his breakfast time to 'spotting talent' among wearers of the cloth.[11]

The Rev. J. T. Rhys may have been in attendance.

The endowment of landlords will have referred to the defeat in the Commons of the Petroleum Bill, reported in the paper the previous day, which proposed to give landowners royalties to minerals discovered by publicly funded exploration of their land, rather than allowing the government to use the money to prosecute the war.[12]

NOVEMBER 1917

On 10 November, Mrs Lloyd George was cutting bread at a troops canteen in London Bridge (see p.313) but did not attend the 14 November committee. She and Olwen were spotted on the London Underground, on 18 November, the *Sunday Pictorial* reporting approvingly: 'Mrs Lloyd George is setting a good example as a petrol-saver and non-motorist for the duration. I saw her with her daughter (Mrs Carey Evans) a day or two ago squeezing into a crowded train on the Underground. Fortunately she hadn't to straphang.'[13]

Was the Underground not only economical but also a safer way to travel? After some early wartime Zeppelin raids, columnist Samuell Pepys Junior resolved: 'henceforth I will always travel underground by night while the warr lasts, being cheper, as 'tis safer.'[14]

The *Pictorial*'s front page reported the death in Palestine of Liberal MP Neil Primrose, with whom she had travelled to Caernarfon earlier in the year and whose wedding she had attended.

As a further economy measure, as opposed to health, it was reported that Mrs Lloyd George had told the *London Express* that women should stop smoking to save tobacco, noting that neither she nor her daughters had ever smoked.[15]

On 19 November, she made a further visit to the day nursery at Woolwich Arsenal, the munitionettes still making shells for a war which would have almost another year to run.[16]

Preparations for a Welsh pageant

Though there was a war on, the pre-Christmas entertainment and fund-raising calendar was getting crowded, Mrs Lloyd George's Shaftesbury Theatre Welsh Pageant in aid of the Welsh Heroes' Fund having to be postponed until 18 December in order to avoid clashing with other charity matinees.[17] The pageant, organised by the producers Messrs Grossmith and Laurillard (who had a lease on the theatre), featured the artists Violet Loraine and Ethel Levey, the ever-supportive George Robey, and many others, including many amateurs, and the band of the Welsh Guards.

The *Sunday Pictorial* gossip columnist had been having tea with Mrs Lloyd George on 25 November: 'Dear Girl in France, who do you think I went to take tea with last week? Mrs Lloyd George. And she makes you have the real sit-down kind that I love, no upsetting it over your best frock.'[18]

More seriously, the columnist gave further coverage to the Bangor science building, the Welsh Heroes Memorial, acknowledging the lead being played by Lady Milsom Rees, wife of the Welsh surgeon and laryngologist who treated many singers, and the Royal Household.

The *Manchester Evening News* ran a *Daily Express* story dubbing the memorial an expensive hobby and noble idea.

> Mrs Lloyd George has a hobby. It is an expensive hobby, for it is expected to cost at least £150,000. When the money is raised – and spent – a noble idea will have come into being in the shape of a vast memorial to the heroes of North Wales who have fallen in the war. The memorial is to take the form of a great science university built round a central hall, in which will be enshrined the name of every fallen soldier, sailor, and nurse belonging to North Wales. Of the £150,000, a total of £53,000 has already been raised.[19]

On Tuesday, 27 November, Olwen joined her in opening another canteen for London's workforce, at the White City. (see p.313) (illustration 43)

In the final week of November she attended a Frivolous Fair and Serious Exhibition, for the Surgical Requisites Association (see p.351), and on 28 November opened the Church Army's sale at Westminster, where a young girl, dressed in a Welsh dress, had a moving story:

> She was much interested in a little girl who presented her with a bouquet. It was explained that the girl's father, a miner, threw up his work to join the Army, and, returning on leave from France, was unable to find his wife and four children before he returned. His officer appealed to the Church Army, and they discovered that the mother had broken down mentally and was in an asylum, and that the children were in the workhouse. The Church Army had taken charge of the children, and it had just been learnt that the father had been severely wounded in France, and had won the D.C.M.
>
> Mrs Lloyd George said that the Church Army had now extended its work to include discharged and disabled soldiers. 'There is a great deal we can all do to help these discharged and disabled soldiers, in addition to what the Government proposes to do, and it would be a great encouragement to those who were fighting to know that there was a great army of people at home determined to help them in every way.'[20]

William Lewis and the Fund were becoming part of that 'great army'. On 30 November, Mrs Lloyd George attended the Shrewsbury conference that established the Welsh National Fund for the Welfare of the Sailors and Soldiers of Wales, coordinating the resources and influence of her Fund, the Troops Fund run by Brigadier Sir Owen Thomas, and the pension authorities of Wales. (see p.249) The focus was steadily moving away from providing comforts in the field to rehabilitation back at home.

I had a dream: Poland calling

As the month drew to a close, Mrs Lloyd George received two letters (preserved in the JTR archive) from the novelist and poet Miss Laurence Alma Tadema, daughter of the Dutch painter Lawrence Alma Tadema, the first from her St John's Wood home.[21]

> 34 Grove End Road, London, N.W., 28 November 1917
> Dear Mrs Lloyd George,
>
> I hope you will not mind my telling you of a rather remarkable dream I had last night concerning your illustrious husband. I dreamed that I had a short but stirring conversation with him, and that, as he turned away, I called him back, saying:
>
> 'Wait, I have something important to tell you. There is a silver wreath hanging over your head, but you seem not to know what is written on the finest of its leaves.'
>
> He looked round. 'What is it?' he asked.
>
> And I answered, 'Poland.'
>
> Mr Lloyd George then turned right back, and his eyes looked as if he was probing a new idea. 'I will think over this,' said he, and then walked quickly away.
>
> It seems to me that this dream is interesting enough to be worth recording, in case it ever comes true.
>
> Believe me, Sincerely yours, Laurence Alma Tadema

That week, the possibility of an independent future for Poland was under intense scrutiny, as the October Revolution had led to the withdrawal of Russia from the war. Germany had plans for a Teutonic republic for Poland.

Her second letter, written two days later,[22] was sent from the Polish

Victims Relief Fund, 11 Haymarket, of which Mrs Lloyd George was a patron:

> Dear Mrs Lloyd George,
> I expect to go abroad next week on matters connected with the Polish Red Cross in France and with the Homes for Polish Refugee Children in Switzerland. I shall therefore not be here during the most important weeks of the Christmas shopping season. I am writing however to enlist your sympathies in the 'Polish Shop' – a new venture of ours. You will find it at No. 26 Regent Street, where, from November 26 onwards, a variety of charming things will be on sale, at moderate prices. May I hope that in my absence you, as a patroness of the Polish Victims Relief Fund, will help us by taking a personal interest in the shop, by calling in whenever you pass, by approving of our display, and by persuading your friends to do likewise?

The Polish Victims Relief Fund was set up in 1915 on the initiative of Jan Paderewski, the musician, to support the needy in Poland. Lawrence Alma Tadema's 1891 portrait of him is regarded as a masterpiece of art. His daughter Laurence was a great admirer of his music and his politics and kept a regular correspondence with him. Paderewski, a campaigner for Polish independence, served as Poland's PM in 1919 for the duration of the post-war peace talks, before returning to his musical career. He developed a good relationship with Lloyd George (he had lunched with Lloyd George in March 1915)[23] even though the Welsh Wizard couldn't deliver Poland's preferred terms at Versailles.[24]

In April 1918, Lawrence Alma Tadema's painting, *The Staircase*, would be included in a 16-day Christie's sale of artworks in aid of the Red Cross.[25] Laurence was appointed CBE in 1918 and was secretary of the relief fund until her death in 1940.

DECEMBER 1917

Olivia Maitland-Davidson kicked off December in fine form in her 'Letters from Eve' in *The Tatler*, sustaining the promotion of the Welsh Heroes' Memorial to those who might have had the wherewithal:

> And while I'm on the great (some think, of course, the only) subject of money, I mustn't forget to tell you of Mrs Lloyd George's new scheme

– which is to raise no less than £150,000 for a North Wales Heroes' Memorial, which at first sight sounds – well, *un peu épais*, what? But when you've heard the P.M.'s wife talking about it... Anyway, listen. It's to provide not only a sentimental but also a practical memorial to the men who have fallen, in the shape of an extension in north Wales of the University College for the teaching and encouragement of science in all its branches. The benefits of the institution will be open to all men and women of all British and friendly nationalities, and a substantial sum will be provided to give free education and maintenance to the sons and daughters of the fallen. There!

Now, £150,000 is wanted. £53,000 has already been subscribed (£20,000 of it by Mr R. J. Thomas). With a monster matinée at the Shaftesbury Theatre on December 18, Mrs Lloyd George hopes to collect some more of the £10,000 that's been earmarked as the very least that's to be expected from London. As for the rest – well, if any of you millionaire men read this paragraph you won't forget to send along a cheque for a thousand or so to 10, Downing Street, will you? It'll be a splendid matinée anyway, and as for the cause – could there be a better one than, with mere filthy lucre, to do some small thing for the children of the men but for whom there'd be no England to love and live for?[26]

A week later Mrs Lloyd George caught the flu, a day after an early morning air raid on London on 6 December, as she recounted to Olwen:

The air raid was the night before I was bad. Wasn't it lucky. Tada had gone to Walton, and at 3 in the morning old Wilkam minus teeth came to call me. Got up, went down, at 3.30 they said all clear, back to bed, called again at 4. Then they came with a vengeance, dropped a bomb on the H. of Commons, one in St James Park...[27]

It was the first anniversary of Lloyd George's premiership.
The *Stirling Observer*'s London report wrote:

INFLUENZA AT 10 DOWNING STREET: The Prime Minister is not the only victim at 10 Downing Street of the raw November winds and of hard work. Mrs Lloyd George, whose sustained efforts on behalf of the present issue of War Bonds have been a light and an example to the womanhood of the country, followed the Prime Minister to the sick room and was in the early part of the week an unwilling martyr to the ravages of influenza.[28]

She was back on her feet for a meeting at the Mansion House on 17 December, called by the Lord Mayor to meet with London's mayors, planning the 1918 St David's Day campaign.

A Welsh pageant for Welsh heroes

On 18 December, the rescheduled Welsh pageant in aid of the Welsh Heroes' Memorial took place at London's Shaftesbury Theatre, gaining good coverage in the society papers, such as *The Sketch*:

> The biggest feature of a striking programme was a Masque of Welsh Mythology, based upon the Arthurian legend, by Mr Louis N. Parker, with music by Mr Ivor Novello, who is seen in one of our photographs as Sir Galahad. The old legend was very picturesquely presented, the author's central idea being the rousing of the three bards by the noise of war, and their summons to King Arthur, some of the Knights of the Round Table, and the ladies of the legend. The King Arthur of the Masque was Mr H. B. Irving, and the Guinevere – rendered in this instance, and in pure Welsh, Queen Gwynhwyvar – the Duchess of Westminster, and the whole company included many well-known actors and amateurs. The performance was a great success, and Mrs Lloyd George is to be congratulated upon a picturesque realisation of a poetic and patriotic idea, carried out for an admirable object.[29]

The Welsh Ivor Novello, on his way to becoming one of the most successful entertainers of the time, was the composer, at 21, of the highly popular First World War song, 'Keep the Home Fires Burning', written in 1914.

A prize draw at Selfridges

On 20 December, it was time to join Gordon Selfridge in Oxford Street, to draw prizes that the store had offered to those who had bought war bonds there in the first two weeks of the month. The *Pall Mall Gazette* correspondent managed to make a drama out of an over-vigorous policeman, a flimsy box and the mystery of who had won:

> THE REVOLVING BOX and THE POLICE SERGEANT: Several hundred holders of War Loan Bonds purchased at Selfridges between Monday,

December 3, and Wednesday, December 12, attended the draw for prize money offered by the firm, which was made by Mrs Lloyd George in the Palm Court this morning. Lady Markham accompanied Mrs Lloyd George.

In thanking Mrs Lloyd George for having consented to undertake the task, Mr Gordon Selfridge expressed his pleasure that Bonds to the value of £3,780,000 had been sold on the premises during the campaign. Every care had been taken to ensure a fair prize-winning chance for each Bond purchaser.

A police sergeant turned the huge revolving box containing the cardboard tickets, but so vigorously did he set about his work that a number of the cardboard slips escaped from the box. There was a brief halt while the box was fortified, and then once again the sergeant twirled the box. This time there was no mishap, and amid cheers Mrs Lloyd George drew out the first winning number.

There were in all five different sets of tickets placed in the box, one for each of the five different Bond denominations – £200, £100, £60, £20, and £5. Only a few thousand tickets went into the box for each of the first three denominations, but over 2,000 cards had to be put into the box for the £5 denomination. Two men it took to drag the huge sack-full of card-slips to the box, and the burly sergeant himself had to lend a hand to tip them into it. In all, 972 prizes were drawn [the paper listed some of the numbers].

Some time was spent in strengthening the box for the reception of the £5 tickets, and as there were signs of impatience among the crowd of excited bond-holders, Mr Gordon Selfridge soothed them with a little jest. 'Before we loan this box to the Government,' he said, amid general laughter, 'I'm afraid we'll have to strengthen it somewhat.'

A *Pall Mall Gazette* representative was informed that no official list of the names of the prize winners will be obtainable for several days. 'Vouchers must first be carefully verified,' he was informed.[30]

The draw over, Mrs Lloyd George soon made her way to Wales for Christmas. She had written the weekend before to Olwen, then staying in Criccieth: 'We cannot come before Friday as the draw at Selfridges is not until Thursday.'[31]

As the year closed, the sportswoman's page of the *Illustrated Sporting and Dramatic News* wrote:

Mrs Lloyd George is a favourite, and she will be more than that, for we Britons dearly love a good woman, and she is just that. We don't talk about her price being above rubies, because we are not Solomons, but, quite commonplace folk as we are, we just love her gentle, kindly face, her fine enthusiasms, and her absolute lack of frills, I mean of the metaphorical kind. For the real frills she probably likes them as well as any woman, and she has quite conquered the chief problem of dress, which is suitability.

All this leads up to the success of her matinée for the Welsh Heroes' Fund. It was largely a personal success. There was a homely, motherly, practical, all-British note through it from start to finish.

I begin to believe that Mrs Lloyd George may quite unconsciously lead us to the old love for the honest, the straight, the true, and away from all the high-browed artificiality which, before war broke out, made us like a nation of semi-idiots, belittling everything natural and nice, and exalting all that was unnatural and well, the opposite of nice. The war began the improvement, and has enormously developed it.

To a good woman, highly placed, it may be left to give the deathblow to exotic frivolity and pretentious culture of the so-called aesthetic.[32]

Whatever the hyperbole, it suggests the straightforward approach of Mrs Lloyd George was very welcome when there was little time for frivolity. The war, even after much appalling sacrifice, was by no means won.

CHAPTER 8

1918: Saving Money, Saving Lives

(January to April 1918)

'It has been said that it is better to put a fence on the top of the precipice than an ambulance at the bottom.'
Margaret Lloyd George, March 1918

JANUARY 1918

THE TROOPS FUND Committee met once in January, chaired by Lord Justice Bankes. Mrs Lloyd George's engagements began in Bangor on 17 January, demonstrating her auctioneering skills by selling a pink tallow candle, for 23 shillings per inch, for a grand total of £4 8s. at a sale in aid of the VAD.[1]

While in Bangor, at the Normal College, she accepted a portrait of her husband in his robes as Chancellor of the Exchequer, painted by Sir Luke Fildes in 1909, observing that 'the portrait was painted in the good times of peace: since then stress and hard work had left their mark on the original.'[2]

The following day, 18 January, she visited Manchester and Liverpool to thank them for their support and to encourage planning for the next St David's Day flag day. (see p.254)

Meanwhile, the PM was responding to the increasing calls for a peace settlement which had been encouraged ten days earlier by US President Woodrow Wilson's 14 Point Peace programme. He asked the Commons: 'If any man standing in my place can find an honourable, equitable, just way out of this conflict without fighting it through, for Heaven's sake let him tell me. My own conviction is this – the people must either go on or go under.'[3]

There were rumours of drama ahead – it had been reported on 17 January that she had written a play, to be performed on the London stage in aid of the Fund.[4] The Welsh-language paper *Yr Herald Cymraeg* was closer to the truth: 'Mrs Lloyd George is said to have co-sponsored a play, soon to be performed in a West End theatre for the benefit of the Fund for the Welsh soldiers.'[5] It would be performed at a London Palladium matinee at the end of May, in aid of the Welsh Prisoners of War Fund.

On 24 January, the *Western Mail* revealed other dramatic plans: 'Mrs Lloyd George, as already announced, has consented to appear in a film drama. Mr Max Pemberton is writing the scenario for the interesting occasion.'[6]

The film may have been *The Life Story of David Lloyd George*, which was announced as a project on 21 February, but which was filmed with actors, and as far as one can tell the journalist and novelist Max Pemberton was not involved.

At the end of the month Mrs Lloyd George co-signed the Saving and Lending Campaign's 'Women's Manifesto to Women', calling on women to avoid waste and cut thoughtless spending. (see p.315)

FEBRUARY 1918

On 14 February, she welcomed her first grandchild, Valerie, daughter of Roberta and Richard. Valerie's brother Owen later wrote, 'not only did she arrive on St Valentine's Day but my father was at that moment at St Valéry, at the Front, so her name was an obvious choice.'[7] She stayed in Cricieth to support Roberta, returning to London on 26 February. Valerie and her cousin Margaret, Olwen's daughter, born a couple of months later, would spend many of their early years together.

On 23 February, she, Sir Joseph and Lady Davies, and Owain Evans, trustees of the Lloyd George American Fund, paid a further visit to the wool workrooms at Blaenau Ffestiniog, Bethesda, and Penygroes. (see p.38)

Women get the vote

The Representation of the People Act, giving some women the vote in parliamentary elections, had received the Royal Assent on 6 February. *The Ladies' Field* ran a supplement, 'WOMAN'S NEW POSITION', with an opening message from Mrs Lloyd George, and articles by Mrs Henry Fawcett, Miss Christabel Pankhurst, Judge Parry and the Rev. Constance Coltman, and others. In October, Constance Coltman had become the first British woman ordained into a mainstream Protestant church, in this case Congregationalist.[8]

In her simple but powerful message, Mrs Lloyd George downplayed the 'novelty', instead underlining the obvious logic that women should play an equal role, and with an eye to the future, stressing that this should continue and grow after the war and not be considered as something to reverse. It was a challenge that would have to be met when the troops came home.

> I have been asked to express an opinion on 'The New Woman Born of the War'. But is there, after all, anything new under the sun? Are not the countless new activities in which a woman is participating to-day simply an extension of that sphere which she has always filled as the complement and help-meet of Man? The war, indeed, has enormously extended the scope of woman's work. We see her fulfilling a hundred duties which never previously fell to her lot; but whether she be replacing a bank-clerk or shipbroker, a chauffeur or field-labourer, a liftman or an errand lad, the sex is still collectively obeying the ancient motto of the individual woman – 'DO THE NEXT THING'.
>
> And if in wartime the energies of woman, her initiative and brains, as well as her industry and muscle, have proved of such incalculable value to the Empire, it must certainly follow that in those schemes of peaceful reconstruction and reorganisation of the social structure, which must follow the war, she will find even fuller scope for her energies, to the good of the Empire and her own happiness. Margaret Lloyd George[9]

Success for women's suffrage would give Mrs Lloyd George the opportunity, and need, to play an unprecedented active electioneering role as a Prime Minister's wife when party politics returned after the war – her 'Next Thing' perhaps.

On 27 February, she was again deputising for the Prime Minister:

Mrs Lloyd George, on behalf of the Prime Minister, was presented with an illuminated address by the members of the Victoria Working Men's Club, Kew Gardens, on Wednesday night, in recognition of the great services which the Premier has rendered to the Empire. Sir George Cave, the Home Secretary, and Lady Cave were present.

In acknowledging the gift, Mrs Lloyd George said it was a token of confidence and sympathy with the Premier in his hard work. 'His burden is a very heavy one,' added Mrs Lloyd George, 'and there are plenty of people ready to criticise when anything goes wrong. We are thankful to say, and it is a great consolation to know it, that the vast majority of the people of this country are wishful to help in every possible way a man who is doing his very best to save his country.'[10]

In her later peacetime political campaigning, Mrs Lloyd George accepted that some criticism was to be expected, but took exception against anything she regarded as *unfair* criticism.[11]

In Wales that day, the Machynlleth Rural Council decided the demands on their resources precluded them from arranging a flag day, charity fatigue setting in.

MARCH 1918

On St David's Day, Mrs Lloyd George finally led the London parade, as extensive as in the previous year, touring London in style, a veritable army of women pinning flags on the workers' lapels and relieving them of their guineas, pounds, shillings and pence. The morning began, as before, by welcoming the children from Chailey with their gifts, at No. 10. (see p.255)

The army of fund-raising ladies was soon on the march again, selling war bonds from tanks to gain the attention of passers-by. (illustration 20) The *Westminster Gazette* publicised the locations:

> The City Tank at the back of the Royal Exchange will be opened in state at 12.30 p.m. on Monday by the Lord Mayor and Sheriffs. The offices of the city's local Central War Savings Committee, at 3, Lombard-street, will be open as a supplementary selling station for Tank Bonds and Certificates, to meet the convenience of those who cannot wait at the Tank.
>
> Mrs Lloyd George, the Duchess of Marlborough, Lady Rhondda, Lady Swaythling, Lady Moir, Lady Dawson, Mrs A. H. Scott, and Mrs Fabian

Ware will assist in the sale of National War Bonds and War Savings Certificates at Marylebone Tank. The Tank will be in Marylebone on March 5.

Paddington is to have a Tank on March 6. It will be stationed outside Whiteley's main entrance.[12]

In addition to her Marylebone stint, on 8 March Mrs Lloyd George was at a table by the St Pancras Tank for half an hour, personally stamping each bond and certificate when sold. Cities competed in a newspaper-promoted Tank Race, £100 million being the target.[13] Reports suggest that the race was won by London (unsurprisingly), followed by Liverpool, then Cardiff and Manchester, and then Bristol, Bradford, Leeds, and Birmingham – the major manufacturing and trading cities of the country.

Tanks also reached some of the smaller places. In JTR's first parish in the mining valley of Garw, where his young children, aged four, seven and twelve were living with their maternal grandparents, the Blaengarw mixed school logbook reported that: 'The school will be closed tomorrow owing to the visit of the tank. The school children of the valley will form a procession and march through the villages to Pontycymmer.'[14]

They might have gathered round the tank and joined the parade. However, the new Fund wasn't appealing directly to the children:

> A laurel wreath was placed over the Roll of Honour – teachers and boys of the school who had gone to war. Brigadier General Owen Thomas' letter was read but so far nothing was done to collect towards the Welsh National Fund for safeguarding the interests of Welsh soldiers and sailors and their dependants, in as much as the Education Committee have forbidden a collection of this nature in schools.[15]

JTR's brother, Harry Rees, would receive the MBE for his war bond selling activities in Ceredigion, prompting his niece Margaret Teify Rhys to write to her father, 'what's an MBE, has Uncle Harry joined the Army?'

President, Women's Free Church Council

On 4 March, Mrs Lloyd George chaired a Troops Fund committee, the next day assuming a further responsibility, the presidency of the

Women's Free Church Council, at the Bloomsbury Central Church. She warned that the calls on her time would limit her contribution, which would prove to be the case. (illustration 30)

The Merseyside press, serving its Welsh community, described the 'inauguration' in some detail:

> Mrs Lloyd George was introduced as the new president of the Women's Free Church Council at a meeting of the body held at the Bloomsbury Central Church yesterday. A choir of women, dressed in Welsh national costume, was present and sang at intervals during the proceedings. Mrs Frean, the retiring president, presented her successor to the audience.
>
> Mrs Lloyd George spoke of the excellent work done in the past year by her predecessor and said that she feared that, owing to the many calls upon her time, she would not prove a very active president. She referred to the increase in the avenues of work open to women, and said that in the factory, in the workshops, and the sphere of Government, women had conquered large tracts of territory. With these increased activities, said Mrs Lloyd George, women's responsibilities have become greater and, in her opinion, the Women's Free Church Council has provided a means for bringing home to millions of women what their share of these responsibilities is. Churches had now to depend upon women to carry on the work while the men were away, and she thought women, who were very human, would do their work well.
>
> Mrs Frean spoke of the work done by the council, which takes care of unmarried women and their babies, and finds homes for the children and employment for the mothers. She stated that the committee were holding a conference shortly with regard to the training of women for the ministry.
>
> Mrs George Morgan, speaking on 'The Girl of Today and Tomorrow', said that she hoped that Mr Fisher's Education Bill would soon be law, for the untrained girl was a serious menace to the State. The girl of the future, no matter how wealthy her parents, would insist upon having a regular occupation, for she felt sure that she would realise that to labour is to get happiness.[16]

While the 1918 Education Act did not deliver all that was expected, it was a step forward towards more universal education, raising the school leaving age from 12 to 14, abolishing all fees in state elementary schools and widening the provision of medical inspection, nursery schools, and special needs education.[17]

The retiring president, Mrs Frean, was a member of the Richmond Hill Congregational Church, Bournemouth, which Mrs Lloyd George had visited in July 1917, and very active with the local babies home and maternity home.

The *Western Mail* reported an anecdote from the inauguration day:

> When introducing Mrs Lloyd George, Mrs Principal Edwards, of Cardiff [wife of the Principal of the Cardiff Baptist College], said the previous evening she had been torn between two emotions. Her aviator son had arrived home on a twelve hours' leave, and seeing that she was worried he inquired as to the cause. Then, attributing it to the following day's meeting, he urged that his mother should go, but sent a message to the Premier's wife that when she made her first visit to France by aeroplane she should come to Wales for her pilot. The meeting greatly enjoyed and appreciated this little personal interlude.[18]

The pilot's offer would not be taken up, as Mrs Lloyd George never flew in a plane.[19] She had put her foot down when Lloyd George considered flying to Paris. Pilot Tregelles Edwards was still flying in the Second World War, a Squadron Leader training pilots, a director of the Cardiff Flying Club, making his living as a stockbroker, and becoming chairman of the Cardiff Stock Exchange.

Free Church Council speech on social rescue

In an undated speech, possibly on the same occasion, Mrs Lloyd George addressed a Free Church Council group on social rescue. This is one of the few remaining speech notes we have both in her hand and in the hand of her secretary JTR.[20]

> This meeting is held for a definite & very important purpose. It has been convened for the object of furthering Social Rescue work under the auspices of the Free Church Council. The need of such work is very great. The last five years imposed a very severe strain on women. The anxiety, the loneliness & an unusual amount of money brought them face to face with daily temptations of the most severe kind. We are not here to pass judgement upon them but to help them out of their trouble. A very great deal is being done for these unfortunate sisters of ours by the Salvation Army, the Church Army & other organisations. We are here not in any sort of rivalry to any other organisation but because the Free Church Council

wants to lend a helping hand in the peculiarly Christian work. We shall, I expect, be told what is being done & also what is proposed to do now. I hope that every woman in this meeting will undertake to give some help in the work. It has been said that it is better to put a fence on the top of the precipice than an ambulance at the bottom. If we want to prevent women falling we must begin with the child. I know of no better way of doing that than by home influence & the teaching of our bands of Hope & Sunday Schools. There is no place where effective preventative work can be done as well as in the Home & the Church.

Mrs Lloyd George used the 'fence on the top of the cliff' metaphor on other occasions – prevention meaning less people to cure.

Comparison of the two handwritten versions suggests that on this occasion JTR wrote out a draft speech on No. 10 notepaper, which she recopied in her own handwriting on the reverse of his sheets, as well as adding one page simply listing the key words. Thus she could either read her speech from the text or, if the occasion allowed, speak more comfortably, prompted by her key words.

What seems clear is that for many speeches she would come well prepared, and then speak formally or informally as appropriate. Her 1927 comment that 'I seldom, if ever, prepare a speech beforehand' is curious, though it is probably true that for many of her electoral tours, her short speeches along the route were delivered *ex tempore*, in English or in Welsh (or both), with a well-honed pitch to her audience.[21]

On Friday, 8 March, she accompanied the Prime Minister to a requiem mass at Westminster Cathedral for the prominent Nationalist Irish politician John Redmond, who had been losing his fight to secure peaceful Home Rule for Ireland.[22] Almost two years since the Easter Rising, the Great War was not the only bitter conflict in play.

To Cricieth and Llandudno

After presiding at a Welsh ladies' choir concert in Wimbledon, raising £125 for the Welsh Heroes' Fund, she returned to Cricieth on 11 March.[23] On the first day back she was speaking alongside William Lewis and the Hon. Violet Douglas-Pennant at a large public meeting at Llandudno Town Hall, hosted by the Caernarfonshire branch of the Troops Fund. (see p.259)

On 14 March, an in-depth interview with Welsh journalist Beriah Evans on rationing was published, where she detailed how Downing

Street was coping with the tighter constraints and offering her advice and perspectives. (see p.317)

On 30 March, a new booklet for schoolchildren was advertised, *The Legend of Llyn y Fan*, a Welsh lady of the lake story, 'available from Mrs Lloyd George at No. 10, the Welsh Troops Fund, or from R. J. Thomas of Garreglwyd, Holyhead, Welsh Heroes' Fund'.[24] The story was included in the Fund's 1915 *The Land of My Fathers* gift book, and was the one story where the illustration was by a woman, Margaret Lindsay Williams, daughter of a Cardiff shipbroker.

APRIL 1918

Mrs Lloyd George stayed in Cricieth throughout April, where Olwen was expecting her first child, Margaret, who was born at Brynawelon on 25 April. Shortly afterwards Mrs Lloyd George chaired a temperance meeting, conveniently in Cricieth. (see p.377)

Olwen relates that her father, in the habit of suggesting names for children, usually late in the day, suggested Margaret should be named Fioled (Violet).[25] This suggests to this author that Lloyd George might have had a word with my grandfather, who in 1913 had named my mother Gwiolydd, a very Welsh translation of Violet – and to this day possibly the only time it has been used as a Christian name. The only other place I have read the word is in JTR's brother's pioneering book on Welsh plants, where he lists various varieties of violets, both as Gwiolydd, and as Fioled.[26] Margaret it was to be, and later she would be partly under the watchful eye of JTR and my grandmother when her mother Olwen returned to India.

CHAPTER 9

1918: Sustaining the Effort

(May to July 1918)

'After four years of charitable war efforts,
the public spirit still strongly survives in the country.'
Newcastle Journal, May 1918

MAY 1918

The Maurice debate

LLOYD GEORGE'S PREMIERSHIP, and Mrs Lloyd George's residence in Downing Street, could have come to an ignominious end in early May if the PM had lost a vote of confidence in the Commons, for which he needed all his skill to win. At its heart was the ongoing power battle between Lloyd George and some of the military leaders. It was brought to a head by Major-General Sir Frederick Maurice writing to *The Times* (contrary to military protocol), accusing Lloyd George of misleading the House of Commons over troop strengths on the Western Front. Asquith took the side of Maurice and the Liberal Party divided three ways, for, against, and abstentions/absence. On 7 May, the day the Maurice letter appeared, Lloyd George sent a card to Mrs Lloyd George while she was at home in Criccieth looking after Olwen and Margaret, one of two such cards in the JTR Collection:

> My dearest M, Another row – a big one. General Maurice's letter. The Government may be put out on it Thursday. But I mean to fall fighting. I am getting sick of this barking & snarling & intriguing. Love D Magi xxxxxxx[1]

On the eve of the debate Lloyd George followed up:

Postmarked 7.45pm, 8 May 1918, to Brynawelon, Cricieth, N. Wales
Hen gariad [Old love], Crisis boiling up. Don't know what will happen. Love to both, D[2]

Lloyd George carried the day, and in the short term it probably strengthened his hand in directing the war effort, relative to the military. But the 'Maurice debate' was a defining moment in the Liberal Party's split. Few of the Liberals who supported Asquith and voted against Lloyd George on this occasion received the coalition 'coupon' in the December 1918 election.[3]

To the Potteries...

The government's survival allowed Mrs Lloyd George to continue her good works, opening the second day of a Red Cross bazaar on 15 May in the Pottery town of Hanley near Stoke-on-Trent. (see p.352)

... and on to Scotland

The travelling Welshwoman next had a weekend in Scotland, accompanying the Prime Minister to Dunfermline, guests of Sir William Robertson, Lord-Lieutenant of the County of Fife. Prior to 'a motor run to Callander and the Trossachs' they visited the Dunfermline College of Hygiene and Physical Education, seeing a display of folk dancing and of Swedish gymnastics (then very popular), as well as the local linen works (their host Sir William being a director). That evening the Rosyth Welsh colony choir gave a concert, while an unusually reticent Lloyd George 'pleasantly refused' to give a speech in Welsh.[4] On 24 May, he received the Freedom of the City of Edinburgh, speaking confidently about the war's prospects.[5]

One young lady who liked his speech – the 16-year-old Miss Megan – wrote from her school in Banstead, Surrey (near their Walton Heath home):

Garratts Hall, Banstead, Surrey, Weds 29 May 1918
My dearest Tada & Mamie, Someone sent me a copy of the speech – in the *Glasgow Herald*, I believe. As far as I have read, the speech delighted me beyond words. It must have made a great impression throughout the

kingdom if only for its optimistic statements & I feel sure that it will give new heart to Brits both home & abroad.

I have not heard from Cricieth for a week at the least. You will, I am sure, be sorry to hear that we are not breaking up until July 26 – three days later than the other date. It seems to be too far away to even think about now but I suppose it must bless my horizon sometime.

Well I must go now. With heaps of love from your loving daughter, Megan[6]

The young Megan (eleven years later, the first female MP for a Welsh constituency) would frequently write appraisals of her father's orations.

Mrs Lloyd George's trip to Scotland meant disappointing the ladies' conference at the annual congress of the Kent County Temperance Federation, at Tunbridge Wells.[7]

May concluded with three more London engagements, beginning on Wednesday, 29 May, with a Downing Street 'drawing room meeting' for the Children's Jewel Fund, of which she was vice-president. Jewels and the like would be donated for sale in support of child welfare.[8]

The following day, 30 May, she opened another kitchen, established in a school canteen in Tottenham (see p.323), and on the final day of the month she and Lady Rhondda attended the London Palladium matinee in support of the Welsh Prisoners of War Fund.[9]

> A Successful Matinee: The Welsh matinee this afternoon at the Palladium stands out as the second best of the war. This is a remarkable testimony, after four years of charitable war efforts, of the public spirit that still strongly survives in the country. Mr Lloyd George was so closely engaged at 10 Downing Street all day that he was unable to look in even for a brief period. Mrs Lloyd George, however, was present. The matinee produced between £6,000 and £7,000 for the Welsh prisoners of war.[10]

The best financial return for a wartime matinee at this point had been that run by George Robey at the Coliseum.[11]

May closed with the Lord Sheriffs of London handing her £8,362, collected in the City on St David's Day.[12]

125

JUNE 1918

On Tuesday, 4 June, she attended the Welsh wedding of Gwladys Hinds, daughter of Mr and Mrs John Hinds MP, at the Castle Street Welsh Baptist Chapel, London.[13] In November, Lizzie (Mrs Hinds), had been the final recruit to the Troops Fund committee.

On 18 June, during a break in Cricieth, Mrs Lloyd George presented certificates to eleven local nurses at a British Red Cross Society meeting.[14] The next day more certificates were given to local VAD nurses.

An appreciation in *The Sketch*

On 19 June, *The Sketch* published another appreciation of the Prime Minister's wife, in its column 'The Way of the World':

> Mrs Lloyd George in Public: Prime Ministers' wives seem to be taking an ever-increasing part in our public lives. Mrs Asquith always was, and is still, one of the social leaders of our day, and has done, perhaps, more than any other hostess to encourage young people who have originality and cleverness. Now Mrs Lloyd George seems to be following the same path. At first she was inclined to be a little shy, but has blossomed out of late in quite a startling manner. I met her the other day at Lady Owen Philipps's wonderful town house, and she discoursed at length, and with something of her husband's exceptional eloquence, on the subject of Welsh industries. The Prime Minister's wife refused to go on the platform and take an official part in the proceedings, preferring, as she said, 'to be for once in a way just simply one of the audience'. I cannot help thinking that this homely act on her part showed a good deal of Mr Lloyd George's genius for doing the right thing at the right moment.[15]

One striking difference between Mrs Lloyd George and Mrs Asquith was her skill in avoiding saying anything that might embarrass her husband, in contrast to Margot's penchant for sharp observations.

The month's most well-attended public event was on 22 June, accompanying the Premier to Westminster Abbey for a service in aid of the National Fund for Welsh Prisoners of War, attended by Queen Alexandra and by Welsh-born Australian premier Billy Hughes. (illustration 49) A 'sell-out' occasion, it was strongly supported by the London Welsh community, the coverage in the *Western Mail* (one of the organisers, alongside the *Evening Express*) including tributes to the organisers such as J. T. Davies, private secretary of Lloyd George, and Alfred Davies, the secretary of the organising committee, a Tory who worked at the Ministry of Munitions, and who during the peacetime coalition would at times assist Mrs Lloyd George's events.[16]

On Monday, 24 June, she was in Cardiff for the first meeting of the new Institutional Committee of Wales for the treatment of disabled sailors and soldiers, and attended the opening of the Inter-Allied Exhibition at Cardiff City Hall.

The Prime Minister's wife was back in London for a busy Thursday, 27 June, firstly presiding over the midsummer Trafalgar Square flower fair which had been running since the Saturday.[17] It provided many photo-opportunities, including Mrs Lloyd George 'redecorating' a Victoria Cross soldier.[18] (illustration 73)

> Mrs Lloyd George, president of the Flower Fair in Trafalgar-square, sold a rose for 150 guineas from her stall. This amount was paid by M. André Charlot, on behalf of the French actors and actresses who are now appearing on the London stage, and the money will be spent on the transport of French wounded.[19]

French impresario André Eugene Maurice Charlot (1882–1956) was best known for his highly successful musical revues in London between 1912 and 1937. A generous patriot with an eye for promotion?

That afternoon Mrs Lloyd George was a guest at a reception given at the Carlton Hotel by Mrs Andrew Fisher, wife of the High Commissioner of Australia, to meet Mary Hughes, the wife of the Australian Premier.[20]

Among the newspaper's Trafalgar Square photos was one of the deposed Tsar of Russia, citing a rumour that he had been executed. That unfounded rumour would soon become reality, at Yekaterinburg, on 16/17 July.

The day concluded by hosting an evening concert in the No. 10 drawing room in aid of the Royal Normal College and Academy for the Blind, Norwood, attended by the PM, with Welsh and English songs and performers, including the Welsh choir from the Royal Naval Division, Crystal Palace.[21] The paper also reported the approval of a National Kitchen for South Norwood, as the food campaign progressed.

On Saturday, 29 June, she again visited the munitionettes at the

Woolwich Arsenal and the women making saddles and tents for the Army.[22] (illustrations 55 to 58)

JULY 1918

The floral fund-raising season continued with a fete, at the Savoy on 2 July, in aid of the Women's Auxiliary Force. The *Sheffield Daily Telegraph*'s 'London Day by Day' column updated its readers:

> THIS FESTIVE MONTH: Today we have plunged into a round of fêtes, which are likely to keep us employed very briskly for the rest of the month. Mrs Lloyd George, who is really making a very creditable attempt to keep No. 10 Downing Street the focus of things, and works almost as hard as her husband, was opening the society's floral fête – at the Savoy, and one of her predecessors at No. 10, Miss Asquith, has made it certain that the St James' Palace fête shall be a gorgeous success, to judge from the number of tickets she has sold. (illustration 76)
>
> But, after all, most are saving our breath for Thursday, when London is to become an appanage of America in celebration of the day when America ceased to be an appanage of London. Perhaps it would have been well to have arranged a rest period to follow, but charity is never tired, and every day for a long time to come is booked. Incidentally, Buckingham Palace is beginning to bulge with the testimony of national interest in the Royal Silver Wedding.[23]

Roll on 4 July – 'Appanage Day' – and a Silver Wedding.

On 3 July, the *Daily Mirror* gossip column coloured in the picture and kept up with women's suffrage.

> UNDERGROUND MELONS: Many of the lunchers at the Savoy yesterday went down to the underground floral fête which Mrs Lloyd George opened afterwards, to buy peaches, melons or grapes from Lady Jane Taylor [a daughter of the Marquis of Tweeddale][24] or boudoir caps and things from Lady Clancarty [an energetic worker for war charities].[25]
>
> THE FESTIVE SPIRIT: Mrs Lloyd George, in a compliment to the fête, wore an appropriate hat with many coloured flowers. I saw her doing the rounds with Lady Townshend and Mrs Parker [Frances, sister of Lord Kitchener] who helps all charitable efforts.
>
> ON THE WAY: Women are quietly getting nearer to seats in Parliament.

1918: Sustaining the Effort

Mr Bonar Law has pointed out that women may now help, with men, to choose candidates. There is nothing now to prevent a woman candidate being elected to the local party organisation.[26]

The *Daily Mirror*'s 'Gossip' column sustained its coverage two days later:

FOR THE BABIES: I had a little chat yesterday with Mrs Lloyd George in Central Hall, Westminster. She seems to have adopted the boy scout code of doing a good deed every hour, for she benefited Baby Week by selling £40 worth of jewellery in a few minutes. Lady Henry was helping her.[27]

The Lady Henry in this instance was Lady Henry Somerset, philanthropist and campaigner for women's rights, temperance and other causes. Mrs Lloyd George would open a fete for her shortly.

On 'Appanage Day' (to cite the Sheffield press), London's Central Hall hosted one of the big 4 July celebrations. At the Anglo-Saxon Fellowship Meeting, Winston Churchill (whose mother was American), and Clementine Churchill led the British contingent. Since becoming Minister of Munitions a year earlier, Churchill had played a significant role in negotiations with the US on their participation in the war. US troops had first arrived in France in June 1917, but didn't play a significant role until October.

The previous day, 3 July, Lord Rhondda, Minister of Food Control, had died. Also deceased at the beginning of the month was another leading Welshman, Glamorgan cricketer and local businessman J. P. Cadogan, one of Mrs Lloyd George's Cardiff hosts in May 1917.

The *Western Mail* published a letter of condolence sent by JTR on behalf of Mrs Lloyd George (albeit referred to as Mrs George).

THE LATE MR J. P. CADOGAN: The following letter from Mrs Lloyd George's secretary has reached us through Mr Gilbert D. Shepherd:

10, Downing-street, Whitehall, S.W. July 4, 1918.

Dear Sir, – I am directed by Mrs Lloyd George to thank you for your letter of the 2nd inst. with reference to the death of Mr Cadogan, and to say that she deeply regrets the loss of so strenuous a worker at a time when there is so much for all of us to do. Mrs George trusts that the noble example set by Mr Cadogan and Viscount Rhondda will inspire many of the merchant princes of Cardiff to take up and carry on their patriotic work. Mrs George has already wired Mrs Cadogan. – Yours faithfully. J. T. RHYS[28]

The Royal Silver Wedding was celebrated on Sunday, 7 July, at St Paul's Cathedral, with a full turnout of royalty, the Lloyd Georges, the Asquiths, and 'many representatives from our Colonies and Allied countries'. On the Saturday Mrs Lloyd George inspected the Dartford Division of the Girl Guides.[29] (illustration 72)

A more 'melancholy' duty, as Mrs Lloyd George would later remark, and frequent occasion would be the unveiling of war memorials and Rolls of Honour. The war still raging, on the evening of Wednesday, 10 July, she unveiled two differing panels at the Garden Suburb Free Church in Hampstead: a memorial to the 18 members of the congregation who had already fallen in the war, and a second panel recognising the members of the congregation who had served or were still serving in the war.

> Mrs Lloyd George, before unveiling the memorials, said the war had left its mark on every church in the land, but they were very proud of the brave boys, and felt that nothing they could do was good enough for those who had done so much for others. Some had fallen, but others were fighting valiantly, and it was hoped that those still fighting would be restored to their people. They mourned the loss of those who had fallen, but in fighting for their country their death had been brilliant, and she hoped their example would induce others to live lives of true patriotism and good citizenship.[30]

On 15 July, she opened a garden fete at Summerfield, Elstree, the home of Lady Prichard-Jones (wife of the Dickins & Jones draper) in aid of St Dunstan's Hostel for Blinded Soldiers.[31]

The National Kitchen, New Bridge Street

On 16 July, *Pathé News* filmed her and other dignitaries visiting the flagship NK National Restaurant on New Bridge Street, Blackfriars, London, possibly the peak of the wartime publicly-funded communal dining programme. (illustrations 38 to 42) On 26 July, she was due to open another National Kitchen, at Holborn Baths, but the Mayoress of Holborn had to take her place.

The next day, Wednesday, 17 July, it was off to Enfield Court, the home of Lady Henry Somerset, to open a garden fete in aid of the War Hospital Depots of Middlesex.[32]

A club for WAACs, Wrens and Penguins

On 18 July, Mrs Lloyd George backed a campaign which was about to reach its goal: setting up a London club where women in the Forces could relax and get together – a girls' social centre for those in war service:

> 'Residential clubs for WAACs, Wrens and Penguins are to be started in London. For some little time, it has been realised that there was a great need for some provision to be made in this way for these girls, and the ever-increasing number of women required to replace the men wanted for the fighting line makes the matter an urgent one,' wrote Mrs Lloyd George and Miss Lucy Markham to *The Daily Mirror*. 'There is great need for a social centre where all the services can meet. This will foster the spirit of comradeship and give an opportunity for the exchange of views to the advantage all concerned.'
>
> Subscriptions, large or small, should be sent the Hon. Treasurer, Sir John Ferguson, K.B.E., the National Bank of Scotland, 37 Nicholas-Lane, Lombard-street. E.C.[33]

The Penguins referred to the women in the Royal Air Force (WRAFs) who didn't fly. The parents of Miss Lucy Markham, Lord and Lady Markham, had made their home near Folkestone available for officers, and sent aid packages to prisoners of war in German captivity. The WAACs (Women's Army Auxiliary Corps), formed in 1917, became the Queen Mary's Army Auxiliary Corps later that year. It was finally disbanded in 1921. Wrens served in the WRNS (Women's Royal Naval Service). Air, land and sea.

Two days later a home for the club was announced:

> The Prime Minister is the patron and Mrs Lloyd George the president of a residential club shortly to be opened at 48 and 49 Eaton Square for the temporary accommodation, when on leave, of women in the three auxiliary services, known the 'Waacs', the 'Wrens' and the 'Penguins'. Provision has been made for nearly eighty residents, including between twenty and thirty officers or administrators. A nominal club membership subscription will be imposed, the scale of residential charges to be as

moderate as possible. It is intended, if sufficient funds are forthcoming from the general public, to establish similar clubs in some of the large provincial towns, where there is a keen demand for accommodation of this kind. Financial support is much needed. Sir John Ferguson is the honorary treasurer, and subscriptions or donations should be sent to him at the club.[34]

A comfortable Belgravian berth. (illustration 71)
Plans for care for soldiers were underway in north Wales:

HOMES FOR WELSH SOLDIERS: MUNIFICENT GIFTS: Mrs Lloyd George has been the means of obtaining a generous gift of whatever sum may be necessary up to £220,000 for the establishment of a home for neurasthenic and another home for paraplegics among Welsh soldiers. Sir R. J. Thomas has also placed at the disposal of the Ministry of Pensions, through Mr William Lewis (superintending inspector for north Wales), a fully-equipped convalescent home for men at Holyhead, in close proximity to his own residence.[35]

Mrs Lloyd George would open the Lady Thomas Convalescent Home at Robert Thomas' Garreglwyd estate in 1919.[36]

Child welfare

The final outing before departing for Wales for the summer was on Wednesday, 24 July, at a baby show in Guildford, Surrey, not that far from the Lloyd George home at Walton Heath. This was more than just another visit of a mothering person to admire babies, as the *Surrey Advertiser* made clear in its front-page column, bringing home the appalling death toll of the war. (see p.355)

The Troops Fund committee had met only three times since the January meeting (which she had missed). While she had chaired all three, the treasurer, Sir Vincent Evans, chaired the 30 July meeting. The committee would next meet, under her chairmanship, in October.

CHAPTER 10

War Begins to Turn

(August to October 1918)

'The crowds were growing and growing, beyond anticipation, and by about half past one, not only had every available seat been occupied, but every inch of standing room was utilised.'

The Herald of Wales, Neath, August 1918

AUGUST 1918

MRS LLOYD GEORGE began her August holiday in Criccieth, before heading south for the National Eisteddfod in Neath, where the PM would also accept the Freedom of the Borough. First, an appointment in Rhyl:

> In connection with the campaign organised by the Ministry of Labour, Mrs Lloyd George on Thursday paid a visit to Rhyl and opened the Women's Service Exhibition in the Town Hall. A procession of nurses and land workers was held in the presence of thousands of visitors, and Mrs Lloyd George drove through the town in a motor-car, accompanied by the Bishop of St Asaph, Mrs Edwards (The Palace), and Mrs R. W. Williams-Wynn. A meeting was held in the Pavilion, and was presided over by Mr Gladstone (Lord-Lieutenant of Flintshire).[1]

> A report in Welsh in *Baner ac Amserau Cymru* [Banner and Times of Wales] indicated that it was hard to hear her voice, but the gist of her appeal was to encourage women to join up for work.[2]

Neath

The Neath National Eisteddfod ran from 5 to 8 August (with record takings – though the doubling of inflation would have boosted that statistic), the Freedom of the Borough ceremony following on 9 August. The authorities were making last-minute plans:

> PREMIER'S PARTY: At a meeting of the Neath Rural District Council, on Wednesday [31 July], Major W. B. Trick said that on his visit to Neath for the National Eisteddfod, the Prime Minister would be accompanied by Mrs Lloyd George and the party would number between 15 and 20. The Parliamentary Committee of the Neath Town Council invited the members of public bodies to attend the ceremony of acceptance of the freedom of the borough by the Prime Minister, but the members would have to be in their seats at 10.45 on the morning of August 9th.
>
> The Premier's party will include Mrs Lloyd George and Miss Megan Lloyd George and the Prime Minister of Australia (the Right Hon. William Hughes). The Premier, Mrs Lloyd George, and Miss Megan Lloyd George will be the guests of Mr T. J. Williams, M.P., and Mrs Williams at Maesygwernen Hall, Morriston.[3] (illustrations 86, 87)

As the citizens of Neath prepared to bestow the Freedom of the Borough on their Prime Minister, the news from the Somme was very hopeful. The headlines were full of a surprise attack made by the Allies, combining, for the first time, tanks, infantry and the air force. For General Ludendorff, 8 August, 'The Black Day in the history of the German Army', decisively turned the war in the Allies' favour. One immediate consequence was that 'the people of Wales' – as one spectator put it – swept into town to see the PM, an invasion larger than even the planners of the ceremony in Neath had anticipated:

> Morriston turned out in force to welcome Wales's great little man – David Lloyd George. Long before the appointed time, huge crowds gathered at the Cross, Morriston, and all around people took up every point of vantage to see and to hear. Flags and bunting and messages of welcome were strung across from street to street – messages in Welsh, *Croeso i'r Prif Weinidog* (Welcome to the Prime Minister). Another banner read, *Cricieth a Threforus am byth* (Cricieth and Morriston for ever).

Not everything was in place...

1918: War Begins to Turn

The casket of a locally-made plate which was to have been presented to Mrs Lloyd George was not ready for the occasion, and it would be sent on. The inscription, which was given to her by Miss Gwenith Alice Williams [the daughter of MP T. J. Williams], was read out as follows: 'Presented to Mrs Lloyd George by the citizens of Morriston on the occasion of her visit to the town, 9th August 1918.'

And on to the ceremony...

The scene was unparalleled in the annals of Castell Nedd; the day a never-to-be-forgotten one. For, added to the enthusiasm over the visit of Cymru's most brilliant son, there was the thrilling war news that the day had brought. Nothing was lacking to bring the sunshine of a new and brighter day into every heart. The gathering inside the hall was a distinguished and even a brilliant one, including no small number of Welsh Members of Parliament, as well as the civic dignitaries and captains of industry of the Principality.

In the afternoon a big singing assembly was held, as the Welsh invasion of Neath continued.

The National Gymanfa Ganu, in the Pavilion at Neath, was the great centre of attraction on Friday, and from the morning until two o'clock in the afternoon there were crowds arriving by trains from various directions, and when tickets, at 6*d.* each, were being issued, it was thought the arrangements would work smoothly. But the crowds were growing and growing, beyond anticipation, and by about half past one not only had every available seat been occupied, but every inch of standing room was utilised. Unfortunately, so overwhelming was the crush at the entrance to the field that thousands rushed into the Pavilion sometime before the opening, and there was an overflow from there to the allotted seats of the bass, tenor, and alto singers, and the seats prepared for the orchestra were taken by others, mostly sightseers.

Did the sopranos get a seat?

When the Premier arrived he was accorded a magnificent reception.

Followed by some repartee...

Mr Lloyd George: 'I came from London this morning to hear you singing.'

Another voice (in Welsh): 'We have been in Neath since four o'clock this morning to see and hear you.' (laughter and great cheering)

Mr Lloyd George: 'Annwyl gyd-wladwyr (dear fellow-countrymen), I am not going to speak now. I came to hear you singing, and if I have a word to say I will say it to-night.'

A voice: 'We cannot be here to-night; we are not Neath people; we are the people of Wales.' (Applause)

Mr Lloyd George held up his hand for silence, and that was a signal for another great ovation from the huge audience. Looking down at the writer, who sat in the corner seat of the Press table, the Premier laughingly said: *'Y mae hyn fel siarad wrth donnau'r mor'* (this is like speaking to the waves of the sea). As soon as the people understood that the Premier was going to speak, however, absolute silence prevailed.

Lloyd George then spoke in Welsh, a short address, reminding them, in effect, that the war hadn't yet got to the point of a final victory, but was going well.[4]

No more objections to the Welsh singing during wartime.

Shortly after returning to London, Mrs Lloyd George went back to north Wales, but neither she nor the media were idle, *The Sketch* quoting her cryptic epigram:

'My experience of social warwork teaches me,' said Mrs Lloyd George to me last week, 'that if charity is still a rarity, vanity is certainly not.' There is much justice in the P.M.'s wife's remark. The war has taught us that, if the uses of advertisement are sweet, they are likewise manifold.[5]

Perhaps a slightly risky observation that could kill the golden goose?

When Lloyd George returned to north Wales later in the month, the people of Criccieth added to the celebrations of Neath:

Mr Lloyd George arrived at Criccieth on Saturday night [24th] and was met at the station by Mrs Lloyd George, Mrs Carey Evans, and Miss Lloyd George. Hundreds of visitors filled the station square and cheered lustily when the Premier alighted from the train. The enthusiastic holiday crowd escorted the party to Brynawelon.[6]

Denbighshire

Mrs Lloyd George then paid a round of visits in Denbighshire, in connection with the work of caring for disabled soldiers and other causes. First she opened a fete at Brymbo Hall, Wrexham, in aid of the North Wales Heroes' Memorial Fund, with Sir Robert Thomas on hand:

> Mrs Lloyd George said it gave her great pleasure to be there that afternoon. They all knew what they were there for, to support that fund of Sir Robert Thomas, and she was sure they were going to give him a handsome sum. It was everything to have a man at the head of a movement of this kind, full of energy and vitality, and possessed of great powers of organisation, and such a man they had in Sir Robt. Thomas. (hear, hear) He had already collected £70,000, and if this movement was going to be a success and a permanent memorial erected to their fallen heroes, he must get another £70,000. She felt sure he would get it, and also that the people would support him.
>
> Our brave lads had been fighting for us and nothing we could do could repay them for what they had done for us. They wanted to make it possible for their children to be educated at our colleges; these colleges had been built on the sixpences and shillings of the working men of Wales, and they were very proud of their democratic colleges, and they wanted their children and their children's children to be educated there, when she felt sure they would be a match for any German who might come along. (applause) She now declared the sale open and wished it every success.[7]

Sir Robert Thomas had been knighted in April.

She then attended a concert at Cefn arranged by the local committee of the North Wales Heroes' Memorial Fund, accompanied by Sir Robert and Lady Thomas and Mr and Mrs David McAlpine, Marchwiel (the half-brother of Roberta Lloyd George). After staying the night with the McAlpines, she visited Wrexham Hospital, and Wrexham Barracks, inspecting the WAACs (since April renamed the Queen Mary's Army Auxiliary Corps).[8] Travelling on to Trefnant, near Denbigh, she opened the new Bryndyffryn hostel for disabled soldiers and sailors, a project run by Miss Mary Heaton (founder of the Vale of Clwyd Toy Company), which had recently received support from the Fund.[9] At the opening Mrs Lloyd George remarked: 'I never go to an exhibition in London without seeing Miss Heaton there in her tall Welsh hat, busily selling her goods.'[10]

SEPTEMBER 1918

A September visit to Manchester, Salford, Bolton, Preston and Blackpool, accompanying the Premier as he accumulated more freedoms of those cities and boroughs, did not go wholly to plan. The Welshman was returning to the city of his arrival in the world. It might have been the city of his departure.

The advance headlines in the *Manchester Evening News* stressed the upcoming 'Strenuous Weekend', making it clear there would be no additional visits to the arranged schedule, and with rest periods scheduled between appearances. Lloyd George was succumbing to the 'Spanish Flu'.[11]

On Wednesday, 11 September, they were met by the city's dignitaries at the London Road Station just after 7pm, proceeding to the Town Hall by way of a pre-announced route. Until the next morning he was to remain undisturbed.

On Thursday, 12 August, the party departed at 11.15 to the Hippodrome, again by a pre-announced route, where he received the Freedom of the City at a ceremony lasting from 11.30 to 1pm.[12]

After lunch at the Midland Hotel it was back to the Town Hall to inspect a guard of honour of volunteers, the Queen Mary's Army Auxiliary Corps (the former WAACs), and women munition workers. Tea was with the members of the Constitutional Club at their club, and at 4pm Mrs Lloyd George received an address of welcome from the Welsh community of Manchester and Salford.

Accompanied by her daughters, she then visited two local hospitals:

> This afternoon Mrs Lloyd George, accompanied by her daughters, Mrs Carey Evans and Miss Megan Lloyd George, visited Brooklands and were conducted over to the John Leigh Memorial Hospital at Woodbourne, where they much admired the arrangements and went through the new wards, now occupied by 60 patients. From Brooklands they motored with Sir John and Lady Leigh to the John Leigh Memorial Hospital for Officers, Altrincham. The hospital now contains between 90 and 100 patients who very heartily received the distinguished visitors.[13] (illustration 63)

This was followed by a 'private house dinner' at the Reform Club which Lloyd George did not attend, taking to his bed at the Town Hall, where he stayed for the next nine days, under the care of the Manchester-based Ear, Nose and Throat specialist Sir William Milligan, and nursed by Mrs Lloyd George:

> The Prime Minister's illness will not allow him to return to London for some days. Mrs Lloyd George, who is with him, is a splendid nurse, and always insists on attending her husband when he is out of sorts.[14]

All the plans for Friday, 13 August, receiving the Freedom of the Borough at Salford, unveiling a war memorial in Peel Park, and on Saturday, 14 August, touring the length of the Blackpool Promenade, lunching with the Mayor, and receiving the Freedom of the County Borough, were cancelled. It was reportedly 'very serious' and 'touch and go'.

The Prime Minister returned to London from Manchester on Saturday, 21 August, still with a respirator. A Downing Street team went up during the week and he was accompanied on the return journey by Chief Whip Freddie Guest and William Sutherland (a private secretary) and Sir William Milligan. His principal private secretary, J. T. Davies, and a small group of onlookers, were on hand to meet him at Euston. The unscheduled Manchester sojourn meant cancelling a visit to see the King and Queen and a stay at Windsor Castle.[15]

Mrs Lloyd George and Olwen returned to north Wales from Manchester, Megan going to London. By the end of the month Mrs Lloyd George herself was unwell, missing appointments and, it would seem, also suffering from the flu. The PM's biographer John Grigg suggested Lloyd George learnt of her illness from the newspapers.[16]

The UK epidemic was then running at ten deaths (from all causes) per 1,000 per week. From early October it took off, peaking close to 60 deaths per 1,000 per week in early November, the rate falling sharply just before 11 November, Armistice Day.

Though illness ruled out in-person engagements, the Lloyd Georges were 'virtually' in Caernarfon on 14 September when nearly half the population turned out to watch early takes of a new film celebrating Lloyd George's first success in being elected MP for the Carnarvon Boroughs. They (or rather the actors Norman Page and Alma Reville, later the wife of Alfred Hitchcock) passed in triumph along the streets and appeared in front of the Liberal Club. This may have been the same film being planned a year earlier.

That film was never released, surrounded by controversy, and was only rediscovered in the Lloyd George family archives in 1994 and finally released in 1996 as *The Life of David Lloyd George* (original title *The Man Who Saved the Empire*). A public engagement delayed by 78 years.[17]

On 15 September, diarist Samuell Pepys Junior gave a different slant on the destination of the parcels going to the PoWs in Germany:

> Walking towards Abinger upon a fair afternoon, I did meet on the way a certain wounded soldier, who asking of me a light to his pipe, we fell to discoursing. He is come out of Germany, it seems, at the last changing of prisoners, and a mournfull relation he did make of what he did suffer among the Germans by lack of victuall and raiment; but a thing worth remembering he did tell, that having a bundle of clothes come from England, the German soldiers that guard him would straightway buy of him one thing and another, and to bid any price allmost; as, for boots, 300 of their marques (15*l*.); for but one shirt, 100 marques (5*l*.); and for an outer coat, 600 marques (30*l*.); to such an extravagance of price as all goods of true cloth and leather do encrease in Germany, and the people (a great part of them) clothed in stuffs wrought of paper.[18]

On 20 September, the papers printed an appeal for jewellery, supported by the familiar trio of Mrs Lloyd George, Lady Rhondda and Consuelo, Duchess of Marlborough:

> Children's Jewel Fund: The ladies who were the original signatories of the Children's Jewel Fund appeal are, I hear, now arranging an exhibition and auction sale of dressed dolls, and would be grateful for donations of china, wax-stuffed, or rag dolls. The exhibition will be divided into sections showing dolls representing historic personages, famous actresses, fashions in dress, uniforms of the Great War, &c. so that individual taste will find a wide-range of choice. Mrs Lloyd George, Lady Rhondda, and Consuelo Duchess of Marlborough are among the signatories.[19]

The American-born Consuelo Marlborough, née Vanderbilt, a cousin of Winston Churchill, was chair of the Economic Relief Committee for the American Women's War Relief Fund.

1918: War Begins to Turn

In the last week of September, the Welsh in Croydon were seeking to attract the Prime Minister's wife to their borough, even if she had upset the local Liberal women in 1914. Sir Vincent Evans, treasurer of the Troops Fund, was a major driver of the society.

> NEW WELSH SOCIETY: Mrs Lloyd George is taking a keen interest in the proposed formation of a Cymmrodorion Society in Croydon, where there is an unusually large colony of Welsh people. She has promised faithfully to come down from Cricieth in order to speak at an inaugural meeting and concert at which there will be a galaxy of musical and oratorical talent. Most of the London suburbs can now boast their local Cymmrodorion societies, and a very flourishing one which exists as far out as Wimbledon has more than once been visited by Mrs Lloyd George. Sir Vincent Evans, the life and soul of the Cymmrodorion movement in London, is being invited to speak before the Croydon society, which will in due course be affiliated with the national body.[20]

A Croydon concert of Welsh music was finally arranged for 19 December, founding the Croydon and District Welsh Society, and presided over by Sir Vincent Evans. However Mrs Lloyd George did not attend, resting in Cricieth after her whirlwind two-week electoral tour that set the precedent of being the first wife of a Prime Minister to campaign widely in a national election. Another missed date in Croydon. (see p.26)

OCTOBER 1918

Illness also prevented her from presiding over a 'great demonstration' at Fulham Town Hall, on 1 October, on women's work in the churches. One speaker was J. Hugh Edwards, Liberal MP for Mid Glamorgan and Lloyd George biographer, for whom she would campaign in December, when he won the Neath seat.[21]

October brought, literally, a new variety for the Mrs Lloyd George story, the 'Mrs David Lloyd George' violet. (illustration 74)

> Mrs Lloyd George's name has, with her consent, been given to new variety of violet which has been grown at Corfe Mullen, Dorset, by Mr J. J. Kettle, F.R.H.S. The seed organs of violets are so close together that in the main they fertilise themselves, but in the case of the 'Mrs Lloyd George' violet,

the grower thinks that ants, in getting at the nectar the back of the flower, must have carried pollen from another variety.[22]

Quite appropriately, the new violet was the result of hard workers. By 1926 it had won many awards in the US and was promising to become 'the most popular violet in the States'.[23]

With the reduction in hostilities reducing the calls on the Troops Fund, the 9 October meeting set up a five-member emergency committee to keep things running. The Fund's committee would not meet again in wartime, next convening in March 1919.

On 10 October, opening a YWCA sale of work at Hamilton Hall, Church End, Finchley, north London, she not only reminded her listeners of the war work done by the women, but that the needs would not go away in peacetime:

> The YWCA had done a good deal in the war, and she could not picture what things would have been like without it. Of course, it was not work which would cease when the war ended, for it would be required afterwards when the work of reconstruction began. There could be no perfect reconstruction without the help of the wonderful YWCA work, and she was sure they would all give their support so that it could be extended and carried all over the country.[24]

On 18 October, a meeting at the Mansion House celebrated the Active Service Club for Women, now in fashionable Eaton Square, London. The recruitment of more women for the war was not letting up.

> A largely-attended meeting in support of the Women's Active Service Club was held at the Mansion House this afternoon, the Lord Mayor presiding, when the principal speakers were Viscount Milner, Secretary for War, Sir Auckland Geddes and Admiral Sims.
>
> Queen Mary sent a message of congratulations, promising to become patroness-in-chief of the club.
>
> Mrs Lloyd George, the president of the club, read a message from the Prime Minister, in which Mr Lloyd George assured the meeting how much the Government appreciated the work done by women. Unless women had come forward, we could never have stopped the German onrush or gained our present winning position in the war. The women who had

rendered such signal war service, added the Premier, had borne their full share in freeing the world from the menace of Prussian militarism.

Lord Milner expressed high appreciation of the work done by women in the war. The fears that women would not be able to bear the strain, that they would not take kindly to military discipline, that they would not present themselves in any great numbers, and, finally, that those who came forward would not be the right stuff, had been most signally falsified by the result. Women had proved themselves to be of great courage in difficult circumstances. Women had helped splendidly, but yet there was need for more women in the services.

'It may seem a strange thing,' said Lord Milner, 'to be calling for war recruits at this moment when the air is full of rumours and hopes of peace. Certainly, there is no man living who more fervently desires an early peace than I do, but I also recognise that there is no more certain way to frustrate the fairest hope for peace than relaxing in any way our war effort the present time. (Applause) At this moment we must put forth every possible effort, must release every possible man for the fighting line, and thus succour every conceivable way our splendid troops at the Front, who are steadily pressing back the enemy with courage and endurance that is beyond all praise.'[25]

The *Sunday Mirror*'s women's gossip corner flagged up the continued campaigning for the YWCA:

Well, there is to be a regular autumn campaign. Lady Frances Balfour is speaking here, there and everywhere – Lady Shelley Rolls is lending her house in Eaton-square for a meeting; while Mrs Lloyd George, the most sympathetic of women, is giving an At Home on November 8 in aid of the association. Funds ought to roll in, don't you think?[26]

Very P. G. Wodehouse at the end there, don't you know.
That day she was pictured with a Welsh doll given by Queen Alexandra for the Children's Jewel Fund.[27]

Mrs Lloyd George has received from Queen Alexandra, the Press Association is informed, a very beautiful Welsh doll for the Welsh section of the Doll Exhibition which is being organised by the Children's Jewel Fund. Accompanying the gift was an autographed letter in which Queen Alexandra states that she is giving the doll as a historical memento of her first visit to Wales over 30 years ago, when the doll was given to her. Queen Alexandra adds that she gives the doll for the benefit of the children of our brave sailors and soldiers.[28]

On 30 October, Mrs Lloyd George was joined at the Jewel Fund's New Bond Street sale by the Dowager Lady Tweeddale, the Duchess of Marlborough, Lady Randolph Churchill, and Lady Henry Somerset.[29] (illustration 68)

The Women's Institute Village Life and Industrial Exhibition at Caxton Hall

October concluded, and November began at Caxton Hall with the WI's Village Life and Industrial Exhibition, the Welsh Day of Monday, 28 October, being opened by Mrs Lloyd George. (see p.332 and illustration 54)

Mary Hughes, wife of Australian PM Billy Hughes, also attended, her husband having to cry off as he was busy critiquing President Wilson's 14 Points for being too generous to Germany, calling for the voice of the other nations to be heard:

> Mr Hughes, the Australian Premier, speaking at Leeds last night, said the acceptance of President Wilson's 14 points by Germany, and the constant reiteration by Prince Max and Dr Solf that Germany intended faithfully to adhere to them, showed that the Germans hoped to gain more from these conditions than from those which the Allies would impose. As yet the voices of the nations who had borne the burden and heat of the day had not been heard. The inspired babel of democracy and peace was deliberately designed to rob the Allies of victory.[30]

Billy Hughes was very much on the 'make Germany pay' side of things. On 3 October, Max von Baden (Prince Max) had been appointed German Chancellor and Dr Wilhelm Solf the German negotiator of peace terms.

Within a week of the Caxton Hall event, Armistice was declared, and the last Imperial German Chancellor stepped down after 37 days in office, ushering in the post-war Weimar Republic.

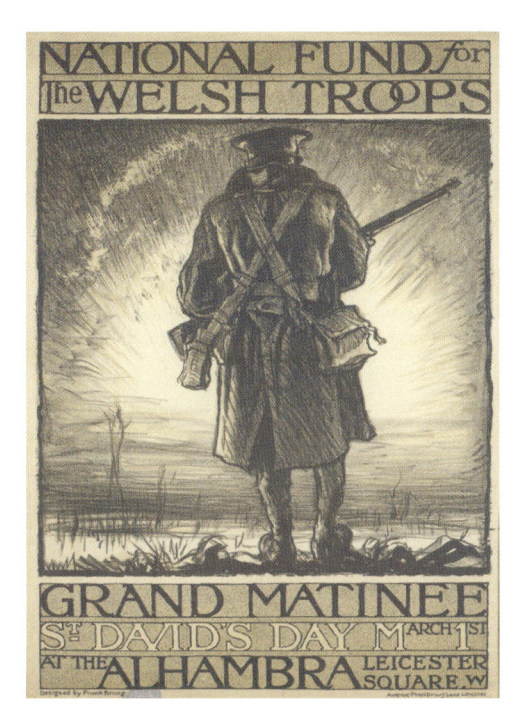

1. Frank Brangwyn's iconic poster for the 1917 London Flag Day West End Grand Matinee. See p.236.
ART.IWM PST 3297 © Estate of Frank Brangwyn All rights reserved 2025/Bridgeman Images

2. Mrs Lloyd George at No. 10, by Olive Edis. See p.104. Taken for *The Prime Minister, A Life*, Harold Spender.
NPG x15464 © National Portrait Gallery

3. Frank Brangwyn's 1914 'Britain's Call to Arms' War Recruitment Poster from the 1915 Fund's gift book, *The Land of My Fathers*.
© Estate of Frank Brangwyn. All rights reserved 2025/Bridgeman Images

National Fund for Welsh Troops

TO PROVIDE ADDITIONAL COMFORTS FOR WELSH REGIMENTS AT HOME AND ABROAD

President:
COUNTESS OF PLYMOUTH

Chairman of Committee:
MRS. LLOYD GEORGE

Executive Committee:

Lady Ninian Crichton-Stuart	Lady Glanusk	Mrs. Reginald McKenna
Hon. Violet Douglas-Pennant	Mrs. Ellis Griffith	Lady Beatrice Ormsby-Gore
Lady Edwards	Hon. Lady Herbert	Mrs. Pryce-Jones

Hon. Treasurer:
SIR E. VINCENT EVANS

Hon. Secretary:
WILLIAM LEWIS

National Fund for Welsh Troops

TO PROVIDE ADDITIONAL COMFORTS FOR WELSH REGIMENTS AT HOME AND ABROAD
(Registered under War Charities Act, 1916.)

Patron:
H.R.H. THE PRINCE OF WALES, K.G

President:
COUNTESS OF PLYMOUTH.

Chairman of Committee:
MRS. LLOYD. GEORGE.

Executive Committee:

Right Hon. Lord Justice Bankes	Mrs. F. T. Hopkinson	Lady Mond
Major David Davies, M.P.	Lady Howard de Walden	Lady Mostyn
Hon. Violet Douglas-Pennant	Mrs. Herbert Lewis	Lady Beatrice Ormsby-Gore
Countess of Dundonald	Countess of Lisburne	Lady (Owen) Philipps
Lady Glanusk	Lady (Francis) Lloyd	Lady Pryce-Jones
Lady Ellis Griffith	Mrs. Lynn-Thomas	Lady St. Davids
Mrs. John Hinds.	Hon. Mrs. A. Maule-Ramsay	Lady Treowen
	Mrs. Reginald McKenna	

Hon. Treasurer:
SIR E. VINCENT EVANS. F.S.A.

Telephone:
HOLBORN 1182.

57 & 58, CHANCERY LANE,
LONDON. W.C. 2

Hon. Secretary:
WILLIAM LEWIS.

January 28th, 1919.

J. T. Rhys, Esq.,
   10, Downing Street,
      Whitehall. S.W. 1

Dear Sir,

    I am in receipt of your letter of the 27th inst and shall be obliged if you will forward parcel to me at the above address.

            Yours faithfully,
               William Lewis.
               Hon. Secretary.

4. Over the four years the Fund's Executive Committee doubled from thirteen to twenty-six members, eventually registered under the War Charities Act, with royal patronage. This 1919 note is the sole remaining communication on file between Mrs Lloyd George's two wartime secretaries, William Lewis and J.T. Rhys.
JTR Private Collection

5. Catching a cold in the Llandudno snow, St David's Day 1915, with Major Richard Lloyd George, Mrs Frederica Thomas, David Lloyd George and Brigadier Sir Owen Thomas. See p. 276.
IWM Q 54471

6. Refugees from Dinant, Belgium, in Cricieth, 1914. See p.31.
© Amgueddfa Cymru-Museum Wales

The Prime Minister Inspects the Napier Car used on Welsh Day by Miss Olwyn Lloyd George

7. Olwen Lloyd George leads the charge on the 1917 St David's Flag Day in London. See p.234. *The Sphere*, 31.3.1917, p.26.
© Illustrated London News Ltd / Mary Evans

8. Megan attempting a sale to her father, French Flag Day, London, July 1915. See p.186.
Olwen Carey Evans Collection 10 (Llyfr Ffoto 1013 C), NLW

9. A Welsh lady on Yr Wyddfa/Snowdon: the 1918 Welsh Flag Day Poster by John Hassall. See pp.37, 255.
ART.IWM PST 13358

10. Olwen Lloyd George auctioneering signed posters at the Floral Hall, Covent Garden, St David's Day, 1 March 1917. See p.234.
Olwen Carey Evans Collection 6 (Llyfr Ffoto 1009 B), NLW

11. Mrs Lloyd George, accompanied by Lady Owen Philipps, arrives at the Stock Exchange on St David's Day, 1 March 1918. See p.255.
Olwen Carey Evans Collection 6, (Llyfr Ffoto 1009 B), NLW

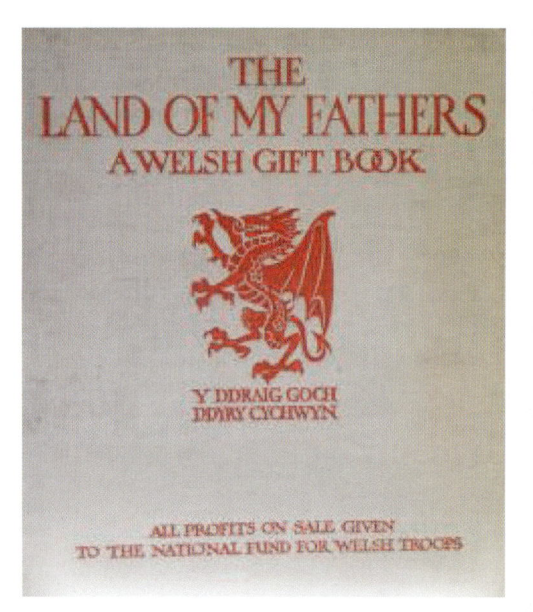

12. *The Land of My Fathers* gift book published in 1915 in aid of the Fund. See p.46
Private Collection

13. G. A. Sawyer, Organiser of the 1918 Welsh Flag Day in London. See pp. 256, 258, 314. *Illustrated London News*, 13.4.1918, p.18.
© *ILN* / Mary Evans

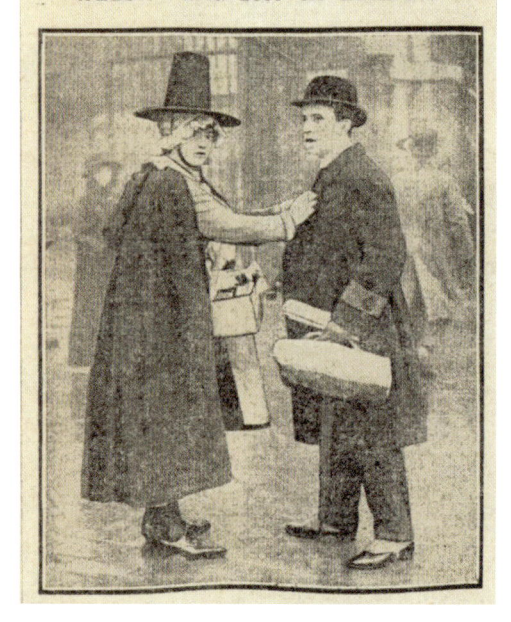

14. 'Miss Olwen Lloyd George selling a flag to a Derby Recruit,' St David's Welsh Flag Day, 1 March 1916. The 1915 National Registration Act, known as the Derby Scheme, aimed at registering all civilians between 15 and 65 for military service. See p.284. *Dundee Evening Telegraph*, 2.3.1916, p.4.
© British Library Board

15. The art of flag selling. *The Sketch*, 19.6.1918, p.5. See p.215.
© *Illustrated London News Ltd* / Mary Evans

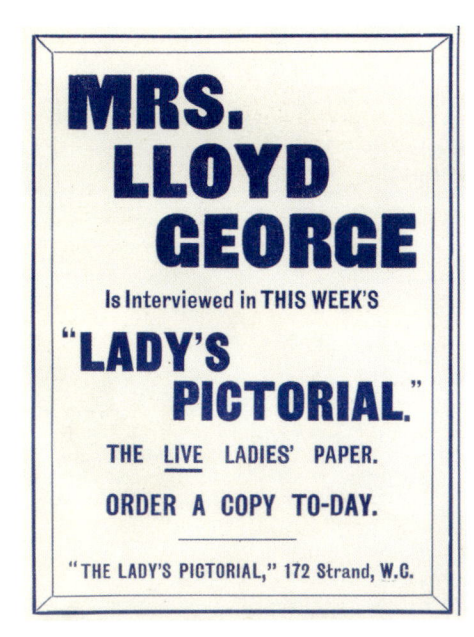

16. Advertisement in *The Lady's Pictorial*. *Illustrated & Sporting Dramatic News*, 13.2.1915, p.697.
© Illustrated London News Ltd / Mary Evans

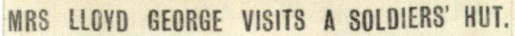

17. Mrs Lloyd George hands out chocolates and cigarettes at the Hampstead Heath temperance hut. See p.212. *Dundee Evening Telegraph*, 25.1.1916, p.4.
© British Library Board

18. Advertising the Postcard Day. See p.192, 204.
ART.IWM PST 10777

19. Constance Hilton, Flag Day organiser 1917, *The Tatler*, 7.11.1917, p.30. See pp.222, 252.
© Illustrated London News Ltd / Mary Evans

20. Tanks on the streets of London, selling War Bonds. See p.117. *Illustrated London News*, 1.12.1917, p.1.
© ILN Ltd / Mary Evans

21. Tanks on the silver screen, *The Battle for the Ancre and the Advance of the Tanks*, 1917. See p.74. *The Graphic*, 20.1.1917, p.5.
© ILN Ltd / Mary Evans

22. 'Presentation to the City of Cardiff of German Gun captured at Loos by the Welsh Guards, 18th November 1915,' from The Welsh Troops Picture PostCard Collection in Aid of the National Fund for Welsh Troops. See p.188.
Private Collection

FRENCH FLAG DAY AT CARDIFF: MRS. LLOYD GEORGE'S VISIT.

23. French Flag Day at Cardiff, 15 July 1915. Beside her, also holding flowers, is Lady Mayoress Mrs J. T. Richards. See p.186. *Western Mail*, 16.7.1915, p.8.
© Reach Plc.

24. The Lloyd Georges visit D. A. and Sybil Thomas, later Lord and Lady Rhondda, at Llanwern, Newport, in 1909. Seated from left, centre row: Sybil Thomas, David Lloyd George, Margaret Lloyd George, D. A. Thomas. Bottom left, their daughter Margaret, later Viscountess Rhondda, suffragette, businesswoman and publisher.
Private Collection

25. Viscountess Sybil Rhondda DBE. Photograph by Hugh Cecil.
IWM WWC D8-3-964

MRS. LLOYD GEORGE AND INFANT WELFARE.

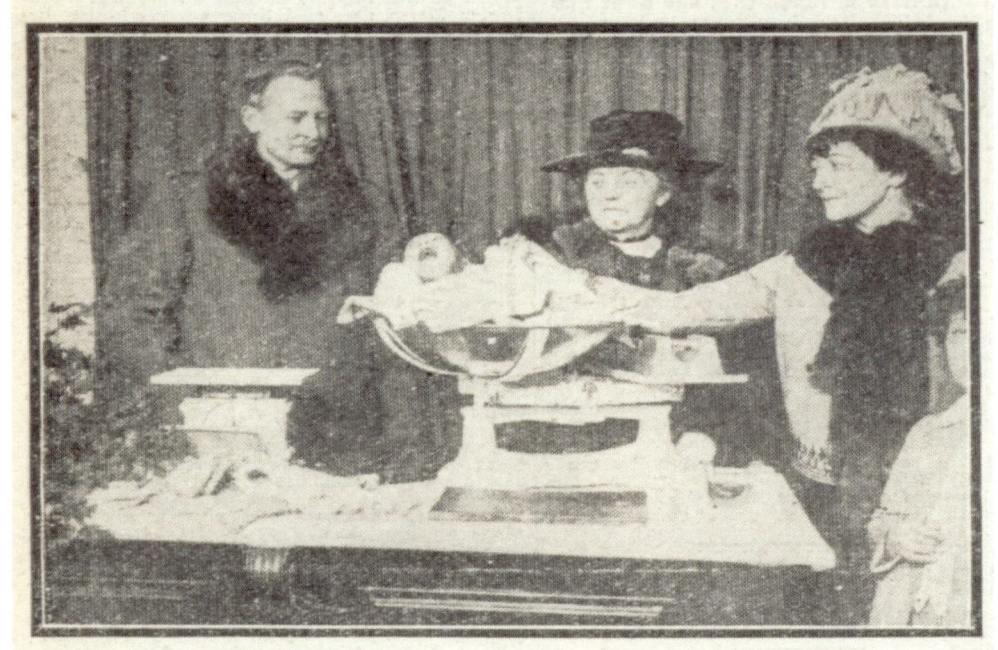

Mrs. Lloyd George at the opening of an Infants' Welfare Centre at Notting Hill, London. She hears a protest against being weighed.—(*Daily Mirror* photograph.)

26. Weighing the baby at Notting Hill. See p.145. *Daily Mirror*, 7.11.1918, p.4.
© Reach Plc.

27. Lady (Julia) Henry's Creche, Woolwich. See p.354. Artist, John Lavery, 1919.
ART.IWM 3084

28. London's East End children and their takeaways, Lycett Chapel, 4 April 1917. See p.297.
© British Pathé Ltd

29. Mrs Lloyd George, in a familiar role in the chair at the National Baby Council meeting, shown in the *Motherhood* film. See p.102. *The Bioscope*, 17.5.1917, p.95.
Courtesy of British Library Board

30. Traditional Welsh dress at the Women's Free Church Council, Bloomsbury. See p.118. *The Sketch*, 13.3.1918, p.3.
© Illustrated London News Ltd / Mary Evans

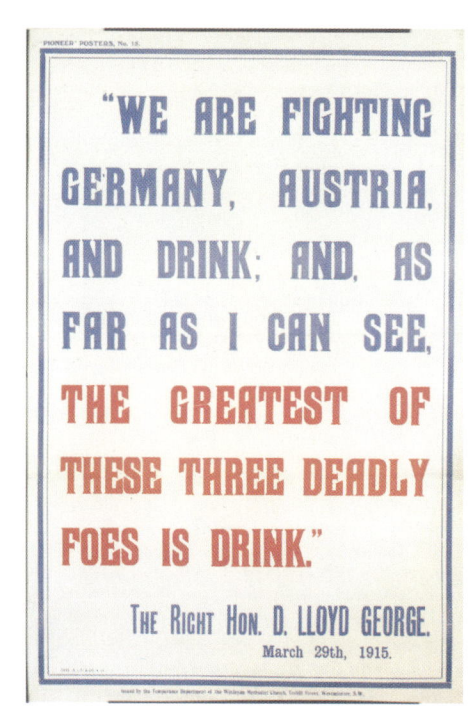

"WE ARE FIGHTING GERMANY, AUSTRIA, AND DRINK; AND, AS FAR AS I CAN SEE, THE GREATEST OF THESE THREE DEADLY FOES IS DRINK."

THE RIGHT HON. D. LLOYD GEORGE.
March 29th, 1915.

31. Wartime temperance poster issued by the Wesleyan Methodist Church. See p.360.
IWM PST 13358

32. Formally opening the club for the women relatives of soldiers and sailors, Camberwell. See p.360.
Olwen Carey Evans Collection 10 (Llyfr Ffoto 1013 C), NLW

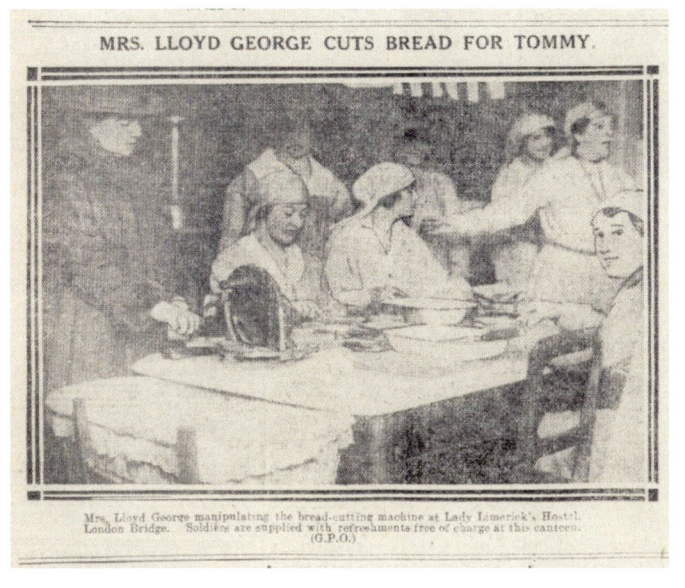

33. Cutting the bread at London Bridge. See p.313. *Leeds Mercury*, 10.11.1917, p.6.
© National World Publishing Ltd, created courtesy of the British Library Board

34. Former Open champion golfer James Braid in the swing for the Fund. See p.193.
Private Collection

35. Sir Vincent Evans, Hon. Treasurer of the National Fund for Welsh Troops. *The Cambrian News*, 16.8.1916, p.15. See p.156.
© Cambrian News Ltd

36. Regulator of all fundraisers. Sir Edward Ward, by 'Spy', Leslie Ward (1851–1922). See p.192. *Vanity Fair*, 30.5.1901.

37. William Lewis, Hon. Secretary of the National Fund for Welsh Troops. *Liverpool Echo*, 31.5.1934. See p.160.
© Reach Plc.

38. Arriving at the NK National Restaurant, Blackfriars, City of London, 16 July 1918. See p.323.
© British Pathé Ltd

39. The broad customer base of the NK National Restaurant, Blackfriars: a soldier, schoolboys, boys in boaters, gentlemen in bowler hats, women from the offices and a bobby, 16 July 1918. See p. 323.
© British Pathé Ltd

AT ONE OF LONDON'S MOST SUCCESSFUL FOOD KITCHENS.

At the New Bridge-street Food Kitchen. Left to right (seated): Mrs. Clynes, Miss Clynes, Mrs. Lloyd George, Sir Vincent Evans, Mrs. Winston Churchill. They tested the quality of the food and the cooking and unanimously pronounced both to be excellent.—(*Daily Mirror* photograph.)

40. Seated at the NK National Restaurant, Mrs and Miss Clynes (the Food Controller's wife and daughter), Mrs Lloyd George, Sir Vincent Evans and Mrs Winston (Clementine) Churchill and others, 16 July 1918. See p.323. *The Daily Mirror*, 17.7.1918, p.1.
© Reach Plc.

41. and 42. The NK National Restaurant, New Bridge Street, Blackfriars, July 1918, a far cry from the soup kitchens. Lighting by the General Electric Company. See p.323. Photography by Adolphe Augustus Boucher of Bedford Lemere & Co.
Historic England Archive

AT THE OPENING OF A CANTEEN AT THE WHITE CITY: MRS. LLOYD GEORGE AND ONE OF HER DAUGHTERS, MRS. CAREY EVANS (RIGHT).

Mrs. Lloyd George, accompanied by her elder daughter, Mrs. Carey Evans, and Sir George Riddell, visited the White City a few days ago and opened a canteen for women workers. Mr. S. J. Waring presided.

43. White City Canteen, front, left to right: G. A. Sawyer, Margaret Lloyd George, Mrs and Mr S. J. Waring, Olwen, and Sir George Riddell. See p.313. *The Sketch*, 28.11.1917, p.36.
© *Illustrated London News Ltd* / Mary Evans

44. Workers attaching runners to canvas tents at the former upholstery department of the manufacturing premises of Waring & Gillow, White City, London, August 1916. See p.313.
Historic England Archive

CHAPTER 11

Peace at Last

(November to December 1918)

'When he returned he was smiling and said only,
"they're going to sign". Then he shook
hands with us all, even with me.'
Margaret Lloyd George, Armistice, November 1918

NOVEMBER 1918

ON 4 NOVEMBER, at the City Girls Club in London, Mrs Lloyd George was talking positively as hopes rose for a passing of a 'long, dark and stormy night':

> MRS LLOYD GEORGE AND BRITAIN'S DEBT TO WOMEN: Mrs Lloyd George, speaking at the City Temple, London, last night, said that to-day the world in general, and certainly Britain in particular, was under a deep obligation to women for what they had done during the past four years of agony and suffering. It had been a long, dark, and stormy night. The night had not passed, but it was passing, and dawn was at hand, and when peace came she could not imagine they would shirk any of the obligations which came with it.[1]

She then hurried to her daughter's bedside. Megan had the flu – for which the death rate had peaked the week before. We can only imagine what was going through her mind.

The same day, her 54th birthday, she had been weighing an infant in the Notting Hill baby centre, promoting the future health of the nation, the baby allegedly protesting.[2] (illustration 26)

Mrs Lloyd George, opening an infant welfare centre in Notting-hill on Wednesday, said that the war had made us realise exactly what it meant to have unhealthy and weak children: so many boys were unfit for the Army. She hoped that we should have a better standard in future, and these welfare centres would be of the greatest assistance. They were needed in all parts the country, as well as in London.[3]

On 6 November, she addressed the London Welsh Women's Temperance Union, at the King's Cross Welsh Chapel, quite possibly accompanied by JTR, it having been his chapel during his early years in London. With an end to war anticipated, not only had she been preparing for her Troops Fund to provide future support for those in need in peacetime, she was looking ahead to new campaigns, as active party politics returned and when women would not only be voting for the first time but standing for Parliament. Here was the chance for women to shape policy on many social issues, including temperance:

> As women will have so large a share of political power in Britain, it is of the utmost importance to take all the means in our power not simply to organise but also to educate them. I hope also that women will not only study how to vote but study the problems which have to be solved so as to bring an original & fresh contribution to the discussion on such questions as housing, health, and above all temperance. This meeting is held under the auspices of the Welsh Temperance Society. We strongly emphasise temperance. Women ought to be able to make invaluable suggestions, and although we cannot exactly see the end of the war still, we all feel somehow 'Mwy sydd eisioes wedi ei dreulio nag sydd ar ôl o'r anial dir' [Literally, 'More has already been spent than is left of the desolate ground']. The end of the war will be the beginning of a new era in the history of the world. What kind of a world is that?[4]

She also showed her humorous side: 'So far, I have not heard of any Member of Parliament who is willing to give up his seat to a lady, but perhaps that will come later.'[5]

The following evening, 7 November, she was the principal speaker at the annual meeting of the Highgate Hospital War Supply Depot, a surgical branch of Queen Mary's Needlework Guild and Hospitals, at Cholmeley School, Highgate.[6]

Across the Channel, her husband was seeking to draw hostilities to an end, the Allies meeting in Versailles to set the terms to be offered the next day to Germany, on 8 November, in the railway carriage in the forest of Compiègne.

Germany was given 72 hours to agree. This was just the start of the long peace negotiations: the Allies would meet in Paris during the first half of 1919 before the peace agreement with Germany was struck at Versailles in July. A further five treaties would still have to be negotiated: the 1919 Treaty of Saint-Germain, with Austria; the 1919 Treaty of Neuilly, with Bulgaria; the 1920 Treaty of Trianon, with Hungary; and finally the treaties of Sèvres (1920) and Lausanne (1923), settling with the dismantled Ottoman Empire and the new Republic of Turkey. The aim, a lasting peace, ran for two decades.

On 8 November, the day Armistice terms were being offered, a Mrs J. Williams of Dulcote, Wells, Somerset, wrote a touching letter of thanksgiving to Mrs Lloyd George:

> Mrs J. Williams wishes Mrs Lloyd George to accept this relic, and would like her to wear it on Peace Day, which seems so gloriously close, and afterwards sell it to the Red X if she so wishes, in thankfulness for the Preservation of her son in 3 and half years' service in France – God Bless you Both. Dulcote, Wells.[7]

The relic was a dark blue silk ribbon embroidered 'George III The 50 Year 1809', marking the golden jubilee of the reign of George III. In reality, it was the start of his 50th year – the first royal jubilee to be significantly celebrated. There was some confusion as to whether it was a year early.

The returning soldier, Reginald Charles Williams, son of gardener James Williams and Sarah Lane, had been a 16-year-old hall boy in service at Dunster Castle in 1911, and would have been 20 when going to France. He died in Dulcote in 1980 at the age of 86.[8]

On the afternoon of Saturday, 9 November, Mrs Lloyd George held an 'At Home' at No. 10 for the YWCA:

> Hundreds flocked to 10, Downing Street this afternoon, the occasion of Mrs Lloyd George's 'At home' on behalf of the YWCA. So large was the attendance that an overflow meeting was held in an adjacent room and an empty grate was rather welcomed than otherwise.
>
> Mrs Lloyd George, after warmly welcoming her guests, said she hoped

the meeting would be a great success, as the YWCA had done such good work during the past terrible four years and three months. They all looked forward to the end of the war and before long they would be looking forward to the demobilisation of the Army, but she felt sure nobody wanted the demobilisation of the YWCA.

The Hon. Emily Kinnard, O.B.E., amused her listeners by one or two little stories in connection with the work which the society is carrying on. One little munitions girl with whom she spoke recently, when asked to describe her life, said it was 'Plumstead, bedstead. Plumstead, bedstead.' Another girl said, 'I didn't believe in no church, I didn't believe in the YWCA, but now I believe in God, because he blew the YWCA here.'[9]

Far from being demobilised, the YWCA continues a century later.

That evening Mrs Lloyd George accompanied the Prime Minister to the annual Lord Mayor's Banquet at the Guildhall in the City of London, as the Allies awaited Germany's response to the peace terms.

GERMANY'S CHOICE: IMMEDIATE SURRENDER OR UTTER RUIN
SPEECH BY MR LLOYD GEORGE: STERN RECKONING FOR THE GUILTY
The annual banquet was given at the Guildhall London, by the Lord Mayor and Sheriffs on Saturday night. In accordance with custom, the guests were received in the library. The floral decorations were simple but effective, and at the back of the dais was fixed a shield bearing the City arms, surmounted by the flags of the Allied nations. The civic procession was heralded by a fanfare of trumpets. The Lady Mayoress was attended by eight maids of honour, who carried bouquets of chrysanthemums. The Prime Minister and Mrs Lloyd George were received with loud cheers, which continued until they had traversed the whole length of the library and reached the dais.[10]

Did she reflect back to the eve of war, when she listened to her husband telling the merchants and bankers in the Mansion House that 'there were always clouds in the international sky, that there were clouds even now, but his view was that common sense, patience, and forbearance would pull us through.'[11]

On Sunday morning, 10 November, the Lloyd George family went down to their Surrey home for their usual brief weekend away.

1918: Peace at Last

The Prime Minister, Mrs Lloyd George, and Miss Megan Lloyd George left early this morning for a brief week-end in the country. Throughout the day Mr Lloyd George was in constant telephonic communication with Downing Street. The enormous public interest manifested in the closing stages of the war was marked by the prescience of a very large crowd in Whitehall at the time they moved off. Mr Lloyd George, with one of these characteristic touches that add much to his personal popularity, patted a curious youngster and chatted briefly with an Australian soldier before entering his motor.[12]

Mrs Lloyd George later recalled the night of 10 November.

The most dramatic moment of our life at No. 10 happened one Sunday evening in November 1918. We were at Walton Heath for the week-end, and I had returned in the afternoon from a drive when Mr Lloyd George said, 'Don't take off your hat, we're going back to Downing Street.' When we got there we had a little dinner party, consisting of General Smuts, Mr Churchill, my husband and myself.

I did not know what news was expected, but during dinner I sensed excitement in the air. Suddenly a message came for my husband, 'You're wanted on the telephone from the War Office,' and he went immediately. The three of us that were left never spoke a word. Mr Churchill paced restlessly up and down the room. General Smuts and I sat in silence. He was not gone many minutes, but to us sitting there it seemed an age. When he returned he was smiling and said only, 'they're going to sign'. Then he shook hands with us all, even with me.

I felt proud at that moment that I had been able to help him even a little in bringing the war to a successful end and the country out of its darkest hour.[13]

On 11 November, the Armistice was declared. In his Notes, JTR recorded Mrs Lloyd George's words:

When I looked down on the crowd on Armistice morning it seemed a road paved with humanity.[14]

The next day, *The Times* carried a message from Mrs Lloyd George to the women of France:

149

MRS LLOYD GEORGE TO THE WOMEN OF FRANCE
Writing to a lady about to proceed to France on a mission to the French Protestant Churches, Mrs Lloyd George, in tendering sincerest good wishes for the success of this 'timely and noble enterprise' said, 'May I through you send a message to the women of France – a message of sympathy, admiration and congratulation – of sympathy with them in the cruel sufferings and appalling losses inflicted on them by the war: of admiration for the fortitude that has never failed them even in the darkest hour: of congratulation that complete and final deliverance is now at hand.'[15]

The JTR Collection includes a letter written on that historic day to the PM, which it would be appropriate to enter into the record here, from his long-time friend and associate, the Lord Chief Justice, Lord Reading, at the time 'in bed with a feverish cold':[16]

On Lord Chief Justice of England embossed paper, 11th November 1918
My dear LG Alas! I am still laid up although I expect to be out on Wednesday. I must send you one line of deep thankfulness for the splendid spirit you have shown throughout these awful years. You have never wavered in your conviction that we should win if only we had faith in the bad as in the good time. You have stood like a rock. Even at this moment it scarcely seems credible that the war is over and that Germany is shattered. Yet it has all turned out so well and above all Great Britain plays her part in battle & in Conference at this most fateful hour.

I have not been allowed to write a line till this moment – but I felt I must relieve my tense feelings by sending my congratulations to you – I think of my departure for America last January – when you said to me if only we can hold out six months till August, the changes will then begin – we shall have weathered the storm and henceforth we shall be moving to victory. Your telegrams to me in these early days are of extraordinary interest now – God bless & keep you my dear friend. I hope to see you Wednesday – as always Reading.

Now for the new House of Commons – it will want all its authority of a fresh mandate to govern in the year or two ahead.[17]

While still Lord Chief Justice (1913–1921), Reading was appointed Ambassador to the US in January 1918. He had led the Anglo-French

Commission in 1915 to seek financial aid from the US, obtaining what was then the largest loan in history, US$500 million.

On Tuesday, 12 November, Mrs Lloyd George and Megan represented the Prime Minister (who could not attend) at the Thanksgiving Service at an overflowing St Paul's Cathedral, attended by the King and Queen and much of the royalty, plus the Asquiths, Sir Eric Geddes (Lloyd George ally and First Lord of the Admiralty), Admiral Sims (Commander of all US naval forces in Europe), and representatives from France, Greece, Italy, Japan, South Africa and Australia.[18]

On Thursday, 14 November, she visited the Cardigan House Club in Richmond, west London, where she inaugurated the club's motor service for the wounded.[19]

The Forces were still in uniform. On Friday, 15 November, she opened a canteen and club at Lillie Road, Fulham, for the Women's Royal Air Force (WRAF), remarking that such institutes were necessary in big towns.[20] The following day, the Prime Minister did join her at the Albert Hall service organised by the Free Churches (as did the King and Queen). The 8,000-strong congregation rose to their feet on the entry of the 'Victory Premier' and Mrs Lloyd George.[21] Diarist Samuell Pepys Junior observed: 'The occasion is a great service of thanksgiving there held by the Dissenters, all their famous ministers praying and preaching in it; but a strange place, I thought, for worshipping God.'[22]

The day after the Armistice, peace seemed infectious, as reported in what would doubtless rank high on any list of 'wish I'd been a fly on the wall' meetings.

MRS ASQUITH AND MRS LLOYD GEORGE: Reunion the order of the day. The most striking evidence which I can produce to prove this, says a *Daily Dispatch* correspondent, is that on Tuesday – the day after the public had acclaimed Mr Lloyd George the chief political instrument of our victory – Mrs Asquith, I am told, called upon Mrs Lloyd George at Downing Street. The significance of this call will not be lost upon those who are intimately acquainted with the personal side of high politics.[23]

The *Newcastle Daily Journal*'s 'London Letter' speculated about Liberal renewal, which was not about to happen.

What Does It Mean?
The praise bestowed by Mr Asquith on the speech of Mr Lloyd George the other day, in which the latter outlined a comprehensive programme of Liberal reform, continues to be a subject of considerable comment in political circles. A good deal has been read into it which a calm analysis of the speech hardly justifies. It is certainly responsible for blunting the edge of Liberal opposition, and it may be that the Right Hon. gentleman desires a return of the old relations which subsisted between himself and his erstwhile brilliant lieutenant.[24]

Later in the month *The Sketch* added a social dimension:

The disappearance of minor social distinctions is one of the accepted marks of the post-war era – people learn in wartime the sort of service and status that really counts. Little flutters may still follow an announcement that Mrs Asquith had called on Mrs Lloyd George; but it is Mrs Lloyd George who has the broadest smile.[25]

On the afternoon of 25 November, she accompanied her husband to Wolverhampton, where he launched the election campaign with his 'Homes for Heroes' speech.

DECEMBER 1918

On 4 December, the Premier's wife was still carrying out her pre-arranged commitments, opening a bazaar in south London, at the Anglican St Barnabas' Church, Clapham Common, where she contributed a signed portrait of the Prime Minister, suggesting, 'it ought to fetch £50', which the Unionist candidate Sir Arthur Du Cros duly paid when he opened the bazaar the following day.[26]

The next afternoon she opened a sale of work at the Enmore Road Congregational Church in South Norwood, and apologised for not staying long as she had to get back to No. 10 for a meeting, adding that, 'when she promised to come she had no idea that it would take place in the middle of the general election.'

On 6 December, the second anniversary of becoming a prime minister's wife, she was in south Wales beginning her two-week whirlwind election tour, to keep herself and her husband in No. 10. The first wife of a Prime Minister to campaign outside her husband's constituency, her ability to draw and entertain a good crowd would be amply demonstrated over the next four years. Women now had the vote and the opportunity was there for her to campaign for her party, the voice and 'presence' of Lloyd George around the country.

Her lifelong campaigning for temperance would continue, and she would not let up on her other welfare-related work.

Postscript

On 26 August 1920, King George V announced that Councillor and JP Margaret Lloyd George was to become a Dame Grand Cross of the Order of the British Empire (GBE) in recognition of her wartime funding work for 'charities, hospitals and other public spirited movements', raising more than £200,000. Lloyd George had written to his wife: 'I signed, yes, your G.B.E. This is the greatest & the highest of all. You wear it on State occasions, a gorgeous sash across your chest.'[27]

***

END OF THE WARTIME DIARY

The story now continues by detailing her main wartime campaigns, cause by cause, the next eight chapters covering her Troops Fund, ably assisted by William Lewis, the Fund's Hon. Secretary, followed by the final six chapters on five further campaigns: recruiting the Welsh Army, supporting the sailors, feeding the nation, providing better healthcare for all, and keeping the country sober. A busy agenda.

Her post-war, peacetime public activities, not least when breaking convention through her political campaigns, and supported by JTR, her private secretary, may be followed in *The Campaigns of Margaret Lloyd George, Wife of the Prime Minister, 1916–1922*.

THE NATIONAL FUND FOR WELSH TROOPS

'There was not a Fund in the country that had been run more economically than theirs.'
Margaret Lloyd George, January 1918

CHAPTER 12

Establishing the Fund and Reactions

(December 1914 to February 1915)

> 'It is hoped that there may be a great
> concentration of effort throughout Wales for
> this most desirable object of adding to the comfort
> of the men who have undertaken the greatest sacrifice
> they can make for their country and Empire.'
>
> *Western Mail*, January 1915

THE NATIONAL FUND for Welsh Troops, often referred to as the Welsh Troops Comforts Fund, was started by Mrs Lloyd George in December 1914 to enable comforts, initially clothing and cigarettes, to be sent to the troops to supplement their official kit and rations. From the onset of war, people had been knitting scarves, mittens and jumpers for their enlisting family members. Clothing stores advertised their range of goods for sale, suitable for the purpose. (illustrations 46, 47) Mrs Lloyd George's organisation drew not only on her network of Welsh and Liberal ladies, but also on the network of MPs and Lords-Lieutenant across Wales.

Key to the Fund's success was the contribution made by its Bangor-born Hon. Secretary, William Lewis. (illustration 37) The role of Treasurer was filled by Sir Vincent Evans, journalist, accountant, and champion of the Welsh cultural revival of the Eisteddfod and the Cymmrodorion Society. (illustration 35) Funds not fully spent by the end of the war were either dedicated to a Welsh children's fund or integrated into the nascent pension system (started by Lloyd George in 1910). William Lewis moved to the new Ministry of Pensions to take this a step forward, before returning to his shipping career in the 1920s.

On 15 December 1914, at her 27 Bryanston Square home in London, Florence, Lady Brynmor Jones, presided over a ladies' committee providing comforts for the London Welsh Battalion, part of the new Welsh Army, attached to the Royal Welch Fusiliers:

> Among those present were Mrs Lloyd George, Mrs Ellis Griffith, Mrs John Hinds [wife of the Liberal MP for West Carmarthenshire], Mrs Timothy Davies [wife of the Liberal MP for Louth, Lincolnshire], Mrs Ivor Bowen [wife of a Welsh lawyer and commander of a London Welsh Battalion], Mrs D. H. Evans [wife of the founder of the eponymous department store], Mrs W. J. Davies, Mrs W. Clarke, Mrs H. M. Emlyn and the Viscountess Parker.
>
> The committee had collected 2,600 pairs of socks, 1,000 handkerchiefs, 15,000 cigarettes, and a number of tobacco pipes. It was pointed out there was still need for many more comforts, especially warm shirts for the men.[1]

A week earlier the London Welsh Battalion had been posted to Llandudno for training, Mrs Lloyd George's son Richard now a Captain in the battalion. During the Boer War, Lady Brynmor Jones had been actively involved in the establishment of a military field hospital, known as the 'Welsh Hospital'.[2]

This gathering of well-connected Welsh women may have been a good warm-up to the meeting hosted three days later, on 11 December, by Mrs Lloyd George at No. 10, when an executive committee was set up for her own comforts fund, the National Fund for Welsh Troops. The organisation and chain of command of the Fund followed the structure established for recruiting the Welsh Army. (see p.274)

> NATIONAL FUND FOR WELSH TROOPS: At a meeting of ladies connected with Wales, held yesterday at 10, Downing Street, London, it was decided to raise a national fund for Welsh troops in order to provide additional comforts for the Welsh regiments at home and abroad.
>
> Lady Plymouth was elected president and Mrs Lloyd George chairman of the committee. The General Committee will consist of the wives or

eldest daughters of peers connected with Wales, the Lords-Lieutenant of the Welsh counties, of the Members of Parliament for Wales, and of chairmen of Welsh County Councils.

The following ladies were appointed to the Executive Committee: Lady Herbert [Albertina, wife of Sir Ivor Herbert, Lord-Lieutenant for Monmouthshire, later Baron Treowen], Lady Edwards [Catherine, wife of the Liberal MP for Radnorshire], Lady Ninian Crichton-Stuart [Ismay, wife of the Liberal MP for Cardiff – he was already serving in France with the British Expeditionary Force], the Hon. Mrs Ormsby-Gore [Beatrice, wife of the Unionist MP for Denbigh Boroughs, then serving in Egypt – succeeding as Lord Harlech in 1938], Violet Douglas-Pennant [philanthropist, National Health Insurance Commissioner for South Wales, and daughter of Baron Penrhyn], Mrs McKenna [Pamela, wife of the Liberal MP for North Monmouthshire], Mrs Ellis Griffith [Mary, wife of the MP for Anglesey], and Mrs Pryce Jones [Beatrice, wife of the Unionist MP for Montgomery Boroughs].

Sir E. Vincent Evans will act as Hon. Treasurer and William Lewis as Hon. Secretary.

All contributions of money and kind should be addressed to Mrs Lloyd George, 11, Downing Street, Whitehall, S.W.[3]

The announcement was given wide national coverage.

Lady Plymouth's husband, the Lord-Lieutenant of Glamorgan, was leading the initial drive for the Welsh Army, which may have prompted her to accept the Fund presidency. Alberta, Lady Plymouth, would attend the Fund's committee on just two occasions. Owners of St Fagans Castle near Cardiff (where the first Welsh VAD was formed, in 1909) the Plymouths established a convalescent hospital there for this new war.[4] Their son, Archer, had been killed in the first month of the war, on 25 August 1914, during the retreat from Mons.

All twelve initial committee members served throughout the war, with the exception of Lady Edwards who died in July 1915. Additional recruits increased membership to 28 by December 1918, the first addition coming at the second meeting, 5 January 1915, when Editha, Lady Glanusk, wife of the Lord-Lieutenant of Breconshire, attended, and in Mrs Lloyd George's absence chaired that meeting (as she would on many other occasions). She may already have been acquainted with the Secretary, William Lewis, Liberal candidate for the neighbouring

Radnorshire constituency. Sir Francis Edwards, the current Radnor MP, who had won the seat in 1900, opposing the Boer War, planned to stand down at the next election.

While members' spouses were mostly holders of official posts in Wales, they had their own skills and connections: for example, MP Edward Pryce-Jones, the husband of Beatrice, ran a pioneering mail-order company, founded by his father, selling woollen goods from their Newtown base. The Welsh were significant players in the country's drapery trade – comforts were their business.

The attendance record at committee meetings varied from 100 per cent (the Secretary); another eight attended more than half, seven at least one-in-three meetings, four less than ten per cent. Mrs Lloyd George attended two-thirds, chairing 19 of the first year's 31 meetings. Pamela McKenna, Beatrice Ormsby-Gore, Mrs Herbert Lewis, and Lady (Ivor) Herbert (later Lady Treowen) were also frequent attendees. Treasurer Sir Vincent Evans attended all but nine of the Fund meetings. Mrs Ruth Herbert Lewis, née Caine, who joined later in 1915, was then also a regular attendee.

Violet Douglas-Pennant attended 42 meetings through to the summer of 1918, when she was appointed commander of the Women's Royal Air Force, the WRAF. Ruffling some feathers, she was controversially dismissed from the WRAF in October 1918 and her career effectively ended, despite a long attempt to restore her reputation. She resigned from the Fund in March 1919.[5]

Lloyd George, contributing £20, was reportedly the first subscriber to the Fund, other early donors including Sir Alfred Mond, £500, and D. A. Thomas (later Lord Rhondda), who contributed £152.10s. from the sale of a two-year-old heifer and a collection taken at Newport cattle market.[6]

The Troops Fund faced two initial challenges: persuading as many people and places in Wales to work with them, many already being very active; and coordinating their activities with others, to avoid overlap, competition, wastage and inefficient delivery to the troops in the field – the latter not easy with regiments moving around, often without notice.

The prestige and contacts under the Fund's umbrella would be important, both in terms of authority and logistics. But a Downing Street address would not necessarily be enough to overcome the ambitions of the major centres of Wales, such Cardiff and Swansea, nor the local priorities of smaller communities. Indeed, that the wife of the Chancellor of the Exchequer should be asking for money was at times contested, especially by those who thought the State should be fully responsible.

William Lewis

William Lewis, Hon. Secretary, had been adopted as the Liberal candidate for Radnorshire, in January 1914, the local *Brecon & Radnor Express* detailing his career:

> THE CANDIDATE: Mr William Lewis is a native of Bangor, and is 44 years of age. He was educated at the Friars School, Bangor [today the oldest existant school in Wales] and at an early age entered the service of a well-known Liverpool ship-owning firm. In 1896 he commenced business as a ship-builder, and about eight years ago he transferred his business to London, where he trades as Lewis, Heron & Co., ship-owners and ship and insurance brokers, 10, Fenchurch Avenue.
>
> In Liverpool Mr Lewis was one of the founders of the Young Wales Society, which has rendered great service to the political and social life of the Welsh community there.
>
> When Mr Lloyd George was the President of the Board of Trade, Mr Lewis was appointed a member of a Board of Trade Departmental Committee, under the presidency of Lord Davenport.
>
> Mr Lewis is a deacon of the Welsh C.M. Church at Willesden Green, and he has rendered great service to the cause of Welsh Nonconformity in the Metropolis. He was secretary and organiser of the Welsh National Bazaar, which was held about 18 months ago, under the presidency of Mrs Lloyd George and the chairmanship of Sir Vincent Evans, which resulted in lessening the debt on the Welsh places of worship by £4,000. Mr Lewis was married in 1898 to Miss Annie Hughes, daughter of the late Ald. Hugh Hughes – then Mayor of Bangor. They have two children, a boy and a girl.[7]

The team running that 1912 Welsh National Bazaar was now reunited to run her Troops Fund: Mrs Lloyd George (Committee Chairman), William Lewis (Hon. Sec) and Sir Vincent Evans (Treasurer). The 1912 event was held at London's Caxton Hall, where Lloyd George had been accosted by suffragettes as he left the building.[8] Not in favour of militant suffrage action against her husband, we may assume Mrs Lloyd George was even less impressed when it disturbed the activities of her church.

Into action

In its first year the Fund's twelve-member executive committee met weekly, outside the holiday seasons, at 3pm on Mondays (with one exception), at 11 Downing St, chaired by Mrs Lloyd George, or another member in her absence, attendance varying from four to nine members, authorising payments, reviewing requests for comforts (by no means all would be granted), inspecting and ordering new comforts, responding to regulatory and other issues, developing strategy for fund-raising and event organisation. The treasurer regularly reported the financial position, and the secretary (or an assigned member) followed up with actions. It was business-like from the start, avoiding the weakness that would hamper many of the new charitable ventures.

In addition to comforting the troops, the Fund sought to support the unemployed around the country, especially Welsh producers of those comforts. The 5 January meeting ordered 700 pairs of socks from the central unemployment body for London, not exceeding 1s. 3d. per pair. John Hinds MP, a draper, and Philip and Owen Williams (from Breconshire), of Messrs. Williams and Davies, well-known London drapers at Earl's Court, were also asked to help in purchasing comforts. Philip Williams also became a trustee of the Lloyd George American Fund, of which Mrs Lloyd George was treasurer. (see p.36)

The meeting approved the dispatch of 950 pairs of socks to the South Wales Borderers (Brecon Territorials) at Milford Haven. Territorials had first been raised after the 1907 Army reforms, essentially as a defensive force.[9]

The meeting tasked William Lewis with finding out the needs of men commanding the power stations on Snowdon and at the Marconi stations at Towyn on the north coast of Wales (the Towyn radio station huts still exist). Mrs McKenna undertook to obtain full information as to the whereabouts of the various units of Welsh troops at home and abroad, and ascertain what comforts were actually provided by the War Office.[10]

A letter was sent to all mayors and chairmen of Urban District Councils throughout Wales, 'inviting their assistance to the objects of the Committee', and an endeavour was to be made to 'secure the sympathy and cooperation of all Welsh religious bodies'.

Arrangements were also to be made for the observance of St David's Day, 1 March, as a flag day throughout Wales, with designs and prices of flags and badges to be obtained. Flag days would become one of the most common, visible and successful of wartime fund-raising activities, including for the Troops Fund.

The Fund's ambitions were published the next day, the *Western Mail* reporting:

> It is hoped that the festival may be celebrated in that way in every town and village of Wales, and in every other centre where Welshmen have a colony.
>
> The idea, of course, is on the lines of the Rose Days which have helped to swell the funds of so many charities, and wherever the scheme is adopted miniature flags will be sold in the streets for the benefit of the Fund.
>
> It is hoped that there may be a great concentration of effort throughout Wales for this most desirable object of adding to the comfort of the men who have undertaken the greatest sacrifice they can make for their country and Empire.
>
> Mr William Lewis, the Hon. Secretary of the committee, will communicate with the mayors and council chairmen, and each locality will develop its own arrangements for ensuring complete success.[11]

The first Alexandra Rose Day, in June 1912, marked the 50th anniversary of the arrival of Queen Alexandra from her native Denmark, to raise funds for her favourite charities.[12] That day Mrs Lloyd George had been selling roses on the Embankment by Westminster Bridge.[13]

The first flag days of this war had already been held, on 5 September in Glasgow, for the Soldiers' and Sailors' Families Association, and in Bristol for the Red Cross.[14]

Comforts were already being sent to the Fund from knitting groups and schoolchildren. The girls of the County School in Aberaeron, Cardiganshire, before breaking up for Christmas, had sent Mrs Lloyd George 50 articles in the form of scarves, belts, and mittens, made by their own hands under the direction of their teachers, for the use of the Army Corps stationed at Llandudno.[15]

The YMCA raises its concerns
The potential for competition with others came almost immediately and was addressed at the 11 January meeting, chaired by Mrs McKenna:

> Sir Vincent Evans placed before the committee certain correspondence that had taken place with the YMCA Cardiff with respect to the selection of St David's Day as the National Fund Flag Day. The Secretary was authorised to write to officials of the YMCA to express the regret of this committee that any question should arise between the two organisations, that the committee fully appreciated the great value of the work done by the YMCA and would deplore anything in the nature of seeming antagonism.
>
> That inasmuch as the appeal of the committee would be to the whole of Wales and to the Welsh-speaking people in English towns upon a purely Welsh National movement, while that of the YMCA was to be confined to So [presumably south] Wales, the committee with much regret could not see its way to relinquish 1 March as its flag day, and trusted that under all the circumstances the YMCA would see its way clear to arrange another date.[16]

Conflicting with traditional celebratory Welsh dinners might also be an issue:

> With regard to a Welsh National Concert to be held in London, no decision was come to, pending information as to whether the usual Welsh dinners were to take place on St David's Day.[17]

In Cardiff, for example, the annual 1 March St David's Day dinner of the Cymmrodorion Society would not be held, but a conversazione and reception was hosted at the City Hall, Attorney-General Sir John Simon, 'a Pembrokeshire man', a special guest. Proceeds from the sales of the 2s. 6d. tickets were to be given to Mrs Lloyd George's Troops Fund.[18]

Cooperating with Cardiff
The meeting of 18 January, chaired by Mrs Lloyd George, sought the cooperation of Cardiff:

In view of a possible difficulty in obtaining the co-operation of Cardiff, it was decided to ask Miss Violet Douglas-Pennant to see the Lord Mayor, and Lady Ninian Crichton-Stuart to write to the Lord Mayoress explaining the objects of this fund and inviting help to ensure the success of the flag day.[19]

The Lord Mayor of Cardiff called a conference to discuss how to respond to the Fund's plans, publishing the carefully worded letter sent 'from the official residence of the Chancellor of the Exchequer', as the *Western Mail* reported on 21 January:

For several days past, the Lord Mayor of Cardiff (Alderman J. T. Richards) and the secretary of the National Fund for Welsh Troops (Mr Wm. Lewis) have been in communication with each other with regard to obtaining local support for the National Fund, and on Wednesday the Lord Mayor received the following further letter, addressed from the official residence of the Chancellor of the Exchequer, which is the headquarters of the Fund:

'My lord, The committee of the National Fund for Welsh Troops is anxious to raise a substantial sum, so that all Welsh regiments serving at home and abroad should be provided with additional comforts, such as shirts, socks, mittens, gloves, Cardigan jackets, sweaters, belts, mufflers, Balaclava caps, handkerchiefs, &c., also pipes, tobacco, and cigarettes.

'We shall be glad to know that you can see your way to form a committee, with an energetic secretary, whose duty will be to raise funds and gifts in kind in the district over which your influence extends. We know that a great many appeals have already been made to the generosity of the public, but hope that you will feel disposed to assist us to provide a sufficient and constant supply of comforts for all the gallant Welshmen who have so nobly responded to their country's call.

'Some of the Welsh regiments are already well provided for with these comforts, but there are other regiments that are sadly in need of them. The object of the Fund is to ensure that all Welsh regiments will receive these additional comforts.

'The committee hope to be able to arrange, with your assistance, for March 1 next to be observed as a National Flag Day throughout Wales in aid of the above Fund. Further details will be sent to you shortly.

'We have much pleasure enclosing a number of suggestions which you may, perhaps, find useful, as they are based upon experience gained in connection with similar undertakings.'

The letter is signed by the Countess of Plymouth (the president of the Fund) and Mrs Lloyd George (chairman of the committee).[20]

Among the Fund's suggestions were a weekly house-to-house collection by volunteers, the placing of collecting cards and boxes in all clubs, shops, etc., benefit performances at theatres, music-halls and cinemas, collections in day and Sunday schools and churches and chapels on a Sunday to be fixed upon, the organisation of a flag day in every town and village throughout Wales on St David's Day, and the formation of ladies' working parties for making the various articles mentioned in the letter.

> LORD MAYOR'S ACTION: As an outcome of this letter, the Lord Mayor has decided to convene at an early date a meeting of representatives of the various organisations that are now separately engaged in carrying out the very work suggested by the London committee. His lordship recognises that at present there is considerable overlapping, and that uniform distribution of the contributions of the public can only be made possible by an amalgamation of effort under one controlling body of management. There are several other important considerations arising out of the letter. For instance, a very successful weekly house-to-house collection is being made, and has been made for several months, throughout the wards of Cardiff in aid of the Prince of Wales' National Relief Fund, and the organising of another similar collection in aid of the new Fund formed in London would seriously interfere with the present work. The conference which the Lord Mayor is about to convene will, therefore, be an important one.[21]

The *Western Mail* report went on to reinforce the concerns about duplication, further detailing other activities underway in Cardiff and nearby.

The immediate Downing Street response included a polite thank-you letter to the Lord Mayor and advising that they were sending a supply of 'parcels to the men of the Monmouthshire Regiment, the Royal Welch Fusiliers, and the South Wales Borderers, now at the Front, and ... comforts to the various Territorials serving at home.'[22]

The 25 January meeting deputed Violet Douglas-Pennant to attend the proposed Cardiff conference, with William Lewis. In addition to inviting the Lady Mayoress of Cardiff (Mrs J. T. Richards) to become a committee member of the Troops Fund, the committee also accepted the design of a Cardiff firm for a small flag for general distribution. Silk and button flaps, with a special red dragon design, would be provided for the occasion.[23]

More socks were ordered from the Welsh Industries Association, but the question of issuing a booklet for the soldiers of Wales, in conjunction with the Welsh Department of the Board of Education, was deemed out of scope.[24] The Permanent Secretary of the Welsh Department, Sir Alfred T. Davies, was a long-time friend of Mrs Lloyd George, so cooperation would probably have not been an issue – the idea might even have been his suggestion.

A separate fund-raising publication would be a later project. The Lady Mayoress did not join the committee but would attend a meeting in June when setting up a plan for parcels for Welsh prisoners of war with the support of the Fund.[25]

Marketing across Wales

The deputation succeeded in getting Cardiff's support, a big step forward, though it would not necessarily mean other major centres, such as Swansea, would follow suit.

William Lewis followed up with one of his typical thank-you letters, duly published by the recipient in the *Western Mail*:

> A letter has been received by the Lord Mayor of Cardiff (Alderman J. T. Richards) from Mr William Lewis, secretary of the National Fund for Welsh Troops, in which he writes:
>
> 'Permit me to thank you most warmly for your exceedingly kind letter, which has given much gratification to Mrs Lloyd George and myself, and which will, I am sure, be equally gratifying to my committee, whom the letter will be read to at their next meeting. The knowledge that Cardiff will take the lead with the Flag Day and Church collection movements ensures the success of both throughout Wales.'
>
> A large parcel from Mrs D. Lloyd George and the committee of the National Society has been received for the Bantam Battalion at Porthcawl.[26]

The Chairman of Porthcawl Council initiated a flag day for the Fund, albeit noting the local efforts already made: 'Personally, I feel, although we have done so much in Porthcawl, we can do a little more by assisting this deserving cause. I am not blind to the fact that we have already raised nearly £1,000 for the different funds at Porthcawl.'[27]

Porthcawl was also billeting Glamorgan's first Bantam Battalion, for men below the minimum recruiting height (between five feet and five feet three inches, and 34½-inch chest). The height restriction had been removed in December after heavy losses at Mons. The Fund would send 24 civilian suits and some woollen comforts to the Porthcawl recruits.[28]

As the Fund's call went out throughout Wales, many local bodies responded positively, but some asked why were these comforts needed for the troops? *The Pioneer*, the weekly socialist newspaper founded in 1911 in Merthyr Tydfil by Keir Hardie, enquired:

> The Chancellor of the Exchequer lives at 11 Downing Street. Why does Mrs Lloyd George not see that it is the duty of the State to provide the soldiers with the luxuries and necessities named above? They are the servants of the State and should not be dependent upon the charity of the rich. When the war is over, and they are back at work, there will be no such appeals.[29]

The Pioneer was echoing the Labour Party's August 1914 twelve-point manifesto, for 'Full provision out of public funds, both for dependant allowances and comforts for soldiers and sailors.'[30]

A debate at Bangor's City Council, in Lloyd George's Carnarvon Boroughs constituency, echoed similar concerns after the Mayor said he had had a letter from Mrs Lloyd George asking, twice it seems, if something could be done to help Welsh soldiers.

> He had replied that Bangor had done very well in this matter through the Women's Patriotic Guild. In reply to that, Mrs Lloyd George again appealed to him to open a fund, and have a national collection on the 1st March, to be called 'The Flag Day'.
>
> Mr Jones Roberts could not understand why the Chancellor of the Exchequer did not provide all the necessary clothing for the troops and that 'it was ridiculous that a rich country like ours, should be begging in this way'.

Bangor's eventual decision to support the Fund may have been swung by the subsequent argument:

Mr Vincent said 'the Corporation provided mackintoshes for its workmen, and surely the Government ought to provide mackintoshes for the troops. At the same time, if the Government did not do it, it was the duty of the people to do it.'[31]

It became an important theme, over time, that the Fund would only supply where there were gaps, and where the War Office could not fill those gaps.

The Builth Wells Council (in William Lewis' constituency) decided in favour, but again only after some debate:

> Eventually it was decided that the Clerk should write requesting the Clerks of Parish Councils and parish meetings in the district to convene meetings of those authorities to make arrangements for collecting funds.[32]

The *Aberdare Leader* reported the lively debate in the Mountain Ash District Council:

> The Clerk submitted correspondence with reference to comforts, garments, etc., for Welsh troops. Mrs Bruce Jones, of the Abercynon Sewing Guild, said they hoped to send on a parcel of clothing in about three weeks' time.
>
> Mrs or Miss L. Howell [*sic*], Penrhiwceiber Sewing Guild, made a like promise, and Miss May Lewis, Garth, Ynysybwl, said they could not entertain the proposal of a Flag Day at Ynysybwl, but they would send very shortly a parcel of garments to Mrs Lloyd George for disposal among Welsh troops.
>
> Mrs Williams, Mountain Ash Sewing Guild, expressed the willingness of her committee to help.
>
> Mr Bruce Jones remarked that it was rather late now to think of making and distributing winter garments.
>
> Clerk: 'They will come in handy for next winter.'
>
> Mr W. Millar: 'I hope it will be over before then.'
>
> Rev. Geo. Neighbour: 'They will want comforts in summer as well as winter.'
>
> Chairman: 'Cigarettes, etc.' (Laughter)
>
> Rev. Neighbour: 'I don't say what.'[33]

Smokes, sweets, soap

Cigarettes, sweets and soap were coming from manufacturers:

> Mrs Lloyd George, chairman of the National Fund for Welsh Troops, has received the following generous gifts: 100,000 cigarettes from the British and American Tobacco Company; one ton of assorted sweets from Lord Devonport; and 12 cwt. of soap from Messrs. Lever Brothers, Limited.[34]

The sweet-supplying grocer, Lord Devonport, would be Food Controller in the days of voluntary food rationing. Lord Leverhulme, co-founder of soap manufacturer Lever Bros., was a great supporter of Lloyd George and the Liberals.

Cigarette-making boomed during the war. Those already warning of the serious health risk were concerned that more young men would become habituated to cigarettes, especially given free distribution. Pipe smoking was more the norm, but in the trenches, cigarettes, dry in their tin (sometimes a life saver when it caught a bullet) were more practical.[35] While Mrs Lloyd George campaigned against drink, another drug was being promoted.

For the gossip columnists, the motherly Welsh lady was looking after her boys:

> Mrs Lloyd George, wife of the Chancellor, is appropriately enough taking it upon herself the task of organising a supply of warm comforts for the men of the Welsh Army Corps. A little note sent from 11, Downing Street, reads: 'Mrs Lloyd George appeals for warm comforts for men of the Welsh Army Corps stationed at Llandudno, Colwyn Bay and Rhyl. They are in need of shirts, socks, mittens, cuffs and cardigan Jackets, also tobacco and pipes. All contributions in money and kind will be gratefully received by Mrs Lloyd George, 11, Downing Street, Westminster, S.W.'
>
> Those who know the Chancellor's wife will realise that the Welsh recruits are going to be well looked after. She is, above all things, a housewife of the rare old-fashioned kind. A great tribute was recently paid to her by an old parliamentarian. 'She is the only woman I have ever known who has turned an official residence into a home,' he said, speaking of the atmosphere that prevails at 11, Downing Street.[36]

Uneven distribution and targeting the faithful

On 25 January, the committee tackled uneven distribution:

> … there was a good deal of irregularity in the supply of comforts, not only between different regiments, but different units in various regiments. This was due largely to the local supply of gifts by friends and others which often meant that half a battalion would be well supplied, while the other half would be without comforts. The committee had, up to now, tried to fill up the deficiency which had arisen in that way, and this would be their policy in the future.[37]

The planned appeal to the faithful was going ahead:

> An appeal for support to the Fund, which, it is hoped, will be commended by the Welsh bishops and leaders of Nonconformity, will be issued during the week, and the committee hopes that every place of worship will be able to make a collection towards the movement on February 28 (St David's Eve).[38]

Debt-burdened chapels, so often supported by Mrs Lloyd George when she opened their own fund-raising bazaars, perhaps regarded the request as competing for the funds they were always seeking.

Clogs and oilskin coats were to be sent to the troops guarding the Menai Bridge.

The 8 February meeting, chaired by Lady Glanusk, was read a letter from Lord Islington, and the Secretary was to see him or some official connected with the Queen Alexandra Field Force Funds. Cooperation with existing and well recognised fund-raisers was important.[39]

Conwy protests: the duty of government

Newspapers carried advertisements for the Fund as well as reporting the reactions from towns and smaller communities. Swansea was planning a Flag Day on St David's Day for the Fund,[40] but the local council in Conwy, within Lloyd George's own Carnarvon Boroughs constituency, had a frank debate over the idea that the soldiers were to be supported by charity, and that the Government was not supplying their needs, not least when working men were struggling with the rising cost of living themselves:

Soldiers' Clothing. CONWAY COUNCILLOR'S PROTEST. 'A Great Wrong.'

At a meeting of the Conway Corporation on Tuesday, it was reported that at a special meeting of the Council a letter was read from the secretary of the National Fund for Welsh Troops, asking the Council's support of the Fund.

A long discussion took place on the question of the troops not being with clothing according to the regulations, and it was resolved that the following resolution be sent to Mrs Lloyd George, the Chancellor of the Exchequer, and Mr William Jones, M.P. [Anglesey-born MP for Arfon, and First Lord of the Treasury] asking them to use their influence so as to induce the proper authorities to provide our soldiers with proper equipments: 'That in the opinion of this council, the local military authorities should have power to purchase garments locally for the troops.'

COUNCILLOR'S PROTEST. Councillor G. H. Edwards said he had been instructed by his Union to forward petitions to the leaders of the Government asking for Government intervention on the question of the inflated prices and the cost of foodstuffs. They had also sent a resolution asking for an increase in wages on account of the increased cost of living. He knew something of the difficulties of collecting contributions from working men. He simply protested against a collection which was intended to be made to supply the troops. He believed they would all agree that this should become a national charge, and that they should not rely on local charity.

The Mayor said that what was referred to in the appeal was comforts to acknowledge the great sacrifice the men had made by joining the army. He sympathised with Alderman Netherwood, whose son had been sent home probably through lack of clothing. Because one or two were underclothed, it was no reason why they should all suffer. He agreed with Councillor Edwards that the Government ought to see to this.

THE DUTY OF THE GOVERNMENT. Alderman Netherwood said it was his contention that it was the duty of the Government to provide the necessary things for the army, such as shirts, underclothing, &c. They as a Council objected to carry out the work which ought to be done by the Government or the War Office.

It was a great wrong to send young men out into the cold with unfit clothing. It was a bad policy on their part. They were ruining the health of hundreds of strong young men, and considered it was a shame to come down and ask a small borough to find the necessaries for the army.

Councillor J. P. Griffith said they were indulging in criticism of the War Office, and he contended that the Council had no conception of the difficulties the War Office had to contend with during the last six months. He was sure the Council would not grudge helping the War Office in providing comforts for the soldiers.

Alderman Netherwood said it was pointed out before, that in other districts the War Office had given power to the military authorities in that district to purchase the very articles that the appeal was made for. There were large stocks of these articles in Conway, Colwyn Bay and Llandudno which the soldiers were short of.[41]

In reality, gaps would not be filled unless voluntary efforts kept trying to do their best, including the children of Talybont, north of Aberystwyth:

REMEMBERING THE SOLDIERS – The children of the Council School, under the guidance of the lady members of the staff, have sent a dozen parcels in response to the appeal from Mrs Lloyd George for comforts for the Welsh troops. Each parcel contained a pair of mittens (knitted by the girls), a khaki handkerchief, a pair of leather bootlaces, a packet of postcards, and a pencil. Another dozen parcels will be ready shortly.[42]

CHAPTER 13

The Fund Settles In

(February to May 1915)

'I cannot pretend to give the nation any expert hint to how long the war will last. If we are wise, people will prepare for the worst, while hoping for the best.'
Margaret Lloyd George, May 1915

OVER THE COMING months the Troops Fund committee, meeting weekly, managed its resources efficiently, selecting which requests to meet, purchasing comforts with care, seeking to avoid unnecessary overlapping or competition, creating a coherent presence in the booming charity 'market'.

As is the nature of volunteer organisations, suggestions and recommendations would be made by friends, but not all would fit with the organisation's own priorities. At the meeting of 8 February, chaired by Lady Glanusk, an offer from Lady Reading, close friend of the Lloyd Georges, of the provision of woollen comforts from a men's working club, was declined with regret, given the Fund's desire to prioritise orders that supported the employment of Welsh women.[1]

William Lewis reported back on 15 February on his discussions with Queen Alexandra's Fund, and it was decided not, for the present time, to enter into any arrangement with the QAFFF beyond the possible cooperation in the dispatch of comforts to the Front. He was instructed to write to the QAFFF's Mrs Sclater as to whether that was possible, expressing the readiness of the Fund to fulfil the requisitions she had received from Welsh regiments serving abroad.

On 22 February, the variety of requests included sending £20 to one brigadier for the procuring of teeth for his men.[2] Mrs Lloyd

George championed dental care during and after the war – the poor state of the nation's teeth had been starkly revealed when men were given medicals on enlistment. The nation's dentists would be enlisted to look after the soldiers, a need brought to Field Marshal Haig's personal attention when he had to go in pain from the Front to Paris for treatment. Dentists' enlistment, in turn, prompted the Royal Dental School in London to start training women for the first time. On 5 November 1919, after performing the 'melancholy duty' of unveiling the Roll of Honour for the 29 dentists from the School who had lost their lives in the war, she was then very pleased to present the top student award to a woman, for the first time.[3]

The movie cameras would soon be out for the upcoming St David's Day Welsh Army parade in Llandudno (at which Mrs Lloyd George caught a bad cold). (illustration 5) Seeing an opportunity to raise funds, the 22 February meeting decided:

> ... not to undertake financial responsibility in connection with cinematograph films, but to leave the matter in the hands of the Educational Publishing Company [the Cardiff company who produced much of the Fund's promotional material, such as flags and posters] to arrange in accordance with their letter. A percentage of at least ten per cent of the proceeds from the display of the films of the proceedings at Llandudno and elsewhere in connection with Welsh troops to be credited to this Fund.[4]

Flag days for the Welsh troops were held around Wales, and in London, Welsh ladies were to be seen in their 'chimney pot' hats.[5] In May, the *Porthcawl News* reported how the town made the 'Top Ten' out of the countrywide takings of almost £5,000:

> FLAG DAY RETURNS. It is now possible to give fuller details of the result of the Welsh Flag Day in aid of the National Fund for providing comforts for the Welsh regiments at home and abroad – a movement inaugurated by Mrs Lloyd George. One or two results have not yet come in, but by to-day the Flag Day returns amount to £4,972 9s. 9d.
>
> At the head of the list are 12 towns which subscribed over £100 each, Cardiff leading with £906 9s. 9d., and Porthcawl tenth with £120. The principal returns (in even pounds) were as follow: Cardiff, £906; Rhondda, £363, Newport, £263; Merthyr, £254; Aberdare, £227; London, £135;

Gelligaer, £135: Abergavenny, £130; Ogmore & Garw, £126; Porthcawl, £120; Mountain Ash, £117; Llanelly, £110; Aberavon, £94; Llandudno, £87; Abertillery, £85; Abercarn, £77; Tredegar, £73; Colwyn Bay, £71; Ebbw Vale, £70.

Between £50 and £70 were subscribed by each of the following towns: Holyhead, Bridgend, Chepstow, Carmarthen, Denbigh, Wrexham, Glyncorrwg, and Pontypool. Seven towns sent amounts ranging between £30 and £50, Carnarvon, Maesteg, Abersychan, Mynyddislwyn, Risca, Aberystwyth and Port Talbot. Between £20 and £30 was subscribed by 36 towns. Twelve towns and villages sent over £5, and there were many smaller subscriptions.[6]

The total exceeded £6,000 when all was counted up across the country.[7]

The committee of 8 March, chaired by Lady Herbert (wife of Sir Ivor Herbert MP, Lord-Lieutenant for Monmouthshire), met with the Secretary for Wales of the St John's Ambulance Society, Herbert Lewis of Cardiff, and discussed how their organisations could cooperate and avoid the overlapping already occurring.

The same meeting was informed that a request of cigarettes for prisoners of war could not be fulfilled as Germany had banned the import of all smoking materials.

The Fund did see its way to purchasing a rugby football for the Welsh Guards. Comforts came in all shapes and sizes.[8]

On 15 March, with Lady Glanusk in the chair, a request from the Rev. Ceitho Davies, Chaplain of HM Forces in Cambridge, was declined on the grounds that they had no power to use their comforts funds for monetary grants with respect to spiritual and religious work. The Rev. Davies may have been disappointed: a Calvinistic Methodist and the first Nonconformist chaplain to be appointed from Wales to the Army, he had served as an unofficial chaplain to troops at Milford Haven before the war, attended a number of meetings of the British and Foreign Sailors' Society when Mrs Lloyd George had been present, and had been attached to the Welsh troops in Northampton when her son Gwilym was stationed there.[9]

Later in the war Bibles and, more often, slimmer Testaments, would be supplied to the troops in the field.

St David was not the only Celtic fund-raiser, as the sketch writer Samuell Pepys Junior reported in his 17 March St Patrick's Day diary entry: 'The streets are full of wenches that sell shamrocks, to help my Lady Limerick's Fund for furnishing hot victuals to soldiers at railway stations, so I had three bunches in my coat before I was come to the Navy Office, and 3s. gone from my pocket.'[10]

Competition for comforts

There was competition not just for funds, but for the comforts themselves. In April, Lady Clare Egerton, daughter of the Earl of Stowe, working to support Welsh prisoners of war in Germany, wrote to the press to protest at the idea of comforts going to the embryonic Welsh Army, which was yet to leave the country:

> Lady Clare Egerton, Trefnant, writes: 'Having written to several sewing parties for clothing for the prisoners of the Royal Welch Fusiliers interned in Germany, I find that most of the organisations have promised all the garments they are making to Mrs Lloyd George for the Welsh Army.
>
> 'As I presume the Welsh Army is clothed, like the rest of the Army, with ample shirts, socks, &c., at the cost of the taxpayer, it would be interesting to know why the clothes are collected for this army, which is the last to be raised, and cannot want the same help as the members the Regular Army who have been fighting since the commencement of the war.
>
> 'Prisoners in Germany urgently require clothes and other necessaries. The depot at Wrexham is sending out as much as they can, but require a great deal more. Any gifts will be thankfully received by the Officer Commanding, The Depot, Wrexham, for this object.'[11]

The Troops Fund would shortly turn its attention to reaching Welsh prisoners of war.

Comfort management

It was not long before the Fund had to 'ration' its supplies. On 12 April, in response to a request from the 18th Battalion Royal Welch Fusiliers (2nd London Welsh), the committee decided:

> that having all along been careful to avoid dealing with units of the Welsh Army already provided for by other organisations, and fearing lest it should be expected to make complete provision for this particular Battalion as its ranks fill up, decided that it could not undertake any responsibility in

regard to either of the two London Welsh Battalions, but inasmuch as the men were reported to be in actual need, the Committee decided to make an ex-gratia gift of 200 shirts and 200 socks.[12]

This may have been a tricky request to turn down, having been sent with a letter from Lady Brynmor Jones, whose own Comforts Fund meeting for the London battalions Mrs Lloyd George had attended in December.

The same April meeting declined a request from the 2nd Battalion Welch Regiment for a monetary grant, though it was prepared to send comforts on receipt of their actual requirement. A request from the 12th Battalion King's Royal Rifle Corps for comforts for about 200 Welshmen was 'carefully considered' but declined on the grounds that they provided comforts only to Welsh regiments, fearing that 'a very wide field would be opened up' if it also had to provide comforts to Welshmen in English regiments.

The committee also deemed 'out of scope' a request for fifes and drums from the 6th Battalion South Wales Borderers. But it was more flexible when the socks sent by Mr J. R. Jones of Ammanford were not in accordance with the original sample, the substitute articles being accepted.[13]

Mrs Lloyd George was unable to attend the two April meetings, but chaired the two meetings in May.

Voices from the Front

Voices of those at war, receiving the comforts, were getting an airing. *Llais Llafur/Labour Voice* reported reactions received in the Swansea region from the Front in Greece, where Welsh miners were using their skills:

> Our readers will remember that some time ago we published an account of work done for soldiers by the Ystalyfera ladies' sewing class. A great number of articles had been sent to the 'National Fund for Welsh Troops' presided over by Mrs Lloyd George. On most of the articles the maker had fastened her name and address, and this has led to the receipt, by Miss Williams, of the Woodlands, of a very interesting letter from Private Tom Jones, son of the late Mr Wm. Jones, butcher, Gurnos, who is at present with the force at Salonica.
>
> Pte. Jones says, 'No doubt you will be surprised to receive this letter

from me. Last week we had an issue of comforts, which had been sent out by some kind friends in Wales. I was fortunate enough to receive a pair of mittens, and you can just imagine my great surprise and delight when I found your card within. These gifts are greatly appreciated by us, especially when they are made by someone with whom we are acquainted. Little did you think when knitting these mittens that they would reach a person from Ystalyfera, who is at present "doing his bit" in this part of the globe.

'I am pleased to tell you that I am in excellent health, although we have had a very rough winter. At present we are having delightful weather, but the heat will soon be unbearable. We are fortunate in being encamped on one of the hills overlooking Salonica. For the last few months we have been engaged in making this place into a veritable Gibraltar. All the military authorities are convinced that the position is now impregnable. Our battalion has gained an excellent name for its work in the trenches. In fact, the general said, were it not for the miners the work could never have been completed in so short a time. The work has been rather monotonous, but the men have done it cheerfully and with a good heart. We are now waiting for the Bulgars, who never come.

'Last Monday at dawn we were awakened by the buzzing of engines right over our camps, and soon we heard the report of anti-aircraft guns. We found that nine Taubes [German aeroplanes] were darting in and out among the white puffs of the exploding shells. Four of the aeroplanes were hit and brought down by our guns.'

Private Jones, in another letter, informs his friends that he has been confirmed at Salonica. Letters of this kind from our 'home' boys will give our ladies renewed energy in their good work. Miss Williams has altogether received 10 such letters, but only one from a local boy.[14]

The Bulgars never did come. The troops spent the first half of 1916 digging a defensive wall around Salonica, nicknamed 'The Birdcage', and the Germans persuaded their Bulgarian allies to hold off, hoping to win the Greeks over to their side.[15]

By May, in the warming weather, chocolates and cigarettes were being sent to the Dardanelles, woollens were being stored for the summer, and knitted body belts, deemed unsuitable by the War Office, were being unpicked for reknitting into socks.[16] Progress was also being made on the book, *The Land of My Fathers*, in Welsh- and English-language editions, to be sold in aid of the Fund.[17] (illustration 12)

The Fund Settles In

Interview on the Fund

On 15 May, the *Western Mail* published a long interview with the Chancellor's wife, six months after the launch of the Fund. This extract, concluding this chapter, provides an excellent resumé of the story so far, recalling the original inspiration for the Fund, the need for a national, coordinated approach from the start, the wide variety of items involved, and the responses across Wales from the well-off to the very poor.

> 'The movement,' said Mrs Lloyd George, 'had, you know, a humble beginning. Some little parcels came to me for distribution among the Welsh troops, and I saw in that fact the desirability of some big national organisation which would bring the generous public of Wales in touch with the men who needed their help. I recognised that some central machinery was desirable to stimulate effort for the alleviation inseparable from military service time at a time of war, and to prevent that undesirable overlapping and competition which too often are a hindrance to enterprises of this kind.
>
> 'There was also the desideratum of removing inequalities in the treatment of various branches of our fighting forces. In the latter regard, evidence was soon forthcoming of the desirability of such co-ordination, for when we got into communication with officers commanding units of Welsh troops both in France and in the United Kingdom, a serious disparity was revealed in the receipt of comforts, not only between unit and unit, but even between men serving in the same unit.
>
> 'For example, men from the chief towns of Wales were found to be much better provided with comforts than their colleagues from the poorer rural districts, while those belonging to large, flourishing churches received gifts far beyond the reach of members of small countryside churches. So we brought into being a National Fund for Welsh Troops, which has been carrying on for what I consider to be a most necessary work for several months.'

The comforts:

> 'Let me tell you what we have already done. We have dispatched to the troops up to May 7 the following articles: 4,245 shirts, 10,120 pairs of socks, 1,152 pairs of pants, 1,248 vests, 3,612 mufflers, 1,078 pairs of gloves, 5,003 pairs of mittens, 962 helmets, 801 body belts, 1,575 Cardigan

jackets, 24 suits of civilian clothes for use of recruits, 115 long oilskin coats, 70 sou'-westers, 120 pairs of clogs, 6,870 tablets of soap, 655 tins of condensed milk, 267,600 cigarettes, 6,392 packets of tobacco, 4,000lbs of sweets, toffee, peppermints, and chocolate, 448 tins of chocolate and milk, 48 large packets of candles, 2,050 tins of boracic ointment and powder, 208 pipes, 300 towels, 500 handkerchiefs, 2,500 writing wallets, a large quantity of sundries, such as boot laces, stationery, razors, strops, shaving-glasses, brushes, combs, thermos flasks, playing cards, matchboxes, cigarette cases, matches, &c.; and medical comforts, such dressing-gowns, bed-slippers, chest-protectors, nightshirts, bedjackets, pyjamas, bandages, cotton wool, pillows, vaseline, kneecaps, woollen jackets. &c., have been despatched to military hospitals in Wales and to the Red Cross Society.'

Responses from the Front:

Mrs Lloyd George handed to me a large bunch of letters which had come from Commanding Officers of all the Welsh regiments, the reserve battalions, and also the battalions forming the 43rd Division, commonly called the Welsh Army Corps. They were all in terms of high praise for what the committee had done, and showed how the comforts dispatched to the men helped them either when fighting in the trenches or when preparing for that experience.

'You will see from those letters,' remarked Mrs Lloyd George, 'that our work is appreciated by both the officers and men, and that the comforts were sent at a time when they were badly needed. But while much has been done for them, more remains to be accomplished. Up to now we have helped practically every Welsh regiment either abroad or at home. More are coming into being, and still more Welshmen are going to take their place in that thin line which holds back the tide of Prussian aggression. Wales, however, must and will give more generous help to fulfil the demands made upon us.'

The financial support:

'Let me say a word about the financial side. I am glad to able to say that the total amount raised at this moment is £10,000. Of course, the Flag Day which was celebrated on Gŵyl Dewi Sant helped very much, and active and sympathetic help was extended to the movement in various parts the Principality. In addition, collections were made in the churches and chapels throughout Wales in aid of the Fund on the Sunday preceding the festival, and as a result of all that effort we were able to realise a sum approximately amounting to £5,000 – £4,972 9s. 9d., to give the exact figure. There are still other returns to come in.'

She then listed the contributions from Welsh cities, towns and villages, as cited in the Porthcawl press (see p.174), before acknowledging the contributions from schools and chapels:

'Let me say, too, how grateful we are to those who organised the school collections in aid of the Fund. Over 200 schools helped with contributions amounting to £100 while 400 churches and chapels contributed between them £600. We were particularly desirous to give the school-children the opportunity of working for the movement. Nothing would help more to stimulate patriotic impulses among them and to give them that sense of duty towards the nation and towards the brave fellows who are fighting.'

Supporting Welsh industries:

'The committee in all their activities have endeavoured to give a fillip to Welsh industries. We have sought where possible to buy flannel and other material manufactured in Welsh towns and villages. One body which has benefited through our work is the Soldiers' and Sailors' Families' Association at Cardiff, although almost every centre in Wales has shared in our orders. Another body which has benefited is the Welsh Industries Association, which is just now taking much interest in the revival of rural industries in the Principality.'

The increasing need:

'Much remains to be done. The number of Welsh troops is daily increasing, as men realise the urgency of the call the nation makes upon them. At present we have between 120,000 and 150,000 men to deal with. A moment's consideration will show you that the £10,000 we have received will not enable us to meet the whole of the demands. Welsh people must do something to ameliorate the conditions under which our men have to fight or to prepare themselves for fighting. We shall have to leave it to most districts to arrange their fund-raising schemes themselves, and we are hoping they will exercise their initiative to our advantage. Carmarthenshire, Glamorgan, and Monmouthshire are, I hear, organising a series of jumble sales, from which we expect to get good results. Let every district in Wales do something to help our fighting men. We have a strong and representative committee at work in London.'

Prepare for the worst, hope for the best:

'I hear there have been criticisms of our work. What work was ever carried out without criticism? There was one suggestion to the effect that we were getting in more money than we could deal with, because it was going to be a short war. I cannot pretend to give the nation any expert hint to how long the war will last. If we are wise, people will prepare for the worst, while hoping for the best. Even if the war collapses to-morrow, we should not have enough money to provide comforts for our men. But, of course, this dreadful struggle is not spent yet, and among all its many duties and obligations I sincerely hope that Wales will not forget such little, but important, items as shirts and socks for her soldiers.'

After promoting the Fund's upcoming book, *The Land of My Fathers*, she continued:

'I know we shall not appeal in vain to the man and woman of wealth in the Principality. But while we are expecting the most from them, this is a matter which everybody should take his or her share, and nothing has pleased me more in this movement than to find almost tragic generosity among the poorest of the poor. I could multiply cases which have come to my notice of great sympathy for our Fund. There is an instance of a poor widow, an inmate of an institution known as the Pilgrims' Rest, who sent her blanket, old and threadbare, of little or no value, but representing all she had to send. And there was the case of the poor old pensioner who sent his half a crown to the Chancellor as his gift to the Fund. This, after all, is the spirit which I want to see manifested in Wales among people of the highest and lowest degree.'[18]

This would be her last appeal made as wife of the Chancellor of the Exchequer, Lloyd George becoming Minister of Munitions ten days later.

CHAPTER 14

Parcels for Prisoners, Flags for the French

(June to September 1915)

'This street collection business is becoming chronic. Between Rose, Pansy, French Flag &c. days and the stock charities, such as Dr Barnardo's Home, the Lifeboat Society, Salvation Army &c., one is bled white.'
Correspondent to the *Western Mail*, July 1915

Welsh prisoners of war

ON 7 JUNE, the Lady Mayoress of Cardiff attended the only committee meeting held that month, 'to consider what action would be taken to provide comforts for the Welsh prisoners of war interned in Germany'.[1] This was not the logistical challenge of getting parcels to mobile troops at the Front, but getting through German controls.

Four days later the *Western Mail* detailed the protocols that were to be followed to ensure parcels would now reach the right destination, thanks to the Welsh Prisoners of War Help Fund, set up in Cardiff by the Troops Fund:

> Last winter the public responded most generously to the appeals for funds to provide comforts for our troops both at home and on the Continent. The severities of cold and wet are now absent, and that call is not at the moment an urgent one.
>
> In the case of the war prisoners in Germany, however, the needs of

these brave men of our own kith and kin are constant, and the conditions of their lives under Hun surveillance call for our most sincere and practical sympathy.

It is, therefore, a pleasure to be able to announce that satisfactory steps have now been taken to ensure a regular transmission of parcels to members of the Welsh units interned in German camps. All that is required is public financial support for the scheme.

According to latest official information, there are over 700 men of the Welsh Regiment, the Royal Welch Fusiliers, and the South Wales Borderers in captivity, and, surely, there is no channel through which donations will elicit deeper gratitude than that now arranged, with official sanction, for the transmission of parcels to the Welsh soldiers in the German compounds.

The article took aim at those not sending help because they thought it might not get through:

Safe transit and delivery being at last guaranteed, provided certain simple rules are observed, the man or woman who delays sending money gifts to the Welsh Prisoners of War Help Fund will be sadly lacking in patriotic duty and in sympathy for the men who are suffering untold hardships, privations, and indignities simply because they were brave enough to take up the rifle in their country's defence.

The plan was then outlined:

At a recent meeting held at 10, Downing Street, under the presidency of Mrs Lloyd George, the committee of the National Fund for Welsh Troops decided to organise and manage a special fund within the Principality, and that the Lady Mayoress of Cardiff be asked to undertake the work. The Lady Mayoress agreed to accept the invitation of the conference, who voted £100 as a nucleus, and her ladyship is now issuing an appeal to the whole of Wales in aid of the Welsh Prisoners of War Help Fund. Letters are being sent to the wives of the lords-lieutenant and to the mayoresses throughout the Principality asking them co-operate by furthering the appeal within their own areas in order that the central fund, at its headquarters at the Cardiff City-hall, may reach substantial proportions.

… spelling out the process by which a team led by the Countess of

Bective, at her family's London home, made sure the aid reached its destination:

> While in London the Lady Mayoress visited 53, Grosvenor-street, where the Countess of Bective, with a committee of workers, is engaged in dispatching parcels to the German internment camps under authoritative sanction and protection. A parcel sent to any private individual is opened and closely inspected by the German authorities, and the slightest transgression of any of the many rules laid down by them often results in the contents of the parcel never reaching their intended destination.

… Parcels, no letters…

> Under the Grosvenor-street scheme however, every parcel bearing the special label agreed upon and Lady Bective's signature, is allowed through without examination, and every facility is given for expeditious delivery. This means that Lady Bective has given her assurance, which has been accepted, that every parcel sent under the aegis of her organisation shall contain only permissible goods, and shall, under no consideration, have written communications enclosed.
>
> In order that the assurance shall be strictly observed, it follows that every parcel must be personally packed by her ladyship's own committee of workers, so that the public are requested not to send gifts in kind, and are encouraged to send only money subscriptions, which are spent in the purchase of suitable foods, &c., selected on expert advice.
>
> The Lady Mayoress of Cardiff was fortunate enough to enlist Lady Bective's co-operation in connection with the Welsh Prisoners of War Help Fund, and all the money flowing into the central fund at the Cardiff City-Hall will be spent in accordance with this excellent scheme of expeditious transmission.

Cardiff City Hall exhibited a sample parcel:

> At the City-hall is a sample 5s. parcel. In the event of the donor desiring a parcel to be sent to any particular soldier, the subscription should be accompanied by his full name, regimental number, regiment, and place of internment, and this special address is added to the official label, as well tas he name and address of the donor, in order to enable the recipients to communicate their personal thanks for the gift.

Special assistance has been placed at the disposal of the Lady Mayoress to carry on the work of acknowledging subscriptions and putting the scheme into full operation, and the public throughout Wales are now asked to support her ladyship's efforts by posting their money gifts to the City-hall without delay, and sustaining their support by regular contributions.[2]

The Countess of Bective, Alice Maria, née Hill, daughter of the Irish peer, the Marquess of Downshire, was the widow of the Anglo-Irish Conservative MP Thomas Taylour, Earl of Bective, a suffrage supporter in the 1880s. The parcels were delivered by the General Post Office and by the American Express Agency. Her packaging scheme had been set up in March, triggered by the fact that packages for prisoners were not arriving. It was initially thought this was due to pilfering by Germany, but the real problem was poor packaging, meaning they often fell apart before arrival.[3] (illustration 48)

Flying the French flag

Cardiff was also the focus of attention on 14 July, Bastille Day, when the city began two days of flag selling on behalf of the British-based French Relief Fund (FRF) in support of the Secours National (French National Relief Fund). Although Mrs Lloyd George was due to attend the first day, she arrived for the second after a short break in the spa resort of Llandrindod Wells with Lloyd George and Megan. On 14 July, Megan was in London selling flags for the French, the press picturing her selling flags to ministers, though failing with her father who already had one. (illustrations 8, 23)

> FRENCH FLAG DAY: MRS LLOYD GEORGE AT CARDIFF:
> 40,000 SOUVENIRS SOLD: LADIES' SPLENDID EFFORT FOR ALLIES
> Mrs Lloyd George paid a visit to Cardiff on Thursday in connection with the city's celebration of the French Flag Day. After a drive in a decorated motor-car to the City-hall, the party proceeded to the docks where they were received at the entrance to the Exchange by Mr T. E. Watson, as president of the chamber of commerce, and the leading members of the French colony in the city. The latter included the Consul of France, M. Monnet, Professor Barbier, Madame Vaillant de Guelis, Sister Barbier of the Royal Red Cross, Messieurs E. Pilsson, M. Wideman, F. Cires, and A. Jolly.

Parcels for Prisoners, Flags for the French

On entering the building, which was decorated with the tricolor, the visitors were warmly cheered by the large crowd of businessmen who filled the floor and occupied the galleries.

Mrs Lloyd George said she was very sorry not to have been able to attend Wednesday's function as she had promised, but she was sure, as she told the Lord Mayor at the station, that the people of Cardiff would make the second day quite as much of a success as the first. She had always realised that Cardiff, when it took up a thing, did it well. She remembered that Welsh Flag Day had been a great success in the town, thanks largely the efforts of the Lord Mayor and Lady Mayoress and their helpers. The Lady Mayoress had taken upon herself to start a fund for the Welsh prisoners of war in Germany. They found that the Welshmen there had no one to look after them, and the parcels that had been forwarded to them had been very gratefully received.

She believed that they in Cardiff made vast sums of money. (Laughter) It was a very prosperous city, and she knew they were anxious to spend the money in the most practical way to help every good cause that was put before them. We all admired the French people and the French army, who had both shown themselves magnificent. We wanted to show them that we were loyal to the core. The French were a nation in which every man, woman, and child had made it their only purpose to carry this war to a successful issue. They had sunk all their differences, and they had gone forward as one man to fight this great war. John Bull was slow to wake up, but when he did wake he was splendid, and there was a great deal for everyone to do in the future before this war was finished. She wished every success to the day, and hoped that a substantial sum would be collected.

A bouquet was then presented to Mrs Lloyd George by Miss Jacqueline Vaillant de Guelis, and a gold brooch in the design of the famous 75mm gun by Master Jacques Vaillant de Guelis, the children of Madame Vaillant de Guelis, the Hon. Secretary of the Cardiff celebration.

Lady Ninian Stuart [a Troops Fund committee member and wife of a Cardiff MP] said they must all realise the great thing France was doing when they recollected that, while the British were keeping some 40 miles of Front, the French were keeping the Germans at bay over a length of hundreds of miles.

Professor Barbier, in feeling terms, voiced the sentiments of admiration which moved the hearts of his fellow-countrymen at the glorious sacrifices which England was making in the common cause, and, amid cheers, turning to Mrs Lloyd George, gallantly requested her to convey his compliments to her illustrious husband. The proceedings terminated by those present heartily joining in the singing of the 'Marseillaise', followed by the National Anthem and cheers for France. A collection was then made among the members.[4]

Professor Paul Barbier was a noted lecturer on the cultural and linguistic connections between Wales and France.

The 32-year-old husband of Ismay, Lady Ninian Crichton-Stuart, would be killed in October that year during the Battle of Loos, supervising the evacuation of Welsh troops from a German trench:

> Ninian stood on the fire step and looked over the parapet in order to direct the machine-gun fire and to rally his men. He was shot through the head and died instantly. Tin hats had not yet been introduced and only became standard issue by the time of the Battle of the Somme in July 1916. Condolences came from as wide a sphere as Mrs Lloyd George to an organ grinder in Cardiff.[5]

His statue was unveiled in 1919 in Cardiff, financed by public subscription. Ismay remarried in April 1917, continuing to attend the committee as The Hon. Mrs A. Maule-Ramsay, her new husband being an army officer invalided back from France and who would serve at the British Embassy in Paris in late 1918.

The attending French Consul, M. Raphael Monnet, also lost his son in the war, in November.[6]

The 75mm gun was an innovative French-designed field gun, much in use during the war. One of the dozen postcards sold in aid of the Troops Fund would feature the November 1915 presentation to the City of Cardiff of a German gun captured at Loos by the Welsh Guards. (illustration 22) Mrs Lloyd George disliked the public display of such 'trophies' in parks where children might play on them. One weapon presented to her she hid behind some bushes.

The Barbier and Vaillant de Guélis families were related by marriage. Marie Stéphanie, née Barbier, now Madame Vaillant de Guélis, organiser of the French Flag Day, and mother of the children Jacqueline and Jacques (who presented the bouquet and brooch to Mrs Lloyd George), was the eldest sister of Uline Barbier, who had accompanied Mrs Kate Freeman of Swansea on the tragic January

Parcels for Prisoners, Flags for the French

evening when leaving Downing Street in a darkened Whitehall. (see p.34)

Marie's husband Raoul, a coal exporter, had already joined the French army in 1914: he died of pneumonia in April 1916 while serving in France. Her daughter Jacqueline, who had presented the brooch to Mrs Lloyd George, died at 22, knocked down by a truck in Cardiff on a dark December evening in 1934. The family made a plea for better road safety, noting the defective lighting, and her aunt Uline may well have remembered that dark Whitehall evening in 1915.[7]

In a world war still to come, Marie's son Jacques, by then a much decorated soldier, died at 38 in a Staffordshire hospital in August 1945, after being badly injured in a car crash in Germany three weeks after the end of the war. In November 1945, Uline Barbier's son Raoul died in Germany, after the war but while still in service with the Army.

After lunch at the Cardiff Exchange Club, Mrs Lloyd George drove with the Lord and Lady Mayoress to visit the King Edward VII Hospital, inspecting the wards for soldiers, women and children, leaving her two bouquets for the patients.[8]

Charity fatigue was now setting in, not only emptying people's pockets but the plethora of causes and organisations was needing some oversight. The *Western Mail* column 'Wales Day by Day' reported one person's plaintive comments:

> 'This street collection business is becoming chronic,' writes a correspondent. 'Between Rose, Pansy, French Flag &c. days and the stock charities, such as Dr Barnardo's Home, the Lifeboat Society, Salvation Army &c., one is bled white. Unless charity bonuses are given in addition to war bonuses it is feared that this extra burden will result in a great deal of unrest, and, possibly strikes, among the poorer-paid section of the community.'[9]

Some regarded such street-selling by ladies and girls as most inappropriate, akin to begging.

Fund-raising for the French revealed further concerns. First, there was confusion when two French Flag Days were announced, one for 7 July, for the French Red Cross, marking a flag day being held in France itself, and one for 14 July, Bastille Day. The French Red Cross appeal was led by the Duchess of Somerset, backed by **PM Asquith**, Lord Curzon, Sir Edward Grey, Princess Christian, the Duke and Duchess of Teck, Lord Crewe and others. The Bastille Day appeal was run by the French Relief Fund (FRF), in support of the Secours National (French National Relief Fund), billed as under the 'High Patronage' of French PM Poincaré, with a list of distinguished patrons, including Lloyd George, Kitchener, Bonar Law, McKenna, Churchill, and Lord Crewe.[10] An attempt to merge the two appeals failed and both went ahead.[11] Aberystwyth would finesse the confusion by selecting the date and cause independently, raising funds for the French Red Cross on 14 July.[12] In London, flags were sold on both days (7 and 14 July), the papers billing Megan's Bastille Day flag selling as being for the French Red Cross. It is very possible the distinction between the different beneficiaries was blurred for those being tapped for their offerings.

Diarist Samuell Pepys Junior was less concerned about precisely which French people were benefiting:

> This day is held the French National Fête, being to commemorate their taking the Bastille prison from King Lewis. The streets full of young wenches in smart cloathes, and selling little French flaggs, mighty pretty; whereof did buy 2, 1d. each, but paid the wench 6d., being for a good end, to wit for the French poor.[13]

Questions of fraud

More seriously, the probity of the FRF came under scrutiny. Though successful in fund-raising, and the organisers handed over one million francs, about £40,000, to the Secours National in September,[14] questions were raised, criticising its 'administrative expenses' that absorbed 29 per cent of its income of £129,376. The FRF Secretary had a police record from 1905, and in 1912 the Treasurer, elected a City of London Alderman, had been rejected having failed to declare certain financial interests. The scandal resulted in a number of the distinguished patrons stepping aside (including Lloyd George) and the Fund was put into administration by the newly-established War Charities Commission. An official enquiry was started, but closed in 1917 due to lack of conclusive evidence.[15] In April 1917, the administration of the FRF was handed over to the trustees of Controlled War Charities, the remaining funds being transferred in 1919 to the British Red Cross.

Some of the monies raised in Wales may not have gone through the books of the UK-organised French Relief Fund. At a special dinner on

Parcels for Prisoners, Flags for the French

29 July, the Mayor of Cardiff handed over a cheque for £6,200 directly to the French Consul M. Monnet, who may have paid it directly to the Secours National in France.[16] Swansea's takings of £550, however, were publicly acknowledged by the FRF. The monies raised in Aberystwyth, where Madame Barbier sang the 'Marseillaise', were sent to the French ambassador of the French Red Cross.[17]

The integrity of the Duchess of Somerset's French Red Cross Flag Day was not called into question, and was billed as the only one officially recognised by the French Ambassador in London.

Fund-raising for the French was not the only exercise that would prove troublesome – a Belgian Soldiers Fund already being under investigation for fraud.[18] Such issues meant that the War Office was now planning to step in to coordinate the raft of charitable activities now booming across the country.

***

Following the April decision not to supply comforts to the London Welsh Battalions, a new request was made in June. But the Fund had limited supplies and Lady Glanusk (chairing the committee in Mrs Lloyd George's absence) ascertained that the War Office itself had plenty of comforts and, in their opinion, 'there is no occasion for this Fund to provide anything in the nature of clothing'.[19] At its 12 July meeting, the Fund resolved that 'this committee will continue to supply additional comforts, including extra shirts and socks to Welsh troops at home and abroad provided that the need for some is vouched for by the Commanding Officers of the Units applying, it being understood, however, that when applications are received, the attention of the Commanding Officers is to be drawn to the large stocks of various comforts said to be held by the War Office.'[20]

Aside from the question of who should be supplying what to whom, the Royal Welch Fusiliers were requesting specially designed wallets for their troops, and Bibles. The Fund responded that the RWF's wallet design would be too expensive, and as the British and Foreign Bible Society had pointed out that Bibles were too bulky to be carried in the pocket, the Fund suggested that Testaments were preferable, and would be supplied that summer, in Welsh.[21]

Fishy donations

While Mrs Lloyd George had caught a cold in Llandudno in March, the profits from more conventional catches in the north Wales seaside town now made their contribution to the Fund. In July, the *Liverpool Echo* published William Lewis' letter to Councillor F. J. Sarson, ex-chairman of the Llandudno Town Council, thanking him for the proceeds of a sale of fish caught in the bay in a competition by the local Sea Anglers' Society, and given in aid of the Fund: 'Mrs Lloyd George wishes me to say that she very much appreciates your kindly thought on behalf of this Fund, and in view of the practical certainty of another winter campaign, shall need all the assistance we can obtain.'[22]

Fishy but not fraudulent donations, one might say.

***

After an August break, the Fund met on 6 September, chaired by Mrs Lloyd George, attended by William Lewis and three others. After considering requests ranging from periscopes (not supplied) to condensed milk, they addressed the need to clarify what they offered in an increasing crowd of multifarious organisations. A letter to the mayors of the boroughs of Wales and the chairmen of district councils was drafted.

A Picture Postcard Day was being planned, selling a dozen cards with images relating to Wales, its troops and the various services offering support, such as the Red Cross. The need to support prisoners of war over the winter was also reviewed.[23] However, further discussion was postponed until the committee 'was in official possession of the intentions of the War Office and of the Committee of which Col. Sir Edward Ward is Chairman.'

Regulation looming

Sir Edward Ward, a military man with a reputation for getting supplies to the right place, was about to be appointed Director General of Voluntary Organisations, a new position in the War Office, 'for the purpose of co-ordinating the work of the various committees and individuals now engaged in supplying comforts and luxuries for the troops and of directing into the most useful channels their kindly energies.'[24] (illustration 36)

He would take up his post on 1 October.

CHAPTER 15

The War Office Steps In

(October to December 1915)

'Father had an absolute mania for parcels. When he saw one he immediately wanted to get his hands on it and open it. Mother caught him red-handed, surrounded by paper, string, and pile of khaki socks. He looked quite shamefaced as she told him off like a naughty little boy.'

Olwen Carey Evans

Golf and a gift book

OCTOBER BEGAN WITH fund-raising on the Llandrindod Wells golf course, with two former Open golf champions, James Braid, from Lloyd George's Walton Heath club, and Ted Ray, Oxhey (Herts) playing two exhibition matches against each other, raising 'close upon £40'.[1] (illustration 34)

The *Brecon & Radnor Express* ran another supportive article, no doubt well briefed by William Lewis:

> It is inevitable that we are faced with, at least, another winter of war. In the dark, dull days approaching, our thoughts will turn more than ever to those, who, having realised their bounden duty to king and country, have left the comforts common to a life of peace and responded to the call which will stand unique in our nation's history. To the vast majority the new life must be comparatively hard to the old routine at home. But it has its compensations. It brings with it the happiness associated with trying to do one's duty, and that joy can be enhanced by friends at home remembering those who are away at the training camps, or on the field

of action. Let us not forget the tens of thousands who have gone from the hills of Wales. There are a variety of ways by which all can help towards sending our men something that will brighten their lot, and remind them that anxious friends are closely watching their career.

The article then urged readers to subscribe to the Fund, reminding them of the work of its Hon. Secretary, 'who is so well-known in Radnorshire', of Lady Glanusk (also local) and Mrs Lloyd George, and promoting *The Land of My Fathers*, the Welsh gift book that 'Mr Lloyd George commends to every Welshman the world over':

> All profits on its sale will be given to this National Fund. It is a book that will appeal to all Welshmen, and, to our English friends, it will serve as an excellent introduction to all that is best in Welsh history, poetry, legend and story. It is a book well worth the half-a-crown charged for it, and the purchaser has the added satisfaction of knowing that he is helping our Welsh soldiers.[2]

The 'anthology of prose and verse passages relating to Wales' included seventeen full-page illustrations. (illustration 12) Committee member Mrs Herbert Lewis was asked if she could promote the book to the Liverpool Welsh National Society.[3]

The charity boom continued: on 15 October, the Lord Mayor of London called a meeting to establish a fund for the relief of Armenian refugees.[4] Mrs Lloyd George would later assist on their 1917 Flag Day.

Sir Edward steps in

But the next challenge for her own Fund was regulation. Sir Edward Ward, now empowered at the War Office as Director General of Voluntary Organisations (DGVO), was making his intentions clear: he would require all fund-raisers to seek 'recognition' from his office. The country's civic leaders, 'the Lords-Lieutenant, Lord Mayors, Mayors, Lord Provosts, and Provosts' would all receive instructions for coordination.[5] *The Times* editorial of 12 October concluded:

> Its prime mission is to tell the people of England to make the things which are really wanted and to make them in such quantities as to admit of their being promptly handled by the transport authorities... In other words, business methods are to be applied which have hitherto been lacking.[6]

In his study of the wartime charity boom, Peter Grant observes:

> He did not want to stifle existing work just to avoid waste and coordinate it ... 'the War Office has no desire to interfere with the patriotic efforts of those who have at the request of Commanding Officers done so much to provide comforts for individual corps.'[7] Sir Edward identified that existing work on troops comforts and medical supplies mainly fell into five categories: 1. Queen Mary's Needlework Guild; 2. The Old Regimental Associations, working for particular units; 3. Red Cross Work Parties; 4. Groups who had worked more or less intermittently; and 5. Bodies of workers unaffiliated to any central organisation – the class forming the great majority.[8]

It was mainly with the last two that he was concerned. With regard to the others, he determined that he would not interfere directly with their work. This decision was also based, no doubt, on their prestige and their desire not to have a government official telling them what to do. Nevertheless, he was able to ensure that their activities complemented those over which he had more direct control. There was no intention to vet charity organisers or scrutinise accounts.

A significant early issue was that of transport and postage costs which were a major burden for local charities. By coordinating supplies at a national level, Ward relieved local organisations of the burden of transport costs, significantly alleviating the problem.[9]

The Welsh Troops Fund was not exempt from complying with Sir Edward's plans – but had other ideas and, given its own position of prestige, sought an arrangement more in line with the longer-established institutions cited above – the Red Cross and Queen Mary's Needlework Guild.

Contact was made promptly, the assistant directors of the DGVO attending the Fund's Executive Committee on 4 October, allowing for an initial exchange of views:

> It was pointed out to the assistant directors that this is the only Comforts Fund of a national character in existence, and that it came into being when it was found that the necessary work was not being done by Welsh local organisations generally, which resulted in very great inequality in the receipts of comforts by the different Welsh Battalions.

In other words, the Fund from the start had set out to be a coordinator on a wide scale.

> The Assistant Directors stated that the actual scheme of the new organisation had not been finally drafted, but it transpired that the Director General did not intend to differentiate between Welsh and other regiments, consequently comforts contributed in Wales and other parts of the Kingdom would be considered for the benefit of the British Army in general. In view, however, of the unique position occupied by the National Fund for Welsh Troops, Sir Edward Ward was favourably disposed to appoint this Fund as a central organisation for the whole of Wales, to which would be sent by him all the requisitions for comforts needed by Welsh troops.
>
> In the absence of definite proposals, the committee refrained from any expression of opinion upon this, and it was finally arranged that the Director General would submit his scheme for the consideration of the committee, and which, if possible, should be circulated among the members prior to the meeting on Monday, October 11th.[10]

This prompt interaction suggests the DGVO was inclined to consider the Fund's 'unique position' as giving it sufficient stature, and perhaps treated more like the established entities. However, the Fund would have to argue its case to avoid any real controls being imposed. That Lloyd George was War Minister may well have made it all the more important that all was done appropriately.

The DGVO duly sent in its formal proposal, with the condition that the Fund obtained the agreement of all the Lords-Lieutenants and Mayors in Wales. The Fund agreed, as the *Llangollen Advertiser* reported:

> The committee considered the scheme of co-ordination of voluntary effort which has been issued by Sir Edward Ward, Director General of Voluntary Organisations. Mrs Lloyd George and the committee are united in the opinion that the scheme has been put forward much too late for the coming winter. The national fund is an organisation which has had a year's experience and is in possession of funds. It has already dispatched comforts to practically every Welsh unit in existence, and is peculiarly competent to deal with the needs of the Welsh regiments. Therefore, the committee feel that they ought to be recognised as the central committee for Wales.

With this end in view, the committee have, through Major General Sir Ivor Herbert, M.P., Lord-Lieutenant for Monmouthshire, got in touch with all the Lords-Lieutenant in Wales, and negotiations are still in progress. The Lords-Lieutenant of Carmarthenshire, Carnarvonshire, Glamorganshire, Merionethshire, Montgomeryshire, Monmouthshire, Pembrokeshire, and Radnorshire are all cordially in favour of the appointment of the committee as the central organisation for Wales. Three other Lords-Lieutenant are consulting their various committees and the replies from two are still awaited. When all the entities of Wales are in accord, it is understood a joint representation on the matter will be made to Sir Edward Ward.[11]

The Lords-Lieutenants of Cardiganshire, Denbighshire and Flintshire were still awaiting responses, while Lady Glanusk reported the response of her husband, that 'Breconshire decides to continue its own organisation'.[12] Lord Glanusk, commander of the 1st (Brecknockshire) Volunteer Battalion of the South Wales Borderers, was now in India.

The Fund is recognised – or is it?

A Fund deputation met with Sir Edward on Tuesday, 26 October:

> WELSH NATIONAL FUND RECOGNISED: The result of the conference which took place on Tuesday afternoon between Sir Edward Ward, Director-General of Voluntary Organisations, and a deputation from the Executive Committee of the Welsh National Fund for providing comforts for the Welsh Troops, is very gratifying.
>
> The deputation, which consisted of Mrs Lloyd George, Sir Vincent Evans, and Mr William Lewis, laid before Sir Edward Ward the claims that the Welsh National Fund be regarded as the central association for Wales, and we are now informed officially that a satisfactory agreement was arrived at whereby the Welsh National Fund will be so recognised. The agreement will be submitted to the committee of the Fund at its next meeting.[13]

This apparently successful resolution would not last long. The Fund's committee re-examined the conditions attached to the agreed 'recognition' as the central association for Wales, and at its 8 November meeting decided not to seek recognition after all, not least as the

DGVO had added further 'red tape', as William Lewis would reveal more publicly in January at a Fund meeting in Caernarfon:

> At first the sanction was promised conditionally upon the support of the various Welsh Lords-Lieutenants being obtained, but when that support was forthcoming the War Office said that the consent of the Mayors and all other persons likely to set up similar organisations must be had.
>
> The committee in London felt that they had other work to do without undertaking all that, and they came to the conclusion that the interests of the Welsh troops would be better served if the committee only consulted their own friends. (Cheers)[14]

New committee members

In November, the independently-minded committee added to its own team, inviting 'the following ladies to join it in its work: Lady Howard de Walden, Lady (Owen) Philipps, Mrs Gwynne-Hughes, Mrs Lynn-Thomas, Mrs F. T. Hopkinson, and Miss Gwendoline Davies, of Llantarnam.'[15] They also planned to consult with Welsh MPs.

Lady Howard de Walden, née Margherita van Raalte, accepted the invitation, but said that she was unable to come on board for a while as she was in Egypt where her husband, Tommy Scott-Ellis, the 8th Lord Howard de Walden and Second-in-Command of the Westminster Dragoons, was posted. In her mid-twenties, wanting to become a nurse herself, she had rented a large house outside the city to establish Convalescent Hospital No. 6, Alexandria, known as the Lady de Walden Hospital, defying the Director General of Army Services' refusal to give her permission to take on a matron and eleven private nurses. Though she did not attend any committee meetings, her Egyptian connections may well have been useful for the Fund.[16]

Mrs Lynn-Thomas, Mary Rosina, née Jenkins, was the wife of surgeon Dr John Lynn-Thomas who founded the Prince of Wales Hospital for limbless sailors and soldiers in Cardiff (and who were both active with the Boer War Welsh Hospital).[17] She would attend only three committee meetings but would have been meeting Mrs Lloyd George from time to time in connection with the Cardiff hospital, often hosting her at Greenlawn, her own family home.

Mai, née Morris, Lady (Owen) Philipps, wife of the Conservative MP for Chester (previously Liberal MP for Pembrokeshire and

The War Office Steps In

Haverfordwest), was an active Fund committee member, and handled the dispatch of comforts to the Welsh Hospital in Bombay, and facilitated railway transport at home.[18] Owen Philipps, a businessman, was a younger brother of Lord St Davids, and had made his money in shipping. Their brother, Major-General Ivor Philipps, at this time commanded the Welsh Army, the 38th (Welsh) Division.

Beatrice Gwynne-Hughes was the wife of the Lord-Lieutenant of Carmarthenshire and an active supporter of the Welsh Industries Association. She warned she would probably not be able to attend committees (which proved true) but made other contributions. Back in January she had been supplying comforts from sewing classes in Llandeilo.

The day after the November 1915 meeting, the newly-invited member, Mrs F. T. (Lilian) Hopkinson, was informed that her eldest son Hugh had died of his wounds at Suvla Bay, Gallipoli, on 6 November.[19] The subsequent Fund minutes recorded she had to defer her reply 'due to a bereavement'.[20] Daughter of a Haverfordwest JP, her husband, a noted civil engineer, was serving with the Ministry of Munitions and the Air Board. Although she attended only six committee meetings (out of 36 held while a member), she contributed greatly as an organiser, not least in running the 1916 Flag Day. In April 1917, she was one of the eight-strong sub-committee that developed the Fund's strategy as it moved from providing comforts to supporting the disabled and their families. In 1918, she was one of the ten Fund members elected to the council of the combined fund that merged the Troops Fund with Sir Owen Thomas' Fund. She became a trustee of the Welsh Troops Children's Fund that ran until 1920.[21]

Miss Gwendolen Davies, Llantarnam, already an active Red Cross fund-raiser, declined the invitation.[22]

In December, an additional invitee, Lady Mostyn, Mary, née Clements, joined the committee.[23] A Lady of Grace of St John, she was an active supporter of the St John's Ambulance Association[24] and President of the North Wales Nursing Association.[25] Lord Mostyn was Honorary Colonel of the 3rd Battalion, Royal Welch Fusiliers.

The Fund's minutes elaborated (but did not publicise) additional conditions that recognition would have entailed:

> The DGVO would accept no financial responsibility of any kind except for the cost of transport of comforts earmarked for these general purposes

199

from the central depot to destination. Inspectors would be appointed by the Drapers' Chamber of Commerce for each district. Every article furnished for the troops would have to be in accordance with standardised patterns and passed by the inspector, and the packing of the comforts would also have to be to his approval. It was expected that, in addition to mittens and mufflers, shorts, socks, pants, vests, helmets and cardigan jackets would also be needed.

It further transpired that it was made clear by the DGVO that the direct upshot of this committee accepting the position of central association for Wales would be that the DGVO would entirely divest himself of responsibility in respect to Welsh troops and would look to us to fulfil all their needs.[26]

For the Fund to have accepted full responsibility, as a voluntary organisation, for all Welsh troops, would undoubtedly have been unsustainable.

Earlier that month the Welsh Army's Major-General Ivor Philipps' request for comforts possibly reinforced the committee's wariness of taking on too much:

... it was evident that the calls upon this Fund from the 38th Welsh Division alone would severely tax our resources, thereby explaining the absolute need for concerted efforts by the whole of Wales if the ever-increasing number of Welsh troops are to be met. It was decided to send a deputation from this committee to meet the Welsh members of Parliament to consult with them as to the best means of enlisting the co-operation of organisations in their respective constituencies.[27]

Anticipating the upcoming festive season, it was probably prudent to deem requests for Christmas puddings to be 'out of scope', though the troops would have welcomed them.[28] Requests granted included 20 long oilskin coats, and 20 pairs of felt-lined clogs for the men in charge of the aerodrome on Anglesey.

In helping suppliers who needed income, a purchase of 'socks made of Welsh wool in the quarry districts where much distress exists', was made, at 1s. 4d. per pair. 'These socks would be much better value as regards wearing qualities and therefore of added comfort to the recipients than the Army pattern sock which the committee has hitherto bought at about 1/– per pair.' One hundred pairs were to be purchased from the Ffestiniog district and 1,000 pairs from the Talysarn district, 'to be properly made and finished to the satisfaction of this committee', most likely from the knitters supported by the donations from the Welsh in America.[29]

At the third time of asking, on 6 December a new request from Lady Brynmor Jones was agreed, 'that on the understanding that this was to tide over present difficulties experienced by the London Welsh Battalion Committee, the Secretary was instructed to forward what mufflers and mittens could be spared.' The meeting was also read a letter from Sir Edward Ward with details as to the method of packing parcels.[30]

A Fund delegation met Welsh MPs on 7 December, and subsequently sent out a circular around Wales asking for support.[31] Swansea was preparing to respond:

> The [Swansea] Town Clerk reported the receipt of a circular from the Parliamentary members of the National Fund for Welsh Troops asking for the co-operation of the council in a conference which would be convened at Swansea early in January, to evolve some scheme to co-ordinate the various organisations throughout Wales who were providing comforts for Welsh troops, to prevent a waste of energy and inequality of distribution, and to ensure a constant and adequate supply of comforts. The Mayor asked the council to appoint delegates, and the number was fixed at three.[32]

Swansea would meet with the Fund in January. While Lord Glanusk's Breconshire was looking after its own troops, the Fund was looking after neighbouring Radnorshire:

> The Radnorshire contributors to the National Fund for Welsh Troops will be pleased to read the following note received by Mr William Lewis, Hon. Secretary to the Fund, from Major Parry, commander of D Squadron, 1/1 Montgomery Yeomanry. 'All the goods are now received. They were most welcome, and, on behalf of my squadron, I beg to thank your society most heartily for them. You will have the satisfaction of knowing that the Radnorshire men are going out thoroughly well equipped.'[33]

A renewed appeal

On 9 December, Mrs Lloyd George published a renewed appeal for funds, stressing the Fund's efforts to cope with the overlapping and inequality of distribution of comforts, and promoting *The Land of My Fathers* as the ideal Christmas present:

> WELSH TROOPS FUND Mrs Lloyd George Makes Fresh Appeal
> To the Editor. Sir, The ever-growing number of Welsh soldiers, of which a very considerable proportion is now serving overseas, has added enormously to the claims upon the National Fund for Welsh Troops, and I have once again to appeal to the generosity and sympathy of all friends and well-wishers for a continuance of the aid that has been freely given to the National Fund since its inception. The letters received from Commanding Officers bear ample testimony to the value of the services rendered by the Fund in adding to the comfort and well-being of Welsh troops who have so gallantly responded to their country's call.
>
> So far, every requisition received has been complied with, but the work done hitherto is small compared with the need of the present winter. Help can be given in various ways – (a) By subscriptions (b) By contributions of comforts, particularly mufflers, mittens, socks, helmets and Cardigan jackets (c) By the purchase of the Welsh gift book, *The Land of My Fathers*, which can be obtained from any bookseller or bookstall. It makes an ideal Christmas gift book.
>
> The Executive Committee has recently been added to, and strenuous efforts are being made to make the Fund in every way a national one, so as to cope with the overlapping and inequality of distribution of comforts which is productive of much waste and dissipation of energy.
>
> All subscriptions and contributions of comforts may be addressed to me at 11, Downing-street, S.W. – Yours, etc. Mrs Lloyd George.[34]

While many requests came directly from Commanding Officers, others would write in. On 13 December, the Fund considered a confidential report from the wife of a staff officer of a Welsh brigade at Salonica on the appalling conditions causing suffering to the troops. The committee decided to spend £1,000 on comforts without delay, dependent on War Office authorities confirming that conditions there were still prevalent. William Lewis was also to ask the MPs for Glamorgan and Breconshire to find out the exact situation from the Under-Secretary for War. In the event, while the need was confirmed as having been real, by then the troops had fallen back to where adequate supplies were available, so the Fund did not follow up.

For the troops, waiting for payday was part of their problem, as Dewi David of the 53rd (Welch) Division wrote home from Salonica in January 1916:

> One thing I like about this camp, there's a few canteens here, run by Greeks, you know, therefore, you can take it from me, the prices are pretty salty. You can get quite a lot of stuff from them, if you have money of course. Unfortunately, I have no money at present – in fact I am absobloominglutely [sic] stoney. Awful plight to be in isn't it, and if we don't have a payday soon, I don't know what I shall do. By the way, Dad, that 10/– note came in jolly handy, another one wouldn't go bad, I assure you.[35]

As he was writing the orderly sergeant came into their tent, asked how much pay they wanted and departed with their pay books.

> He has saved my life – bless him. Just as I was shouting about being stoney, too. 'Smarvellous, Corn in Egypt, what do you say.

Reflecting cooperation in the 'supply chain', the Fund agreed to buy a stock of wool held by the Welsh Industries Association, and acknowledged the Fund's 'considerable obligation' to the YMCA for help in shipping thirty bales of comforts to troops in Gallipoli.[36]

Shipping was not only a logistical challenge but expensive. William Lewis had recently applied to the Railway Executive Committee for the Fund to be on the list of approved societies permitted free railway carriage of comforts to the military forwarding depots at Southampton and Devonport. It took until October 1917 to be 'put on a similar footing to Queen Alexandra's Field Force Fund'. The Fund then had to obtain a lorry to deliver their bales to the railway company, who had previously collected them.[37]

This slow process suggests Sir Edward Ward was not particularly disposed towards further concessions to the Troops Fund, nor to grant a privilege which others enjoyed as a result of accepting recognition.

Postcards

Picture Postcard Days were planned for the Fund:

> Llandovery Town Council: A letter was read from the Countess of Plymouth and Mrs Lloyd George suggesting that the council should arrange a Welsh Troops National Picture Postcard Day to provide additional comforts for Welsh regiments at home and abroad. It was decided that the suggestion be adopted, and that the event should take place on the Christmas Market Day (December 23rd), the arrangements to be left in the hands of the committee who acted in connection with the Flag Day movement in March last.[38]

In Llandudno ladies were preparing to sell the postcards, but stormy weather meant that it was 'feared that the result will not be as successful as previous flag days'.[39] The Fund's committee decided to make a more concerted effort for postcard sales on St David's Day 1916.

For Christmas 1914, Aberaeron schoolgirls had been doing their bit. In 1915 the farmers of Aberaeron, 'with smiling faces', brought their live produce to market to raise money for the Fund:

> Farmers and others responded bountifully to the call of the local committee for produce etc. to be offered for sale by Mr W. J. Phillips, auctioneer, who also acted as secretary and organiser, in aid of the National Fund for Welsh Troops, organised by Mrs Lloyd George, and with Mr William Lewis of 11, Downing-street as organising secretary.
>
> The sale was conducted by Mr W. J. Phillips from a lorry placed in front of the Town Hall on Monday. The bidding was brisk and cheerful from start to finish, long after dark. The foods comprised goods and chattels varying from sheep to a horse shoe and comprised turkeys, geese, ducks, guinea fowls, poultry (live and trussed), about five or six tons of potatoes, turnips, parsnips, carrots, celery, hares, rabbits, suiting quilts, sheets, rocking chairs, tables, wheat flour, oatmeal, oats, cheese, butter, eggs etc. The farmers showed a commendable readiness to help. In most cases they carted in their own goods with smiling faces.[40]

The final observation phrase, 'In most cases', perhaps was an allusion to the tensions that existed in wartime with respect to the patriotism of farmers, as Gwyn Jenkins observes:

The main complaints about farmers ... were associated with accusations of profiteering ... as a consequence of the increase in prices for agricultural produce and their alleged tendency to protect their sons and their most expert farmhands from enlistment...[41]

The press tour the Downing Street warehouse

Shortly before Christmas, the Fund opened its No. 11 warehouse doors to a correspondent of the Liberal *South Wales Daily News*, yielding further favourable publicity:

BUSY SCENE IN DOWNING STREET
The *South Wales Daily News* correspondent visited 11, Downing street, a few days ago, and writes:
'I was enabled to see the preparations for the dispatch of comforts to the Welsh troops abroad by the Welsh National Fund. Mrs Lloyd George was there, and, also, Mr Wm. Lewis, on whom for months the bulk of the work and organisation had necessarily fallen. Few of those who have sent comforts can have any idea of the magnitude of the task.
'Though the consignment under weight at the time of the visit was but for a couple of battalions, one of the largest rooms in Downing street was a veritable warehouse, with hundreds and thousands of mufflers, mittens, and socks – one could feel little notes from the fair knitters tucked away in the foot of a good many of the last named – of a quality that money could hardly buy. All these had to be packed according to War Office regulation, first wrapped in waterproof material, and then made up by expert packers from the warehouses into bales, with "dogs' ears" at each corner for handling.
'It was a revelation of the vast amount of work which the Fund and its organisers have for months been performing daily.'[42]

Professional packers had been employed for the work, at 1s. per hour.[43] (illustration 48)
Olwen Carey Evans recalled a further logistical challenge, her interfering father.

Father had an absolute mania for parcels. When he saw one he immediately wanted to get his hands on it and open it. The sight of so many parcels coming into Number 11 dazzled him, and although he knew very well what they contained, he couldn't resist opening one. Mother caught him red-handed, surrounded by paper, string, and pile of khaki socks just as she came down to breakfast. He looked quite shamefaced as she told him off like a naughty little boy.[44]

Since the summer the Troops Fund had met fourteen times – Mrs Lloyd George in the chair on all but three occasions as they navigated the War Office challenges. The year-old Fund was well established, raising funds through Flag Days and other activities, carefully dealing with the 'competition' from other charity efforts, maintaining its independence albeit with cool relations with the new DGVO – all thanks to the business-like efforts of William Lewis, supported by the influence of Mrs Lloyd George and her cohort of well-placed ladies, and their spouses.

CHAPTER 16

Coordinating with Wales

(January to December 1916)

'The organisation was peculiar to Wales, its administration would be entirely free from red tape, and, as far as possible, all the articles and materials required would be purchased in the Principality.'

William Lewis, Swansea, January 1916

Swansea for the Swansea boys

THE 14 JANUARY Fund Committee, chaired by Mrs Lloyd George, prepared for William Lewis to travel to Swansea to consider coordination with the local Fund.[1] The committee would meet 21 times during the year, Mrs Lloyd George in the chair in all save two.

The membership had now risen to 21, latest recruits including the Countess Dundonald (Winifred Cochrane, née Hesketh), born at Gwrych Castle, Abergele, Conwy, a philanthropist who in 1914 opened the Countess of Dundonald Hospital for the wounded at Eaton Square. In December she had offered space at her Portman Square home as a depot and office for the Fund, which was declined on the grounds that a move from No. 11 would not be a good idea.[2] A Welsh speaker, she was a supporter of the Eisteddfod, and President of the Vale of Clwyd Toys company (founded before the war),[3] and of the Denbighshire division of the Welsh Industries Association.

With a planned wide appeal for subscriptions across Wales, there was concern, shared by Swansea, this might compete with local appeals:

Convened by the Mayor of Swansea (Ald. Merrells) at the suggestion of the Welsh Parliamentary Party, and Lady Plymouth and Mrs Lloyd George (on behalf of the National Fund for providing comforts for the Welsh Troops), a representative conference was held at the Swansea Guildhall, on Friday afternoon, for the purpose of considering some system of co-ordinating all the various organisations in order to prevent waste of energy and inequality of distribution which is the inevitable result of a lack of co-operation, the attention being directed to the matter especially because of the increasing number of Welsh troops.

The Mayor said he thought there was some necessity for a co-ordinated scheme to prevent overlapping. Mr Lewis (representative of the national movement) was present, and he thought they would be able to convince them of the necessity. It was feared by some that, by a national scheme, local enthusiasm would be damped. He thought that while they might join the national movement, the local movement could also still go on.

The great difficulty at Swansea was to find out if all the local boys were adequately served, and he believed they were; but though they might be fortunate so far as Swansea is concerned, it might be that some other parts were not so well placed.

William Lewis made his pitch:

Mr Lewis said the Fund had received from Swansea and district every help and sympathy. They wanted to be of service to the Welsh soldiers and to obviate the inequality of the distribution of comforts. The object of the conference was not to interfere with any local association, but rather to supplement local effort. The constantly growing number of Welsh troops and the uncertain duration of the war made it essential to provide comforts for the troops.

Few of the boroughs of Wales had the wealth of Swansea, and no other county had the wealth of Glamorganshire. His committee was able to see the work being done in all the counties and most of the districts of Wales; but the details of the work and how it was being done was the object of the co-ordination proposals.

The interest in the Army in Wales was a great deal more personal than before the war, and they anticipated 200,000 Welsh troops for whom provision would have to be made. If they only spent 5s. each, that would exhaust £50,000.

The need was growing, but there had been no attempt in Wales at co-ordination, and that applied to the individual counties, one part not knowing what the other part was doing. Some men in Welsh regiments were drawing from three separate funds, while men from poorer parts were only drawing from the county fund. The requisitions from Commanding Officers showed that the efforts had not been sufficient to meet all the demands of the men; recently very heavy demands had been made upon them.

He instanced what had been done in a national way. When the Fund was inaugurated he first thought that it was the Government's duty to provide the comforts; but he had changed his mind, and it would have been a great loss if the women of Wales had not had the opportunity of doing work which they had done and were doing so nobly.

The proposals were that each town should be co-ordinated and the various committees should co-operate with the Fund as a central organisation. It was not proposed to do anything to prevent dispatching goods, as were being done now, but the Fund would like to keep a record of everything going to each regiment and, then, if it was found there were over-supplies, it was suggested the supplies should be diverted to other Welsh battalions.

Further, it was proposed to open a depot in London to which parcels could be sent for dispatch to individual soldiers; these would be baled and forwarded regularly, thus saving the donors postage (except to London) and facilitating dispatch.

While there is no evidence that the Fund did dispatch to individuals, the Cardiff PoW scheme did send to individual prisoners of war.

Mr Lewis spoke of the Fund's efforts in the direction of encouraging Welsh industries, how they bought Welsh goods and how their scheme was preferable to any War Office scheme, for he thought no matter of that nature should be undertaken by an office which had obviously other work in hand, and it was desirable there should be no red tape methods.[4]

Then followed a long debate, with an underlying theme that Swansea should look after Swansea troops first. That, however, would leave Swansea with the logistical challenge of connecting with them in the field, the Mayor pointing out that:

… more than 53 per cent of the Swansea boys were serving in English and Irish Battalions.

Local MP Sir Alfred Mond confessed that:

> ... he did not see why the Commanding Officer at the Front could not see to a more equal distribution of comforts being sent out, when it was found that some men had plenty while others had none.

The Mayor reminded him that:

> ... Commanding Officers' opinions on comforts differed; one C.O., if he had his own way, would not allow parcels or even a cigarette to the men.

While some believed Swansea, a rich borough, should take a wider view, and set an example to encourage more coordination elsewhere, a 'Swansea men first' resolution was passed unanimously:

> That a Mayor's Fund be established to provide comforts, etc., for Swansea men with the Colours; that, all the various Guilds and Committees in the Borough concerned with the comforts, etc., be invited to co-ordinate their efforts, and that having provided for the needs of Swansea soldiers and sailors, whatever surplus is left to be allocated to the National Fund of which the meeting is in hearty sympathy.[5]

In other words, rather than the Fund supplementing the work of Swansea, Swansea would supplement the Fund with any remaining surplus. In reality, each would do their own thing. It did mean yet another fund was being set up, this time by Swansea.[6]

William Lewis may not have obtained the agreement sought, but this would not hamper the Fund's activities elsewhere, and he continued to travel through the Principality seeking support. In February, Lady Mond, wife of the Swansea MP, was invited to join the committee.

While Swansea was helping the Swansea boys, the Free Church Girls Guild of Cricieth were making comforts for Welsh soldiers and sending them to Mrs Lloyd George.[7]

Some observers in Carmarthenshire's Maescrugiau suggested that those that didn't see the value in helping might be ashamed, if not publicly named:

> Both the Sewing Guilds of the district have received thanks from Mrs Lloyd George, to whom several packages of comforts have been sent for

the benefit of Welsh troops. About 50 ladies from each class. There are some folks who do not sympathise with these good objects, and display their meanness and sublime ignorance by turning their backs when requested to help. They are worthy only of supreme contempt.[8]

In Wrexham, auctioneers Messrs. Frank Lloyd & Son planned a large jumble sale for February, to be opened on the first day by Mrs Lloyd George.[9] Advertisements called for 'DONATIONS of Gifts of Furniture, Silver, China, Antiques, Works of Art, Books, Linen, Glass, etc. for the Sale', but in contrast to Aberaeron, 'no Live Stock invited'.[10]

William Lewis on red tape and anti-Welsh spirit

At a meeting in Caernarfon (which Mrs Lloyd George attended) William Lewis explained why the Fund had changed its mind with respect to GCVO recognition, his comments reported by the *Brecon & Radnor Express,* headlined: 'Mr Wm. Lewis and "Red Tape"; Anti-Welsh Spirit':

> Mr Wm. Lewis (Hon. Secretary of the National Fund) said that there had been a great deal of overlapping owing to the want of organisation. His own opinion at the outset was that each county should look after its own battalion, but he had since found that such a method would be ineffective because of the sudden strain to which a particular county fund might be put. As an instance, he cited the case of about 5,000 Welsh troops who had run short of food and had no proper equipment. Without any delay, the London committee decided upon the expenditure of £1,000 upon comforts for those men. (Cheers)
>
> The Fund had already in hand about £10,000. The organisation was peculiar to Wales, its administration would be entirely free from red tape, and, as far as possible, all the articles and materials required would be purchased in the Principality. They also hoped to work in hearty co-operation with the organisation formed by the War Office, which had Sir Edward Ward as the director general.
>
> The fact of the matter was the director general was not anxious to draw any distinction between the Welsh troops and the rest of the British Army, but with all due respect he [Mr Lewis] would say that the attempt to sink the individuality of Welsh troops in this matter was quite in keeping with what occurred in connection with the Welsh Army Corps and the attempt to deprive the R.W.F. [Royal Welch Fusiliers] of its distinctive flash.[11]

The distinctive flash was a decoration worn on the bearskin of the RWF: a War Office proposal to remove it was successfully resisted earlier in 1915, it being permitted except in the theatre of war.[12]

The St David's Society in New York was doing its bit:

> The St David's Society has decided to hold a social meeting on St David's Day, March 1st, instead of the usual lunch, at the Aldine Club, 200 Fifth Ave. Some of the city's most talented Welsh people are guaranteed to take part in singing, oratory, &c. The proceeds to be sent to Mrs Lloyd George in order to satisfy the needs of the victims of the war – Colwynian.[13]

A further indication of attention being given to the 'victims of the war', not just troops in the field.

On 24 January, Mrs Lloyd George was 'rolling up her sleeves' on London's Hampstead Heath, handing out cigarettes and chocolates to recruits stationed in huts for training. (illustration 17)

> Mrs Lloyd George made an excellent amateur waitress on the occasion of her visit to Hampstead Heath, where the ladies of the locality have a temperance hut for the soldiers stationed there.[14]

Such huts were set up all over the country at training camps and in central London.[15] Built as temporary accommodation, a century later there has been an effort to restore the surviving examples.

At a Welsh Troops fund-raising event at the Calvinistic Methodist Church in Hammersmith – a lecture, in English, on 'Cambria's Part in Empire Building', by the Rev. Wynne Evans, Pastor of the Albion Congregational Church – she made it clear that the Welsh Troops Fund didn't just benefit the Welsh and did coordinate with the War Office:

> ... in the Welsh troops there were Englishmen, Scotchmen and Irishmen in the same way that there were Englishmen and Scotch in Irish regiments, so that every nationality would have its share.[16]

She pointed out that the supplies they sent out were often not 'extras' but replacing original kit: 'They knew what the War Office supplied to the men, so they came to make up for the lost kit.' She may not have mentioned that by then they were also supplying footballs, boxing gloves, mouth organs, games such as draughts, dominoes and ludo, and soon, gramophones and records. The Mayor of Swansea had requested accordions and mouth organs, which the Fund said it would pay for, but the Mayor had to obtain them and dispatch them.[17]

Marketing to Wales

Fund committee members wrote to their local papers. In this letter published in the *Carmarthen Weekly Reporter*, and elsewhere, recent recruit Beatrice Gwynne-Hughes stressed that the Fund was now regarded by Sir Edward Ward as a 'central' body alongside the War Office, and one which helped in the task of coordination.

> National Fund for Welsh Troops: To the Editor, *Carmarthen Weekly Reporter*. Sir, Your readers have probably seen the last circular issued by Sir Edward Ward, the Director of Voluntary Organizations, urging that all subscriptions and donations and parcels of comforts for troops should be sent direct to the War Office or through some central body such as the National Fund for Welsh Troops, to prevent the enormous over-lapping which takes place when private organisations or efforts send parcels to units and regiments already receiving comforts from the central organisation. It saves time and trouble, as units are so constantly being moved from one point to another, that it is only the War Office or some organization such as the National Fund for Welsh Troops, in constant communication with the War Office, who can know where to send to these units direct; many parcels too get lost and damaged in being forwarded from one camp to another.
>
> Both the War Office and the National Fund, on principle, only send to units and not to individuals, except on the special request of the Commanding Officer such things as are absolutely needed. Every man thus gets what he really needs but there is no unnecessary waste.
>
> I hope that other villages and districts will follow the excellent example set by Llandeilo and the Rifle Club in Golden Grove in organizing entertainments for the above National Fund. Auction sales might also be arranged for the same purpose. A great sale of flags and post cards has been arranged to take place on St David's Day. If any committees would undertake to sell flags and postcards on St David's Day, or on the nearest fair or market day, these could be obtained by writing at once to the Hon. Secretary, National Fund for Welsh Troops, 11, Downing St., W.C. Beatrice Gwynne-Hughes, Member, Executive Committee, National Fund for Welsh Troops, Tregeyb, Llandeilo, February 21st, 1916.[18]

Her letter also acknowledged a number of gifts and contributions from local donors. Though she had joined the committee in November 1915, she did not attend any committee meetings. Her husband died on 2 January 1917, aged 58, when they had been visiting Bath, where she was seeking treatment for rheumatism.

Brigadier-General Sir Owen Thomas' new 'movement'

In the last week of February, a national conference was organised by Brigadier-General Sir Owen Thomas, early convenor of the Welsh Army, and held at Shrewsbury to discuss his proposed new 'movement' which he had announced in December to safeguard the interests of Welsh troops during and after the war. Included would be the raising of a fund to help Welsh troops. On the face of it, this seemed to offer direct competition with the Troops Fund. However, in correspondence with Mrs Lloyd George, the Brigadier assured her that he had 'no intention of any interference with the workings of the Fund'. William Lewis and Sir Vincent Evans attended the Shrewsbury meeting and were reassured that this would be so.[19] By the end of 1917, Sir Owen Thomas' Fund would be consolidated with the Troops Fund, coordinating with the Pensions Ministry to help the disabled soldiers and their families prepare them for a life after the war, a transition that became a priority for William Lewis.

A question of patronage

On 29 February, Mrs Lloyd George, now with a cold, missed the London Welsh Stage Society's matinée performance, 'under the Fund's patronage', at the Haymarket Theatre, attended by Queen Alexandra, with Welsh actors, musicians and singers performing three Welsh-themed, largely musical plays and a ballet.[20]

For some reason, the Fund committee had needed some persuasion to grant the organisers their patronage. In November, W. A. Bayley of the London Welsh Stage Society had proposed a 'Dramatic Performance in a London Theatre' on behalf of the Fund, without financial responsibility for the Fund as long as the committee would help sell tickets. This the committee 'could not see its way to undertake', nor would it 'entertain' his suggestion of placing an advertisement of the Fund in the *Ladies' Field* magazine. In response, Bayley requested if it could be announced as 'Under the patronage and with the Consent of the Executive Committee of the National Fund for Welsh Troops', to which the Fund suggested that 'an announcement to the effect that the proceeds would be in aid of the Fund should suffice'.

The persistent Bayley tried again in January for permission to say it was 'under the patronage of the Committee', which was deferred for a week before agreement was given. A fortnight later, and a fortnight before the curtain came up, on 29 February, the eve of St David's Day, it was announced that Queen Alexandra and the Lord Mayor had also offered patronage for the event. While it is not clear what made the Fund cautious, perhaps there was concern that it would prove an extra burden on the team running the Flag Day the next day, as opposed to complementing the Welsh celebration.[21] It may also have been seen to conflict with the Fund's own St David's Day evening rally at the London Opera House.

The Welsh invasion of London

The 1916 first of March St David's Flag Day stepped up to a new level from the very first one held in 1915, though Mrs Lloyd George, nursing her cold, had to direct operations from No. 11. During the February build-up, Joseph Lyons, owner of Lyons Corner Houses, had provided a room with refreshments and some entertainment at his restaurant, the Trocadero, off Piccadilly, for a preparatory get-together of the helpers. Lyons may well have been planning for an innovation in view of slackening wartime trade:

> The concert tea had its beginnings at the Trocadero. During the First World War the banqueting rooms were under-utilised, and in 1916 tea was served for the first time in the Empire Hall along with a full concert programme. It was not long before fashionable London realised that, with its music, its delightful teas, and the pleasant atmosphere, the Empire Hall held attractions that were too good to miss. Indeed, the Trocadero's concert teas became so popular they were soon copied by many other hotels and restaurants across London.[22]

The Globe went to town on the Welsh invasion of London, noting that nearly all pedestrians were wearing a decoration 'either out of sympathy or in self-defence': (illustration 15)

'Cymru am Byth!'

'Y Ddraig Goch Ddyry Gychwyn'

No, this is not a freak of the linotype. It's an old friend in a new dress designed by Mrs Lloyd George to tax the London public and raise money for the National Fund for Welsh Troops. 'Wales for Ever!' 'The Red Dragon Leads the Way,' are the war cries of the Welsh in this new invasion of the Metropolis. A large proportion of the 3,000 damsels engaged in extracting coins from people's pockets to-day were Welsh, and the national costumes, shawls and chimney-pot hats announce the fact in unmistakable terms.

St David's Day began with an uncomfortable drizzle, but in the sunshine that came later the Welsh women reaped rich harvests from the sale of flags, postcards, and daffodils. Nearly every pedestrian wore a decoration, either out of sympathy or in self-defence. The flag became the signal of surrender. The wearer had paid and he passed on. Many of the large business establishments, such as Robinson and Cleavers, Peter Robinson's, Liberty's, and Waring and Gillow's, were utilised as bases for operations. At some of the stands an interesting Welsh gift book, *The Land of My Fathers*, found ready sale.

In honour of the day the band of the Welsh Guards played outside Buckingham Palace this morning. An early raid was made upon the Ministry of Munitions, and a huge sale in that particular department was the reward. Mr Lloyd George was buttonholed early. A number of young ladies in Welsh national costumes selling flags had a busy time in the Law Courts. They walked boldly past the attendants through the Central Hall, and wandered into the corridors where counsel in robes, as well as litigants and jurymen, were invited to purchase.[23]

The paper's front page also covered the imminent launch of the Government's new savings campaign to finance the war; hence, perhaps, the allusion above to tax.

The chief Flag Day organiser in 1916 was recent committee recruit Mrs F. T. (Lilian) Hopkinson, whose son had died in Gallipoli in November.[24] Mr Leason Thomas, Secretary of the Glamorganshire Society, was invited to take on the necessary secretarial work.[25] The *Haverfordwest and Milford Haven Telegraph* interviewed their townswoman:

INTERESTING INTERVIEW WITH THE HON. ORGANISER: A representative of the *Telegraph* has just been privileged to have an interesting chat with Mrs Hopkinson, the honorary organiser of the Welsh Flag Day movement, promoted for the purpose of raising funds for Welsh troops now serving with the colours.

Mrs Hopkinson, who is a daughter of Mrs James Thomas, Rock House, was good enough to give us much information which cannot fail to prove of interest to readers of the *Telegraph*, having regard to the fact that several Haverfordwest ladies took an active part in the selling of flags, post cards, &c.

Associated with the Hon. Organiser of the event were Mrs Lloyd George, Miss Olwen Lloyd George, Mrs Hugh Thomas, and other well-known ladies.

'There were many pretty incidents,' observed Mrs Hopkinson, in connection with the 'Day'. 'For instance some small boys in a Board School made a collection of half-pennies, and sent them to me as they were "Welshmen"; a soldier from Southampton sent 1s. for a flag to take back to France, while a lady in Manchester remitted 2s. 6d. for a flag for each of her three Welsh servants; again £3 raised in a very poor district in the south of London came as a pleasant surprise, and showed what could be done in quiet a unostentatious way by a very hard-working business Welsh woman ... Our returns,' continued Mrs Hopkinson, 'now reach over £5,500, the result of four to five weeks of very hard work.

'We had many anxious moments but many humorous incidents also occurred from time to time – for instance when someone wrote on the previous Saturday asking if I didn't think it well "to put off the Flag Day while the slushy weather was on". I should like to mention that my offices were lent me free of rent, and that the staff was entirely a voluntary one, with the exception of one paid typist. All these workers gave their whole time to the work and it is but another example of what women can do and do very efficiently.'

Mrs Hopkinson also handed our reporter a list of the sums collected by the various lady workers, with the districts allocated to each. They are as follows:

Mrs Charles Price, Part of Trafalgar Square, £21 2s. 2d.;

Mrs Bromfield, St James's Street and Pall Mall, £56 7s. 11d.;

Miss Mamie Wilson, St Martin's Lane, £17 12s. 8d.;

Miss Katie Thomas, Whitehall and Parliament Street, £178 14s. 0d.;

Miss Fanny Noott (niece of the late Mr John Harvey), Westminster Bridge, £22 4s. 11d.;

Mrs Oliphant Goldie, Blackfriars, £54 16s. 7d.

Mrs Hugh Thomas, Miss Gwen Matthews, the new Lady Rhondda and Miss Edith John R.A.M., kindly sold flags, &c., for Miss Katie Thomas.

Lord St Davids, at 3, Richmond Terrace, lent his house as a depot, and entertained about 60 ladies to luncheon and tea.

'Mr Fred Warren,' added Mrs Hopkinson, 'very kindly gave me one thousand copies of his poem, "The Welsh Call to Arms", to be sold in aid of the Funds, and this made a very considerable addition to the total realised. The poem itself proved highly attractive and was greatly praised by several people.

'I asked Queen Alexandra if she would send me a letter of encouragement, and she very graciously did so and gave me permission to have it printed. I also asked her to accept post cards of the Prince of Wales at the hands of two ladies who would be wearing the identical gowns worn by two women who were present when the French effected a landing at Fishguard in 1707. The Queen felt so interested in the dresses that she expressed a wish to receive the ladies in her drawing-room. I had the honour of presenting them, and Her Majesty expressed the liveliest interest in their quaint attire.'[26]

Fred Warren was an accountant and poet from Haverfordwest.

The street collections might seem modest at first glance, but the £17 12s. 8d. St Martin's Lane collection in the West End would be around £1,500 in today's money, and the £178 14s. 0d. on Whitehall and Parliament Street, with four to five collectors, including 'the new Lady [Sybil] Rhondda', around £15,000. D. A. Thomas had been created Baron Rhondda in January.

In the London suburbs the response was at times more muted:

Welsh Flag Day passed off very quietly in Streatham. Not many sellers were in the streets. A good many questions were raised as to the dragon on the flag. Most people expected to find a leek, or, as it was expressed, something 'oniony'.[27]

In the evening the London Welsh had a party:

DEMONSTRATION AT THE LONDON OPERA HOUSE: St David's Day in London for 1916 will not soon be forgotten. Londoners bought the small Welsh flag (the Red Dragon) by the thousand, so that on the streets and in trains nearly every person wore the Welsh colours.

The great rally at the London Opera House at night was one of the biggest events that has happened in the history of the London Welsh community. This building, the largest available in London, with seating accommodation for over 3,000 people, was packed. The chair was taken by Lord Harlech, who was supported by Mrs Lloyd George, Sir Francis Lloyd and Lady Lloyd, Lord Justice Eldon Bankes and Lady Bankes, Lord Lisburne, Major Robert Jones, and Dr Lynn-Thomas of Cardiff. There were several Members of Parliament present, including Mr John Hinds, M.P., Mr Haydn Jones, M.P., Mr Ellis Davies, M.P., and Mr Timothy Davies, M.P.

The band of His Majesty's Welsh Guards was a great attraction and the immense audience was delighted with their performance. It was their first appearance in public [founded in 1915], and London Welshmen and Welsh women gave the Band and the Conductor a cordial reception. The singers were Mr Ben Davies and Mr Ivor Foster, who are always welcome at London Welsh gatherings. One item that was received with much cordiality was 'Comrades', by a glee party from the Second Battalion Welsh Guards. The performance was encored. The Welsh boys from the Tower of London sang 'The Soldiers' Chorus', which was equally well received.

The meeting was in every way a huge success; but keen disappointment was felt at the absence of the Minister of Munitions and of well-known members of the House of Lords and the House of Commons. It is well known that Mr Lloyd George is hard at work and finds little time for leisure in these strenuous days; but his presence at this gathering would have encouraged his countrymen to do even greater things in the future in celebration of their national day. The Committee, of which Dr D. L. Thomas was chairman, Mr Philip Williams, treasurer; and Mr Evan Richards, and Mr H. Pughe Roberts, Hon. Secretaries, is thoroughly representative of all Welsh societies in London and of all parties and creeds.[28]

The evening event raised £170, almost matching the takings from the politicians, civil servants and other workers passing through Whitehall and Parliament Street. The London Opera House, on the Kingsway, was renamed the Stoll Theatre after its takeover that same year by theatre impresario Oswald Stoll. While Mrs Lloyd George's fund-raising of over £200,000 was a significant achievement, Stoll raised more than £260,000 during the course of the war. The biggest single fund-raiser was *The Times* newspaper, bringing in £16.5 million of the £21 million raised for the Red Cross.[29]

The *Llanelly Star* front page added positively: 'Subscribers to this Fund may rest assured that every penny is judiciously expended and that the comforts go to the proper quarter and the right people.'[30]

Welsh Flag Days were happening elsewhere, especially across Wales, 26 women rattling the tins in Llangollen, doubling the previous year's takings, even in the 'flattest' time of year.

> Welsh Flag Day at Llangollen proved a great success, as we all anticipated that it would do, and Mr A. Parry Morgan and the members of the Welsh Literary Society who, at the request of the Urban Council, engineered the affair, are to be heartily congratulated on their achievement. Of course the amount is not large when compared with the amounts collected at Llangollen on other Flag Days but it must be remembered this is the very flattest time of the year at Llangollen, and that other appeals were made when there were plenty of visitors in the town.[31]

'Carmarthen Under the Searchlight'

The Liberal *Carmarthen Weekly Reporter* asked if the locals were doing their bit – or whether the calls for charity were reaching the limits of what people were able or prepared to meet. Its regular column, 'Carmarthen Under the Searchlight', surveyed the accumulation of fund-raising challenges, wondering why 'for some occult reason' Carmarthen was hosting many different countries' flag days except that for the Welsh:

> I am told that the Carmarthen public have not subscribed at all handsomely towards the last appeal for the Carmarthen Soldiers' Welfare Fund. This is a pity; but at the same time it does not at all constitute any reflection on the generosity of the Carmarthen public. A fact looks very imposing until you come to investigate it. For instance, if a man says he never touches a drop of beer, you are impressed with his sobriety, while possibly the fact is that he drinks brandy.
>
> When the British Forces were first sent to Cyprus about forty years ago there was a terrible epidemic. A question was asked in Parliament whether it were true that 800 men were laid up with fever. The Minister in reply stated that there were, according to the latest returns, only 35 men in hospital. This was quite true. The hospital could only hold 35, and the

rest of the poor fellows had to lie wherever they could. There were 800 men ill; but the Minister who said that there were 35 men in hospital was telling the truth.

It is true that the Carmarthen public did not subscribe at all generously towards the latest appeal for the Soldiers' Welfare Fund. But there are a few other little facts which ought to be known. The Carmarthen public at the start of the war subscribed handsomely towards the Prince of Wales Fund. Then they subscribed towards the British Red Cross. Then they decided to support forty or fifty Belgian refugees!

After that came the Soldiers and Sailors' Families Association. The Carmarthen public did something for that. Then there came the Soldiers and Sailors' Help Society. The Carmarthen public did a little for that. Then there was a Soldiers Club started at Carmarthen, and the Carmarthen public assisted in that. Next came an appeal for the Belgians in Belgium and the Carmarthen public did their bit for that. Next came appeals for funds for the local Red Cross, and the Carmarthen public did something again. An appeal was made for Welsh prisoners of war in Germany, and the Carmarthen people were again to the fore.

After that came the Red Cross sales. An appeal for the Carmarthen Soldiers' Welfare Fund was made about this time and was responded to generously. Then we had a Russian Flag Day and a French Flag Day. After that an appeal was made for the Serbian Relief Fund, and an envelope was left at every house in the town. The Carmarthen public responded nobly to this.

About this time an appeal was made by Mrs Lloyd George for a Welsh Flag Day. This was for the purpose of providing comforts for the Welsh troops. It was decided not to have a Welsh Flag Day at Carmarthen. We had had Russian, French and Belgian Flag Days; but for some occult reason, the line was drawn at a Welsh Flag Day in Carmarthen on St David's Day. I don't profess to understand this extraordinary phenomenon. But, there is the fact. After it had been decided not to help the National Fund for Welsh Troops, a second appeal was made for the Carmarthen Soldiers' Welfare Fund. This second appeal failed.

There may be many explanations. It may be that the Carmarthen people are 'cleared out' and have no more money for any further funds. Or it may be that the Carmarthen people resented the decision about the Welsh Flag Day and decided to have no more to do with welfare funds, seeing that they did not have an opportunity of subscribing to the National Fund. Or again it may be that the appeal was affected by the disclosure of the curious fact that the men of the Carmarthenshire Battalion get nothing out of the Carmarthen Soldiers' Welfare Fund – surely an extraordinary anomaly. And there is the further fact that churches are sending out parcels on their own account to individuals at the Front, and that they prefer to expend their money in that way as they know exactly who gets it. There is a lot to be said for this attitude. If Carmarthen boycotts the National Fund and goes in for a fund of its own, it is only a step further for every family to have its own welfare fund for its own soldier.

The explanation may possibly be quite different to anything which I have suggested. But when the Carmarthen public have subscribed generously towards countless funds, the fact that one particular appeal has failed is no reflection on the generosity of the Carmarthen public. What was there about that particular fund which caused its failure amid so many successes? *ALETHEIA*[32]

While it seems that Beatrice Gwynne-Hughes' letter of 25 February hadn't yet spurred Carmarthen to answer her call, clearly the good citizens had been emptying their pockets for a while.

The column, under its pseudonym *Aletheia* (in Greek philosophy, truth, or disclosure), then shone its critical searchlight on the arguments put forward by conscientious objectors, the controversial issue of the moment.

Looking for warehouse premises

Warehouse space in Downing Street was limited and enquiries were being made around London to those owning large houses, and at major stores (often Welsh run), for space and help in packing parcels. T. J. Harries, off Oxford Circus, a firm later absorbed into John Lewis, had looked promising, but when that did not materialise a request was put to Harrods, where a suitable room was found, previously occupied by the New Zealand Fund. It would be managed by Miss Constance Mabel Hilton, 32, the Balham-born daughter of a second generation Portland cement manufacturer, of Faversham, Kent.

Personal losses

Miss Hilton, whose future husband was currently a prisoner of war in Germany, had been working on the recent Flag Day – and would do so again in 1917 and 1918. Four of her brothers served in the war – one brother had died at Ypres, in February 1915. A second brother would die in June 1916, and a third in April 1917. Her fourth brother survived the war and served again in the Second World War.

Not surprisingly, other committee members were experiencing personal loss in the war. On 6 July, Mrs Lloyd George had welcomed the latest recruit to the Troops Fund committee, Lady St Davids, who had recently become the second wife of John Wynford Philipps, Lord St Davids, his first wife having died in March 1915. His eldest son had died in the second Battle of Ypres in May 1915. On 7 July 1916, the day after the committee meeting, his second son, Lady St Davids' stepson, would die fighting in the woods of the Somme.

On 14 November 1917, Lady Treowen, formerly Lady (Ivor) Herbert, attended the meeting unaware that her only son had been killed in Palestine two days earlier: the news would arrive a week later. She did not attend any further meetings during wartime. The Treowens also had a daughter and by 1918 their Montgomeryshire farm in Wales was entirely run by women. In late September 1918, she obtained a Fund grant of up to £50 for an Abergavenny sewing class to purchase wool and other materials for comforts – albeit the war almost being over.[33] At the December 1918 election, the press noted that her husband, now a peer, could not vote, and saw her off in her car as she went to cast her vote. In 1920, she attended two meetings of the Fund.

Lloyd Georges for sale

In a further fund-raiser, portraits of Mrs Lloyd George and of Olwen, by Swansea-born Welsh artist Gwenny Griffiths, were on sale at the Mendoza Gallery, Old Bond Street, London, on 17 to 19 May, organised by Mrs Hopkinson and William Lewis, alongside works of other Welsh artists, including Sir William Goscombe John, Frank Brangwyn and Margaret Lindsay Williams, in addition to a portrait of Richard Lloyd, Lloyd George's uncle, by Christopher Williams (a frequent painter of the family), and specially-commissioned paintings of Sir Eldon Bankes, of Mr F. T. Hopkinson (the organiser's husband), and of Lady Arthur Pearson.[34] Mrs Lloyd George herself was in Wales but her husband called in.[35] The gallery had been provided without charge. Following the sale, William Lewis was authorised to auction unsold paintings at a reasonable reserve price – in the event he sold a number privately at a higher price than would have been likely by auction.[36] Overall, the sale raised £437 19s. 2d.[37]

On 19 May, William Lewis indicated he would step down as the Liberal candidate for Radnorshire, due to 'changed circumstances in consequence of the war'.[38] No doubt he had his hands full with the Troops Fund. The incumbent Liberal MP, Sir Francis Edwards, who had planned to retire (husband of Fund member Lady Catherine Edwards, who had died in 1915) agreed to stay on until a successor could be found. In 1918 the seat was merged with neighbouring Breconshire, and Brecon & Radnor was won unopposed by the Brecon incumbent, Sidney Robinson, a Lloyd George-supporting Coalition Liberal.

To sustain a pristine reputation in the competitive charity world, on 17 July William Lewis and Treasurer Sir Vincent Evans drew the Fund's attention to the recommendations of the 'report of a special Committee set up to enquire into the operations of charitable funds such as this', which included the publication of audited accounts. A leading City firm, Whinney, Smith & Whinney (auditors of the London & Midland Bank, and of the Queen Mother's Alexandra Day Fund) agreed to take on 'honorary auditorship' of the Fund.[39] On 11 July, the committee had been given a detailed breakdown of all the contributions made to the Fund to date, totalling £61,521, 7s. 3d., almost half raised through the 1917 Flag Day efforts.[40]

The Birkenhead tramways had sent in £39.16.11 raised from a week's collection they had run on the local tramcars for the Fund.[41] In March 1917, the Birkenhead tramcars would raise another £51 for the YWCA to help the women munitions workers.

Further afield enquiries were underway to determine the needs of the troops in Egypt, Salonica and Mesopotamia. A staff major recently returned from Egypt reported that the men were particularly in need of Virginian cigarettes.

> Egyptian cigarettes are issued but the men do not like them. As a matter of fact the tobacco seemed to be impregnated with a drug ... and given the climate ... Thirst quenchers made by Boots Cash Chemists are much appreciated and much needed, for in some places the men only get a pint of water a day, and in his opinion all troops in the East ought to be supplied with these or similar preparations if a sample was submitted for the inspection of the Committee. (illustration 46)
>
> It appeared that the 1st Glamorgan Yeomanry are 300 miles south of Alexandria in the desert, that everything, even water, has to be taken on camel back, and it was therefore strongly urged that cigarettes and

thirst quenchers be sent to this particular unit, and if possible to all other regiments in Egypt. He emphasised the great difference in the temperature between northern and southern Egypt, and gave, as his opinion, that not much clothing was needed for the present. He said that summer comforts could be sent out up to October and winter comforts immediately afterwards in order to cope with extremes of temperature, for the cold is intense in winter in Salonica and in northern Egypt. In his opinion, too, the medical service was far from satisfactory.[42]

By September, the Glamorgan Yeomanry in Egypt had duly been sent 5,000 cigarettes and 480 bottles of thirst quenchers – in addition to twelve deliveries to Welsh troops in Europe of other comforts (ranging from socks, shirts and mittens, towels, games, hairclippers and scissors, shaving soap, pipes, gramophones, helmets, tins of fruit, handkerchiefs, and one fly sprayer outfit and refills), and to the 34 (Welsh) Hospital in Bombay, 5,380 cigarettes and 1,058 other articles for hospital use.[43]

William Lewis was disposing of some of the Fund's Picture Postcards, still in hand, in the US, advertising in the *Welsh American*, a dollar for a packet of cards, accompanied by an autographed letter from Mrs Lloyd George. There had been one unforeseen obstacle when the Liverpool Censor Department refused to send the cards. In time this problem was overcome, though William Lewis was authorised, if need be, to offer money back to purchasers or deliver after the war.

Offers of comforts came from suppliers looking for an outlet for their stock, company liquidator George F. Wyatt offering nine tons of chocolate, and Columbia Graphophone [the new technology was still settling on its name] Co. 12-inch records deleted from their current lists. In October, the Fund ordered half a ton of chocolate and 80 parcels of Welsh and English records. Comforts were also being delivered to the home-based Royal Defence Corps, guarding ports, bridges, and prisoner of war camps.

Lady Plymouth, Mrs Lloyd George and Lady Mond also arranged a concert for the London Welsh community at the house of Lady Cowdray, 16 Carlton House Terrace, raising around £194 4s. 6d. for the Fund, just a little more than the night at the opera in March.[44] The concert had been planned for the Savoy Hotel but a double booking meant Lady Cowdray had to come to the rescue.[45]

Mrs Lloyd George herself was looking after everybody at the concert and wore dark blue taffeta with a rosewreathed hat. Her daughter, Olwen, helped energetically and sold programmes. The ballroom was so well filled that there was a little alarm lest some of the audience should be crowded into Lady Cowdray's cabinets of lovely old Chelsea. After the concert – a very good one – there was tea on the cool terrace.[46]

On 7 August, in Pwllheli (along the coast from Criccieth), Mrs Lloyd George proposed the vote of thanks at the Town Hall where Brigadier-General Owen Thomas chaired a concert in aid of the Belgian Wounded Fund:

> Referring to the voluntary Fund which is being raised in Wales on behalf of broken Welsh warriors, General Thomas said in the first twelve months of war 200,000 men answered the nation's call in Wales. He felt great moral responsibility in regard to these men. He visited their homes and knew what it meant to these people to take away their breadwinners. He pledged the nation's honour that they would not be allowed to suffer great hardship on their return to their country, and he was determined to do all in his power to help them. (Applause) It was our duty to see that the Government did look after these brave men, and with the voluntary fund now being raised, he hoped to render assistance to those in special need and outside Government relief. The men who volunteered at the beginning of the war and their dependants were the best asset the country possessed, and it was a sacred duty to take care of them. (Applause)[47]

On 23 August, as regulations progressed, the War Charities Act (1916) had been passed, and on 21 September the Fund approved its submission for registration as a charity (now compulsory), receiving its certificate in January 1917.

The 12 October Fund meeting, attended by a core group of Mrs Lloyd George, Lord Justice Bankes, Mrs Herbert Lewis (on the committee since September 1915), Treasurer Sir Vincent Evans, and Secretary William Lewis, addressed the strategic issues now facing the Fund. In addition to the ongoing efforts at cooperation across Wales, William Lewis pointed out that:

> ... a new difficulty had developed during recent months through the drafting of a large number of Welshmen into regiments other than Welsh,

that is in English, Scotch and Irish, and as this Fund had up to the present dealt only with Welsh regiments, dissatisfaction was bound to arise when it was found that men from localities that subscribe to the Fund do not participate in its benefits, because they are attached to other regiments, and that this undoubtedly tended to strengthen the claims of Sir Edward Ward's organisation.

The committee had in the past made efforts to obtain official recognition, and a greater measure of sympathy from the War Office, and had met with some degree of success, and the Secretary suggested that the committee might now endeavour to do what Queen Alexandra's Fund succeeded in doing, namely to have the War Office directly represented upon the committee, and that it might perhaps be possible to get Major David Davies to agree to become a member, as his services would doubtless be of considerable value.

He also suggested that the committee should consider the advisability of endeavouring to arrange for the opening of a depot in France, and if possible in the East, where comforts for Welsh troops could be stored and their distribution undertaken by responsible military authority.[48]

Major David Davies MP, of Llandinam, appointed parliamentary private secretary to Lloyd George in July, would play an important role for the Fund as it shifted its focus from supplying comforts towards supporting the disabled and their families. Grandson of the industrialist David Davies of Llandinam, and brother of the philanthropists Gwendoline and Margaret Davies, he had raised and commanded the 14th Battalion of the Royal Welch Fusiliers, at home and in France, until June 1916. He had government experience, having participated in the 1911 parliamentary debates on Lloyd George's Insurance Bill with respect to the interests of Wales.

NOVEMBER 1916

In November, Mrs Lloyd George chaired two Fund meetings, where it was decided that, given the Fund's current resources, they would not make further appeals to individuals for now, but concentrate on another St David's Day Flag Day in Wales and London in 1917. As Lilian Hopkinson was unable to lead the London campaign again, a sub-committee was established and, in December, Miss Constance Hilton, who had helped Mrs Hopkinson in 1916 and had been helping manage the Fund's warehouse, and who had lost a second brother in France in June, took charge.

An idea of contacting the large employers of labour who were benefiting from war and whose employees were benefiting from the Fund, was considered but not pursued.

The more health-conscious members of the committee may have approved of the decision not to send cigarettes and tobacco to the Welsh Hospital at Netley, athough Lady Owen Philipps sent £5 as a gesture.[49] Not all comforts were available, the Secretary recording in the minutes that all comforts had been dispatched 'with the exception of the canvas shoes which Mr Philip Williams had utterly failed to obtain from any wholesale dealers in London'.[50]

An unfortunate clash of dates

As in March 1915, there was a clash of dates with the YWCA who were supporting a flag day for women munitions workers on 27 February. William Lewis was tasked to write and suggest that 'in view of the 1st March being the recognised day for a Welsh effort it was singularly unfortunate that they should have chosen a date two days prior, and expressing the hope they could be good enough to make other arrangements'. However, when William Lewis consulted Mrs Hopkinson to suggest to whom he should write, she advised that such a protest might only cause friction, and if left alone the others might assist on St David's Day. In the event, by February, by which time there were increasing demands to improve the wages and conditions for women munitions workers,[51] the clash of dates remained unresolved, to the regret of the west London *Richmond Herald*:

> It is greatly to be regretted that the collection organised by the women of England on behalf of the YWCA Fund for providing more hostels, canteens and rest rooms for women munitions workers should fall in the same week as the Welsh Flag Day. The YWCA appeal is to be made next Tuesday, and two days later is St David's Day. As far as Richmond is concerned, the public are to be appealed to on both days. The Mayoress has in hand the arrangements for the Welsh Flag Day, and Lady Yoxall those for the Women's Day. The Women's Day is not exactly a flag day – there are, I believe, to be stalls at which articles of various kinds are to be sold – but at the same time it seems likely that the day's doings will affect adversely the collection that is to be taken on St David's Day.[52]

Pansies would be on sale, as opposed to daffodils.

> Twelve million pansies have been prepared for Women's Day to-morrow in aid of the Women's Wartime Workers' Fund. Among the sellers will be women munition workers in factory garb.[53]

We may assume that Mrs Lloyd George, and the ladies on her committee, regretted the clash with a worthy women's cause and with the YWCA.

Finally, in 1916, on 5 December, with the troops facing their second Christmas away from home comforts, the quirky diarist Samuell Pepys Junior reminded his readers that those at home might also want to think hard as to how much of their own Christmas could they send:

> This day observing in our flatt the greatest litter of string, brown paper, and boxes of card board, and enquiring of cook what should be the reason thereof, it comes, she says, of the Xtmas parcels that she and the mrs. will dispatch to Germany to the 2 prisoners, being my brother Tom and cook's leftenant. The most ridiculous thing ever heard of, that they would thus waste our money and victuall these times, being that the Germans will allow no sending of Xtmas parcels (very sensibly, I think), and 'tis ordered that all parcels be now sent to prisoners by the Rosicrucians' office. So telling them; and presently enquiring further what they send, and going to our larder, here be plum porridge, minced pies, sweatmeats, and a great store of all possible dainties prepared, and, what is the foolishest, spriggs of holly and misseltoe for decking them out come Xtmas. The which I bade them keep for our own eating, and thank God for it, rather than it be eaten of German swine.[54]

As the year ended, an additional challenge for getting the comforts to the soldiers at the Front was revealed in the *West London Observer*, highlighting a problem which still challenges mail order and online shopping today – will the clothes fit? (illustration 45)

CHAPTER 17

Olwen Flies the Flag

(January to March 1917)

'At Covent Garden we found just the same reception from the florists, fruiterers, and vegetable dealers as the butchers had given us. The best hotels and restaurants can't come near them for genuine generosity.'
Olwen Lloyd George, St David's Day 1917

To Chancery Lane

LLOYD GEORGE'S ELEVATION to the premiership meant a move next door to No. 10 Downing Street. The three interconnecting rooms at No. 11, enjoyed since inception, would no longer be available for the Fund. William Lewis decamped to two rent-free furnished rooms at Sir Vincent Evans' Chancery Lane Safe Deposit Company, from where he would now operate. The Fund would only be responsible for rates, cleaning and utilities, the support of two secretaries resulting in a small rise in the Fund's overheads. His move may have triggered Mrs Lloyd George to review her own secretarial needs, not least as her workload increased. In the spring, JTR would join her as her private secretary.

In addition to a change of premises, the Troops Fund now was steadily transitioning from provision of comforts to the treatment and retraining of disabled soldiers and sailors.

Mrs Lloyd George chaired the two January Fund meetings, attended by recent recruit Lady Francis Lloyd (Mary, née Gunnis, of Leckie, Stirlingshire), the wife of Sir Francis Lloyd, a Royal Welch Fusiliers colonel whose responsibility in the war was the protection of London from Zeppelins – known as 'the Man who Ran London'.[1]

'The Man who Ran London' could not protect the city from the second annual Welsh invasion of flag-sellers, its organisation already underway. On 17 January, Mrs Lloyd George addressed a Mansion House meeting hosted by the Lord Mayor, bringing together London's boroughs to plan the next campaign. Welsh Flag Days were also expected in Manchester and Liverpool, given their large Welsh communities, and elsewhere in England. In December, Welshman F. C. Hamer, of the *Manchester Guardian* and President of the National Union of Journalists, had written to William Lewis offering to help reach the large Welsh community.[2] In London Mrs Lloyd George promised to sell flags outside the Mansion House on the day from 10.30 till 1 o'clock,[3] a promise she would not be able to fulfil.

Messrs Robert Lewis, 'cigar importer & tobacconist, manufacturer of cigarettes, meerschaum pipes &c' of 20 St James's Street, trading since 1787,[4] offered the ground floor of their West End premises at 22 St James's Street as the Flag Day campaign HQ, the Fund indemnifying them from any claims such as rates and taxes and agreeing to give it up at any time 'should their Superior Landlords (the Crown) object'. In a separate initiative, the managing director of one of London's largest dairy companies, who was sending out cheques to 5,000 farmers, offered to enclose an appeal on behalf of the Fund, which was duly signed by Mrs Lloyd George, to accompany his covering letter. He also contributed 100 guineas to the Fund.[5]

The music hall singer and impresario George Robey, an avid fund-raiser himself, wrote to Mrs Lloyd George, apologising he could not assist in managing the planned St David's Day concert, but making a contribution nonetheless: 'I should be delighted for you to put this cheque in your collecting box on March 1st, to start the day's work, and let me have, from you, just one flag that I can keep as a souvenir.'[6]

Preparing for St David's Day

During February, on successive weeks, Mrs Lloyd George visited west London, preparing for the London Flag Day. Ealing had a strong Welsh community and the Lloyd Georges had lived there at times in their early days in London. William Lewis joined her for the second visit on 16 February.[7]

The previous day, 15 February, a well-attended Fund committee, a dozen members being present, signalled the Fund's transition. The next day, Sir Owen Thomas, who was also looking ahead, convened a meeting of his own Fund. The Troops Fund minutes noted that:

> ... they might find themselves in a position to supplement, as occasion and need arose, the Government grants, and that to avoid duplicate organisations, it was desirable to attain if possible some measure of cooperation between the Fund and Sir Owen Thomas' scheme. The committee expressed its opinion that the future work of the Fund would very largely lie in this direction.

William Lewis, for whom helping the disabled had become an increasing priority, would meet with Sir Owen, Mrs Lloyd George and Violet Douglas-Pennant to discuss the idea.

At the February Fund meeting he reported on Flag Day events planned elsewhere, mixing praise with criticism:

> The movement had been taken up very universally throughout Wales. Swansea alone of big towns had refused, under the guidance of the Mayor, as the town proposed providing for its own men, despite the fact that this Fund had sent, on various occasions, comforts to the Units particularly connected with Swansea as well as to individual soldiers, at the official request of the ex-Mayor.
>
> The action of Wrexham was also disappointing, for although it was known that we intended to hold a Flag Day, the authorities there had arranged to hold a Flag Day on their own account in aid of the RWF [Royal Welch Fusiliers]. In view of the enormous demands that had been sent to this committee from the many battalions of this regiment, it was apparent that the men would have fared badly had they been dependent upon Wrexham alone and been deprived of the great assistance rendered by this Fund.
>
> On the other hand ... the Lord Mayor of Manchester and the Mayor of Salford had placed themselves at the head of the Flag Day movement in their own and neighbouring boroughs, and that the Manchester Tramways Committee, whose trams serve a perfect labyrinth of large adjacent boroughs, had consented to hold a week's collection in all their cars, and further that the Welsh people of Merseyside had thrown themselves with vigour and enthusiasm into the movement.
>
> A Welsh Flag Day was also to be held in Liverpool, Bootle, Birkenhead, Wallasey, and other smaller districts. Nottingham and several smaller centres in England had also arranged for a Welsh Flag Day.[8]

The Prince of Wales had recently consented to become Patron of the Fund, his secretary sending £50 as a contribution. The Fund had now received over £28,000 in cash donations, and with a Flag Day imminent it was decided not to make a special appeal to likely donors for now. St David's Day would bring in another £28,000, almost doubling funds raised to date.

With William Lewis driving the changing strategy, and the process of distributing comforts becoming relatively routine (dealing with each request as appropriate), the Fund's Executive Committee now met just once a month, and in May, and the summer months of August and September, not at all, in contrast to the first two years' often weekly meetings.

Olwen flies the flag

Once again, Mrs Lloyd George could not take the lead for the London Flag Day, being in Cricieth, preparing for the funeral on 3 March of Lloyd George's uncle Richard Lloyd. Thus her daughter Olwen led the St David's Day charge on the streets and markets of London, supported by an estimated 7,000 volunteering ladies. (illustration 10) The day's takings would amount to £12,800, more than double the 1915 countrywide takings of £6,000.

In the morning Lloyd George was at No. 10 to receive what would become the annual party of children with disabilities bringing their gifts from their Heritage Craft School at Chailey, Sussex.

> Two gaily decorated motor-cars drove up to No. 10, Downing-street this morning, containing the children from the Heritage Craft School, Chailey, Sussex, under the care of Mrs Kimmins, wife of the Chief Inspector of L.C.C. schools, founder and honorary secretary of the school.
>
> One tiny dot handed to Mr Lloyd George an address framed in Sussex oak and embellished by the Welsh dragon. The address read:
>
> Dear Mr Lloyd George, – Every cripple at Chailey is with you – to the very last crutch. Whatever we can do to help you end this war please be sure we shall gladly do. We are busily getting ready to take in more wounded soldiers for what the grown-up people call educative convalescence, but what we call learning to forget their troubles and to earn their own living alongside us. Our motto is 'Lastus Sorte Mea' [Happy in our Lot]. We all wish you a happy St David's Day, but the Welsh cripples send the loudest cheer.

The cripple boys, some of whom are now working on the land connected with the farm school, sent a bouquet of their leeks, and the cripple babies in the Montifori School, not to be outdone, sent some daffodils.

Another address from the girls of the Llangattock Heritage Craft School, Chailey, read as follows:

The cripple girls of the Heritage Craft School, Chailey, beg that you will use this blotter and muffler that we have embroidered for you on St David's Day, 1917. We all look forward to your visit to Chailey. Many of us come from Wales, and we are all doing our best to save and do without everything that we possibly can, that can help you. P.S. – Of course, we are all planting our gardens with vegetables.

The Premier, who seemed greatly pleased with the addresses, smilingly returned thanks. He said that he wished the school every success, and hoped that the children, too, would all be a very great success. The children subsequently called upon Princess Louise (a patron), at Kensington Palace, and Lady Llangattock.[9]

The rather wonderful phrase 'educative convalescence' denotes Grace Kimmins' novel approach of pairing a child born without a limb to wounded soldiers who had lost the equivalent limb, allowing the child to mentor the adult in adapting to the loss.[10] Wartime spawned many medical advances. Chailey Heritage School, like many of the 'start-ups' of a century ago (it was founded in 1903), continues today.

Olwen travelled in style in the family Napier car. (illustration 7) The *Pall Mall Gazette* gave the day a supportive write up, David the Prime Minister rivalling the patron saint in capturing the headlines:

LLOYD GEORGE'S DAY: Welsh Flag Day was an unqualified success. Although the Prime Minister and his wife were unable, owing to the death of Mr Richard Lloyd, to take an active part, it was emphatically 'Lloyd George's Day'.

MISS LLOYD GEORGE ARRIVES AT 6 A.M.: Long before most Londoners were out of their beds this morning, Smithfield and Covent Garden markets had found a new significance for March 1, the Welsh National Day. St David's Day had, in the vivid imaginations of the markets, developed into Lloyd George's Day.

A splendid reception was accorded Miss Olwen Lloyd George, when, at the head of a bevy of Welsh beauty, she entered Smithfield Market at a few minutes before six, accompanied by Mr Henry, who had been entrusted by the Welsh Flag Day committee with the organisation of the market sales, Miss Hilton, the organising secretary to the committee, Miss Forster, and many other ardent workers for the cause of the Welsh troops. Miss Lloyd George was soon in a whirlpool of business.

When she herself sold a flag, no one offered less than the largest of our silver pieces, and here, there, and everywhere she had to make pretty little impromptu speeches.

DISCOVERY: A charming description of Miss Lloyd George's triumphant progress was given to the *Pall Mall Gazette* representative by Miss Forster. 'They simply overwhelmed us,' said Miss Forster, 'and everywhere our leader went she was cheered first for herself, and then, perhaps, louder than ever, for her father.'

We soon found out that St David's Day was a small thing alongside Lloyd George's Day. 'It's not that I'm Welsh, because I'm Scotch, but it's because it's your father's day,' said one very big and very tired-looking salesman, as he gave Miss Lloyd George a 10s. note for a tiny daffodil.

A SHOWER OF COINS: 'And it's not only because of St David's Day, and because of my father, but because of our Welsh troops, too, that I thank you,' said Miss Olwen, 'and amid the cheers that followed we were all assailed with a perfect shower of shillings, half crowns, and Treasury notes. There never was such generosity that of these fine men in the Smithfield and Covent Garden markets – for when we went on to Covent Garden we found just the same reception from the florists, fruiterers, and vegetable dealers as the butchers had given us. The best hotels and restaurants can't come near them for genuine generosity. Including cheques, I think I may say that I received at least £1,500 in less than hour.

Wherever we went it was always the same cry: "Lloyd George's day! Why, of course, missy!"'

Later, the West End and the City followed the lead of the early morning markets. All the most fashionable streets were patrolled by daintily dressed society women, many of them in the picturesque Welsh National costume. One side of Regent-street, for instance, was under the charge of Lady Prichard-Jones and the other under Lady Milsom Rees, and here, shortly before eleven, an amusing little incident occurred.

A DELIGHTED OLD GENTLEMAN: An elderly gentleman approached three flag-sellers in succession, and, tendering a £1 note, spoke volubly in Welsh. Each of the three had to signify their inability to understand

235

him, and he passed on disconsolate. He came to yet another saleswoman, younger, and perhaps even prettier than the others. Again the quick query in Welsh, and this time an even more voluble and delighted response in the same language. Slowly the gentleman returned the Treasury note to his pocket and produced instead something crisper and infinitely more substantial. So the Fund became richer by a £10 note.

AT THE STORES: In Conduit-street Lady Rhondda, aided by a number of friends, did excellent business, while thoroughly satisfactory sales were reported from a number of the departmental stores. At Harrods, Lady Reading and Miss Gladys Cooper were the chief sales women; while at Selfridges, the Hon. Mrs Geoffrey Pearson was in charge.

MISS LLOYD GEORGE AT THE STOCK EXCHANGE: The City did its full share as usual. Miss Lloyd George motored to the Mansion House, where she was received by the Lord Mayor. After spending about an hour outside the Mansion House, selling flags and daffodils, which were readily bought up, she accompanied the Lord Mayor to the Stock Exchange, where she had an enthusiastic reception, and was speedily relieved of her stock. Photographs of Mr Lloyd George and of his daughter, Miss Megan, although offered at a shilling, fetched a much higher figure. Wooden leeks and real and paper daffodils were in great demand.[11]

In the afternoon there was a show at the Alhambra Theatre, Leicester Square.

BY ROYAL APPOINTMENT: THE QUEEN AT THE ALHAMBRA: FINE SINGING BY THE WELSH GUARDS' CHOIR: Large crowds cheered Her Majesty the Queen as she arrived at the Alhambra Theatre to attend the grand matinée arranged as the pièce de résistance by the Welsh Flag Day committee. Within the theatre the fashionable awaited Her Majesty's coming. Among others present were: The Countess of Dundonald, Lady Harlech, Lady Merthyr, Grace Lady Newborough, Lady Tredegar, Lady Francis, Mrs Cazalet, Miss Chetwynd, Mrs Howard Corbett, and Mrs Elmsley Carr.

The programme itself was full of the best things the London amusement world has to offer, but no item more obviously pleased Her Majesty than the singing of the Welsh Guards' Choir, who, under the conductorship of Sergeant W. T. Jones, rendered with true Welsh spirit two of the most popular Welsh national airs, 'Men of Harlech' and 'Cydgan y Morwyr' [The Sailors' Chorus].[12]

The matinée poster has become a highly recognised work by Frank Brangwyn. (illustration 1)

In the East End a donkey, given by a Mr Pugh, was raffled, bringing in two thousand sixpences [£50] for the Fund.[13] Committee member Lady Owen Philipps, who had recently bought the first shell manufactured in Wales under Lloyd George's munitions scheme, put up the shell for re-sale.[14]

A well-attended committee on 2 April, chaired by Mrs Lloyd George, covered a typically wide range of issues. A request by Major-General Ivor Philipps for a grant to the 38th Welsh Division in France for buying typewriters was turned down, though the committee was willing to supply Mess mugs. Five hundred pounds was approved for the Royal Welch Fusiliers Prisoners of War Association – in the event this grant was not needed. Flintshire passed on some complaints from individual soldiers about the distribution of comforts, while numerous Commanding Officers sent letters of thanks for the Fund's support. Discussions were also underway with respect to engaging the retailer Bryan Bros. of Cairo to act as a depot for the Fund in Egypt, given heightened shipping problems due to more frequent submarine attacks. In October it would be reported that the insurance premium for transport would be a heavy 207 per cent.

Bryan Bros, of Cairo, was founded in 1886 by John Davies Bryan from Caernarfon and two brothers. By this time, also present in Alexandria, Port-Said and Khartoum, it was one of the most notable department stores in the Middle East. Their building in Cairo still stands.[15]

In April Mrs Lloyd George's daughters Olwen and Megan both took to the London streets raising money for comforts for the troops in the Middle East, on Mesopotamia Day.[16]

Looking ahead

A sub-committee comprising the officers, Mrs Lloyd George, Sir Vincent Evans, and William Lewis, supported by Lord Justice Bankes, Major David Davies MP, the Hon. Violet Douglas-Pennant, Mrs Hopkinson and Lady Owen Philipps, was now charged with planning what should be done with the Fund's money in the future. William Lewis was already engaged in discussions with David Davies as to how the Fund could promote the interests of disabled soldiers.

On St George's Day, 23 April, Mrs Lloyd George, Olwen, Violet

Douglas-Pennant, and William Lewis, joined several hundred members of working parties at a meeting in Caernarfon of the county's district associations formed to support Welsh troops. After Mrs Lloyd George reviewed recent fund-raising and their plans for the Fund, William Lewis reiterated his critical line, that the War Office had broken faith with the Welsh people, going back on a promise to put Welsh soldiers in Welsh regiments commanded by Welshmen, making it harder for the Welsh Comforts Committee to do its job.

In a lighter touch it was noted that the fund-raising was clearly assisted by having links with a certain address in London.[17]

CHAPTER 18

Treatment and Retraining

(March to December 1917)

'The proper solution of this problem is, in its way, as important as the proper ending of the war.'
William Lewis, March 1917

WILLIAM LEWIS WAS now setting his sights on establishing a single national scheme for Wales for the treatment and retraining of disabled soldiers and sailors, ideally under the newly-established Pensions Ministry, perhaps with a Welsh Department.

Correspondence with David Davies

His correspondence with Fund committee member David Davies MP reflects his increasing frustration with bureaucracy (not least when 'substituting bustle for business')[1] with the divisions within Wales, and voicing his own sense of duty to provide for those whom he had urged to risk their lives for their country.

On 19 March, confessing 'to mental indigestion' after a weekend reading all the Pensions Acts and Parliamentary debates, William Lewis concluded:

> The one outstanding fact is that, despite the apparent and vocal determination of the nation to act with justice and generosity to the men broken in its service, the disabled soldier will, after all, in some measure, be dependent upon voluntary funds – bluntly – upon charity.[2]

He expressed his own moral commitment to the disabled:

> I am intensely interested in the Welsh soldiers. I was too old to join the Army myself, but I spoke at many recruiting meetings to induce others to go, and I feel a moral responsibility to do everything in my power to help, in any small way, to lighten the burden that many of them will have to bear for the remainder of their days. I am, henceforth, quite prepared to devote the whole of my time and whatever energy and organising experience I have to their service.[3]

Adding a few days later:

> The proper solution of this problem is, in its way, as important as the proper ending of the war.[4]

North versus south

One hurdle facing a national scheme for Wales was that local and regional interests were moving towards separate north and south Wales schemes, coordinating with county committees. On 27 March he wrote:

> What we feared is actually taking place, and all kinds of wild-cat schemes are evidently afloat. Had a scheme been drafted first of all for universal application to Wales as a whole, and men sent down to explain it in Wales, who knew the people and the idiosyncrasies, we might, with a little tact, have brought the whole of Wales into line. As it is, it is evident that Denbigh is putting forward the grouping of North Wales Counties alone, which is playing right into the hands of South Wales, to the detriment of the soldier.[5]

He did acknowledge that he was not totally innocent of some regionalism and possibly conflicting objectives:

> You know that an extremely ambitious scheme of raising £150,000 for a North Wales Memorial to fallen soldiers has been launched. I have been asked to act as Honorary Secretary of a London committee to help this along, and have agreed. But I have little expectation of this large sum being obtained; and with all possible respect to its promoters, I do not think it ought to succeed if the raising of this sum should, in any degree, imperil the success of the National Fund we have in view for the benefit of the disabled Welsh soldiers.[6]

Treatment and Retraining

The North Wales Memorial, or Welsh Heroes Memorial, was for a science block at the university in Bangor to provide access to education for all children irrespective of means, a project championed by Robert Thomas. The north/south issue would be discussed in May at a meeting hosted at No. 10 to promote the project.

In a 15 June letter to William Lewis, Swansea barrister E. Marlay Samson, a key player in seeking support for the disabled in Wales, but more relaxed about north and south entities, later gave his own perspectives on the memorial project:

> I see North Wales has already decided on a National Memorial for the North, a new Science Block at Bangor University. Personally I think institutions to help disabled men would appeal to the South Wales public more as a War Memorial than an Educational purpose, however worthy. I wish we could have had a really great national scheme of aftercare as a Welsh Memorial. I fear, however, that it is too late, as North Wales has decided otherwise. It will be all the more necessary therefore to rely on the National Fund if the Joint Committee are to carry on aftercare work to the greatest advantage.[7]

On 4 April, William Lewis launched into Denbighshire once more, citing Talleyrand in a handwritten note to David Davies:

> I should have thought that Denbighshire has had enough of the North Wales stunt. A couple of years ago I endeavoured to get Wales under the direction of the Lady Mayoress of Cardiff to run one National Fund for Welsh Prisoners of War, & this Fund contributed £100 for that purpose but Wrexham would have nothing to do with Cardiff control. The result is that the RWF Prisoners of War Assoc. is practically bankrupt. We are giving them £500 this week. The Welch Regt Fund at Cardiff has only 240 men to provide for the Wrexham lot have 498. So that the wealthy part of Wales has exactly half the burden of the poorer part. The descendants of the Bourbons who forgot nothing and remembered nothing [Attrib. Talleyrand] are evidently to be found in the county where the N. Wales Asylum is also located.[8]

William Lewis on the debt of Wales

William Lewis then drafted a coherent and impassioned article for the press (it would seem unpublished), summarising the challenges

241

inherent in the return of so many wounded soldiers. The 47-year-old Calvinistic Methodist who had spoken on the recruitment platforms (see p.281) began by acknowledging Wales' debt to the Forces:

> The Debt of Wales to Her Disabled Sons
> The question of dealing with the disabled soldier and sailor is attracting much attention, but scarcely can it be said that the attention is as great or the enthusiasm so keen as was displayed in the latter months of 1914, when respectable, patriotic and highly prosperous middle-aged men crowded the platforms of town and village, to call in clarion notes upon the younger and (so they said) more fortunate men to respond to the call of King and Country, and painted in glowing colours how Britain would in turn repay its debt to them and to their families should it fall to their lot to have to pay some of the hideous penalties that war inevitably exacts. We know what response the young men of Britain made. They went out in their thousands, and hundreds of thousands, to defend liberty, to destroy militarism, to put down wrong, and to exalt righteousness.
>
> Thousands have returned broken in body or mind, thousands more will follow. Without their ready sacrifice Britain would have lost the war – unless adequate reparation is made to the men shattered in her service, she will have lost her soul.
>
> In no part of the Kingdom was more enthusiasm shown than in Wales, the home of a peace-loving people. Clergy and ministers vied with politicians and soldiers in pointing the path of duty. The present Prime Minister called for a separate Welsh Army Corps, and in the twinkling of an eye it had leapt into being. From pit and quarry, from field and workshop, from bank and office, from school and college in every town and village, an almost endless array of young Welshmen flocked to the Colours. Battalion after battalion was added to her famous regiments, and those who were left behind added cubits to their stature as they told how great a proportion of the population of their country had turned their backs upon all future prospects in life, and, without staying to count the cost, had faced all the terrors of the unknown.

He called for Wales to act, united:

> Today comes the test. Will Wales with one heart and voice, forgetting all past differences and division, knowing no geographical or social distinctions, bend herself to the task of making the lot of the disabled

easier to bear, and of bringing a glimmer of sunshine into lives darkened by the tragedy of maimed limbs, of bodies racked by pain and disease, and of disordered minds. If ever there was a call for united national action, it is today. If ever a problem demanded the setting aside of every form and grade of provincialism and parochialism, it is this. Why should there be a need for emphasising unity? Because the number of men affected is so great, the forms of disablement are so varied, and the difficulties of treatment so complex.

Another 'Roll of Honour':

Men may return apparently sound, but in the course of time some form of mental or physical disablement directly traceable to their war service may appear, so that the extent of liability will for a long time be problematical. A register will have to be compiled (another Roll of Honour); it will then be found how many of them have lost their sight, how many their hearing, some will have lost the power of speech, hundreds will have lost one limb or more, the health of hundreds will be impaired by tuberculosis, rheumatism and other ills, consequent upon exposure, hundreds will be the victims of varying degrees of paralysis, of epilepsy, and of the innumerable forms of nervous troubles, many will have lost their reason, the minds of many more be dulled.

Shortage of staff and equipment:

All will require special treatment and attention. Doctors and nurses and necessary institutions and equipment will be scarce, and such as are available will have to be carefully conserved. Existing facilities will have to be utilised to their fullest extent, and many provided in addition where they can be of the greatest general service. If this be attempted sectionally, the success of any one section will only be attained at the expense of another, to the lasting detriment of the men. Can there be any doubt that the committees already set up in Wales – as they realise the greatness of the task imposed upon them, and imbued as they all are with a sense of their deep responsibility to secure the best possible treatment for the men entrusted to their care will decide that the first step is close cooperation and united action.

Training as well as treatment:

But apart from the matter of treatment there is also the question of training. It is hoped that a great majority of the disabled may be trained to follow some form of occupation, different of necessity perhaps to that of the able-bodied. There will be probably in many instances at first a disinclination on the part of these unfortunate men to undergo the training that will make them once again useful members of the community. Many will consider that they should be left alone to eke out such existence as will be possible to them on the pension payable by the Government. Such a course would be disastrous to them and to the country, and it must be rigorously combated. Competent instructors will be difficult to obtain and this, in itself, coupled with the scarcity of doctors and nurses will do much to bring about joint action, for in a majority of cases treatment and training can proceed simultaneously.

For rich and poor:

The aim of Wales must be to provide the highest medical skill, the most complete and efficient care, the most effective and thorough training of each of her disabled men, whether he be a citizen of a wealthy city, or the son of the labourer's cottage on the lonely mountainside. When the training and treatment is completed, there will still be the problem of future employment, which will probably entail the setting up of new industries, and a fresh re-organisation of the country's resources which will demand the aid of the keenest business intelligence and the best trained intellects Wales can produce.

Local responsibility, acting together:

Let the local committees not consider that their sphere of action and of usefulness and responsibility will in the least degree be lessened. The real care of the men of their particular county and borough will still be theirs, all that they are asked to do is to act together in providing the necessary machinery, in the setting up of which, and in its control, they will all have a voice.

A State-established national scheme for Wales:

The State has recognised the vast importance of this problem, and has created a new ministry for the express purpose of dealing with it, and has placed at its head a man whose sympathy with the disabled is universally acclaimed. A body formed under his guidance (for it is definitely stated that he strongly favours a National Scheme for Wales) speaking for the Welsh nation will always be assured of sympathetic consideration and of ready help.

A recognition of the immensity and complexity of the problem is the first and surest step towards the finding of its proper solution. If Wales attempts a plan of shreds and patches it will stand convicted of a lack of vision, and where there is no vision the people shall perish.[9]

He sent a similar draft to David Davies, with the note:

Dear Major David Davies, I don't know whether you will have the time or the patience to read the enclosed which is a copy of what I have given to the *Western Mail* and *S. Wales Daily News*. Please don't say 'Eye-wash' if you do read it. I want it to appeal to the imagination as well as to the business interest of any Welshman who happens to read it.

Yrs Ever, William Lewis

He later added:

I feel instinctively that so far public opinion in Wales on this question is nebulous and uninstructed.[10]

The *Western Mail* reported:

PROPOSED WELSH SECTION: It is understood that proposals will be submitted to Mr Barnes, the Pensions Minister, in favour of the establishment of a Welsh section in the Pensions Department. In connection with the provision to be made for disabled soldiers in Wales, an influential deputation (including Mrs Lloyd George and Major David Davies, M.P.) has had an informal discussion with Mr Barnes, and has offered him the fullest assistance devising a national scheme which, while taking account of the special conditions and needs of the Principality and recognising the principle of Welsh autonomy, will secure for Wales the full advantages of any State provision.[11]

Pensions Minister George N. Barnes, a Glasgow MP, was a former leader of the Labour Party and supportive of Lloyd George's 1911 Act.

On 21 May, the *Manchester Guardian* published a long interview with David Davies, expressing many of William Lewis' views with respect to the needs of the disabled. He noted how the state was still relying on the voluntary sector:

> It appears that the Government have decided that the capital required for these institutions must come from voluntary sources. Consequently, it will be necessary to raise a National Fund ... Personally, I think the State should have put up all the money that is required for the purpose.[12]

In June, William Lewis suggested to David Davies: 'I think that it would be worthwhile for you to see the *Herald* and *Labour Leader*, both Labour papers of somewhat extreme type, but both possessing a certain following, and both readable papers.'[13]

At the beginning of May, William Lewis had expressed his personal view that the Troops Fund had 'now outgrown its somewhat limited scope of real usefulness', and while disappointed that during his time in Downing Street he had not moved closer to the action, he was neither an axe-grinder nor harbouring any great ambitions for a civil service position:

> Dear Major David Davies
>
> I am a little exercised in mind regarding the suggestion you have more than once made, that I should in some way identify myself in an official capacity with the future care of disabled Welsh soldiers, and as I find it difficult to speak clearly on this and other points, when in your office or in the presence of a third person, I am constrained to write.
>
> Judging from the remarks made to you by the Rt. Hon. Barnes and the gallant Sir Ivor [Herbert], it is widely thought that I belong to the large and widely flourishing brotherhood of axe-grinders, and that my zeal for the future welfare of the soldiers is somewhat tempered by self-interest. In justice to myself let me say that such is far from being the case. I have for the past few years endeavoured to the best of my small ability to be of service to Wales. I commenced by serving the 'Corff' [Body] in London. I ran a couple of bazaars to aid the struggling Welsh churches in this Babylon. I went to Radnorshire full of an enthusiastic belief in the political destiny of my country, and returned a wiser and poorer man. I then took up this Fund, which has now outgrown its somewhat limited scope of real usefulness. If I can be of use in helping to set up a really

efficient scheme for Wales in connection with her disabled men, I shall be quite content afterwards if need be (to quote that bright organ of public opinion, the *Radnorshire Standard*, in the days of David Williams when I first appeared there) 'to return to that sphere of decent obscurity which I previously adorned'!

I have not the slightest ambition to become a small cog in the cumbrous machinery of the Civil Service – the grave of initiative and the forcing bed of dull stolid automata. A daily diet of Barnes and Boscawen would very soon make a neurasthenic of me. I confess that I had at one time hoped that Mr Lloyd George would have made use of me during the war, but although I was under his roof for two years, he evidently did not consider that my service would be of any value.

Faithfully yours
William Lewis.[14]

However, by 29 June, William Lewis was looking ahead again, as Pensions Minister Barnes was now moving on to join Lloyd George's five-member cabinet and William Lewis seemed to be putting his hat in the ring (or perhaps he was suggesting someone else):

Now that our highly esteemed friend Mr Barnes has been called up higher and admitted into the very holy of holies, I presume we shall have to start *de novo* in the matter of the disabled Welsh soldier. You probably know who is to take the Ministry of Pensions on and I shall be very glad if you will supply him with the necessary dose of ginger. I have sent my nomination for the post to Mrs LlG and, had she the necessary power, I know that she would act upon it cheerfully and promptly. Faithfully yours,
William Lewis.[15]

Anyone for cricket?

The Fund committee met on 7 June, the strategy sub-committee reporting on progress, William Lewis detailing the various comforts sent to Welsh troops in France, Salonica and Egypt, from foodstuffs and clothing to candles, writing wallets, gramophones and records and, for the 38th, in France, enough shirts, trousers, belts and caps to equip two cricket teams (and two cricket sets to the Welsh Guards). The Welsh troops in Egypt had been moved to Palestine, so further enquiries were being made to see what was practical.[16] William

Lewis reported on meetings held with Pensions Minister Barnes and on correspondence with Colonel Sir Robert Jones, Inspector of Military Orthopaedics, being well briefed on the experience to date in rehabilitating the wounded and what was needed.

The Fund was also finalising its accounts, with a view to publishing them in full.

The Countess of Lisburne, a new committee member, who had helped with the Flag Day, attended the meeting, one of just two she would attend. At the end of May she had attended a meeting of the friends of the Poor Disabled Soldiers War Committee at the home of Mrs Cazalet, a good friend of Mrs Lloyd George.[17] The Countess, the former Mlle Regina de Bittencourt, was the daughter of a wealthy Chilean, then on his country's Legation. The 7th Earl of Lisburne, from Cardiganshire, was serving in the Welsh Guards and she assisted a number of war charities, including taking the wounded for drives.[18]

On Wednesday, 4 July, Mrs Lloyd George presided over the Fund sub-committee following meetings with the Pensions Minister and correspondence between David Davies and Sir Arthur Griffith-Boscawen, Parliamentary Secretary to the Pensions Ministry. The committee asked Sir Vincent Evans and William Lewis to point out to Sir Arthur that in their view:

> ... there appeared to be no reason why the Red Cross Society should not undertake to do for Wales what apparently it had arranged to do for England and Scotland, i.e. provide money for the setting up of the necessary institutions for training and treatment ... [and that the Troops Fund] would not be in a position to undertake such work.

and to tell him that:

> ... while accepting as inevitable the setting up of separate joint committees for north and south Wales, they very much hoped that ultimately, means would be found to form a joint committee that would bring both north and south Wales into close co-operation.[19]

William Lewis also was meeting the local War Pension committees in north Wales, particularly with Montgomeryshire and Denbighshire, and corresponding with Marlay Samson of Pembrokeshire.

While there were virtually no requests coming in for comforts,

William Lewis wrote to all Commanding Officers in the Egyptian Expeditionary Force that a firm in Cairo would be taking on the supply of comforts on behalf of the Fund.

A partnership in the offing

After another Fund sub-committee on 11 July, the full Executive Committee met a week later. After deciding to buy up as much stock of socks, shorts and underclothing at the lowest price possible (anticipating limited supplies of wool and flannel), it was agreed to use part of their accumulated funds to supplement the allowances and contributions of the State, and to approach the Welsh National Fund for Soldiers and Sailors (Sir Owen Thomas' Fund) and the various pensions committees to form a central committee to administer the joint funds and 'to be the sole authority to appeal for further public support'.

The Fund committee met again on 11 October, chaired by Lady Glanusk. Total cash received to date had now exceeded £60,000, and the range of comforts extended to include mouth organs, Oxo cubes, tea tablets, nickel mirrors, indoor games, boxing gloves and fingerless gloves. A conference was planned for 19 October to meet representatives of Sir Owen Thomas' Fund and the north and south Wales committees to pursue amalgamation plans.

The Shrewsbury conference

On 30 November, Mrs Lloyd George chaired the Shrewsbury conference which established the Welsh National Fund for the Welfare of the Sailors and Soldiers of Wales. She continued to emphasise the responsibility of the State as well as the value of voluntary assistance.

> WELSH SERVICE MEN AND THEIR DEPENDANTS: NATIONAL FUND INAUGURATED
>
> A national conference, representative of all interests in Wales, was held at Shrewsbury on Friday to start the Welsh National Fund for the welfare of the sailors and soldiers of Wales and their dependants. In the Fund will be united the National Fund for Welsh Troops, of which Mrs Lloyd George is chairman, and the Welsh National Fund inaugurated by Brigadier-General Sir Owen Thomas. It is intended to aim at raising £250,000 for the Fund.

On the motion of Mr D. S. Davies, of Denbigh, Mrs Lloyd George was elected chairman of the conference, and those present included Brigadier-General Sir Owen Thomas, General Sandbach, Mr William Lewis (London), Mr Ellis Jones Griffith MP, Lady Trevor, the Hon. Violet Pennant, the Mayors of Bangor and Aberystwyth, Mr Hugh Lewis (Newtown), Mr William Edwards (chairman of the Anglesey County Council), and Mr A. Seymour Jones (Wrexham). Mr William Lewis was elected secretary.

Mrs Lloyd George said two considerations appeared to be firmly and generally held throughout the country; first, that the State should not be allowed to escape in any particular way from its due obligations to the men who answered its call; secondly, that in addition there would still be considerable need for assistance to be rendered through voluntary funds.

Her experience during the past three years had been that Welshmen the world over were eager to assist any movement for the betterment of the future existence of those who had borne the burden and the heat of the day and of their families. Money had been sent to her from all parts of the world, from China to Peru. One day a totally unexpected cheque for £1,500 was received by the Fund of which she was chairman as a contribution from an inter-allied bazaar at Chicago.

The first decision they had to arrive at that day was as to whether a national organisation was necessary, and she did not think there were two opinions on that point.

Their next duty was to ensure that the machinery set up for the conduct of the organisation would be such as to earn the confidence of the nation generally, as well as of the men for whose benefit it was being created. (applause)

General Sir Owen Thomas moved that a fund, to be known as the Welsh National Fund for the welfare of the sailors and soldiers of Wales who had served in the war, and their dependants, be constituted, and that one of the objects be to advance money either on loan or as a gift, or partly the one or partly the other, where thought well, to give the men a new start in life.

He reminded the conference of the scheme inaugurated in February 1916, and said that the scheme that day was practically the same. They were changing the administration because circumstances were greatly changed since early in 1916. Wales responded magnificently to that scheme, and they had a list of some 50,000 subscribers. Mrs Lloyd George's scheme was the first in the field, and that Fund was already a very substantial

Treatment and Retraining

one. The executive of his Welsh National Fund had definitely arranged to amalgamate with the National Fund and work as one. Those joint funds would form a splendid nucleus for the grand scheme which he hoped would be launched there that day. He had to go in a fortnight to South Africa, but on his return he would visit every county in the Principality on behalf of the scheme.

A committee was formed, and on the motion of General Sandbach, it was decided that the Prince of Wales be asked to be patron of the Fund. Mrs Lloyd George was elected chairman of the committee.[20]

Due to catching the flu, she missed the 10 December Fund meeting, chaired by Lord Justice Bankes. However, on 17 December, she may well have attended the sub-committee that fine-tuned the relationship between the Troops Fund (which still retained a separate identity) and the new amalgamated Welsh National Fund, as agreed with Sir Owen Thomas' Fund at the joint conference in Shrewsbury, careful to ensure no future confusion:

> ... that the Troops Fund [or Comforts Fund] must continue in existence to perform the definite work for which it was formed, and for which it had collected money. It must also keep such control over monies already collected, as will ensure its being able to carry out its work to completion.
>
> It is most anxious that the Welsh National Fund [the new entity, or Welfare Fund] shall be, and be recognised as the only voluntary organisation in Wales to provide for the welfare of the soldiers and sailors in Wales who have served in the war, and their dependants, and is prepared to render it all the financial assistance in its power.
>
> Under no circumstances will the Comforts Fund endeavour to compete with the Welfare Fund. No appeal by the Comforts Fund will be made by that body in Wales and no attempts will be made to undertake any of the work which is undertaken by the Welfare Fund.
>
> When the work of the Comforts Fund is completed, the intention is to dissolve the Fund, and hand over any balance then in its hands to the Welfare Fund.[21]

That same day she attended the meeting of London mayors, hosted by the Lord Mayor and Mayoress at the Mansion House, planning the 1918 St David's Day Flag Day.[22]

The Hon. Organiser for the 1918 Flag Day would be G. A. Sawyer, a silversmith who frequently assisted the Lloyd Georges on financial issues, a director of Mappin & Webb and of S. J. Waring's furniture company, Waring & Gillow, who provided 'palatial premises' in Conduit Street for Flag Day helpers. (illustration 13) The former Miss Constance Mabel Hilton, now Mrs J. S. Franklin, the 1917 organising secretary, had been taking the lead so far. She had lost a third brother, on the Somme, in April, but on a happier note, in November, she married Lieut. Franklin, who had returned from two years of captivity in Germany.[23] (illustration 19)

CHAPTER 19

From Comforts to Care and Children

(January to December 1918)

'The Fund was going on to try to help the sailors and soldiers and their dependants after the war. There would be a lot for voluntary workers to do in this way without relieving the State of any of its obligations.'
Margaret Lloyd George, Bangor, March 1918

THE YEAR'S FIRST Fund meeting, on 10 January, chaired by Lord Justice Bankes, finalised plans for the upcoming Flag Days: 50 Welsh Testaments were sent to ten Army chaplains, and comforts were delivered to the Isle of Man, to France, to the Runcorn Vicarage Hospital, to the POW camp in Newtown, Kerry, Ireland, to wounded Welsh soldiers in Brondesbury Park Hospital, London (local to William Lewis' home), and to Miss Edith Thomas, for the Cricieth Comforts Fund. Edith was the elder sister of Leah Thomas, Liberal activist and suffragist who would be one of the first two women elected to Cricieth Council, in 1919, polling just ahead of Mrs Lloyd George.

Some requests were approved conditionally: a grant to the Soldiers and Sailors' Free Buffet at Euston Station had been made conditional on the outcome of a separate appeal in the *Evening Standard*. As the newspaper's appeal had raised £8,000, the Fund deemed their contribution no longer necessary. Similarly, their offer of support was gratefully turned down when a London Welshman seeking money for band instruments for the 18th Welch Regiment had raised the full £78 needed.

Looking ahead in Manchester and in Liverpool

On 18 January, Mrs Lloyd George visited the north-west metropolises, Liverpool and Manchester, both with substantial Welsh 'colonies', to discuss Flag Days and plans for the amalgamated Troops Fund.

> A Tribute to Manchester's Generosity: To-day, Mrs Lloyd George, wife of the Prime Minister, visited Manchester for the purpose of expressing the thanks of the Welsh people to the workers for the Welsh Flag Day some months ago, and also to inaugurate a National Fund in aid of Welsh troops. The distinguished lady addressed a packed meeting of workers at the YMCA Hall in the afternoon. Mrs Lloyd George was accompanied by Mr William Lewis, who has taken a prominent part in the work of the Welsh funds.
>
> The Chairman said the appeal to Manchester had resulted in the raising of £3,570.
>
> Mrs Lloyd George opened by thanking the Welsh community of Manchester and Salford and all their English friends who had helped so liberally in the 'Flag Day' effort. She wished to enlist their sympathies and practical support for the Comforts Fund for Welsh troops, which they hoped would have an even better year than last. In addition to sending comforts, they wanted to help in every way possible the men who had been discharged from the army and navy, and a new national scheme was being started for that purpose.[1]

That evening she dined privately at Liverpool Town Hall with the Mayor and Mayoress of Liverpool, before a public meeting at St George's Hall, Liverpool, with Welsh Flag Day workers.

> In Liverpool last night, Mrs Lloyd George, addressing a meeting of workers of the Welsh National Flag Day, said that on the three occasions they had Flag Days, over £40,000 had been raised. In one case a woman sent her weekly allowance of 5s. They hoped to raise a quarter of million pounds, and there was plenty of scope for voluntary workers now and after the war. Many of the men would come back to their homes and find that their businesses had gone, and it was necessary to give these men a chance start again. That would be a much better policy than providing an allowance or pension.[2]

Mrs Lloyd George assured her listeners that 'there was not a Fund in the country that had been run more economically than theirs'.[3]

Charity fatigue, Machynlleth wobbles

As St David's Day loomed, charity fatigue was apparent. On 27 February, at the Machynlleth Rural Council, when a letter was read from Mrs Lloyd George asking them to arrange a Flag Day and collect subscriptions for the Welsh Troops Fund, the matter was deferred. The council also deferred a decision on housing: in wartime there wasn't time or money for everything.[4]

But the show went on nearer London: 'Mrs Lloyd George attended a concert yesterday [28 February] at Acton in connection with the Welsh "Flag Day". Before the concert she lunched with the organisers, and the meal was supplied from the local communal kitchen.'[5]

The final Welsh invasion of London

Having reviewed the troops in a cold Llandudno on the 1915 St David's Day, been confined to No. 11 by a cold in 1916, and missing the 1917 Flag Day due to the funeral of Uncle Richard Lloyd, on 1 March 1918 Mrs Lloyd George finally drove off from No. 10 in Lloyd George's flag-bedecked Napier car used by Olwen the previous year, though with the roof on due to the weather. Notices at the Stock Exchange reminded everyone of her forthcoming visit. (illustration 11)

The children from Chailey made their annual visit to No. 10 with gifts.

> A touching incident was the visit to 10, Downing-street of a party of children from the Heritage Craft School, Chailey, Sussex, who brought a number of presents for the Prime Minister. They included a wooden stool decorated with the red dragon of Wales and ingeniously carved with his toes by an armless boy. From the girls came a daintily embroidered and fully equipped cradle which Mrs Lloyd George accepted for her grandchild. The Prime Minister heartily thanked the children.[6]

The Times, not as detailed a publisher of Mrs Lloyd George's activities as the regional press, covered the campaign closely, including which lady was manning which flag-selling site across the City, the West End, Hampstead and Finchley. The changing focus of the Fund was made clear:

MRS LLOYD GEORGE'S TOUR: St David's Day was observed as Welsh Flag Day in London yesterday, when collections were made in aid of the National Fund for the provision of comforts for the Welsh troops. The gifts are to be distributed irrespective of the nationality of the men in the Welsh regiments, and part of the money collected will go to help disabled men and those who return to find their occupations gone.

Mrs Lloyd George, president of the Flag Day committee, made a tour of the various depots. Shortly before 11 o'clock, accompanied by Miss Lloyd George, Lady (Owen) Philipps, the Hon. Violet Douglas-Pennant, and Mr G. A. Sawyer (the honorary organiser), she drove in a decorated motor-car from Downing-street to the Mansion House. Escorted by the Lord Mayor, and accompanied by Mr A. W. Hersee (the City organiser), the party proceeded to the Stock Exchange, where they were warmly welcomed and where a liberal collection was made.

A visit was next paid to the Baltic, where a list has been opened which exceeds £1,000. At Lloyd's, Mrs Lloyd George was presented with a cheque for £2,537. The list at the Coal Exchange is not yet closed, but an inkstand presented by Messrs. Mappin & Webb was sold by auction by the secretary and fetched 55 guineas.

At each of these business centres Mrs Lloyd George and the Lord Mayor made brief speeches. After the City visits Mrs Lloyd George and her party went to Finchley, where they were met by Mr Edward Duveen, honorary organizer for Hampstead, and received by a guard of honour consisting of girls in Welsh costume. A number of well-filled purses from the women of Hampstead were presented to Mrs Lloyd George by the Marchioness Townshend, Miss Duveen, Miss du Maurier, Miss Mildred Sawyer [daughter of G. A. Sawyer] and other ladies.

On the return to the City, a call was made at the Prudential Assurance Company's offices, where Mrs Lloyd George was received by the directors and given a cheque for 125 guineas, which will be supplemented by further sums collected by the staff. After luncheon with the Lord Mayor at the Mansion House the party resumed the tour, visiting the Corn Exchange where a cheque for 100 guineas awaited them, and Houndsditch, where Mr S. Britton, representing the Jewish community, presented Mrs Lloyd George with a casket containing Treasury notes. On leaving Houndsditch the Lord Mayor, Mrs Lloyd George, and the other members of the party drove to the Strand Theatre, where there was a matinée performance of *Cheating Cheaters*, at which Queen Alexandra was present.

The American play, *Cheating Cheaters*, was not about getting revenge on rogue charity funds, but of two neighbouring families of crooks trying to rob the other, unaware they shared the same profession.

As in previous years, there was little chance of avoiding a flag seller, a veritable roll call of society ladies, City worthies, peppered with stars of the stage and screen, at the leading shops and hotels strategically located to tap into the moneyed classes and the commuting workers, and not far from some refreshment and shelter.

'Ladies in waiting'

> Flag Day souvenirs were sold at a large number of depots, where the helpers in charge were as follows: Lady Rhondda, Bond Street; Lady Brade, Whitehall; Lady Stanley, Selfridges; Lady Cave, Buckingham Palace Road; the Lord Mayor, the Sheriffs, Mrs Wilkins and Mr A. W. Hersee, The Mansion House; Lady Cooper, the Guildhall; Alderman and Mrs Edward Moore, Bishopsgate; Lady Dallas, Leicester Square; Lady Lloyd Mostyn, Charing Cross; Lady Griffiths, Víctoria Street; Lady Armitage-Jones, St James; Countess de Montefiore, Strand Palace Hotel; Countess du Monceau, Russell Hotel; Lady Davison, Kensington; Lady Price, Prince's restaurant; Lady Milsom Rees, Savoy Hotel; Lady St Davids, Pall Mall; Lady Alexander, Mlle. Genée, and Miss Violet Loraine, Carlton, Ritz, and Piccadilly Hotels; Mrs Allington, Strand; Mrs Archdale, Trocadero and Criterion restaurants; Countess di Castelfalfi, Hyde Park Hotel; Miss Margaret Cooper, Piccadilly Hotel; Miss Irene Vanbrugh, Ritz Hotel; Lady Mannering, Claridge's Hotel; Miss Eva Moore, Berkeley Hotel; Mr Edward Duveen, Hampstead; and Mrs and Miss Ffoulkes-Jones, Mrs Lloyd William and Mrs Greenwood, Grosvenor Hotel.

The suffragette Helen Archdale, later editor of Lady (Margaret) Rhondda's *Time and Tide* magazine, was posted at two of the later favourite dining haunts of the suffrage and literary movement, Trocadero and Criterion.

The Times continued:

> About 4,500,000 national flags and standards were offered by the 10,000 women helpers at a penny apiece, and 500,000 silken banners at 3d. Buttons and bannerettes with portraits of the Prime Minister, picture

postcards of Welsh scenes, silk aeroplane flags, white metal leeks, gilt aeroplane brooches and daffodils were among the souvenirs of the day.[7]

The *Illustrated London News* noted the efficiency of the Flag Day's organiser, G. A. Sawyer, in keeping the costs down, the point Mrs Lloyd George had stressed in Liverpool.

> Mr Sawyer has just collected £15,500 for Mrs Lloyd George's fund for providing comforts for Welsh regiments. It is interesting to note that the organising expenses have been only a fraction over one per cent, and the cost of flags, boxes, trays, etc., amount to nine per cent, the total expenses thus being ten per cent, which is exceedingly satisfactory. Mr Sawyer's view is that all flag days should be, where possible, conducted on strictly honorary lines.[8]

Meanwhile, Swansea, having chosen the previous year to fundraise primarily for the Swansea boys, was now doing its bit for the new combined Welsh National Fund:

> WELSH FLAG DAY: How Swansea is Helping a Deserving Object: This is the National Flag Day in Swansea of the Welsh National Fund for the welfare of sailors and soldiers, the object of which is to assist where Government allowances are insufficient. Of this Fund, the Earl of Plymouth is president, Brigadier-General Sir Owen Thomas, vice-president, Mrs Lloyd George, chairman, and Messrs. W. White and Marlay Samson, K.C., Hon. secretaries.
>
> Swansea has received 50,000 1d. flags, 15,000 3d. ones, 2,000 metal leeks (sold at 6d. each), and 4,000 buttons at 6d. A supply of leeks and daffodils made by discharged soldiers, which arrived early, went like wildfire, and are now sold out.[9]

Eight Welsh battalions had been disbanded, but as the men were deployed elsewhere it would not interfere with the Fund's operations. The recent list of comforts included new bladders with footballs. For the previous year's Flag Day movement, under seven per cent of the £29,509 raised was spent on flags, cabinets, collecting boxes etc. Total Fund office expenses had risen, with two typists employed at the Chancery Lane offices (albeit less than one per cent of receipts) to be covered, unlike the free rent and staffing enjoyed at Downing Street.

To Llandudno

On 12 March, Mrs Lloyd George, William Lewis and the Hon. Violet Douglas-Pennant spoke at a large public meeting at Llandudno Town Hall, hosted by the Caernarfonshire branch of the Fund. The Premier's wife noted, after the typical 'very hearty reception', that 'it was a great pleasure to come to a nice quiet town like Llandudno from London, where there was the constant danger of the raids'. In 1940 it was Llandudno's location, beyond the range of German bombers, which prompted the move of tax offices to the town, still there today.

She reminded her listeners that the task for volunteers wouldn't end with the war:

> The Fund was going on to try to help the sailors and soldiers and their dependants after the war. There would be a lot for voluntary workers to do in this way without relieving the State of any of its obligations. Returned soldiers, who had left everything to fight for their country, would be helped to start again in civil life. There was nothing too much to do for the brave men who had been fighting and making it possible for the people at home to live in peace. (applause)

And just as she had told the Bangor Women's Patriotic Guild in May 1917 'to make hay while the sun shone' (see p.305) she urged her audience to raise the money now, despite charity fatigue:

> This was the time to collect the money, while the war was going on, for it was possible that when peace was declared people would not be so ready to give. For that reason the executive was now trying to get a big surplus with which to help the fighting men on their return.

After remarks by William Lewis, the Hon. Violet Douglas-Pennant continued on how the Fund would be filling the 'glaring gaps' not covered by the State, and look after the next generation:

> THE SONS AND DAUGHTERS OF HEROES: They had to think what they were going to do for the men when that great and glorious day came that comforts would be no longer needed. Their Fund was going to give a helping hand such as they could not expect the Government to do. It was going to fill the glaring gaps that were left by the Government departments. It was going to be the privilege of the fathers and mothers who had sent

out their sons now to work together so that their sons should feel that what they had fought for had not been in vain. They must not treat the 'boys' as if they were just crocks and wrecks. (Hear, Hear)

They had also to think of those that were left behind when the men did not come back. They had got to see to it that the children of those men had even a better education than if their fathers had lived. The sons and daughters of heroes must not be left to go behind because their fathers were not there to see to them. (applause)[10]

On 24 April, in Parliament, Pensions Minister John Hodge (successor to George Barnes) confirmed, in reply to a question by David Davies, that William Lewis had been appointed as pensions inspector for north Wales.[11] William Lewis may not have achieved his goal of a single fund for Wales, but would have a hand in its administration.

An Institutional Committee for Wales

The Pensions Ministry set up an overarching Institutional Committee to combine the various voluntary efforts in Wales to assist disabled soldiers and sailors, Mrs Lloyd George serving as the representative of the Welsh National Fund (the newly combined Troops Fund with that of Sir Owen). The committee would be chaired by Sir Arthur Griffith-Boscawen representing the Ministry, with six representatives nominated by the Joint Disablement Committee of South Wales and Monmouthshire, four from the North Wales Disablement Committee, and representatives for the British Red Cross Society, The Order of St John and Jerusalem, and for the medical service (Western Command).[12] Similar committees had been established for England and for Scotland.

A structure at least was in place for supporting the disabled.

On 24 June, Mrs Lloyd George attended the first meeting, held in Cardiff, of this new Institutional Committee for Wales.

> Mr Marlay Samson said there were probably in south Wales alone no fewer than 25,000 men who had been discharged from the services as disabled.
>
> The Chairman stated that the Order of St John was prepared to make a grant of £10,000 to the committee, and the Swansea Hospital Committee was prepared to erect an annexe for the treatment of disabled men. It was agreed to approve the Swansea scheme and to contribute.

Mr J. H. Davies, Aberystwyth, mentioned a scheme for the creation of a convalescent institution at Aberystwyth. He hoped to be able to inform the next meeting that arrangements had been made for the taking over of large premises with 100 bedrooms on the Marine Parade. The cost would be £16,500. Sir John Collie said the scheme was most admirable and a committee from south Wales was asked to report. A report was also received on a Wrexham scheme.[13]

This particular Aberystwyth project would not be realised.[14]

While in Cardiff, she and Sir Arthur Griffith-Boscawen attended the opening of the Inter-Allied Exhibition at Cardiff City Hall, opened by the Minister of Pensions, John Hodge. Exhibits by Belgium, France, Italy, Serbia, Canada and South Africa were on display. The exhibition presented 'remarkable evidence of what may be justly termed modern miracles that have been performed in repairing the ravages of warfare'. There was also a demonstration of re-education to suit the war-disabled.[15]

After the war Mrs Lloyd George would campaign at successive by-elections to get Sir Arthur (when becoming a Tory minister in Lloyd George's Coalition) back into Parliament.

Grant assessments

On 26 June, the Troops Fund reviewed their contribution to the new Welsh Institutional Committee, and decided to make grants not exceeding as a whole the grants from the British Red Cross committee and the Order of St John of Jerusalem, as long as they received definite proposals as to the purpose, and that an equivalent amount was provided by the Treasury.[16] This discipline would be adopted on 20 July by the new Institutional Committee, so that grants would comprise 'at least half from the Treasury, one quarter from the Institutional Committee and the remaining quarter from the Troops Fund'.[17]

The Troops Fund committee was meeting less frequently, the routine work being carried out by William Lewis, but in Mrs Lloyd George's holiday absence, on 30 July a special meeting was convened, chaired by the Treasurer, Sir Vincent Evans, with six members attending, to consider three appeals made to the Welsh Institutional Committee.

The Convalescent Hospital at Colwyn Bay had requested £400 for equipment, contributed *pro rata* by the Institutional Committee 'partners' on the formula in play – the Treasury paying 50 per cent, and the Institutional Committee, and the merged Troops Fund 25 per cent each. The grants were later withdrawn as the medical branch of the Ministry of Pensions had found the proposed premises unsuitable.

Two hundred and fifty pounds was granted to the Vale of Clwyd Rural Industries, Trefnant, the Pensions Ministry approved training facility in toy, furniture and basket making.

The formula for £7,500 for a hospital accommodation annexe for the Swansea General Hospital was a little different, with £3,500 from the Treasury, and £1,000 each from the Institutional Committee and the Troops Fund being supplemented with £2,000 from the town of Swansea.[18]

It being summertime, the same meeting approved a new supply of cricket equipment (two cricket bats, two balls, six stumps and two pairs of bails) to the 38th (Welsh) Division (as in June 1917). And two sets of boxing gloves.

47 Varieties of comfort

The minutes detailed the 47 varieties of comforts dispatched since the Fund's inception, including one collapsible cooker. Most numerous were, unsurprisingly, 803,515 cigarettes, 106,142 pairs of socks, 30,215 writing wallets, 30,020 packets of tobacco, 24,274 mittens and gloves, 20,548 shirts, and 20,675 handkerchiefs.[19]

Information from officers on leave suggested the need for garments would be limited over the coming winter, but 'things like gramophones, footballs and, if possible, luxuries such as cocoa and potted meats would be acceptable'. A letter was to be sent by the Secretary to each Welsh unit's Commanding Officer.

With fewer meetings, on 9 October an Emergency Committee was established, comprising the officers – the President, the Countess of Plymouth; the Chairman, Mrs Lloyd George; the Treasurer, Sir Vincent Evans; and the Hon. Secretary, William Lewis – and Lord Justice Bankes and Lady Owen Philipps.

Working with partners

At the October meeting, the Fund decided that the Swansea Hospital grant would only be paid when the other contributors, the Treasury, the Institutional Committee and Swansea town, had paid. Grants to

Caerderwen Hospital, Neath (£155), to Plas Darland, Wrexham (£200), Plas Acton Hostel, Wrexham (£125), and to Curative Workshops, Wrexham (£87.10.0) were approved conditional on the Treasury paying at least double the amount.

In the latter case the committee was 'by no means satisfied that they ought to be asked to contribute towards payment of rent, but as the amount in question was not large they agreed in this instance but were anxious that this should not be taken as forming a precedent'.

Consideration of a grant for a Cardiff Hostel was deferred, 'pending certain enquiries', it being felt that 'the City of Cardiff should not find it necessary to ask for aid from such a Fund as this'. Also deferred was an application for comforts for Christmas parcels from the Clapham Junction branch of the Women's Temperance Union.[20]

The Fund would not meet again in wartime, next convening in March 1919.

The Welsh Troops Children's Fund

Some comforts were provided until mid-1919, when the Versailles Peace Treaty was finally signed and the majority of troops had returned home. In March 1920, the bulk of the Troops Fund's monies were placed in a trust, The Welsh Troops Children's Fund, to benefit children, up to attaining the age of 21, with one or both parents Welsh or resident in Wales, and one or both who had served in the war in any capacity. The trustees were given a relatively wide remit to assist on education and apprenticeship, clothing suitable for employment, medical aid and travel expenses. The nine trustees included Mrs Lloyd George, Lady Owen Philipps, Marlay Samson, Mrs Hopkinson, Sir Vincent Evans, and William Lewis. At least three were always to be from north Wales, south Wales or Welsh people residing outside Wales. The balance of six men and three women was not to be changed.[21]

As the country turned its mind toward reconstruction, turning swords into ploughshares, munitions factories back to peaceful manufacturing, guns back to butter, children would be important. Not surprisingly, diarist Samuell Pepys Junior uncovered one particular opportunity revealed in a conversation:

> He tells me they have a mighty fine design of making children's pramms in lieu of ayre planes, with good assurance of profit in it by the great number of warr marryings. Moreover, a certain friend of his, who stands

to be choasen with Ll. George's ticket, will move the new house that they grant 100*l*. for every child that is born, being our first need in the reconstructing, to have more babies; and of every such 100*l*. he do reckon 10 ginnys secured to their company for a pramm.[22]

Planes into prams, me thinks…

William Lewis returns to shipping

On 19 December 1919, Mrs Lloyd George and the committee members presented William Lewis with a canteen of cutlery as a token of their thanks for all his work.[23] He returned to shipping after the war, where he continued a successful career, living in London, becoming chairman and general manager of the Pacific Steam Navigation Company, serving on several boards, and a member of the Court and Council of the University of Wales. His *Times* obituary in 1934 noted that he was 'a prominent figure in the British shipping world, where he was greatly respected and was regarded as a very able businessman as well as a very kindly one'.[24]

RECRUITMENT, SAILORS, FOOD & ECONOMY, HOSPITALS & HEALTHCARE, TEMPERANCE & WARTIME SOBRIETY

CHAPTER 20

Recruitment
(1914 to 1916)

'If the country found it necessary to go in for conscription, she would not like to be one of those young men who had waited to enlist.'
Margaret Lloyd George, June 1915

IN ADDITION TO providing comforts for the country's soldiers and sailors, Mrs Lloyd George actively supported the recruitment drive, in particular raising the new Welsh Army – an ambition pursued by Lloyd George, and raised by Brigadier Owen Thomas, himself an Anglesey farmer. The Nonconformist chapels were, in the main, encouraging men to join up for this 'just' war. But there was also passionate opposition to war. It was a division, especially within Liberal ranks, that would come to a head when reliance on volunteers – 'Your Country Needs YOU!' – was supplanted with conscription in 1916.

Her recruitment efforts were not confined to the Army, but also encouraging women to grasp new opportunities and make their contribution, whether in nursing (at home or at the Front), working on the land, in factories and in as many other professions as possible. The increase in the number of women working outside the traditional sphere of the home not only helped win the war but strengthened, by example, the case for allowing equal opportunities for women in all walks of life.

Recruiting an Army
The war would unite the country, rousing people into action, but it would also divide them, not least with respect to conscription to the

Forces. While Mrs Lloyd George's support of welfare organisations was wholly in character, her support for a show of gunboats (see p.30) and recruitment campaigning might seem surprising. However, unlike the Boer War (which Lloyd George had strongly opposed, as an Imperial war), this new conflict was more broadly accepted, and presented, as a 'just war'. One Nonconformist in the vanguard was the Calvinistic Methodist, the Rev. T. C. Williams from Menai Bridge, referred to by Richard Lloyd George as 'one of my mother's dearest friends' for whom 'Brynawelon was a second home.'[1]

Gwyn Jenkins argues, in his recent analysis of wartime Ceredigion, a county previously 'believed by many to be imbued with the spirit of peacemaking, rooted in firm Nonconformist religious beliefs', that:

> The perceived threat from an expansionist Germany, coupled with the glorification of the British Empire, not least in schools, led to this growing militaristic spirit and, with it, expectation of war. This spirit was largely centred in the urban areas of the county and among the local gentry, as was the case in most parts of Britain. It was not necessarily a spirit which welcomed warfare as a means of settling disputes, but was rather rooted in a belief that it was necessary to be prepared to defend one's country, community and family. Such approval of military defence allowed even those who might have been expected to disapprove of warfare to embrace the armed forces as a necessary response to perceived threats.[2]

In south Wales the anti-war movement was stronger among the mining community and where the Labour Party was more dominant.

SEPTEMBER 1914

In September, Margaret Lloyd George, the chapel-going welfare campaigner, was in full support of recruitment.

> Last Friday evening, at the Pwllheli Town Hall, a rousing meeting in support of the recruiting movement was held. The Rev. E. W. Evans, Nevin, presided. After a speech by the Rev. John Williams, Brynsiencyn, Mrs Lloyd George spoke: she was glad the Welsh people were not deaf to their country's call, and hoped that recruits from Wales would be further augmented. Nobody knew better than Welshmen how to fight for

freedom, and it behoved them to do their utmost to assist England and the Empire in its noble task of preserving the integrity of a small and weak nation like Belgium. In championing the cause of the weak, Providence would see to it that not only the nation would be saved, but her complete victory over her enemies be assured. (applause)[3]

The Rev. John Williams, Brynsiencyn, criticised for wearing full army uniform in the pulpit, earned himself the sobriquet of 'David Lloyd George's chaplain'.

After more speeches several young men volunteered with the Territorials. While Mrs Lloyd George was already recruiting, her husband had yet to speak publicly on his support for the war, having been a staunch opponent of the Boer War. Just over a week later, on 19 September, Lloyd George made a notable speech at the Queen's Hall, London, firmly backing the war. At ostensibly a recruitment event for Kitchener's army, Lloyd George called for a Welsh Army to be raised, with an eye to the Welshmen of London and beyond.[4] Ten days later he followed up in Cardiff:

> 'I should like to see a Welsh Army in the field.' This simple sentence in Mr Lloyd George's memorable speech at the Queen's Hall, London, 10 days ago, had its sequel in Cardiff this afternoon, when machinery for raising a Welsh Army Corps of 50,000 men was set in motion by the Chancellor of the Exchequer himself, with the approval of Lord Kitchener.[5]

Kitchener was opposed to armies being set up outside the formal armies, but gave in after a major dispute with Lloyd George. Eventually, the 'Welsh Army' amounted to a single battalion, the 38th Welsh Division, of some 18,500 men, in addition to the existing three Welsh regiments, the Royal Welch Fusiliers, the South Wales Borderers and the Welsh Regiment (to which many recruits would be attached). The Welsh Guards were later created in February 1915, becoming the fifth regiment of footguards (joining the Grenadier, Coldstream, Scots and Irish Guards) – and recruited from those regiments.[6] On 12 September, Gwilym Lloyd George was commissioned a lieutenant in the Royal Welch Fusiliers, and in February became the aide-de-camp to Major-General Ivor Philipps, the Commanding Officer of the 38th. In 1916, Gwilym transferred to the Royal Garrison Artillery. Also on the 12th, his elder brother and engineer, Richard, joined the Royal

Welch Fusiliers and was commissioned into the Royal Engineers in September 1916. (illustration 50)

OCTOBER 1914

Lloyd George joined his wife and daughter Megan at a Cricieth recruitment meeting on 1 October. *The Cambrian News* captured the prevailing mood.

> SURPRISE VISIT. Mr Lloyd George, accompanied by Mrs Lloyd George and Miss Megan Lloyd George, arrived unexpectedly in Cricieth on Thursday night by motor car and, hearing of a recruiting meeting at the Town Hall, immediately repaired thither. The building was packed, and the door was closed and guarded by a police constable on the inside. Hearing a rap at the door the constable urged the knocker to try the back door, as it was hopeless to try to get in through the front door. Thrice Mr Lloyd George knocked and thrice he was told to try the back door. Then the constable, hearing a shout of 'Lloyd George' from the crowd outside, opened the door, and Mr Lloyd George entered, to the astonishment of the meeting, including Mr Lloyd George's brother, Mr William George.
>
> A speech by Mr Lloyd George was insisted on, and, speaking in Welsh, he referred to the difficulty he experienced in gaining access to the meeting, remarking that it was like trying to pass a sentry at the Front. (Much laughter) The meeting was presided over by Mr O. T. Williams, J.P., chairman of Cricieth Council, and the speakers included the Rev. John Williams, Brynsiencyn, Sir Henry Lewis, and Colonel Owen Thomas.
>
> A speech was also given by Sergeant Williams, Carnarvon, a native of Pwllheli, who fought in Mons and who is invalided home. Sergeant Williams, 'who returns to the Front on Monday said he retained his nerve in Mons, but to speak with the Chancellor there in front of him quite unnerved him.' (Laughter) The sergeant, however, made a good speech as well as a good impression on the audience.
>
> Mr Lloyd George, who was received with a perfect storm of cheers, proposed a vote of thanks to the speakers. He said he came there not to make a speech, but to make common cause with his neighbours in the great fight. Proceeding, he said: 'I had looked forward, after a weary time, to come among you in August and early September to enjoy the peacefulness and calm of the mountains, the hills, and the sea breezes, when suddenly war of nations was upon us. One day, if you looked east,

everything was as clear as the dawn; not a cloud anywhere, but in an instant, as it were, all was changed, and bloodshed, burning of homes, killing of innocent people, and devastation everywhere. I am not ashamed to say we never entertained such evil thoughts of the people who are now at war against us.'

And after relating a recent meeting with the Belgian Chancellor, Lloyd George continued:

You will be surprised to be told that for every Belgian soldier lost on the field of battle, three unoffending, innocent people have been ruthlessly killed in that country. It is evident that the whole German scheme was to rush Belgium in order to crush France before returning to attack Russia.

I am not one of those who are in favour of war. I have stood on this platform to protest against war, as you know, and if I believed now that this was not a just war it was my duty to say so. I am, however, perfectly convinced that this is a righteous war. It is a great burden to keep up a large army and a large navy; but the time has come for us to have a large army as well as a large navy. At the start we had 200,000 men in the field. We never had so many men in a foreign war, but we shall have a million before long on the Continent of Europe. (Cheers) It took fifteen years to break Napoleon. I do not think it will take anything like as long as that to vanquish the Kaiser; but, long or short, England is going to see it through. In recruiting, Scotland came first in numbers, England second, and Wales third. At Cardiff there was to be a conference to start a Welsh army. One county alone would furnish 20,000, and the adjoining county already had promised 8,000. If Carnarvonshire would do its share there should be 3,000 soldiers from it to make up Kitchener's army, and if there was one man less it would be a shame to Eryri. (Loud cheers)[7]

In 2022, Eryri was adopted as the official name for Snowdonia.

Colonel Owen Thomas was promoted to Brigadier General and took responsibility for training the new Welsh Army Corps. In 1918, the fund he established to support the soldiers would be merged with Mrs Lloyd George's Troops Fund. In December 1918, he surprisingly won the Anglesey Parliamentary seat for the Independent Labour Party, defeating the long-serving Liberal MP and Lloyd George ally, Sir Ellis Ellis-Griffith.

Recruitment remained 'voluntary' until conscription was imposed in early 1916, the war well into its second year of carnage.

Northampton

On Sunday, 15 November, Mrs Lloyd George and the Chancellor visited their son Gwilym in Northampton, billeted there with the new Welsh recruits undergoing training.

> The Chancellor was recognised by a large number of people. On Black Hill an individual in whom the war has not killed personal animosity to the Chancellor, said within his hearing, 'That's the bloke that's put a penny on our beer.'[8]

Mrs Lloyd George returned on the Wednesday:

WELSH NIGHT AT THE TOWN HALL: Mrs Lloyd George, the wife of the Chancellor of the Exchequer, who was accompanied by the Right Hon. Herbert Lewis, M.P. (Parliamentary Secretary to the Local Government Board) and Mrs Lewis and Mrs Tom Ellis, the widow of a late Liberal Whip, visited Northampton on Wednesday evening.

Mrs Lloyd George opened the new winter equipment for the troops, erected on the Racecourse by the YMCA. The tent, a large one, will be a splendid club for the troops in the coming cold weather. It is strongly built of wood, lighted with oil lamps, and heated with stoves. Here the men will be able to sit and smoke and read, there are postal arrangements, concerts held, and services on Sunday. Many a man will be glad of such a place of rest in the next few weeks after long hours of arduous training.

Mrs Lloyd George also addressed the troops at a concert in the Town Hall. There was not an inch of standing room left when Mr Lewis opened the proceedings with a brief speech in Welsh, and called on Mr David Ellis, one of the Welsh party who gave the concert, to sing 'God Bless the Prince of Wales', in the native tongue.

Mrs Lloyd George then made her brief speech, first in Welsh and then, for the sake of the 'foreigners' in English. 'I have been telling the Welsh boys,' she said, 'that I am very much afraid Northampton people are spoiling them. You are very, very kind to them. That is what we all hear in Wales. Many mothers have told me that they hope their sons will stay in Northampton, the people are very, very kind. Wales is a nation which has very great traditions, and has given many brave soldiers to the Empire.

I am quite sure they will uphold those great traditions, that they will be brave and courageous wherever they go.'[9]

The late Tom Ellis MP was the founder of *Cymru Fydd*, the campaign for Welsh Home Rule, and was succeeded by Lloyd George and Herbert Lewis when he stepped down.

She also urged them to remember the advice of 'that great soldier Roberts', and keep away from drink. Field Marshal Lord Roberts, one of the most successful military commanders of his time, was a temperance campaigner, not least as a means of improving discipline among his men. He had died four days earlier, of pneumonia, aged 82, visiting Indian troops in France. His state funeral would follow the next day, Thursday, 19 November.

Not everything went smoothly in Northampton for the Welsh recruits, many of whom had been given leave to go home and then were suddenly recalled:

> The men were much upset by their sudden recall on the way home and wondered at the cause. On the previous Saturday all the horses had been handed over to the authorities, but were fetched back. It was understood that the Battery was to hold itself in readiness to move off if called upon.
>
> On Wednesday last week there was more excitement. As the men fell in after dinner, the order was given that the Battery was to move off at four that afternoon. The men were dismissed and ordered to pack their kits, leaving them at their billets, and taking only a shirt with them. Kits were at once got ready, and the Battery was mounted in full marching order a good half-hour before the specified time.
>
> At a little after four the Brigade moved off for, as they thought, a lively time. They left the Racecourse at one end and marched round to go through Northampton, when the order was given to return to the lines through another entrance. It was then realised that it was, after all, only a false alarm. The horses were unharnessed, watered and fed, and the men returned to their billets hardly knowing whether to enjoy the joke or not.[10]

Training to be able to move at a moment's notice when the time came?

A local perspective on the visiting Welshmen (aside from the gentleman complaining about the penny on his pint) was written later by a Northampton soldier, Frederick James Hodges, who joined up in 1918 and fought in the Battle of the Somme:

> All Over by Christmas
>
> When the Great War commenced, in August 1914, I was a schoolboy aged fifteen at the local Grammar School. Suddenly the town was full of soldiers – the Welsh Division arrived by rail and were billeted in the homes of the local inhabitants. At my home, we had two who shared a bed and had their meals with the family.
>
> On the racecourse, near my home, there was tremendous military activity and we Grammar School boys, on summer holiday, spent all our time there. There were huge ration dumps in and around large marquee tents; large heaps of freshly baked loaves; whole cheeses, and the carcasses of animals were being cut up on trestle tables erected on the grass near the tennis courts. Most of the soldiers wore their smart blue dress uniform; only a few had khaki. They were Territorials, popularly known as 'Saturday Afternoon Soldiers', who went to camp annually for a week.
>
> All along the St Georges Avenue border of the racecourse, drinking troughs were set up with water from the mains for the hundreds of horses and mules. Wooden stables were erected on the football pitches; army farriers were shoeing horses; mules were being broken in, and bugle calls and trumpet calls became a familiar sound from Reveille to Lights Out. Long columns of men, wagons, and guns began to move through the town, often holding up all the traffic and giving the civilians a legitimate excuse for being late for work. Young Welsh soldiers began courting Northampton girls and some eventually married and settled in the town after the war was over. One of them, named Williams, became Mayor of the Borough.
>
> No one had the least idea what was really involved in Britain being at war with Germany, and the prevailing mood was often expressed by the phrase 'It will be all over by Christmas'.[11]

The 20-year-old Newport-born future Northampton Mayor, Percival Williams, didn't have to go far to get his girl, being billeted at the Angel Inn, where his future wife, Phyllis Tonsley, then just 17, lived with her widowed mother, the proprietress. They married in 1919, later ran the hotel and became Mayor and Mayoress in 1946. Her father had been Mayor in 1898.[12]

Racing had ceased on the racecourse in 1904, and when the troops left in 1917, leaving the ground well and truly churned over, the area was divided into wartime allotments.

For Northampton it was 'all over before Christmas', in that the Welsh troops all departed on 20 December.[13]

FEBRUARY 1915

Recruiting the Welsh Army

In early February, Mrs Lloyd George spelt out, for the *Daily Chronicle*, the Welsh Army recruitment plan, its success so far, and lauding the history of the Welsh regiments. The Troops Fund had adopted the same 'chain of command' throughout Wales. The *Llangollen Advertiser* reported:

> 'In the first two months of the war,' Mrs Lloyd George says, 'Wales sent 40,000 men into the army. That in itself is a whole corps, but, toward the end of September, a small provisional committee summoned to Cardiff the wonderful business conference of peers and working men, soldiers and civilians, Churchmen and Nonconformist, who came to the conclusion that Wales ought to start afresh and raise a new army corps of her own.
>
> 'It was in this way that our national executive recruiting committee came into being, and I should think that such a committee was something unique in the way of committees. Its purpose was nothing short of carrying through for the Welsh counties the arrangements for raising, organising, feeding and clothing their country's little Army, the expense being borne by the War Office, to whom, when completed, the corps was to be handed over for higher training.'
>
> CIRCULARIZED COUNTIES
> 'The way in which the Welsh national committee went about the affair was simple. They circularised the Lord Lieutenants of all the counties, asking each of them to form three local committees of their own. The duty of the first committee was to get the men; of the second to arrange and prepare accommodation for them; of the third to supply each recruit with one pair of boots, a greatcoat, two flannel shirts, two pairs of socks, one towel, one piece of soap and one knife, fork and spoon. The aim of the county recruiting committee was to raise three army divisions, each

made up of 12 battalions of infantry, two field and one signal company of Royal Engineers, three field ambulances of the Royal Army Medical Corps, and one divisional train and one reserve park of the Army Service Corps. Accordingly, as they came from north Wales, mid Wales or south Wales, the new infantry recruits have, where possible, been formed into fresh battalions of the Royal Welch Fusiliers, the Welsh Regiment, or the South Wales Borderers, names which must have done much to attract their latest members.'

REGIMENT 200 YEARS
'Of the three, the youngest is the Welsh Regiment of mid Wales, which is now close upon two centuries old. It took part in the Afghan War, and it fought at Alma, Inkerman, and through the siege of Sebastopol. Both the South Wales Borderers and the Royal Welch Fusiliers were raised in March 1689, and both of them, curiously, won fame in Flanders at the very beginning of their history. The Borderers served through the first siege of Namur in 1695, and from then, down to the splendid heroism of Rorke's Drift, it has brought greater and greater renown to Wales.

'I need say nothing of the Royal Welch Fusiliers, all over the world, beyond recalling the fact that their first fighting was also in Flanders and that, besides Namur, Lille and Douai are places in the present war where the Fusiliers long ago won renown.'[14]

She closed her article with an appeal for comforts. In this war Namur, in Belgium, had fallen in the first three weeks.

Captain Richard's light and dark messages

Her son Captain Richard Lloyd George added a lighter twist to the recruiting process, speaking at the Llandudno Town Hall to the Tabernacle Welsh Baptist Church:

… his father was a Baptist and his mother was a Methodist which, as far as he could understand it, was why he happened to be a Baptist himself. (Laughter) A little while ago it appeared that there were more Baptists among the soldiers in Llandudno than men of any other denomination. When he told that to his mother she tried to explain it by saying that the Methodists had all joined before the Welsh Army was formed. (Laughter)

But then he acknowledged the gravity of the challenge:

Turning to the more serious side of the situation, he said he was one of those who thought that the dark days, the real dark days, of the war had yet to come. It might be a pessimistic sentiment, but he was convinced that the clouds were only just beginning to gather.

'One got a very wrong impression in this country. We saw recruits pouring in, and men training and drilling in every town of any size, and we naturally thought that Germany could not possibly stand up against it all. Here was one fact against that. Germany was one of the strictest countries in Europe in the matter of conscription, and picked out the very best men to form the conscript army. When the war broke out, from the men who were not liable for military service in Germany, the army enrolled two million volunteers, two million men who joined of their own free will to fight in a war of aggression. He did not want to frighten the civilian part of the audience; if he did they might have a nightmare, and they would be having reports again in the brigade office in the morning that there had been aeroplanes in Llandudno. (Laughter)

'But they should look the facts in the face. The more social gatherings they had', he said, 'the better it would be for them. The Germans were great believers in singing. In some places where the trenches were very close, our men could hear the Germans trying to learn the British songs. On a dark wet night, when everything was fairly quiet, the British could hear garbled versions of "Tipperary" and "Who is your lady friend?" and other songs floating across. (Laughter) When he was in the ranks he used to look forward to a sing-song in the evening, when they could forget the fatigues of the day and what the colonel had told them. (Laughter) If they enjoyed themselves at entertainments such as that and determined to forget their troubles and tribulations, they would be better men and better women and better soldiers if there should be any set backs or disasters.' (Applause)[15]

At the 1917 Aberystwyth Eisteddfod, his father would defend wartime singing in one of his most notable, impassioned, speeches.

St David's Day, Llandudno

On St David's Day, while some sold flags in Wales and in London, Mrs Lloyd George accompanied her husband, reviewing the Welsh Army in

Llandudno. A bitterly cold day, she predictably caught a cold. However Llandudno might have been safer than London, which had snow and a serious flu outbreak that month. (illustration 5)

The seaside town rolled out its red carpet:

> The Llandudno Urban District have unanimously decided to present to Mr Lloyd George an address of welcome and of appreciation of his services to Wales and to the Empire since the war began. The address will be in Welsh and English, and in the form of an album, containing, in addition to the text of the address and the signatures of the members of the Council, some ten photographs of the town and district which were taken towards the end of last season. A gold and enamel brooch will be presented to Mrs Lloyd George, representing the regimental badge of the Royal Welch Fusiliers.[16]

An 'address' would customarily be a verbal tribute, accompanied by a written version, often handsomely illustrated, and bound.

The Lloyd Georges also attended a special joint Nonconformist service held at the Llandudno Pier Pavilion, where on St David's Day Mrs Lloyd George presided at an eisteddfod.[17]

In London, on St David's Day, very appropriately, the Welsh Guards mounted the guard at Buckingham Palace for the first time, three days after their formation. A week later the Troops Fund agreed to supply a rugby football to the Welsh Guards (exercise and recreation being important).

Great Thoughts

She added some humour to the recruitment campaign in the publication *Great Thoughts – A Weekly Paper for People Who Think*:

> Speaking of Welsh women and the war, the wife of the Chancellor says: 'The treatment of Belgium by the Germans has roused the Welsh women indeed. Then, too, they are not now afraid of being left a burden to others or the parish as they were at the start of the war. The Government's generous arrangements have freed them from that fear. In some villages I know, where men at first hung back after the women saw what good money came regularly to the families of the few who had gone, when they grasped that the wives and children left behind were actually better off, financially, than themselves whose men-folk were still working at home,

these women soon began – it makes me laugh to think of it, but people do like such a good joke! – these women soon began to urge their own husbands and sons to join the Forces too! And to-day there is hardly a man left in those villages who could possibly be accepted as a soldier, sailor, or combatant of some kind!'[18]

Recruitment at Greenway

In stark contrast to the garden parties of the last hot summer of peace, the largest event on Mrs Lloyd George's June 1915 calendar was 'the Great Patriotic Meeting' at Greenway Manor, Radnorshire, on Friday, 18 June. The message was that men should enlist, that conscription was not a preferred policy, but would come if needed. People and communities, not surprisingly, were often divided on the issue of whether those able to fight should volunteer. By now losses at the Front and a dwindling number of eligible young men signing up meant some form of compulsion was imminent.

From the many speeches, two are reproduced here. First, Mrs Lloyd George, after stressing the clear difference between this conflict and the Boer War, left her audience in no doubt about German cruelty, called on the youth of Wales to sign up, the men for the army, the women to come to work with, she suggested, the prospect of equal pay. This may have been her final appearance on an army recruitment platform.

In a longer address, William Lewis, the county's Liberal candidate for Parliament, and Troops Fund Secretary, delivered a hard-hitting 'call to arms', stressing the 'justness' of the war and the duty of the people towards the State.

The *Western Mail* headlined its report 'Day of Conscription: Mrs Lloyd George's advice to the Youth of Wales':

> A meeting under the auspices of the Central Committee for National Patriotic Organisations was held in the grounds of Greenway Manor, Penybont, Radnorshire, by permission of Mr J. L. Greenway, J.P., when stirring patriotic addresses were delivered. The grounds had been decorated with the flags of the allies, and there was a great muster of people from the surrounding districts.
>
> The chair was occupied by Sir Powlett Milbank, Bart (Lord-Lieutenant of the county), supported on the platform by Mrs Lloyd George, Colonel Venables Llewelyn (Commanding Officer of the Glamorgan Yeomanry),

Mrs Venables Llewelyn, Mr William Lewis (London), Mr J. L. Greenway, J.P., and others.

The Chairman said he found upon looking through the recruiting returns that 60 per cent of the men who had enlisted in that county were married men. That was not right, and it was the duty of every unmarried man to go first. They had Mrs Lloyd George with them that afternoon, and he knew that no name would appeal to Welshmen more than the name Lloyd George. His name also appealed to Great Britain and the Empire. If there was a man able to get munitions in the country it was Mr Lloyd George, who was already getting them. (Applause)[19]

The Brecon and Radnor Express continued:

Mrs Lloyd George (who was cordially received) moved, 'That this meeting of men and women pledges itself to do its utmost to bring the war to a victorious end.' She said she felt very shy and frightened to stand before such a large audience. She was very terrified when she saw her name in big letters on the poster calling the meeting. She felt sure that it must be her husband that was coming down and not her. (Laughter) She was no speaker, but had simply come there to try and induce the young women of this county to take up work which would relieve young men so that they could go and join the colours. (Cheers)

There were still a large number of men of military age in Wales who had not enlisted. Wales had done remarkably well. They had done better than any other part of the country in proportion to their population. (Cheers) They were proud to think that their country had done well, but they could still do better.

She was told that at the fairs and markets in Wales there were a great number of men of military age who had not enlisted. Officers had gone round to try and induce them to enlist, and the reply had been that they would come when they were fetched. They were waiting for conscription. They were proud of their voluntary system. (Cheers) But, if the country found it necessary to go in for conscription, she would not like to be one of those young men who had waited to enlist. (Cheers)

She had been told that some parents were keeping their sons from enlisting. She wondered whether that was true. She wondered whether they, in the country districts, realised what a terrible war this was. They were providentially protected by the sea, and they had not got the enemy on their soil, as they had on the Continent. And, perhaps, that made some more or less indifferent. True, they had had a few bombs here and there to wake them up a bit, but they saw nothing of the horrors of war.

Some thought it was not much more than the Boer War. But they were using more ammunition in a few days in this war than was used all through the Boer War. The Germans were out to rule the world, and they ought to realise that as soon as they possibly could, and every man ought to do his best to fight this wild beast let loose in Europe.

The Germans were not fighting fair. They did not confine their fighting to the use of guns, rifles, bayonets, &c. They were using poisons against their brave soldiers, and she thought they should turn upon the Germans with the same weapons as they had used against the British, the French and the Russians. (Cheers) They must turn the Germans out of the fair country they had devastated.

Some of them were, at first, very reluctant to believe some of the stories of atrocities. They hoped they were not true. They could indulge that hope no longer. There was a report made public now which was conclusive of the German guilt. Eight people of sound judgement and experience had taken evidence from about 1,000 people, and had examined papers and diaries left about by the German soldiers, and they had come to the conclusion that there had never been such cruelty in war for 300 years. The Germans had gone back to the Dark Ages, and, sad to say, these were the deeds of a so-called civilised country.

She then called on the young women to join the workforce.

Being face to face with this great need, they wanted young women to be willing to relieve young men. In the towns the young women had taken up work as ticket collectors, tram conductors, lift attendants, &c. She had seen pictures of girls working in the hay-field. No work could be more clean or healthy. No dainty girl would soil her dress or her hands in hay-making, and she hoped that, wherever farmers were short of labour, women would be only too glad to go to help them. Gardening was also very congenial work for women, and she was glad to see that this was being taken up. Women were also going to do other farm work. In Continental countries they often saw women working on the fields in times of peace, and in wartime they had to rely on them almost altogether to till the ground and garner the harvests. The clerks on the Great Western Railway had stated that they would be willing this year to give up their fortnight's holiday to help farmers. She thought that was very noble of them. (Hear, hear) She was glad the Board of Trade was helping in some of these directions, and that it was intended to give the women the same wages as men.

More technical training, less piano-playing:

> She was glad, too, that instruction was to be given to prepare young women for technical work. They wanted more of such instruction, and less of piano-playing and some other things. (Hear, hear) The summer holidays were approaching, and they were hoping that the teachers and elder pupils would be ready to co-operate, so far as they could, in the great struggle which was going on.
>
> There was a great need for sand-bags to protect their soldiers in the trenches. They had not had enough. A great number of women were employed in making these sand-bags, and their soldiers, with the larger supply they now had, felt more safe than they had done before. This demand for sand-bags would last as long as the war lasted. They also wanted respirators to protect the soldiers from the horrible German gases. She felt sure that they were all prepared to do all that they could to help their brave soldiers who were fighting for their country. (Cheers)[20]

The address of William Lewis

William Lewis, another Calvinistic Methodist from north Wales, and Liberal candidate, delivered a patriotic call to arms. After a few minutes honouring those on the platform (including highlighting Mrs Lloyd George's many campaigns) he spelt out the 'justness' of the war, and the obligation to join the Forces, without pulling any punches:

> At meetings in Radnorshire I addressed prior to the war, I dwelt upon what I considered, rightly or wrongly, to be the duty of the State to the people. Surely, an obligation is placed upon me now to emphasise the duty of the people to the State. (Hear, hear) Individual rights no longer exist, universal responsibility takes their place. This meeting is asked to pledge itself, that is to say, each individual present pledges himself or herself to do everything in his or her power to assist the Government – the National Government of the day – to bring the war to a speedy and victorious end.
>
> What does this mean? In the words of the Prime Minister, delivered in the House of Commons on Tuesday night, 'We have each and all of us to respond with whatever we have, with whatever we can give, with whatever

we can sacrifice.' These are not idle words to adorn a peroration. They are words full of grim truth, and I have no doubt that, once this is realised, Radnorshire will not be behind any part of the country in its response. The appeal that is now being made is to patriotism, aye, and to something greater even than patriotism. It is an appeal even to the conscience, and it is this that I would desire to emphasise in the few words I have to say.

...

It is unnecessary for me to dwell upon the origin of the war. Let this fact speak for itself. In previous wars we have not been an united people. During the Crimean and South African wars there was a strong minority that believed we were in the wrong. To-day, on the other hand, for the first time in the modern history of Britain, we find all differences of opinion obliterated, all classes and creeds united in a grave determination to carry to a successful issue the challenge that has been forced upon us (cheers) and the resolution to which I am speaking is to bind you and to bind me to convert the determination into action.

This, then, Mr Chairman, is our starting point. The war, so far as Britain is concerned, is a just war, and, to the extent that anything spiritual belongs to war, it is surely a noble thing to find the nation prepared to sacrifice itself, without counting the cost, in the defence of honour, of justice and of right.

Whom are we fighting? Here, again, there can be no difference of opinion. We are fighting an enemy intoxicated with the lust of power, a people without moral restraint, advocates of the gospel of force, scoffers of the gospel of love, a nation without scruple, without faith, without pity, and without soul. Can any man or woman remain indifferent at the bare possibility of such a race becoming predominant among the nations of the earth?

If, then, our cause is a just one, if our enemies be such as I have endeavoured to describe, what have we got to do? First and foremost, we have each one of us to acquire the moral courage to do what is right. We have to do what is right by our Motherland, we have to learn the value of sacrifice, and we have to defend the faith in which we have been nurtured. We have in this country entered into and possessed the fair inheritance of freedom. It came to us through the sacrifices of the few for the sake of the many in the past. The fate of coming generations of Britons is in our keeping to-day. Will they say of us in the days to come, 'They fought the good fight. They kept the faith.' (Cheers) Remember this, the State can compel each of us to do his part. It will be to our

Recruitment

eternal disgrace if in the hour of trial, in the time of stress, we refused to do it voluntarily.

I am told that young men have said that they will not go until they are fetched. All I have to say, if this be true, is that they are not worth fetching. (Cheers) It would soil a soldier's uniform to put on such a man. (Cheers) If there be any young man who has realised the diabolical methods of warfare adopted by the Germans, who has been told how innocent civilians have been butchered, how women have suffered that which is worse than death, how children have been tortured, who has read of the deliberate murder of men, women and children by the sinking of the *Lusitania* without feeling his whole soul stirred, and every nerve and sinew in his body braced with a holy determination to do his part to put an end to such atrocities, to protect the weak against the strong, to stand for righteousness, justice and truth – if there be such a man willing to let others suffer so that he may be safe, I tell him that he is a coward – unworthy of the traditions of his race. (Cheers) Every young man in Radnorshire has heard his country's call. Seven hundred have responded, and an equal number, it is said, have for some reason or other turned a deaf ear. I am not here to condemn, but to endeavour to persuade. I do not believe that the young men of Radnor are cowards, and I am sure, sir, that you, with your long and fuller knowledge of them, will confirm this.

Why, then, do they hold back? Nearly three million men have joined the Army and Navy since August last. Each one has left his home, whether it be Buckingham Palace or the peasant's cottage, each one has relinquished farm, or shop, or factory, or bank, or office, or school, or university, each one has willingly gone and laid his life upon the altar of his country, each one has learnt the great lesson, possibly without knowing it, that the spirit of sacrifice is an indispensable constituent in the life-blood of a nation – without it the nation becomes anaemic and decadent, with it the nation is virile and strong. These men have gone, but I doubt not that almost every one of them could have found some excuse had he wished for remaining at home. It was because they did not do this that we are able to meet to-night at Greenway Manor. I exhort every young man to ask himself earnestly and seriously this question: 'What is my duty? What ought I to do?'

Let him do this, let him listen to the reply of his conscience, and let him act accordingly, and the complaints regarding the response of the men in rural districts will soon cease.

I am told that there are mothers who are preventing their sons from playing the men's part. I wish to speak very tenderly of a mother's love for her offspring, but I do think that the mother who is willing to see other mothers bereaved and other homes desolated, so that her own home may be kept inviolate, has not yet learned the noblest function of motherhood if she stands in the way of her sons participating in the sacrifice that should be the lot of all.

It has been said that the man who can make two blades of grass grow where one grew before is a public benefactor. However true these words were in the past, they are doubly true to-day. The farmers have here their opportunity to serve their country, and, by diligence, labour and intelligence to make the best use of their land in order to ensure a sufficiency of food-stuffs, so that famine and want may not visit our beloved country. A call has gone forth from the Government for the exercise of the strictest economy and thrift by one and all, high and low, rich and poor, and I doubt not this call will be obeyed.

In some counties a census has been taken of every man, woman and child, with a view of ascertaining what service each can render. You may, sir, find it possible to see that this is done in Radnor. In conclusion, let this resolution, which will doubtless be passed here to-day, be in the nature of a binding obligation upon each of us. We belong to a race of noble traditions, a race that has never submitted its neck to a foreign yoke, that has kept its shores inviolate, that has never failed to do its duty, and that has ever been ready to defend the right. All that is asked of us is that we in our day prove ourselves worthy of these traditions and of the trust that has been imposed upon us.

God give us men. A time like this demands strong minds, great hearts, true faith: and ready hands. (Cheers)[21]

In 1918, William Lewis would recall the times he called for men to enlist, inspiring him to work towards supporting the returning disabled soldiers, sailors and their families, and calling on the State once again to do its duty towards the men.

Three days later, the Bill for a National Registration Act, known as the Derby Scheme, was introduced, aiming at registering all civilians between the ages of 15 and 65. Farming was not an exempt occupation unlike some industrial jobs. Initially to help manage the increasing labour shortage, the information was also used when conscription for the Forces came in 1916. The National Register was taken on 6 September. The register was destroyed after the war. In a similar manner, in September 1939, at the outbreak of the Second World War, a national census was taken, detailing everyone's occupation.

Conscription led to many notable fissures in relationships, not least among Welsh Liberals and undoubtedly was a test of faith for those who put aside their pacifism to support a 'just war' but found conscription a step too far.

On 27 January 1916, the Royal Assent was given to the Military Service Act, imposing conscription on all single men aged between 18 and 41, but exempting the medically unfit, clergymen, teachers and certain classes of industrial worker. Conscientious objectors – men who objected to fighting on moral grounds – were also exempted, and would be given, in most cases, civilian jobs or non-fighting roles at the Front. A second Act, passed in May, would extend conscription to married men.

Most conscientious objectors argued their case on religious belief, with a minority objecting to the war itself. Neither group were popular, especially the latter. Tribunals were set up which could give exemptions for those in particular professions, but any others who failed to answer the call if it came, even serving in uniform in a non-combatant role, were subject to two years in prison with hard labour. Decisions by tribunals would, understandably, often be contentious, leading many anti-conscription activists to turn from stopping conscription *per se* to helping conscientious objectors.[22]

The call-up would start in March – the Act was to come into operation after fourteen days, and after twenty-one days all affected would be considered as having enlisted.

A Somerset clergyman, with a Welsh-sounding name, had his own way of arguing his case:

> The vicar of the Somerset mining village of Coleford, near Bath, the Rev. J. H. Evans, has issued a remarkable challenge. Having received an anonymous letter urging him to practice what he preaches and join the army, the vicar, explaining the position of the clergy, invites the writers to disclose their identity, when he will put on the gloves and meet them individually in the ring.[23]

MAY 1916

On 11 May, Mrs Lloyd George and Australian Premier Billy Hughes accompanied Lloyd George to a meeting in Conwy where he gave a major speech on the necessity for compulsion (conscription now in effect), 7 June would be the last day for volunteering.[24]

On a flippant note, *The Globe* carried a clipping from Down Under:

> Novel Appeal to Women: Women should relinquish the companionship of men eligible for the military service who have refrained from enlisting, suggests the Australian Director-General of Recruiting.[25]

In his memoir of his mother, Richard Lloyd George gave his perspective on her attitude to killing.

> My mother hated the thought of war – not only as the mother of two sons of military age, but also because of her peaceful upbringing. But she came to hate the Godless brutes who plunged the world into four and a half years of carnage more than she hated war itself.

Then, after relating a story of how she would not let him kill off a flock of scrawny chickens, he continued:

> But, had I been able to convince her that one of those wretched fowls was suffering from a disease which would presently infect the whole flock, she would not have hesitated for a moment about having the afflicted hen killed. So with the Huns! Once she realized they were spreading the pestilence of war all over the world, she was a wholehearted believer in destroying them.
>
> Perhaps I am the only one (besides my father) who can understand how my mother's attitude towards killing – anyone or anything – insensibly influenced him in those summer days of 1914. But when they both awoke to a realization of the fact that only by killing Germans could the germ of war be eradicated from the world's masses, they both knew the ghastly business had to be done. There was, most definitely, no element of pacifism about either of them.[26]

CHAPTER 21

Safe Havens for Sailors

(December 1916 to December 1918)

'The debt the nation owed to the men who sail the seas, both in the Naval and the Merchant Service could only be acknowledged but never discharged.'
Rev. J. T. Rhys, March 1917

ON 5 DECEMBER 1916, the day before No. 10 beckoned, Mrs Lloyd George launched a new appeal, on this occasion for the British and Foreign Sailors' Society (BFSS), to assist the mothers, widows and orphans of sailors. Supporting the sailors would become all the more urgent in February 1917 when Germany began to wage unrestricted U-Boat warfare on all shipping, adding to the existing pressure on food supplies already constrained by poor harvests in the US and the UK.

The Nonconformist BFSS, about to celebrate its centenary, provided safe havens and pastoral support for the country's sailors around the world and in British ports. Its hostels and institutes provided food, lodging, education and recreational activities. Given that the BFSS was an experienced organisation, the appeal did not demand a great deal of her time and attention, though, despite this, her mailbag quickly became larger than that of the PM as a result of this one appeal.[1]

Often referred to as the 'YMCA at Sea', the Society was the second on her list of seven 'movements in which I have been interested, mostly active', drawn up by JTR in his Notes for her never-to-be-completed autobiography.

JTR joins the BFSS

As noted earlier, just before she launched her appeal, JTR had stepped down from his Swansea pastorate, on 27 November, and joined the BFSS as one of the two London Metropolitan Superintendents.[2] The BFSS would keep him in the Nonconformist fold. Its organising secretary was fellow Congregational minister, the Rev. T. Eynon Davies, whom he knew well, both having trained at the Memorial College, Brecon, both having served in Aberdare, south Wales, and the Rev. Davies had officiated at JTR's wedding in 1904. London was familiar territory for JTR, having spent ten years training and working as a draper there until 1896, attending the Welsh chapel in King's Cross, where he would first meet Lloyd George.

JTR also worked with Lady Rhondda (illustration 25) in this campaign, as *The Cambrian News* would acknowledge in 1918:

> The Rev. J. T. Rhys, late of Swansea, who for the past two years has been doing war work in London, has rendered valuable services to distressed sailors. When the intensive submarine campaign began, he undertook to organise relief for torpedoed sailors, and probably addressed more audiences than anyone else on that subject. He raised enough money to provide substantial relief for thousands of torpedoed sailors, being very energetically supported in this by, among others, Mrs Lloyd George and Lady Rhondda.[3]

It was later said that it was his work with Lady Rhondda which led to his appointment to the Downing Street secretariat when Mrs Lloyd George needed a new private secretary.

JTR developed some affinity with the sailing fraternity when in Swansea. In 1909, he travelled for his summer holiday on a series of steamers from south Wales to Bordeaux and Santander, then back up the Channel to Rotterdam and home, getting closer to the daily life of the sailors.

On 22 March 1917, JTR was in Southall, west London, acknowledging the heroism of the sailors and the critical work of the BFSS.

> THE HEROISM OF OUR SAILORS: Rev. J. T. Rhys, speaking at the Southall Brotherhood on Sunday afternoon, said the debt the nation owed to the men who sail the seas, both in the Naval and the Merchant

45. Wartime perils of online shopping, coincidently (or deliberately?) published alongside a public letter from Mrs Lloyd George calling for support for her comforts fund. See p.229. *West London Observer*, 29.12.1916, p.2.

© British Library Board

46. Comforts for the soldiers. See p.24. *Nottingham Journal*, 15.7.1915, p.1.
© Reach Plc.

47. Comforts for sale. See p.156. *The Bystander*, 9.12.1914, p.36.
© Illustrated London News Ltd / Mary Evans

48. Packing food parcels for prisoners of war: in this instance at the Australian Red Cross premises in Regent Street, London, January 1917.
Source: Historic England Archive

TWO WELSH PREMIERS PHOTOGRAPHED.

49. Megan, David and Margaret Lloyd George with Prime Minister 'Billy' Hughes of Australia, and the Dean of Westminster, after the June 1918 Service at the Abbey in aid of the Welsh Prisoners of War Fund. See pp.55, 126. *Western Mail*, 24.6.1918, p.6.
© Reach Plc.

MRS. LLOYD GEORGE HELPS A GOOD CAUSE.
Mrs. Lloyd George selling the little paper lamps to Australian soldiers yesterday in aid of the Red Cross Funds.

51. Lamp Day, Friday, 11 May 1917, Mrs Lloyd George selling paper lamps in Waterloo Place, by the statue of Florence Nightingale, born 12 May 1820. See p.83. *The Daily Graphic*, 12.5.1917, p.7.
Private Collection

50. Lieutenants Gwilym and Richard Lloyd George, 6th Battalion, Royal Welch Fusiliers, 1915, at Downing Street. See p.268.
Olwen Carey Evans Collection 10 (Llyfr Ffoto 1013 C), NLW

52. Opening the first Women's Institute hall in the UK, at Penrhyndeudraeth, Caernarfonshire, with Olwen, Miss Alice Williams and her uniformed brother Sir Osmond Williams, Lord-Lieutenant of Merionethshire. See p.99. *Sunday Pictorial (Sunday Mirror)*, 26.8.1917, p.14.
© Reach Plc.

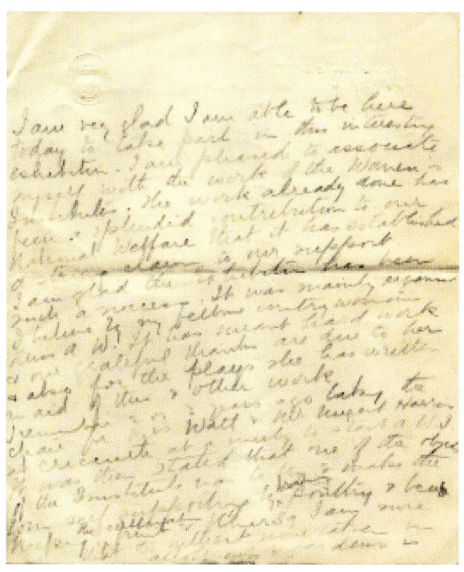

53. First page of Mrs Lloyd George speech at the WI Exhibition, October 1918. See p.332.

JTR Private Collection, copy in the Rev. J. T. Rhys (Margaret Lloyd George) Papers, NLW

54. WI Exhibition, October 1918. Mrs Goodman, Queen Alexandra, Princess Mary, Miss Alice Williams and Mrs Alfred Watt on the opening day. See p.332. *The Landswoman, The Journal of The Land Army and the Women's Institutes*, 1.12.1918, p.42.
British Newspaper Archive, image created courtesy of the British Library Board

55. With the munitionettes, Woolwich Arsenal. See p.127 Headline from *The Daily Mirror*, 1.7.1918, pp.4–5.
IWM Q 108419

56. The saddlemakers at Woolwich, June 1918. See p.127.
IWM Q 108420

57. Visiting the women tentmakers at the Woolwich dockyard, June 1918. See p.127.
IWM Q 108443

58. With the only women tinners (i.e. metalworkers) in England, during a visit to the Equipment and Ordnance Stores in Woolwich, June 1918. See p.127.
IWM Q 108421

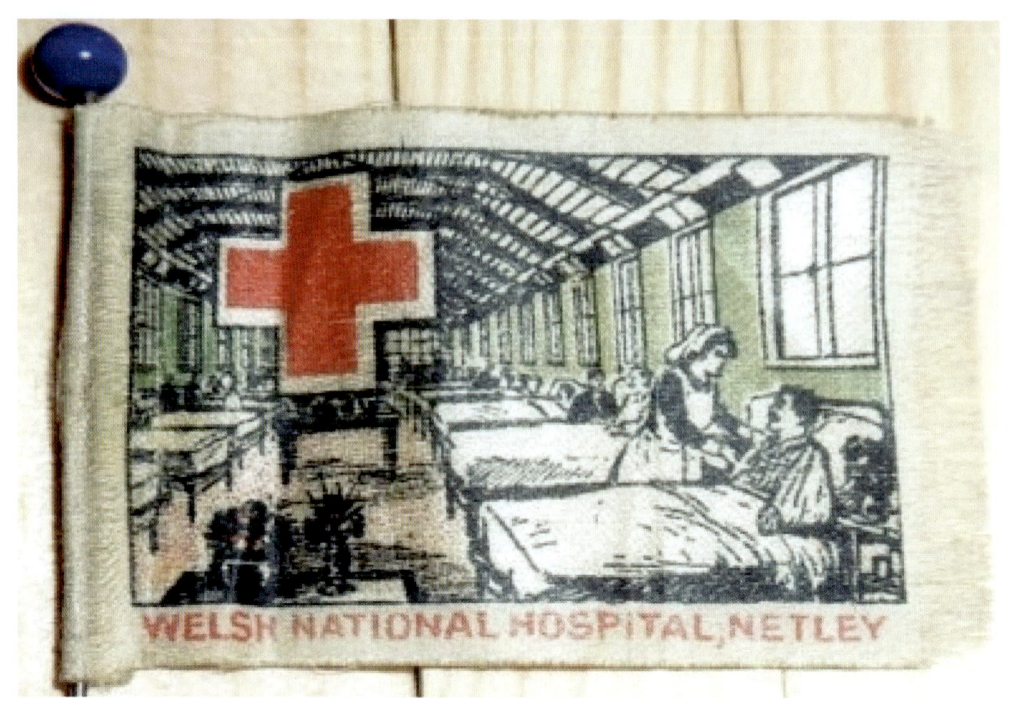

59. Flag sold for Welsh National Hospital, Netley. See p.341.
www.netley-military-cemetery.co.uk, courtesy of Julie Green

60. At the Welsh Hospital, Netley, 17 September 1915, seated with left to right, Lady Mond, Matron Miss E. G. Evans, commander in chief, Col. A. W. Sheen and Megan. See p.341.
Olwen Carey Evans Collection 6 (Llyfr Ffoto 1009 B), NLW

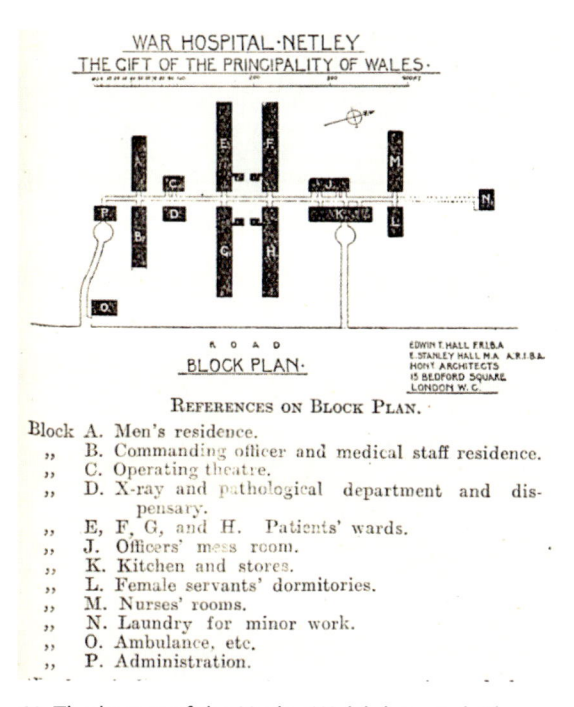

61. The layout of the Netley Welsh hospital. *The Hospital*, 24.10.1914, p.95.

62. Dispensary, Welsh Hospital, Netley. See p.341.
www.netley-military-cemetery.co.uk, courtesy of Julie Green

63. Manchester, 1918, visiting the John Leigh Memorial Hospitals. Sir John Leigh is standing next to Olwen, and behind Mrs Lloyd George, who is seated between Lady Leigh and their daughter Marjorie Joan. See p.138.
Olwen Carey Evans Collection 6 (Llyfr Ffoto 1009 B), NLW

64. Dr John Lynn-Thomas, inspiration for the Prince of Wales Hospital for the Limbless and Disabled, Cardiff. See p.347.
Walter Stoneman NPG x186065
© National Portrait Gallery, London

65. Staff at Wern Red Cross Hospital, Porthmadog, 1917, Olwen standing fourth from left, behind Mrs William George, and Mrs Bolland (the VAD commandant, in black), with Dorothy Drage, quartermaster, the other side of the commandant. See pp.73, 337.
© The Royal Welch Fusiliers Museum

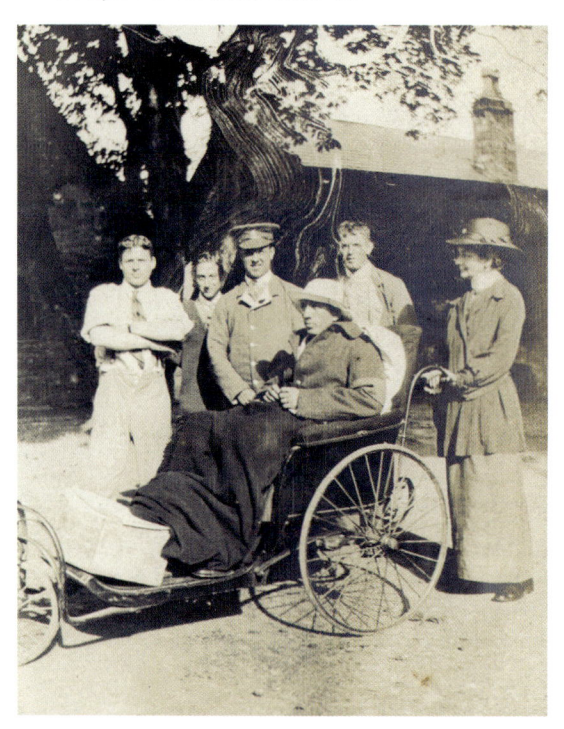

66. Patients at Wern. See pp.73, 337.
Olwen Carey Evans Collection 6 (Llyfr Ffoto 1009 B), NLW

67. Olwen leaves for Red Cross duty in France, including scrubbing the station platforms.

See pp.43, 339. Olwen Carey Evans Collection 6 (Llyfr Ffoto 1009 B), NLW

A GROUP OF DISTINGUISHED COUNTERWOMEN.

Left to right: Dowager Marchioness of Tweeddale, Duchess of Marlborough, Mrs. Lloyd George, Lady Randolph Churchill, and Lady Henry at Children's Jewel Fund sale in New Bond-street, London, yesterday.—(*Daily Mirror* photograph.)

68. With the Dowager Marchioness of Tweeddale, the Duchess of Marlborough, Lady Randolph Churchill, and Lady Henry, at The Children's Jewel Fund, New Bond Street. See p.144. *The Daily Mirror,* 1.11.1918, p.4.

© Reach Plc.

Toys from Trefnant, Vale of Clwyd. See p.37.

69. A harpist from a set of Gorsedd of the Bards figures

© Amgueddfa Cymru-National Museum Wales

70. A swinging toy looking remarkably like Lloyd George, the words Red Tape discernible on the top bar.

Still from Trefnant Vale of Clwyd Toys, YouTube video, by Keith Smith, 2016, https://www.youtube.com/@keithsmith8335

NEW CLUB FOR WOMEN WAR WORKERS.

A corner of the newly-opened Active Service Club for Women, in Eaton-square, London. Mrs. Lloyd George is making a special appeal for funds to enable it to carry on its necessary work.

71. London club for the women in the Forces, Eaton Square. See pp.131, 142. *The Daily Mirror*, 19.10.1918, p.5.
© Reach Plc.

MRS. LLOYD GEORGE AND THE GIRL GUIDES
On Saturday the Premier's wife inspected the Dartford Division.

72. A bold feather in Mrs Lloyd George's cap, with the Dartford Girl Guides, from the paper's fashion page. See p.130. *The Graphic*, 13.7.1918, p. 52.
© Illustrated London News Ltd / Mary Evans

AFTER THE V.C. FROM THE KING—A ROSE FROM THE PREMIER'S WIFE : SERGEANT HAROLD JACKSON, V.C., "REDECORATED" BY MRS. LLOYD GEORGE.

74. The *Viola odorata Mrs David Lloyd George*. See p.141.

Image courtesy of Clive Groves, Groves Nurseries, Bridport

73. The Premier's wife redecorates a Victoria Cross soldier at the Trafalgar Flower Fair, June 1918. See p.127. *The Sketch*, 3.7.1918, p.3.

© Illustrated London News Ltd / Mary Evans

75. Italian Flag Day, December 1916. See p.67.
ART.IWM PST 10918

76. Savoy Floral Fete, July 1918. See p.128.
ART.IWM PST 13192

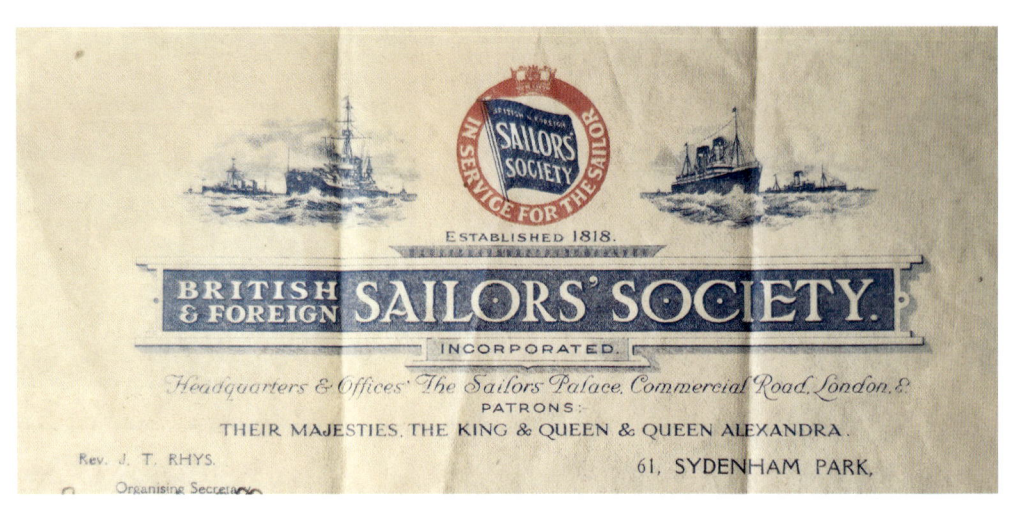

77. BFSS letterhead of JTR, Organising Secretary.

78. BFSS souvenir flag.
© Amgueddfa Cymru-Museum of Wales

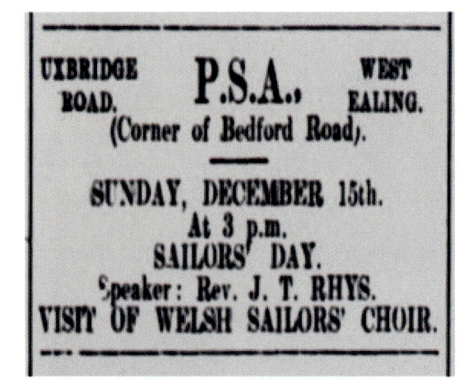

79. J.T. Rhys, London Metropolitan Organising Secretary of the British and Foreign Sailors' Society and Private Secretary to Margaret Lloyd George.
JTR Private Collection

80. Entertaining the Pleasant Sunday Afternoon audience in West London. See pp.290, 292. *Ealing Gazette*, 14.12.1918, p.4.
© British Library Board

81. Statue of Cranogwen at her birthplace, Llangrannog, unveiled by the Monumental Welsh Women campaign in 2023. See p.365.
Molyneux Associates

82. Agnes Slack, temperance campaigner. See p.364. Frontispiece of her biography by her niece Aelfrida Tillyard, 1926. Published by W. Heffer & Sons Ltd, Cambridge, England.

83. Red Dragon lapel pin.
© Amgueddfa Cymru-Museum Wales

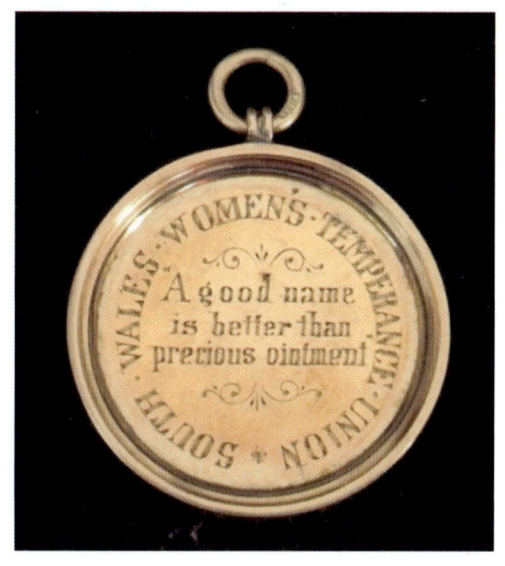

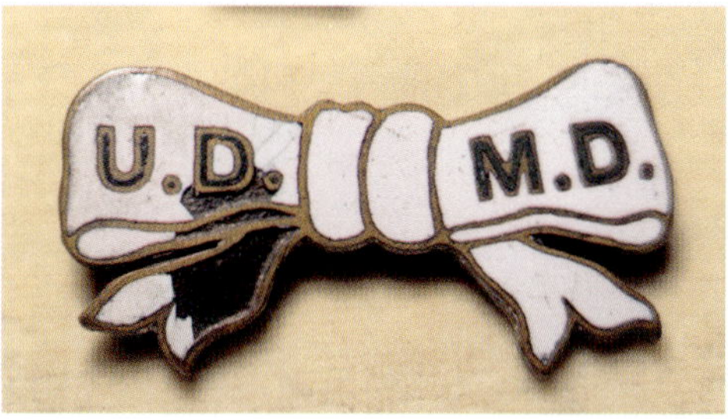

85. JTR's white ribbon lapel pin, with the initials of the union, *Undeb Dirwestol Merched y De*.
JTR Private Collection

84. The South Wales Women's Temperance Union / *Merched y De* medallion of Jane Annie Rhys, née Jones.

86. Miss Gwenith Williams presents an inscription for a casquet to Mrs Lloyd George, at Morriston, Swansea, August 1918. See p.134.

Maesygwernen Album (Llyfr Ffoto 254 B), NLW

87. The celebratory scenes in Neath, August 1918, a decisive breaktheugh in the war coinciding with Lloyd George receiving the Freedom of Neath and the family attending the Neath National Eisteddfod. See p.134.

Olwen Carey Evans Collection 6 (Llyfr Ffoto 1009 B), NLW

Safe Havens for Sailors (1917 to 1918)

Service could only be acknowledged but never discharged. It was a priceless service rendered at great personal sacrifice and amid constant perils. The British and Foreign Sailors' Society, which was now in its hundredth year, sought to ameliorate the lot of the sailors and protect them from moral dangers, and provide them with spiritual ministrations. At the present moment it was giving its energy without stint to succour those who were torpedoed, and to brighten the lot of the sailors who were interned in Germany. It was a matter of infinite pride that sailors who had suffered from German torpedoes never shrank from joining other ships at the earliest possible opportunity.[4]

On 7 May, Mrs Lloyd George handed over a cheque for £37,219 (over £2 million today) as a result of her appeal, at the BFSS annual meeting at the Mansion House.[5] We may assume JTR, as BFSS London Metropolitan Superintendent, was in attendance, by now either working for Mrs Lloyd George or about to be appointed. Also speaking was Marie Corelli, who had written a book, *Eyes of the Sea*, for sale on behalf of the Society.[6]

Ten thousand pounds, more than one quarter of the funds raised by her BFSS appeal, was given in the first few weeks by the Liverpool shipping broker Robert Thomas, also well known to William Lewis, who had worked for Robert's father's shipping firm. He continued to be a generous philanthropist, a major instigator and sponsor of the Welsh Heroes Memorial in Bangor, converting an uncompleted mansion on his Garreglwyd estate, at Holyhead, Anglesey, into a convalescent home for disabled soldiers and sailors, which would be opened by Mrs Lloyd George in 1919.[7] Robert Thomas was knighted in June 1918, and became the Coalition Liberal MP for Wrexham (1918–1922) and later Liberal MP for Anglesey (the seat later held by Megan Lloyd George). But his business collapsed in the 1929 crash.[8]

In May 1917, the convoy system for protecting ships from U-Boats was finally starting, after much pushing from Lloyd George against Admiralty opposition.

Funds continued to come in from abroad. In January 1918, the Maharajah of Scindia sent £1,000 to Mrs Lloyd George's appeal, and the London and River Plate Bank, Buenos Aires, sent £400 in response to a similar BFSS appeal by Lady Beatty, the wife of the Commander-in-Chief of the Grand Fleet.[9]

At the end of March 1918, JTR spoke at a concert in aid of the

BFSS given by the County Secondary School, Sydenham (his home neighbourhood). Mrs Percy Illingworth (widow of the late Postmaster-General) took the chair.

> The Rev. J. T. Rhys said that it was quite impossible to describe fully either the terrible experiences through which our sailors went in these days or our feeling of admiration for their strenuous services and sustained heroism. It was without precedent in the history of the world, and no language could be found to do justice to the men. The Sailors' Society was doing all that was in its power to minister to the needs of these men, and he appealed for help for the Society to carry on until there would be no further need to provide relief for torpedoed or mined crews. (applause)[10]

On 5 May, JTR chaired a south London meeting in aid of the BFSS hosted by the Hither Green PSA, to hear the Royal Navy Voluntary Reserve (Crystal Palace) Welsh choir. Standing in at the last moment for David Davies (the MP who was working with the Troops Fund), JTR quipped that he lacked the latter's three attributes, being neither a major, MP nor millionaire. A collection of £18 6s. 5d., supplemented by £20 from David Davies, was raised for the BFSS.[11]

PSA, rather delightfully, stood for the 'Pleasant Sunday Afternoon' Brotherhoods, first started in 1875 by a draper-turned Congregationalist deacon (JTR would have had some affinity there) to offer men relatively short (less than 45 minute) sessions, with the aims of attracting them to the church and/or offering literacy education. The movement spread around the country, each society adapting to local conditions and not purely a religious activity. The Welsh chapel in Eastcastle (formerly Castle) Street, near Oxford Circus, still hosts a monthly Saturday Afternoon Society. Perhaps we can discern an echo of the sobriquet 'Saturday Afternoon Soldiers' given to the Territorials?

BFSS bazaar, Cardiff

On 8 June, the *Western Mail* reported that Margaret Lloyd George would open a bazaar in October (planning well ahead) for the Cardiff branch of the Sailors' Society. By now 1,055 ships and 31,000 sailors had been assisted by the Society, along with the provision of 103,000 meals and 82,000 articles of clothing, at the cost of £6,000. The cost of railway warrants had been £3,000. Parcels worth £31,000 had been sent to prisoners of war in Germany.[12]

Safe Havens for Sailors (1917 to 1918)

On 24 October, the 12.40 GWR train whisked her to Cardiff to fulfil her promise:

> MRS LLOYD GEORGE AND SEA HEROES: Mrs Lloyd George arrived at Cardiff on Wednesday, and had a most cordial reception when, at the City-hall, she declared open the Trafalgar Bazaar in aid of the British and Foreign Sailors' Society. The primary object of the bazaar is to raise funds to provide a Cardiff section in the Welsh wing of the Sailors' Rest and Hostel to be erected in London as a war memorial to our sailors by the women of the Empire.
>
> The Society had now decided to open a hostel for sailors in London, at a cost of £50,000. This was the offering of the women of the Empire to the brave men who had stood gallantly by us in our hour of need.[13]

The bazaar, organised by the Ladies Guild of the Society,[14] was linked with a nationwide tribute under the patronage of the Cardiff Shipowners and Docksmen to Admiral Nelson, who died on 21 October 1805. The bazaar raised £2,500 in aid of a Cardiff section in the Welsh wing of a new Imperial Hostel in London.[15]

Sailors in Shepherd's Bush and Staines

JTR continued campaigning for the BFSS alongside his No. 10 duties. On 15 September 1918, while Mrs Lloyd George cared for her flu-ridden husband in Manchester's Town Hall, he was speaking on the subject of 'S-O-S' in Shepherd's Bush with the Welsh Sailors' Choir, raising funds for the BFSS.[16]

JTR and the choir were together again in October, at the Town Hall in Staines.

> WELSH SAILORS IN STAINES: On Saturday and Sunday a choir of thirty Welsh sailors visited Staines under the auspices of the Staines United PSA. On Saturday evening the Friends' Meeting House was crowded to the doors. The Rev. J .T. Rhys gave some particulars of the work of the Society, stating that during the war over £30,000 had been spent succouring torpedoed men. The choir, composed entirely of Welshmen, had given over one hundred concerts without any fee of any kind.[17]

On 5 December 1918, almost a month since the Armistice and two years precisely since Mrs Lloyd George launched her BFSS appeal, she called a meeting at No. 10 in aid of a campaign, led by Beatrice, Lady Dimsdale, that appealed to 'the women of the Empire' for £10,000 in aid of a rest home for seamen in London (for which the October Cardiff meeting had also been raising funds). The Imperial Hostel would be another war memorial delivering welfare.

> Mrs Lloyd George, who has all along taken a very keen interest in the welfare of the sailors belonging to both branches of the service, has arranged to have a great meeting at Downing-street on December 5th to further the interests of the Imperial Hostel for the Port of London. Mrs Lloyd George has already raised for the British and Foreign Sailors' Society war work over £45,000, and she is confident that by this meeting she will attain her cherished ambition of raising the amount of £50,000.[18]

In the event, that afternoon Mrs Lloyd George was in south London opening a sale of work at the Enmore Road Congregational Church, Clapham, and JTR may well have had to apologise for her absence at No. 10. She did leave the sale early, saying she had to get back for a meeting, so it is possible she arrived late.

The No. 10 meeting was chaired by Sir Eric Geddes, First Lord of the Admiralty. Lady Dimsdale would lay the foundation stone of the Empire Memorial Sailors Hostel on 13 March 1923. The large BFSS building, emblazoned 'The Mission', still stands on Commercial Road, Limehouse, as does the work of the Sailors' Society, now into its third century.

On 15 December, it was again Sailors' Day in west London, with JTR and the Welsh Sailors' Choir entertaining attendees of the Pleasant Sunday Afternoon in West Ealing.[19] (illustration 80)

CHAPTER 22

Food and Economy
1917

'The Frenchwoman's secret, I have heard,
was the great attention she gave to the stock-pot.'
Margaret Lloyd George, 5 March 1917

WHILE THE TROOPS Fund, the Welsh Army and the British and Foreign Sailors' Society sought to win the war on land and at sea, the war also had to be won at home. As with recruitment, food rationing began with voluntary action and persuasion, before compulsion was brought to bear. Communal kitchens were set up by people across the country, followed by State initiatives culminating in heavily subsidised, 'national kitchens'.

Mrs Lloyd George's food and economy campaigning picked up soon after she entered No. 10. It was a natural cause for the Welsh countrywoman, housewife, mother and keen gardener to champion, and she would often join forces with Sybil, Lady Rhondda, whose husband, D. A. Thomas, the newly-ennobled Baron Rhondda, would be persuaded by Lloyd George in June to take over as Food Controller to put more drive behind the process. Voluntary rationing had included unpopular ideas such as 'meatless days', but Lord Rhondda would go further, introducing sugar rationing, meat rationing and price control measures before accelerating the capacity of public dining.[1]

The campaigning was also educative. A 'Women's Manifesto', urging the well-off to show restraint in consumption and avoid waste, and the organisation of exhibitions and teaching facilities to improve housekeeping skills, sought to make limited supplies go further – even though some thought that if women stayed at home and stopped politicking, then all would be well.

It was also the time when, by coincidence, the nascent Women's Institute, the WI, was taking off, having first taken root in north Wales, where Mrs Lloyd George and the Agricultural Organisation Society established the UK's fifth WI, in her home town of Cricieth. On the eve of the Armistice, the WIs would hold their first major national exhibition, in London's Caxton Hall.

MARCH 1917

On 5 March 1917, the new chatelaine of No. 10 chaired a full house at St James's Theatre, London. Her speech was covered widely, including by *The Times*:

> An audience of women, which filled the St James's Theatre from the gallery to the stalls, gave a warm greeting to Mrs Lloyd George yesterday when she took the chair at a war-housekeeping meeting, organized by the women's sub-committee of the Lord Mayor's War Savings Committee. Those on the platform included the Duchess of Rutland, the Duchess of Abercorn, Lady Lansdowne, Lady Devonport, Lady Mersey, Lady Sandhurst, Lady Reading, Lady Rhondda, Lady St Helier, Lady Mond, Lady Moir, Lady Tuck, Lady McClure, Lady Lloyd, Lady Lane, Lady Nott-Bower, Lady Campbell, Lady Alexander, Mrs Creighton, Mrs Plowden, and Mrs Arnold Glover.

> The Frenchwoman's secret – the stock-pot:

> Mrs Lloyd George said they were there to save the foodstuffs of the country, which might be made to go much further by careful housekeeping. Both in France and Germany women paid more attention to the details of housekeeping than women in England. It was said that a Frenchwoman could provide a meal for her family out of what a British woman wasted. The Frenchwoman's secret, she had heard, was the great attention she gave to the stock-pot. In the schools now, we were training little girls to cook and bake, and when she visited a school lately the girls gave her a loaf of delicious bread they had made. If, when these girls married, they continued to bake their own bread, they would save a great deal of flour, for home-made bread was very economical. It was a great mistake for girls who earned their own living – girls who were typists or teachers – to think they need pay no attention to housekeeping.

Grow our own food:

Agriculture had been neglected in this country. We had depended far too much on our Navy, under whose protection we were able to obtain food from other countries, and we had not thought it worthwhile to grow our own. This must be changed and every district must grow its own vegetables, and as far as possible its fruit and wheat. Certain parts of this country were ideal for fruit growing, and apples grown in some districts of England were far sweeter than those from any other part of the world.

Rationing, and 'no treating':

They should realise, too, the importance of rationing. Every bit of meat and every lump of sugar saved was helping to win the war. If one person in a family ate less than the others, he must not hand the surplus on to someone else. That was treating, and treating was illegal.

Mrs C. S. Peel of the Ministry of Food followed up:

Mrs C. S. Peel, speaking in her official capacity as one of the women directors at the Ministry of Food, said she could say there was no need for panic. Panic and hoarding were a disgrace to the nation. They were not asked to undergo any serious sacrifice or inconvenience, but if the voluntary rations were followed, this country would be saved the horrors of privation and the rationing system as they had it in Germany. Entertainment was only possible when one's friends did not consume another meat meal when they reached home. If one lunched at another person's house and had meat, it should be followed by a meat-less dinner.

Pledge cards:

Speaking of the plans of the Ministry of Food, Mrs Peel said economy should be blatant, and Lord Devonport had ordered the printing of cards bordered in red, white and blue, which could be shown in the windows of those who pledged themselves to observe voluntary rationing loyally and honestly.

Upstairs as well as downstairs:

A very difficult problem was the position of employer and employee when, as in the case of domestic servants, wages were given partly in money and partly in board and lodging. In houses where there had been a high standard of living, servants could not be asked to cut down this standard unless a similar economy was practised in the dining room. A mass meeting of domestic servants would be held presently in a large theatre, when a committee would be formed of servants from great houses and another of stewards, who could give great help in the matter of food economies.

A great campaign was also being organized to give help and advice to everyone who asked for it. She and her co-director, Mrs Pember-Reeves, would work with every organization that could help them. They were also preparing to have the advice of experts available for officers' messes where it was found that the messing bills were excessive.

What about the wounded, and the dog?

Many questions were handed up from the audience. A V.A.D. commandant asked if a small hospital might exceed rations and was told that wounded soldiers could hardly be brought under food rations. A suggestion that bakers should make loaves of substitutes for wheat flour and mark them as such in their windows Mrs Peel said she would bring before the Food Controller. A question as to whether dogs' food should be deducted from their owners' rations aroused a storm of protest and was left unanswered. Before the close of the meeting Mrs Peel again invited those present to send her suggestions and recipes.

Lady Mond, proposing a vote of thanks to Mrs Lloyd George, said that in her hospital the men were well satisfied with the amount they had from the rations.[2]

Lady Mond may have been referring to the Welsh wing at Netley Hospital or, on a smaller scale, the facilities in the convalescent facilities at her home, Melchet Court.

The Times also printed six bread recipes, reporting on the leaflets that gave tested recipes suitable for coping with voluntary rations, available from the Association of Teachers of Domestic Subjects.

The *Food Ministry Public Kitchens* handbook would also criticise the 'appalling ignorance' of the British people in preparing attractive food, neglecting other cuisines, most notably those of 'the pleasant land of France – the shrine of all true chefs'.[3]

Communal kitchens

Alongside rationing, the provision of communal dining facilities was promoted, again proceeding step by step, building on the communal soup kitchens set up before the war by the Salvation Army and other volunteer organisations, and culminating with 'national kitchens', run as business propositions, subsidised by Treasury funding, and providing reasonably-priced, well-cooked food.

Troops moving around the country also needed feeding, and the first railway canteens were set up in Banbury and in Perth in September 1914.[4] In addition, mouths abroad had to be fed, as Mrs Lloyd George had acknowledged in her November 1915 interview with Percy Alden on the work of women:

> I referred to canteen workers in England, but a very large number are in France. There is a large canteen in the Gare du Nord and a Salle de Recreation at Compiègne. Wherever there is need and wherever the opportunity offers, the women press in to help. Although there may be failures, in most cases they are equal to any burden that is thrust upon them.[5]

In the East End

On 4 April, Mrs Lloyd George and Lady Rhondda were in east London opening three communal kitchens. The London evening paper, *The Pall Mall Gazette*, reported at length:

> MRS LLOYD GEORGE IN THE EAST END: WARM PRAISE BY THE PREMIER'S WIFE: Three communal kitchens were opened in London to-day, two by Mrs Lloyd George in the East End, and one by Lady Rhondda in Cripplegate. Mrs Lloyd George's engagements necessitated her travelling through some of the most unsavoury streets in that part of the Metropolis. At the opening of the Lycett Chapel War Communal Kitchen, in Mile End-road, she was accompanied by Lady Askwith, Mrs Page (wife the American Ambassador), Sir J. Benn, and the Mayor of Stepney.
>
> In this locality the Rev. James Jackson has for some time been providing 1,000 children with penny dinners each week, and while the Premier's wife

was speaking, children were constantly passing in and out with basins and jugs for the purpose of carrying cooked foods away. (illustration 28)

The Precious Children

Mrs Lloyd George said she did not know anything more economical than kitchens such as these for the saving of food and the same time for the provision of nourishing food for the children of the poorer masses. The nation had always looked upon children as precious, but in these times they were more than ever precious, and through these kitchens she was sure they would save hundreds of little lives. She was in full sympathy with the movement.

God Bless America

Sir John Benn, in welcoming the presence of the wife of the American Ambassador, said he had read with joy and gratitude the message from America. [US President Wilson had just made it clear that the US would enter the war on the side of the Allies – though it would be more than a year until US troops had their first engagement.] The message would live as one of the greatest sermons in the history of the world. It would hearten us, and would echo as a message to the brave boys at the Front. We did not yet realise the great influence it would have on the war. Our feelings were 'God bless America'.

At 'Paddy's Goose', in Shadwell High-street, there were a number of men, typical East End inhabitants taking their midday meal, when Mrs Lloyd George arrived. They stood up from their tables and removed their hats as she entered, and punctuated her subsequent speech with applause. Mrs Lloyd George, in declaring this kitchen open, said that some of the puddings and meat pies looked most tempting. Nobody could possibly prepare such meals in their own homes at such prices. Mrs Page had been telling her of the use of cereals in America, and she hoped they would be introduced into this country.

The public food kitchen which Lady Rhondda opened on the premises of what was formerly the Crown public house, Whitecross-street, Cripplegate, had been provided by the Salvation Army.[6]

The Lycett Chapel was later a warehouse and demolished in 1971. Over the road was the Welsh Calvinistic Methodist Chapel: the building survives but Mrs Lloyd George might be less impressed to see her denomination's building surviving as a public house.

Food and Economy (1917)

The American Ambassador, Walter H. Page, appointed in 1913, was someone who saw eye to eye with Lloyd George, and according to Richard Lloyd George, 'my mother met him frequently and liked him'.[7]

Sir John Benn was the Leader of the Progressive Party, son of a Congregationalist minister, a former MP for Devonport and for St George's Tower Hamlets, a member of the London County Council, the father of William Wedgwood Benn (his successor as MP for St George's Tower Hamlets), grandfather of Labour MP Tony Wedgwood Benn, and great-grandfather of Labour MP Hilary Benn. The Benn dynasty. The Progressive Party was aligned to the Liberals.

The report on Lady Rhondda's visit to a pub-turned-kitchen added further perspectives on the campaign, including the prices.

> Salvation Army to Serve 17,000 Dinners Daily: Lady Rhondda opened at midday another food kitchen organised by the Salvation Army for the supply of cheap food, at Whitecross Street, in the great parish of St Luke's, premises which were formerly used as a public house. According to Colonel Laurie, who is in charge of this department of the Salvation Army's activities, no fewer than thirty-two such kitchens will be opened by the end of the present week in the Metropolis and the provinces, serving 17,000 hot dinners daily. The prices charged are according to the following scale: Soup, 1d.; sausage and two vegetables, 3½ d.; meat pies 2d. and 3d.; shepherd's pie 3d.; haricot beans 1d.; peas 1d.; potatoes 1d.; rice 1d.; tapioca 1d.; raisin pudding 1d.
>
> Colonel Laurie explained that the movement began five weeks ago in Spa-road, Bermondsey, and was an attempt to provide mothers who were at work with hot and nutritious food. These kitchens would be self-supporting. The Salvation Army would not make a profit because they were supplying the meals at cost price. They were dead nuts on the two p's – pauperising and profiteering.
>
> The dinners were intended to be eaten off the premises, though the Army had no hard and fast rules on the subject. Two children came to one of the kitchens the other day and asked if they could eat their soup there. In reply to the question why they desired to do so, they replied, 'Mother is in bed with a new baby, and there are ten of us now!'
>
> A crowd of women and children waited to be served by Lady Rhondda with their dinners.[8]

Spa Road, Bermondsey, was a major waste paper recycling depot run by the 'Army'. At first the word kitchen was used to indicate food that was not intended to be eaten on the premises – unless, as for the two children, home was too crowded!

Camberwell

On 18 May, Mrs Lloyd George and Lady Rhondda were again in tandem, at a communal kitchen in Camberwell, accompanied by Megan and local MP Tom Macnamara. As Parliamentary Secretary to the Admiralty, U-Boats were at the forefront of Macnamara's mind:

> THE SUBMARINE MENACE, STILL TO BE FOUGHT: Mrs Lloyd George, accompanied by Miss Lloyd George and Lady Rhondda, yesterday visited a communal kitchen established a week ago at Kempshead Hall, Albany-road, Camberwell, and formally declared it open.
>
> Dr Macnamara, Parliamentary Secretary to the Admiralty, in opening the proceedings, said that Germany's threat to starve us into submission would not slake the grim determination of the British. While he was quite sure that their grit and spirit were admirable, he felt bound to say a word of warning:
>
> 'The returns of losses issued yesterday and yesterday week,' continued Dr Macnamara, 'must not cause you in the slightest degree to relax your efforts in this direction. These returns speak for themselves, but do not draw any hasty conclusions from them. Do not let them delude you for one moment into the belief that the submarine menace is already turned aside and set at naught – it is not. These returns will be gravely disappointing to the enemy, who started this monstrous campaign with such hysterical and fiendish confidence that at last it had forged the weapon which would bring this country and her Allies to their knees. It would be worse than folly on your part to assume that the vital part you can play in beating the submarine menace is no longer urgently necessary.
>
> 'If you are a workman or workwoman in the shipyards, engineering shop, munition factory, your reply to Germany's threat must be to redouble your effort, and toil right to the absolute limit of your physical strength.'[9]

The menace was still far from 'naught', the same newspaper reporting further Allied shipping losses in the Mediterranean.

Food and Economy (1917)

A kitchen by royal appointment

Two years into the war, feeding the population was a challenge across all of society, and on 21 May, Queen Mary opened an experimental 'Kitchen for All' at 104 Westminster Bridge Road, Lambeth, established under the auspices of the Ministry of Food. She was accompanied by Food Controller Lord Davenport and his wife, by Lady Rhondda, and by Mrs Davidson, wife of the Archbishop of Canterbury.[10] The location was by the Underground station of the same name, then being renamed Lambeth North. The Food Ministry's Mrs Peel later recalled that an old man, who had been served by the Queen without him realising who she was, returned later when this was pointed out to him, to solemnly wave his hat three times to her.[11] Contemporary newspaper reports noted the returning customer was an old woman. The canteen proved very popular, the suffrage paper *The Common Cause* reporting that it was referred to as 'a sort of local Ritz'.[12] The kitchen was able to cater for 2,000 people a day, with a staff of two cooks, two kitchen-maids, a superintendent and a cashier from whom customers bought coupons on entering, rather than paying cash after eating.[13]

A tougher approach

The opening of the flagship 'Kitchen for All' would prove to be one of Lord Davenport's final outings as Food Controller. He was not in good health and was soon to be replaced by Lord Rhondda. Restricting the public's choices is never easy, as diarist Samuell Pepys Junior observed in his idiosyncratic manner in his diary of 16 June:

> My Lord Rhondda (that was Mr Thomas) will be the Comptrouller of Victuall, in room of my Lord Devonport, which, that he dares do it, is thought the bravest thing allmost done in the warr by any, not being a soldier or sailor, being the most unthankfull office possible.[14]

Lord Rhondda, a successful Welsh businessman, was reluctant to take the job, his own health causing anxiety, and keen to continue his work establishing a Ministry of Health. William Beveridge, who would lay the foundations of Britain's post Second World War welfare state, wrote in his contribution to Rhondda's biography: 'The official lives of Food Controllers in other countries had been generally unpopular and short.'[15] The brutal reality was that while the appointment would make Lord Rhondda a household name, it would be his last work, as he died a year later just before the opening of the campaign's flagship National Kitchen on New Bridge Street, Blackfriars, by Mrs Lloyd George. While he had been all for voluntarism in the early years, he would now take tougher action on rations and give a more commercial push to communal dining.

War Economy exhibition in Bangor

War Economy exhibitions also were organised to help people economise. On 30 May, in Bangor, Mrs Lloyd George's presence helped to attract good media coverage:

> THE BANGOR WAR ECONOMY EXHIBITION: An exhibition which will be opened daily until Saturday was inaugurated yesterday afternoon in Bangor by Mrs Lloyd George. It was held in the beautiful Prichard-Jones Hall of the University College of North Wales at Bangor, and in its preparation and organisation the local War Savings Association and the Women's Patriotic Guild, as well as other bodies, participated with commendable energy and spirit.

Cooking competitions, including those designed to revive lost skills:

> In connection with the exhibition a series of competitions have been arranged, prizes being offered for the finest and most suitably clothed babies, the best collection of recipes for Welsh home-made remedies, the best cup of home-made food for children, and the best old Welsh cookery recipes, including a recipe for making oatcakes with a view to reviving the lost art. Cookery contests and contests in the production of home-made makeshift household utensils, toys, and so forth are also arranged for.

Make do and mend ideas...

> The exhibition included an interesting stall full of the Welsh toys made in the Vale of Clwyd, and stalls on which examples appear of coal-saving devices, home cobbling, and garments produced from the unworn parts of old stockings and other articles of clothing. To save the wearing into holes of stockings at the heels and toe, pieces of cloth cut in the manner shown on one of the stalls are stitched on to act as heel and toe protectors.

Food and Economy (1917)

Not just speech making, see what you can get from the regulated amounts:

A number of stalls are set apart for wartime cookery exhibits. On one of them the Women's Guild show one day's meals for one person prepared in conformity with the Food Controller's scale. The meals are breakfast, dinner, tea, and supper, and the dishes as set out are likely to give a much better idea to a housewife who inspects them than a great deal of speech-making and literature of what one person should be limited to in the matter of food in order to comply with the regulations. It is obvious from a glance at this table that an ordinary man ought to thrive quite well on these rations.

And there's always a handy proverb:

The Queen Mary Needlework Guild have also a stall to illustrate their activities in the good causes. Exhortations to economy are given on the stalls and on the walls. The prudent Welsh proverb 'Tafl a'th unllaw, casgl a'th ddwylaw,' 'Cast with one hand, gather with both,' may be quoted as an example.

Learning how to save:

The Mayor of Bangor (Mr R. J. Williams) presided at the opening ceremony, and paid a tribute to the work which the women of his city had done in connection with the exhibition and for war purposes generally. 'To learn how to save' was the object in view in asking the people to visit the Prichard-Jones Hall during this week.

An emotional appeal for the help of all in warding off the menace of food shortage was given by Mrs Tippett, of the Food Control Campaign.

AN AWAKENED NATION
Mrs Lloyd George formally declared the exhibition open. She said the terrible war had revealed to us the resources of our own country, as to which we had grown very indifferent. We had been content to buy vegetables and meat from other countries; but she was glad that now a great deal was being done to increase the home production of food.

More gardening, and to continue after the war?

Men and women were hard at work in their gardens wherever she went, and especially around London. She felt sure that this sort of thing would go on after the war, and that the people who had begun to take an interest in gardening would continue to do so. The situation, as Mrs Tippett had said, was a serious one, and everyone should do his or her best to help in producing food and preventing waste.

Lessons from the London communal kitchens:

She had been helping in three or four communal kitchens in London, and was sure these would be very great institutions for the poor in large towns. People could buy in them a plate of soup for twopence, a meat pie for twopence, and a sago pudding for twopence. No mother could cook dinner for her children at that price, and it meant a great saving in fuel besides. In that exhibition she was sure people would get ideas how to prepare inexpensive dishes which would be nourishing and substantial if properly cooked. The boys and girls of the country should be well fed if it was possible to do so, because they were the greatest asset the country possessed. (applause)

Subsequently, there was a demonstration of cooking vegetarian dishes by Mrs Wokes, of Liverpool, a 'Talk on Substitutes for Bread and Flour' by Miss Mary Jones of the Carnarvonshire Domestic Science Classes, an address on 'Co-operative Production in Agriculture' by Mr E. R. Davies (the secretary of the Carnarvonshire Education Committee), and a children's play, *Patriotic Peace*, by the scholars of the Menai Bridge Council School under the direction of Miss Longfield Jones.[16]

Typically, Mrs Lloyd George used her experiences elsewhere to encourage her listeners.

Bangor Women's Patriotic Guild

On the same day, she visited the Bangor Women's Patriotic Guild at the local YMCA. Founded to supply comforts to troops very soon after the war began, it was the Guild's own fund-raising back in February 1915 which the Mayor had cited as evidence that Bangor was already doing its bit when she persisted in asking them to run a Flag Day for the Fund. On this occasion the Mayoress recalled the Guild's positive response.

Mrs Lloyd George paid a special visit to the Bangor Women's Patriotic Guild at the YMCA. The Mayoress (Mrs R. J. Williams), in welcoming Mrs Lloyd George, said that the guild had sent garments and comforts of all kinds, not only to the National Comforts Fund for Welsh Troops, in which Mrs Lloyd George is specially interested, and for which the guild recently raised £60 by means of a Flag Day, but to other sections of the Army and Navy.

Some part of the guild's work reached every Front where Allied or British forces were fighting, and letters of grateful acknowledgment came from Commanding Officers in France, Egypt, Mesopotamia, from our allies, the Alpini, at home, and abroad.

A large framed portrait of Mr Lloyd George had been given by the guild to the ward in the Invalides, Paris, equipped by the French kindred emergency fund.

Mrs Lloyd George expressed the pleasure she felt in meeting the working members of the guild and in hearing details of their organisation and work. She greatly approved of the guild's wide scheme of assistance, because the wider the interests the more sustained and varied because of the individual member.

AFTER-WAR NEEDS
She was of the opinion that there would be a real need for such organisations as that of the Women's Guild after the war. The need for their work would continue, but funds would not be so easily raised. Therefore, she advised the guild to keep up their output of work, and to 'make hay while the sun shone', financially, in order to have funds ready to help the disabled heroes who returned to civil life.

Referring to the Welsh Comforts Fund, Mrs Lloyd George explained that the comforts are not sent to individual soldiers of any battalion, but to the officer commanding, who saw to their distribution. The fact that hundreds of letters of thanks were received almost daily showed that the gifts were pretty evenly distributed.

The Welsh Flag Day had proved such a wonderful success, realising some £30,000, that the committee controlling the National Fund had decided to allocate a certain amount to be used after the war to help disabled men. The visits to hospitals for limbless men and to others for men grievously disabled had convinced her of the duty and privilege it was to help such heroes. The courage and cheerfulness of the men were beyond all praise. (applause)

And the 'war tea' complied with the rules too…

A 'war tea' was partaken of, in which everything provided was made by the guild members in strict accordance with the Food Controller's orders. Only economy recipes had been allowed.[17]

The National Economy Exhibition: County Hall, South Bank, London

On Tuesday, 10 July, Mrs Lloyd George presided at the National Economy Exhibition, at the South Bank's New County Hall, started in 1911 and formally opened in 1922 as the London County Council headquarters.

Her comments on the state of the kitchens at Downing Street almost a decade earlier received wide coverage:

> MRS LLOYD GEORGE ON SCULLERIES AND BATHROOMS
> Mrs Lloyd George, who presided last night at the National Economy Exhibition, remarked:
> 'When we went to 11, Downing-street, nine years ago, we found a big scullery there, with not a window, not a gleam of light, nor ventilation of any kind. It took me some little time before I could persuade the Board of Works to build me a nice little scullery. I did not rest till I got it. Now there is a nice little complete scullery, with a glass roof, and a window which opens out into the garden. Perhaps you would not believe me if I told you that when Mr Asquith came to 10, Downing-street, nine years ago, there was not a single bathroom in the place.
> 'That is enough about Downing-street – I think it has improved a little since we have been there.'[18]

Mrs C. S. Peel, of the Food Control Department, spoke on 'The Labour-Saving Home of the Future'. The National Economy Exhibition would continue for a while, demonstrating how food could be conserved in simple ways.[19]

The next evening Mrs Lloyd George opened another YWCA canteen, at the Tolmer's Institute, Drummond Street, Euston, equipped by the National Amalgamated Approved Society for the use of its 800 female clerks:

Food and Economy (1917)

> The canteen consists of a large airy dining-room, built rather like a church, with a timbered roof, stained windows, and harmonious grey walls; and a rest room furnished with comfortable wicker armchairs, intimate little tables having bright cretonne covers, a Japanese rug suite, and a truly encouraging array of cheerful crockery.[20]

The 'London Letter' column in the *Cambridge Daily News* praised the voluntary work of the YWCA, 'in perfect harmony' with the State.

> Yesterday added one more to the rapidly increasing list of YWCA canteens. It opened in the afternoon under the auspices of Mrs Lloyd George, Mrs Waldorf Astor, and many other distinguished ladies. The opening of a YWCA canteen is not attended with pomp and circumstance, but those who are responsible for it regard it, quite rightly, as an event of great importance.
>
> The growth of the YWCA's work has, they claim, done more for the happiness of the new armies of women workers than all the care of officialdom. I am not suggesting that the work of the YWCA in any way clashes with the 'expert' supervision of the Welfare Department. On the contrary, the two activities are in perfect harmony. But voluntary organisation among the girls themselves, many of whom are members of the YWCA, has gone far to make possible the general betterment of conditions after working hours.[21]

On 16 July, it was announced that retail food prices had more than doubled in the past three years of war.[22]

Domestic science training

In September, considerable coverage was given to Mrs Lloyd George's letter to the *Daily Telegraph* on domestic science and the need for women to improve their domestic skills.

> DOMESTIC TRAINING: MRS LLOYD GEORGE'S APPEAL
> To the Editor of *The Daily Telegraph*
>
> Sir – In recent articles in the Press, there have been presented the lines on which the young educated girl of the day might develop to her own advantage and that of the country at large. Certainly imagination has been quickened, and to take advantage of this new birth new channels of

activity must be provided or much of the boundless energy of youth may be lost.

'A profession for every girl, like every boy':

It is for the older generation to realise that every girl, like every boy, should have a profession and that a thorough training in a subject, no matter what the subject may be, makes for development of character, and in no way detracts from the finished whole. There is room in the world for all types, and scope for everyone with youth and health, opportunity and encouragement at her back.

Wealthy parents, no less than their poorer neighbours, will be wise to take full advantage of the careers open to women. Nursing, medicine, architecture, horticulture, banking, departmental work and teaching, give endless variety of choice, but the greatest of these is teaching, calling as it does for all the best qualities of heart and brain and hand.

Never was the cause of education so much in people's minds [the reforming 'Fisher' Education Act would pass in 1918]; never was there such a call to save to the uttermost the children of the nation, bodily, mentally, and spiritually; and never were there hopes centred so high as they are at the present time. Education has for so long been the Cinderella of the professions, badly equipped, badly endowed, nobody's child; but our eyes have been opened, and all classes are calling out for more light.

Among the very branches of educational work, none have deserved better of the public at large than those of domestic science. It is helping in this time of crisis in every conceivable way, and has penetrated into every stratum of society.

Upon the women of this country, no less than upon the men, is laid the necessity of fighting enemies of stern stuff; in the case of the women want and hunger for themselves and their children, unless scientific knowledge is brought to bear upon the question. The various food campaigns all over the country have done much to open the eyes of the people to the shortage of food and the national defect of ignorance in cooking; but the trained people who are wanted to present the truth in a convincing and uncontrovertible way are comparatively few in number, and many have been lent by education authorities to other departments requiring help in practical food questions.

The shortage of teachers in training:

There is needed at the present moment for a large army of women qualified by training and natural gifts to undertake the teaching of domestic economy; the supply is not equal to the demand, even now, when for years the training schools have been pouring a steady stream of intelligent, qualified women into the ranks of the teaching profession. Now, when more and still more are required, the numbers coming forward for training are lamentably short. The facilities for training in cookery and domestic economy, both in London and the provinces, are ample, and are not being used to anything like their full extent. I would, therefore, like to ask parents who are weighing the future of their daughters to consider whether they would not usefully be trained for such work as described above. Work in offices and banks, labour of all sorts (most of it of a transitory nature), are deflecting into blind-alley occupations the girls upon whom the educational future of the children depends; there is no one to sound the alarm. The terrible mortality of infants and children due to improper feeding is a scandal to our civilisation; and could be minimised if knowledge of this important branch of education were more widespread.

The subject is worthy of grave consideration and we are looking forward in the hope that in future more consideration may be given to domestic subjects, both for their own educational value, and for the state of the race.

Yours faithfully, M. Lloyd George

10, Downing-street, Whitehall, S.W., Sept. 1[23]

One hurdle that would have to be negotiated in 1918 was that the Ministry of Food would start poaching staff from the domestic science colleges in order to offer cookery instruction at the national kitchens themselves – though that may have been an effective and alternative means of training the population at large.[24]

The London correspondent of the *Irish Kerry Evening Post* was supportive:

> Her plea for domestic science has been read with a good deal of interest. The Premier's wife has been devoting herself very vigorously to this subject during the last twelve months, and has appeared on many platforms to advocate the views which are set down in her letter today. Baby Week did a great deal to give publicity to the demand for trained instructors in domestic science.

Mrs Lloyd George now makes an earnest appeal to parents to consider whether their daughters could not usefully be trained for such work, and I have no doubt that the appeal will not be fruitless. It is obvious, however, that the position of those who embark on work of this kind is at present no less uncertain than that of the other workers to whom Mrs Lloyd George refers.[25]

'Aurora', of *The Hendon and Finchley Times*, gave the story considerable coverage in the Ladies Column on an advertising page mainly for private schools, noting the obstacles, not least money:

Mrs Lloyd George has been writing to the Press on the subject of Domestic Science. She urges upon the parents of the country the unique opportunity there is now for their daughters to go into training so as to become teachers of what is known as Domestic Science.

While the young men are fighting in one direction, she argues, the necessity is laid on the young women of fighting enemies at home – the enemies of want and hunger. Shortage of food, combined with national ignorance of cooking, opens up a vista not beautiful to contemplate, unless the matter is taken in hand and combated by intelligent educated women who know how to get the best results from whatever food may be available.

The truth has to be driven home that a shortage is likely to continue for some time longer, and only trained women know how to meet such a prospect. The war has opened up so many unexpected ways in which women may get a living, that the sex has flocked to them in multitudes, oblivious of the fact that the end of the war will see all or nearly all of these avenues closed, while that of Science will be open for all time.

The financial constraint:

There is another. As at present constituted, training at a Domestic Science centre, with a view of teaching, costs a considerable sum of money, and when the training is complete and the pupil is equipped to take up her teaching duties, the emolument offered is altogether incommensurate to compensate for the time and effort that have been put in to acquire the knowledge.

If a girl only undertakes a course of study so as to be able to better conduct her own home when she is married, all well and good; but there are few parents who are willing or can afford to give their daughters a training costing two or three hundred pounds to start them as teachers, and then to see those girls only able to command a salary of £80 a year, perhaps rising to £120, when there are other professions, not requiring nearly so expensive a preparation, that are open to any girl with ambition.[26]

In other words, an opportunity for women after the war when they have to give up the jobs they are doing, but who can afford such an education? Few can train to be teachers if teachers don't get paid enough.

A writer by-lined as 'Mater' couldn't resist a dig at the suffrage movement:

MRS LLOYD GEORGE AND CHILD WELFARE: To the Editor of the *Derby Daily Telegraph*.
Sir, – The valuable advice given to women recently by Mrs Lloyd George should be seriously taken to heart. She said, 'There is needed at the present moment for a large army of women qualified by training and natural gifts to undertake the teaching of domestic economy,' and she continued, 'The terrible mortality of infants and children due to improper feeding is a scandal to our civilisation.'

One wonders whether the woman agitators of former days, or their societies, will set to work now on the lines indicated by Mrs Lloyd George. Surely it were better to inculcate those maternal and domestic qualities which, being more natural, should be more congenial than controversy, vote-hunting, and party politics. In this work, too, there is no room for partisanship, and the effects must inevitably be beneficial to the home-life of the nation and the welfare of the race, bodily, mentally, and spiritually – Yours truly. Mater.[27]

The *Gloucestershire Echo* ran a similar response, from Nottinghamshire, on its front page:

MRS LLOYD GEORGE AND CHILD WELFARE: TO THE EDITOR OF *THE ECHO*
Sir, – A correspondent in your recent issue did well to remind us of the wise words of Mrs Lloyd George on the above matter. It is a sad commentary on our boasted civilisation that the most important duties of womanhood should be treated practically with indifference. In these days far too much

is said and written of 'political rights' and too little of social duties and domestic economy.

One has to speak with bated breath these days, but it may be pardoned if one suggests that the suffrage movement is responsible for a great deal of the trouble. The outlook is not an inspiring one unless saner and safer ideas are promulgated among the future mothers of our race.

It is not yet too late to take stock of the position; it might not be a great disadvantage if our legislators in the Upper House carried out what was attributed to them at the Trade Union Congress the other day, holding the Reform Bill for maturer consideration.

It is certain that after the war women's duties and responsibilities in private life will be of more importance to the nation than in politics. Indifference in the home makes inefficiency in the State.

J. LLOYD JONES. Ortygia House, Long Eaton, Nottingham, October 1st, 1917[28]

The letters reflect the prejudices against which the women's movement was campaigning.

The Daily Mirror was more supportive, recounting a different anecdote, reflecting the way Mrs Lloyd George was encouraging her gender and the country's cooks.

No. 10, Downing-street: Mrs Lloyd George is a practical housewife, and knows everything about cooking and housework generally. On one of her regular trips down into the kitchens, I am told, one of the servants said to another: 'Well, she's the first Prime Minister's wife who knows what's what. P'raps,' she added, with a thoughtful air, 'one of us may come here on the same job 'fore we die!'[29]

Precisely the sort of revolutionary thinking that 'Mater' wanted to nip in the bud.

And while we consider the culinary life of Downing Street, another anecdote is worth telling. Mrs Edith Nepean, a writer of Welsh stories, in English, recalled:

Some time ago she [Megan Lloyd George] and Mrs Lloyd George came to see me, and there were macaroons for tea. A few months later I was at Downing-street at about tea-time, and was asked to stay. While I was hesitating Megan disappeared. Presently she returned and, emptying a bagful of macaroons, exclaimed triumphantly: 'Here are your favourite cakes. Now you will stay.[30]

Born in Llandudno, Mary Edith Nepean's first novel, *Gwyneth of the Welsh Hills*, was published as a serial earlier in the year, then as a book in 1918 and filmed in 1921. She had been encouraged in her writing by Lloyd George.[31]

Sugar supplier and bread-slicer

As food constraints tightened, was the PM's wife the last resort? On 9 November, the *Lichfield Mercury* relayed an appeal from a Staffordshire resident under the heading 'Powers of a Prime Minister's Wife': 'Madame, Mrs Lloyd George, I don't want to beg, but to ask you, as the Prime Minister's wife, can you assist to get me some sugar?'[32]

On 10 November, *The Leeds Mercury* pictured Mrs Lloyd George cutting bread at a canteen for the troops, this time at Lady Limerick's Hostel, London Bridge, with the heading 'Mrs Lloyd George Cuts Bread for Tommy' – or as in the caption, 'manipulating the bread-cutting machine'. Lady Limerick was an active campaigner and most of the stations had such a canteen or buffet, in London often run by a lady of note.[33] (illustration 33)

New White City canteen

On Tuesday, 27 November, there was another canteen to be opened, for the workers at the site of the factory of furniture makers Waring & Gillow, at the time turned into a wartime manufacturing facility. (illustrations 43, 44)

> Accompanied by her daughter, Mrs Carey Evans, Mrs Lloyd George opened, at the White City, on Tuesday, a canteen which will provide hot meals for 8,000 war workers. The verse in the Bible, said Mrs Lloyd George, which suggested that those who would not work deserved no bread to eat, appealed to her with growing force. If the Food Controller found it necessary to take further measures in regard to the bread supply, she was positive that he would deal generously with those people who worked.[34]

She was accompanied by Sir George Riddell, and by Mr and Mrs S. J. Waring, of Waring & Gillow. In 1920, Mrs Lloyd George would present Mrs Waring and Lady Riddell at Court, at the same time as presenting Megan into 'Society'.

Also attending was G. A. Sawyer, who had organised the 1918 Welsh Flag Day in London. A director of Waring & Gillow, he was awarded a CBE in 1921 for his efforts.[35]

Despite this public and private provision, restraint on consumption could not be relaxed with the war in its fourth year, and was not just about food. In December, 'Eve' of *The Tatler* had a sharp eye for what might be coming:

> Apropos of Piccadilly and its crowds of lovely girls... 'nother row on 'cos we dress too much in wartime. The Duchess of Atholl says it's too perfectly frightful, she thinks, and someone's made a perfectly priceless suggestion that there should be a Dress Ministry at once, with Mrs Asquith and Mrs Lloyd George as controllers and us on the staff. Which really would be amusing, what? To start with, lovely contrast in Controllers – the P.M.'s nice, small wife, all gentleness and unassumingness and earnestness and the rest; and her predecessor all decision and opinions and emphasis, not to speak of her being herself the possessor of a not altogether democratic wardrobe.[36]

Mrs Lloyd George, the 'Dress Controller' perhaps?

CHAPTER 23

Food and Economy
1918

'Setting up one food cupboard for the whole nation, has brought everyone together within the bond of one large family... if we are to enjoy equal privileges, then we all have to make an equal sacrifice.'

Margaret Lloyd George, March 1918

Women's manifesto to women

AT THE END of January 1918, Mrs Lloyd George co-signed the Saving and Lending Campaign's 'Women's Manifesto to Women', which called on women to avoid waste and cut thoughtless spending, with well-to-do women to lead the way. The money saved should be lent to the State by buying National War Bonds or War Savings Certificates.

The Nottingham Evening Post published the manifesto in full:

> The following manifesto has been issued by a committee of women to emphasise the duty of the sex in the great economy campaign.
>
> We realise that women and girls of every class are eager to do all they can to support the fighting forces. The year 1918 will probably be decisive in the history of the war and we venture to call upon women to lead the way in a sphere of national service which is of the first importance, the practice and teaching of economy. Thousands are rendering this service already, but there are still far too many, men and women alike, whose thoughtless spending is weakening the cause of the Allies.
>
> The facts are obvious. Needless expenditure on articles requiring labour and material at a time when both are scarce and all that can be

spared are wanted for our fighting men, is to sacrifice their lives in blind ingratitude.

We earnestly appeal to well-to-do women to lead the way. The example of many is counteracted by the ostentatious display of a minority. This is especially true with regard to dress. Changes of fashion imply serious waste of labour and material. We beg all women to deny themselves for the sake of victory and to support loyally all restrictions which the Government may impose for this end.

The money saved should be lent to the State. The matter is urgent and we have written, in the belief that the women and girls of Great Britain, in grateful memory of the men who have laid down their lives in the war, and to show their sympathy with those who are now fighting, can and will abstain from all unnecessary personal expenditure, and will set aside the money thus saved and invest week by week in National War Bonds or War Savings Certificates in order that every material help may be sent to the men at the Front. The manifesto is signed by (among others) Mrs Lloyd George, Miss Beatrice Chamberlain, the Duchess of Portland, and by the presidents or chairmen of 21 national women's organisations, political and social, of widely different shades of opinion.[1]

Other signatories included Lady Londonderry, Lady Rhondda, Lady Haig, Lady Jellicoe and Lady Beatty, whose dress sense was already well-known to 'Eve' of *The Tatler*, reviewing this economy measure for its fashion-conscious readers:

Talking of frills, you've heard, I s'pose, of the newest economy campaign against the new fashions. Mrs Lloyd George, who of course doesn't go in much for clothes; the Duchess of Portland, who rather does, but I suppose she had to do something to keep even with the duke for being teetotal for the duration; Lady Londonderry, great on women and the land affairs; Lady Rhondda, the marvel of the age who doesn't eat anything two days a week; Lady Carson; Lady Kinnaird, YWCA official; Lady Haig, who is a strict dress economist; Lady Jellicoe, also not a frock-fury; and Lady Beatty are among the appealers who implore women not to buy clothes but on war loan.

'Changes of fashion imply serious waste of labour and material.' Which is all about the new tight frocks, of course.

But what is one to do? Go about in a five-yard round skirt and look a washout? But even *that* might one sink to *if* it'd help win the war. But *would* it? After all, what are *fifty* 20-guinea frocks against an eight million-a-day war?[2]

Quite. This was the nearest Mrs Lloyd George got to playing the role of 'Dress Controller', as 'Eve' suggested in December.

In 1929, Mrs Peel, Co-Women's Director at the Ministry of Food, recalled that the wealthy had already been economising, while those for the first time in employment were spending: 'In spite of the Economy Campaign, the *Draper's Record* published the fact that more money was spent by women on clothes in 1917 than in 1915. It was certainly not spent by the upper classes, who became shabbier and shabbier, but by women who for the first time had money to spare.'[3]

Margaret Lloyd George on rations

The State was also about to take further steps to counter food shortages. On 25 February 1918, Lord Rhondda's National Kitchens' Order instructed local authorities to establish national kitchens 'as a matter of urgency and as a form of insurance against acute food shortage'.[4] Rationing was getting stricter and it was important that everyone was seen to be doing their bit, not least in No. 10.

The following interview with Mrs Lloyd George may have taken place before compulsory rationing came into effect (December 1917 to February 1918) but it perhaps was part of the warm-up to the campaign.

The interview (first published in Welsh in March, here translated by Dr J. Graham Jones) was conducted by Beriah Evans, a long-time supporter of Lloyd George, secretary of the Welsh Nationalist movement *Cymru Fydd*, journalist, and prominent at National Eisteddfods. The result is classic Mrs Lloyd George: clear homely advice, careful not to criticize government policy, and taking the opportunity to champion education, especially for girls, and everyone must do their bit. Although she didn't think the National Kitchens would work in villages, she did support the idea of school lunches.

> Rationing Food Fairly: Mrs Lloyd George relates how the Prime Minister's family coped under Lord Rhondda's food regime by Mr Beriah Evans.
>
> In a recent conversation with me, Mrs Lloyd George explained her opinion about the work of Lord Rhondda as our Food Controller, and she

gave interesting details about the home life of the Prime Minister and the difficulties faced by his family under the rations scheme. She said:

'The Food Ministry has rendered an important national service by impressing upon the mind and conscience of every family in the kingdom the necessity now for all of us to stand or fall together. Lord Rhondda, by setting up one food cupboard for the whole nation, has brought everyone together within the bond of one large family, one general brotherhood. He has placed us all on the same footing, and has made us realise that, if we are to enjoy equal privileges, then we all have to make an equal sacrifice. Common sense dictates that the food cupboard of one family should not be allowed to overflow with plenty while the cupboard of his neighbour is empty.

'I can assure you that there is no hoarding in our house in Downing Street – and of necessity it is very difficult to make food arrangements there. Very seldom do we know who will be there for breakfast, or lunch, or possibly for dinner. We do not purchase half as much meat as we used to. The butcher's shop where we bought our meat in London had sold everything and had closed at nine o'clock last Saturday. We can get fresh meat in Cricieth only once a week. When there, I usually do my shopping on a Thursday for the family's needs for the following week. In Plas Hen, Chwilog, we have to depend on a butcher who comes around once a week for orders.'

Plas Hen was where Richard Lloyd George and his wife, and now their daughter Valerie, lived at the time, close to Llanystumdwy, Lloyd George's former home.

'The success of the housewife in looking after the home and the family depends to a large extent on her being well organized and able to anticipate what will be needed in wartime and its shortage as in the days of peace and plenty. Hitherto our main difficulty has been the shortage of butter and margarine. The ration of this is certainly small, especially where there are children who eat a lot of bread and butter. But even then a wise mother can meet to some extent with this difficulty by providing other kinds of food to replace the sandwich.

'We as a family have often suffered inconvenience because of a shortage of butter; but complaining does not help things. Mr Lloyd George likes to spend Sunday in the countryside at Walton Heath, and it is more difficult to have things there than in London. I usually go there every Friday,

Food and Economy (1918)

taking one maid with me from Downing Street, and taking butter or margarine with us from Downing Street. Megan, who is away in school, always spends Sunday with us, and often a friend or two stay with us over Sunday. We have succeeded in doing quite well on the whole, with rather a lot of inconvenience and discomfort at times, it is true, but there is no purpose in complaining and worrying about it.

'Our coal has been cut back since October. This makes a great deal of difference in our cooking arrangements, and we have had to be very economical with the coal. As for milk, we have to live on half what we used to have, and often we have none at all. The milkman never comes until the afternoon now. We have stopped making milk puddings of all kinds, but there are plenty of recipes for other tasty foods to replace them. Every experienced family knows how to cope with the small, unexpected needs of home life.

'If Lord Rhondda anticipates an imminent shortage of any kind of essential or popular food, his duty is to ration it. In the case of all essential food, everyone must be placed on the same level. By working happily together, by being ready to suffer and sacrifice together, that is the only way we can emerge safely from our national crisis. It is a very easy task to criticize the Food Controller, and to find fault with his regulations; anyone can do that; but it requires an ability far higher than the norm to devise a scheme that is better than his scheme. And now that he has had such an extensive experience, and has gathered so many facts and essential information concerning our food resources, and has set up a committee of individuals to supervise him, I, for my own part, will be perfectly willing to allow him to decide what needs to be done in order to ensure the necessary supply of food.'

Town versus Country
'There is an essential difference between the customs of life in the town and in the country. In the towns and the industrial areas, the shop is usually so convenient that people can get their food from the shop almost on a daily basis. It is very different in the countryside. There the working man will usually provide a joint of bacon and a dish of butter at the start of the winter. It would be a wholly unjust matter to accuse the ordinary working man of 'hoarding' food – unless he would continue to purchase these foodstuffs from the shop while he still has the joint and the supply of butter in the house. Rather than penalising him, we should encourage him to practise the necessary economies. The same regulation should be

applied to the farmer by allowing him to provide for the needs of his family as previously, whether it be bacon or butter, or any other food which he produces. But he should place on the market everything which he produces over and above the ordinary needs of his family.

'Then there is the question of the milk. Milk is a food especially for children. We must care for the children as a top priority; they are the hope for the future. Milk for the children should therefore be the top priority for the dairy. Having secured enough milk for the food, then butter and cheese should be made from what is left over. I am afraid that the children in the villages are now being deprived of the milk which they previously used to have, as the farmers send it to the towns to be sold.

'The "Public Kitchen" scheme should be adapted to all the big towns. Such a kitchen, where the food is cooked for the whole area, rations the food, time, work and money. It would save coal and gas, the food would be better and it would be better cooked, and would be much cheaper than it often is in the houses at home. A substantial dinner can be obtained from the public kitchen for about half of what it would cost at home.

'But the scheme is not suitable for a rural area. Yet I would like to see the "school lunch scheme" becoming more general throughout the country. All the potatoes and vegetables could be grown in the school garden; the gardening training would be as good for the boys as would be the cooking training for the girls. An excellent dinner can be made for a penny a head. I opened a "School Kitchen" in a rural area shortly before the war, and, although the price of the dinner was a penny a head, it paid its way. I suppose it would cost more now, but it would become cheaper and generally better than at home.'[5]

The Food Ministry did also push for canteens in villages, but only when there was sufficient population density and transport, and under certain conditions, including the provision of soup and food that could be easily 'taken into the field', such as Cornish pasties.[6]

Although the women's movement at times queried the unelected Mrs Lloyd George's authority to speak on their behalf, she was, as wife of the Prime Minister, close to the thinking in Government circles. Rationing was a sensitive issue, where a loose comment could embarrass the Government, but where a soft approach may have been just what was needed to help deliver a hard message, the underlying tenor being that the rules apply to all: 'One food cupboard for the whole nation.' There was definitely method in her messaging.

Lady Rhondda's 'At Home' for national kitchens

While Mrs Lloyd George was in Wales, Lady Rhondda, wife of the Food Controller, gave an 'At Home' on 14 March at the National Kitchen on Buckingham Palace Road, attended primarily by domestic science teachers. JTR was present. Initially named the Central Kitchen, the kitchen had just been established there, at the National Training School of Cookery, adjacent to Victoria Station, on 4 March.[7] The *Western Mail* covered the 'At Home', which was also attended by Charles Spencer, the businessman selected by Lord Rhondda to drive the national kitchens programme:

> Lady Rhondda, who is extending practical support to the national kitchen movement, gave an 'At Home' this evening at the National Kitchen, 72, Buckingham Palace-road, to representatives of the teaching profession who are interesting themselves in the question of food economy.
>
> The guests comprised chiefly those members of the profession who are working in the interest of the torpedoed sailors for the British and Foreign Sailors' Society, under the direction of the Rev. J. T. Rhys, formerly of Swansea.
>
> Lady Rhondda spoke on the development of the movement, and suggested that Wales should take up the national kitchen scheme, expressing the hope that Alderman Spencer, Director of National Kitchens at the Food Ministry, would turn his attention to the Principality.
>
> Alderman Spencer remarked that the local authorities in Wales and in other parts of the country were the people who should carry out this work. He thought the result of the present movement would be a credit to Lord Rhondda and the department over which he presided.
>
> The Rev. J. T. Rhys commended the work Lady Rhondda had undertaken on behalf of torpedoed sailors in a cheerful and self-denying manner. He was amazed at her ladyship's mercy, industry, and self-sacrifice.[8]

Charles Spencer had accepted Lord Rhondda's invitation in November 1917 to head up the Food Ministry's mass dining project on condition that it would be 'untrammelled by red tape' and run as a 'business proposition'. Not happy with the word 'communal', Spencer suggested many alternatives, from which the title 'National Kitchen' was chosen, alongside the 'NK' brand. As Lord Rhondda would tell the *Manchester Guardian* in January 1918: '"Community kitchens" implied on the one hand, a culture of charity, and, on the other, communism.'[9]

JTR'S tale

JTR later recalled a similar occasion, probably at Buckingham Palace Road:

> Owing solely to the fortunes of war, I can claim to have spoken at meetings with the Dowager Lady Rhondda more frequently than any other speaker. When Lord Rhondda was Food Minister I called to ask him if he would address a meeting I was organising. He said he gladly would, but public speaking was not quite in his line. 'Ask my wife. She is a first-class speaker, but don't tell her I suggested it, for she hates public speaking.' I did so, and for many months Lady Rhondda and I addressed meetings, morning, noon, and night, in almost every borough in London. She spoke in a most informing way on how to economise in the matter of food, and on the cultivation of various foods in particular. We often had to speak six times in one day, and Lady Rhondda was often so exhausted that, at the end of the day, she could scarcely crawl into her car to be taken back to Ashley Gardens.
>
> There hangs a story at the end of that campaign. Lady Rhondda expressed a wish one day to meet some of the ladies who had been helped at those meetings, and authorised me to arrange a dinner at a certain West End hotel for a hundred or more guests. I consulted friends, drew up our lists of guests, and approached some hotels for tenders.
>
> Alas, the Minister of Food put his foot down. It was preposterous to propose a dinner when there was still a shortage of food. And the wife of the Food Minister! But as not infrequently happens, the husband was outwitted by the wife. Lady Rhondda arranged for a demonstration of a vegetarian dinner at one of the best-known colleges for Domestic Sciences and Cooking in London, and we dined without violating either the letter or the spirit of the law, and we had a happy time. I remember sitting between the wife of an Archbishop and the wife of a statesman who subsequently became Chancellor of the Exchequer.[10]

JTR's dining companions may have been Edith Murdoch Tait, Mrs Davidson, wife of the Archbishop of Canterbury (who had attended the Royal opening of the Westminster Bridge Road experimental kitchen in May 1917), and Ivy Chamberlain, wife of Austen Chamberlain. If not too exhausted, Lady Rhondda might have walked home, a modest stroll from Ashley Gardens.

On 20 May, Mrs Lloyd George was complimenting another

kitchen, established in the canteen of the Down Lane Council School, Tottenham:[11]

> Mrs Lloyd George, opening today a National Kitchen in Tottenham established by the Food Control Committee, said she had visited a number of National Kitchens in the London area, and said that she considered that it was the finest and most up-to-date that she had seen, and the food was excellent. She also spoke of the great importance of providing food for the rising generation.[12]

The National Kitchen, New Bridge Street

On 16 July, with *Pathé News* in attendance, Mrs Lloyd George and a distinguished party had lunch at the flagship NK National Restaurant on New Bridge Street, Blackfriars, London (running from Blackfriars Bridge up to Fleet Street and Ludgate Circus). Their visit as diners, as opposed to opening the venture, was to demonstrate that the kitchens were for all, serving good-quality food. Charles Spencer had written to Lord Rhondda in January 1918: 'There is no one the working woman looks up to like a Lord. We should have to get noble Lords and Ladies to patronise the communal kitchens and have the fact well press-campaigned.'[13] (illustrations 38 to 42)

Possibly the grandest of the wartime kitchens, details of the interior survive, General Electric making a record of their modern lighting. You can see why restaurateurs bridled at this State-subsidised competition, although *The Mirror* newspaper's 'Sunday Pictorial' noted a surprise bonus for the local trade: 'One unexpected result of the opening of the National Kitchen last week was to bring an enormous increase of business to other restaurants in the City. This was due to the immense overflow of people who were unable to get served at the National.'[14]

This one was called a Restaurant not a Kitchen, albeit using the NK 'brand'.[15] The premises had been taken over from Spiers & Pond, a long-established major catering business, especially at railway stations, and this was possibly the site of their successful Ludgate Hill Station restaurant, already an elegant establishment back in 1866, a 'popular haunt for bohemian and literary types', praised by Dickens as one of the first places in the country where the railway traveller could get 'wholesome food, decently served'.[16] Spiers & Pond went into receivership in 1916, sold some operations (including their notable

Criterion Restaurant on Piccadilly Circus, which they had founded in 1873), but had since returned to business.[17]

> Mrs Lloyd George, accompanied by Mrs Winston Churchill, Mrs Clynes, Mrs Spencer, wife of the Director of National Kitchens [Charles Spencer], and Sir Vincent Evans, dined to-day at the National Restaurant in New Bridge-street. The party partook of an excellent meal, comprising fried fish with hollandaise sauce, and new potatoes, and sago jam, at a total cost of 1s., and they expressed themselves as being delighted with the meal. Mrs Lloyd George, who spoke with enthusiasm of the work of the restaurant in supplying cheap meals to the workers of Fleet Street, remarked that anybody who came there could get a sound, substantial meal, and she expressed the hope that there would more of such institutions established.
>
> Mrs Clynes also was pleased with the arrangements and declared she was astonished at the quality and the quantity of the food. 'I am a North Country woman,' said Mrs Clynes, 'and I know what a good meal is and what good cooking is; both of these can be obtained here.'[18]

Mrs Clynes was the wife of the new Food Controller, J. R. Clynes, leader of the Labour Party who had succeeded the recently deceased Lord Rhondda. Diarist Samuell Pepys Junior, lamenting the rising cost of living, expressed his sympathies with the new incumbent:

> The price of margareen is this day encreased to 1s. 2d. the lb., which is, God knows, such a price as I had never thought I should live to pay it for margareen; and a bad beginning, I think, for Mr Clynes, he now made Comptrouller of Victuall.[19]

Nationalise the caterers?

In October 1918, *The Herald*, 'The National Labour Weekly', would set out its own vision for the future of the National Kitchens when reviewing the success of the New Bridge Street Kitchen. It is reprinted in full below, with italics from the original, as an entertaining and insightful example of the political debates of the time over ownership, welfare, and the relative roles of public and private sectors.

> TAKE OVER LYONS! Cheaper Food and Better Food
> WHEN the National Kitchen and Restaurant was started in New Bridge Street, London, the catering trade grumbled uneasily at what they

considered reckless adventure into their preserve. But when the National Kitchen disclosed the results of its first quarter's trading, the catering trade was thoroughly startled. And good cause it had to be. But of that in a moment.

The line the caterers took against National Kitchens was, of course, a purely disinterested one. The National Kitchens would absorb public money. Was that right in wartime? The National Kitchens were charity. Did the British worker want charity? And one firm, realising perhaps that its customers' sympathies were not likely to be easily aroused on behalf of the catering trade, made the generous argument 'What is being done now in MY trade may next be done in YOURS' – as if to say: 'We, of course, would grin and bear it; but think of the precedent, old chap! We must save you from State interference.' They even went so far as to declare from many posters that Might was not Right. And only the most hardened cynic could read between the lines of these altruistic arguments in the text:

'What of my Dividends?'

Consider for a moment the Might – that has been the caterers – and whether it has had anything to do with Right. The most important catering organisation in London is that of J. Lyons and Company Ltd. It is also the most prosperous of its kind. Its dividends even in wartime are 25 per cent, and last year it added £40,000 to its Reserve Fund. True, before the war it was making 42½ per cent, but that is scarcely a good defence. Lyons pre-eminently deserves our attention, and every city in the country its equivalent case.

The 130 odd Lyons' branches serve millions of meals a week. [When Mrs Lloyd George opened the National Restaurant there was already a J. Lyons restaurant over the road.] They serve them mainly to the clerk, the office girl, the shop assistant, the foreman. They are institutions, therefore, of very great national importance. They have, under pressure of war conditions, lessened portions, decreased quality, reduced service, and greatly increased prices. That some of this process was inevitable we, of course, admit: but why should they make 25 per cent profit? This is an apposite question for the worker who, for want of better – and let us freely admit, there are no better capitalist businesses of this kind – has had to feed at the Lyons' establishments. His bill and his appetite have given him broad enough hints. And now comes the National Kitchen to prove the facts to the end of the handle.

A Comparison

The worker goes to his mid-day dinner at the National Kitchen. What can he get for about a shilling? He chooses, from a fine variety of dishes, a plate of soup (2d.); haricot oxtail (6d.); with marrow or peas or carrots (2d.); two slices of bread and butter (1d.); a cake (1d.); and a cup of tea (1d.) – making in all a halfpenny more than shilling. The food is hot, of fine quality, and of generous proportions.

Or he goes to Lyons. His soup costs 4d.; oxtail, 9d.; potatoes, 2d.; bread and butter, 1½d.; cake, 1½d.; and tea 2½d. – a total of 1s. 10½d. And he won't have had food as good, as hot, or as plentiful.

At the National Kitchen, the customer carries his own food to his table, and so saves a little overhead cost for the concern – and much time for himself.

Now, the provision of such good food, and such cheap food, may seem financially impossible to those who are accustomed to the caterers' prices. Does it pay? Obviously if it does not pay, and the Ministry of Food is subsidising it out of public funds, the charge against the caterers falls to the ground.

It Pays!

In fact, it pays. It doesn't 'just pay', it makes an exorbitant profit. The National Kitchen has so little to do with charity that it is making out of its customers what would be, if it were an ordinary concern, *a dividend of 70 per cent, per annum*, after all expenses, depreciation, interest on capital, &c., have been provided for. In eighteen months the whole capital cost of this concern will have been paid for out of profits! And it serves an honest meal at a reasonable price.

The proper feeding of millions of workers in great cities and small is a matter of the utmost importance to the State. It is a responsibility which the State has allowed to be clenched in private hands. But now the New Bridge Street Restaurant has shown what is possible. Our duty to the workers is plain. We must have not one, not a dozen, but thousands of these restaurants throughout the country.

The need exists. The model exists. The power exists. *The machinery exists.*

The need is in the underfed and over-charged workers.

The model is in the National Kitchen at New Bridge Street.

The power is in the hands of the Ministry of Food.

The machinery is in the restaurants, hotels, shops and general establishments of the great caterers.

Food and Economy (1918)

The first step for the Ministry of Food to take is to NATIONALISE LYONS!

The shops are there. The customers are there. *And, so far, the private profit has been there.* Let the private profit go.

'Stop the Home Fires Burning'
We do not deny that there will be difficulties – artificial difficulties.

The catering concerns include some of the greatest advertisers in the country; and that the Press cannot forget. Apart from that, the difficulties are amazingly few. And think what the results would be! Such a scheme would mean a daily blessing to millions of people. It would strike at the heart of monopoly. It would be a social education, for the 'rich' and the 'poor' would have to foregather together on the equal terms of their common human needs. It would make an enormous saving of coal, through better organisation, and the growth the 'food-away-from-home' habit. It would mean an enormous economy in the foodstuffs themselves, by token of better cooking and organisation. Moreover, it would be an enormous addition to the revenue of the country; for the Ministry of Food has proved, not only that it serves its customers better, but that it is better qualified to run a catering business, and at a greater profit than the caterers themselves – that it has done it once, and can do it again. The Lyons' concern is flourishing, but others are not. Let them undergo, in due course, a healthy course of nationalisation!

The method of nationalisation is perfectly simple. Every shareholder in these concerns would be given War Bonds to the value of *the actual amount they invested in the business*. Thus, those who had invested when shares were at par would, at last, have a term put to their exploitation of the public. They would get the fair War Bond interest of 5 per cent, that which they ought never to have had more. Those, on the other hand, who but lately invested would not suffer for they, too, would get 5 per cent on whatever they had put in, whatever the nominal value of their holding. Exploitation would thus be eliminated, and at the same time no one would suffer.

Waste
It has long been the general view that public services – like waterworks, trams, gas and electricity – should be withdrawn from private hands. It has long been proved what great results accrue to the public when this is done. Food distribution is, at any time, a service as essential as

these, but in wartime, and in an island country, it exceeds any of them in importance. There was lately a series of posters put about with the idea of making people realise their responsibility to the seamen if they wasted what it costs privation and lives to bring to our tables. Waste now – and always – is monstrous; but something just as monstrous is making private profit out of commodities carried at such a cost.

The National Kitchen and Restaurant, we say, has proved that it could pay dividends at the rate of 70 per cent per annum. (Some capitalist newspapers, it may be remarked in passing, have gone so far as to say that this is a 'sound return'.) It feeds its customers and it outdoes even the Lyons' concerns in the way of profit. That, it may be argued, is a reproach to the National Kitchen – but it is surely a worse one to the great-headed businessmen who run the catering concerns! If the Ministry of Food could convert the Lyons 25 per cent into 70 per cent, it would be able, without loss on the sum total of its business to open kitchens, afford service, supply food, in any places where the local conditions might make a paying proposition impossible. It could contribute an enormous sum to the Exchequer every year. It could make a fair distribution of food, regardless of price, to the whole population. And, incidentally, it could give its servants a first-rate wage and first-rate conditions.

We conclude with a boast which fell from the lips of Mr Montague Gluckstein when he addressed the Lyons shareholders in June 1917: 'You are, no doubt, interested to learn that while the consumption of food has been less, the cash receipts have considerably greater.'[20]

As for the employment implications, *The Sunday Pictorial* had asked:

What Say the Waitresses? If the national kitchen business grows to any extent, will waiters and waitresses be required? Waiting on one's self does away with useless labour, and frees men and women for productive work.[21]

Joseph Lyons had at least joined the campaign against waste, back in 1916:

Messrs Joseph Lyons are exhibiting a small poster in all their 200 teashops, restaurants, and factories to this effect: 'To waste is to be pro-German, so if you can't fight, contribute your bit by exercising economy and avoiding

Food and Economy (1918)

waste in everything, in business and in private life.' Meanwhile, the price of tea, toast, etc., rises by halfpennies.[22]

Neither *The Herald*'s vision of the nationalisation of the catering trade, nor the spread of national kitchens, came to pass. In March 1919, Spiers & Pond would be wrangling over a price for the New Bridge Street Restaurant, and by late 1919 all national restaurants had closed.[23] J. Lyons prospered, with waitresses part of its image, notably the 'nippy waitress' in a 1924 modernisation drive – not for them *The Herald*'s endorsement of the NK idea of taking your own food to your table. Spiers & Pond (rumoured to have been a J. Lyons takeover target in 1911) had also been well known for attracting its barmaids, described by Dickens as 'bright-eyed, cheerfully obliging nymphs'.[24] In 1951, in a further modernising, pioneering move, J. Lyons became the first business to use a computer, the LEO 1 (as in Lyons Electric Office) computer. The last Lyons Corner House closed in 1977.

For *The Herald*, the opportunity to promote the concept of nationalisation was not one to be missed: in July 1917 the Fabian Sidney Webb had written a powerful essay crediting the wholehearted support for the war effort by the Labour movement, and volunteerism, for the way distress had been averted during the war.[25] He was then working on Clause IV of the Labour Party's constitution, which embedded nationalisation as a key tenet of socialist policy (the same clause whose amendment symbolised New Labour's ambitions 80 years later).

The opening of the National Kitchen in New Bridge Street, a legacy of Lord Rhondda, probably marked the peak of the wartime restaurant boom, just one year on from the success of his predecessor Lord Davenport's Westminster Bridge Kitchen. The war had just three months to run. Ten days later, on 26 July, Mrs Lloyd George was due to open another National Kitchen, at Holborn Baths, Endell Street, Shaftesbury-avenue, but the Mayoress of Holborn had to take her place.[26] The previous day the Mayor had had an informal luncheon there, expressing his own views on the national restaurant concept:

> The restaurant, formerly a swimming bath, will hold 200 persons, and the cost of conversion and equipment is estimated at £1,800. [The Mayor] said that the money spent on the kitchen would be borrowed from the State, and would probably be paid back in 10 yearly instalments, free of

interest, so that no part of the cost would fall on the rates. He questioned whether it was wise of the Government to establish those kitchens, and believed that it would have been cheaper to control restaurants and eating-houses. They intended, however, to make the best use they could of that institution.[27]

Public baths were often selected as locations for public kitchens. Holborn Baths continues today, a leisure centre with pool and cafeteria.

By the time of the Armistice there were 363 officially registered national kitchens. Within six months 120 had closed. Their demise ironically was accelerated by the extension of rationing (as people had to use their meat coupons in the kitchens) and there was strong opposition from restaurateurs, citing unfair subsidised state competition.[28] The attractiveness of communal dining took a further knock with the 1918 influenza outbreak. Mrs Peel reflected that, after the war, while some middle-class people might actually economise by eating out, this was less of an option for working-class people, on more limited income.[29]

The food reformers at the Ministry had also imagined other long-term change:

> Probably at some future time it will be difficult to believe that each household did its own separate marketing, buying small amounts of food from retail dealers at hundred per cent above cost price, that every hundred houses in a street had each its own fire for cooking, and that at least a hundred human beings were engaged in serving meals that could have been prepared by half a dozen trained assistants.[30]

The post-war years would continue to be a time of austerity, food shortages, and food price inflation. Rationing was only slowly wound down and the Ministry of Food itself was finally closed in March 1921. Mrs Lloyd George continued her housekeeping campaigning, calling for the retention of allotments, more training in domestic science, and frowned on the increasing tendency for housewives to rely on tinned food from the corner shop. With perhaps some irony, during the April 1921 coal strike, shortly after the Ministry was closed, Mrs Lloyd George was appointed to an Emergency Kitchens Committee set up by the Board of Trade 'to encourage the provision of cheap cooked foods in districts when the need is apparent'.

The need for welfare was as great as ever. The communal national kitchen phenomenon tested cultural, economic, social and political boundaries, and made an important contribution in a time of emergency. Only two decades later, the country's new Prime Minister, Winston Churchill, would revive the concept in the face of renewed conflict.

The country's women come to town

By the summer of 1918, the country's Women's Institutes were planning to 'come to town' for the first time, for an October exhibition of not only jam but their food 'banking' innovations, as the *Sheffield Daily Telegraph* described:

> The Premier's Home-made Jam: Mrs Lloyd George, I hear, will be much in evidence when the villages are 'brought to town' shortly. There is to be a more than usually interesting exhibition of wartime revivals – the preserves, toys, and baskets which villagers have had to provide for themselves because they cannot get them in any other way. The Premier knows the jam is good, because on one occasion when Mrs Lloyd George was discussing the work in progress she took up a pot of excellent whole fruit jam, asked the price, and carried it home to Downing Street for the Prime Minister's breakfast.
>
> Another phase in which Mrs Lloyd George is interested is the new-style village 'bank', which deals not with money, but fruit and vegetables. Under a cooperative preserving system the village women 'pay in' their home-grown produce, presenting later their 'cheque' for pickles and jams as they require them.[31]

The *Reading Mercury and Oxford Gazette* reported:

> In Oxfordshire and elsewhere, the Women's Institutes movement is co-operating with the Workers' Educational Association in arranging a series of lectures. At many of the institutes instruction is being given in basket making, and bacon curing and bee keeping. Excellent progress is being made with the arrangements for the exhibition of women's work organised by the National Federation of Women's Institutes to be held at the Caxton Hall, Westminster, London, S.W.1 ... particulars can be obtained from the organiser, Miss Alice Williams, Hon. Secretary, National Federation of Women's Institutes, 72, Victoria Street, S.W.1.[32]

The Newcastle Journal stressed the work of the Women's Land Army:

> Women's Work: In the Village Life and Industrial Exhibition to be opened in Caxton Hall towards the end this month, the Women's Land Army will be a prominent feature in the life-size illustrations of the work of national importance women are performing for the nation. This aspect of women's labour bulks largely in the exhibition at the Whitechapel Art Gallery, so admirably organised by the Women's Work Sub-Committee of the Imperial War Museum. The lay figures of the uniformed lasses of the Land Army, and the stuffed farm animals in their charge, form very striking pictures, and have largely contributed to the popularity of the exhibition.
>
> The Caxton Hall gathering, illustrative of village life, will be on independent and original lines, and in view of its importance has secured a flattering measure of influential support. The Queen has arranged to visit the exhibition, and will probably be accompanied by one or more members the Royal Family. Mrs Lloyd George and Mr W. M. Hughes, Australia's Prime Minister, will be among the 'openers' of the exhibition on successive days.[33]

On 3 September, diarist Samuell Pepys Junior recorded that his family were also doing their bit: 'My wife and our girls this day mighty busy jamming fruit (blackburies and marrowes the most of it).'[34]

The Village Life and Industrial Exhibition, Caxton Hall

Queen Mary opened the exhibition on the first day, accompanied by Alice Williams and Mrs Watt. (illustration 54) Mrs Lloyd George was both a great admirer and friend of the Queen, as Ffion Hague observes: 'In her fund-raising and hospital work she would have found a natural point of contact with Margaret,' and both were keen gardeners.[35]

Mrs Lloyd George opened the exhibition on Welsh Day, Monday, 28 October. Her handwritten speech notes survive in the JTR Collection:

> I am very glad I am able to be here today to take part in this interesting exhibition. I am pleased to associate myself with the work of the Women's Institutes. The work already done has been such a splendid contribution to our National Welfare that it has established a strong claim to our support. I am glad that the exhibition has been such a success. It was

mainly organised I believe by my fellow countrywoman Miss A. W. [Alice Williams]. It has meant hard work & our grateful thanks are due to her & also for the plays she has written in aid of this & other work.

I remember 2 or 3 years ago taking the chair for Mrs Watt & Mr Nugent Harris at Cricieth at a meeting to start a W.I. It was then stated that one of the objectives of the Institute was to try and make the town self-supporting in poultry & beekeeping, the cultivation of fruit and flowers. I am sure that the interest now taken in allotment gardens is in itself sufficient to justify the efforts made at the start by Mrs Watt and Mr Harris. The exhibits will greatly help to advertise the work that is being done by women all over the country. The women are doing all they can to be helpful in suggesting new ideas & to try to solve the difficulties of our food problems & the high cost of living.

We are having to be economical & we make use of things we never dreamt of in the piping times of peace. Now that women will help us to legislate, I hope they will have something to say to the House planning association & that they will see that a garden be attached to every house. I hope the people of this country are not going back to pre-war days but that they will insist on holding their allotments. We see in this hall the results of these allotments, the splendid fruit and vegetables grown & the competition has been very keen. I trust we shall go on to perfect our Women's Institutes so as to benefit the country at large.[36] (illustration 53)

For the history of the Women's Institute, this speech is a small treat, citing the key founders, the importance of Cricieth and Wales as the 'birthplace' of the WI in the UK, and again encouraging the newly suffraged women to use their power to influence policy.

Caxton Hall held an important place in the history of women's suffrage. On 19 February 1906, the first suffrage procession in London of three to four hundred 'poor working women from the East End for the most part', marched to Caxton Hall, which they had hired, and subsequently proceeded to the House of Commons (where they were not admitted), to demand that the King's Speech should include a suffrage measure.[37] Thereafter, at the beginning of each parliamentary session, the Women's Social and Political Union (WSPU) hosted a 'Women's Parliament' at the Hall, before going on to Parliament to deliver a petition to the prime minister in person – an attempt which never succeeded.

The WI Caxton Hall event was given wide press coverage. *The*

Suffolk and Essex Free Press reported on the food, the toys and the revival of rural crafts:

> At the first annual meeting of the National Federation of Women's Institutes just held in London, it was stated that the number of Institutes now numbered over 700. The movement is spreading throughout the country with amazing rapidity, and is already exercising a most beneficial influence on village life and industries.
>
> This week's exhibition at Caxton Hall, London, organised by Lady Denman, Chairman of the Federation and Miss Alice Williams, Hon. Secretary, by common consent was one of the most striking displays of women's work ever brought together in England. The fruit, vegetables, eggs, preserved foods, cakes, cheeses etc. were warmly praised by connoisseurs and largely bought by the general public. Commercial toy makers were surprised by the excellence and novelty of the toys, soft and hard, made in English villages – a company has, by the way, been started to develop the British-made toy industry so successfully initiated by the Women's Institutes. Village-made fabrics formed another attractive feature of the exhibition: and among its other effects hardly fail to be a marked revival in rural arts and crafts. Examples of the latter, as well as fine home-made cheeses, were sent from places where, prior to the starting of a Women's Institute, nothing of the kind was done.
>
> Her Majesty the Queen, whose warm sympathy for everything which concerns the welfare and progress of British women is well known, visited the exhibition, as did Mrs Lloyd George.[38]

The Cardiff-based *Western Mail* celebrated Welsh success:

WELSH WINNERS AT THE WI: Striking evidence has been given at the exhibition now being held at Caxton Hall, London, of the value of the National Federation of Women's Institutes, and also of the great interest aroused in Wales in the work of the Federation. On Welsh Day the exhibition was opened by Mrs Lloyd George, who said that she was particularly pleased to be associated with this movement, partly because of its appeal to women and partly because of the part played in it by Wales. Women had already rendered great national service by suggesting new methods of economising, and so helping solve the food problem and the cost of living.

Of the six banners awarded for special merit, Wales won not less than three – by the Deudraeth Institute for the largest number of prizes per institute, by North Wales for the greatest number of industries represented, and by Ffestiniog for the most original industry. The officers for Wales are: Mrs Lloyd George, president; Mrs Drage, chairman, and Mrs William George, Hon. Secretary.[39]

The WI movement was of course integral to the war housekeeping campaign and continues today. A women's initiative whose time had come? In contrast, emergency communal dining has ebbed and flowed with crisis, but as modern campaigners such as Dr Bryce Evans remind us, the lessons of wartime could help meet the challenges of 21st-century food austerity and the need for a healthy diet.

CHAPTER 24

Hospitals and Healthcare
(1914 to 1918)

'It is more dangerous to be a baby
in England than a soldier in France.'
Margaret Lloyd George, January 1918

HEALTHCARE WAS A lifelong cause for Mrs Lloyd George, not least supporting the provision of care for mothers and babies, from maternal care to crèches for working women (not least the munitionettes), and safe spaces where women and children could relax away from the temptation of drink.

In addition to supporting two hospitals, the Prince of Wales Hospital for the Limbless and Disabled, in Cardiff, and the Welsh wing of the Netley Military Hospital, on Southampton Water, Mrs Lloyd George made frequent visits of support for other hospitals and care facilities, as well as publicising the work of women in healthcare throughout the war, at home and abroad. The latter dimension is well covered in an interview she gave in November 1915 which is reproduced in this chapter.

Recruiting nursing volunteers

At the outset of war, on 4 August 1914, Mrs Lloyd George, daughter Olwen, and sister-in-law Mrs William George attended a Cricieth meeting to set up a voluntary aid detachment (VAD), recruiting civilian volunteers to nurse military casualties. VADs were first set up in 1909, with the help of the Red Cross and the Order of St John.[1]

Hospitals and Healthcare (1914 to 1918)

All classes are displaying an admirable feeling of unity at Cricieth. On Tuesday evening, Dr Lloyd Owen (medical officer of health) convened a meeting for the establishment of a voluntary aid detachment in the town, and the attendance included Mrs Greaves (wife of the Lord-Lieutenant) and Mrs Lloyd George. More than twenty members were enrolled at the meeting. Mrs Bolland was appointed commandant, Mrs William George, Lady Superintendent, and Mrs [Dorothy] Drage, quartermaster. Miss Olwen Lloyd George will be one of the cooks, and Dr Gladstone Jones has undertaken to deliver lectures.[2]

John Greaves, wealthy slate mine owner, and first commoner Lord-Lieutenant of Caernarfonshire, and his wife Marianne, lent a nearby property to establish the Wern Military Hospital, initially for 25 patients, rising to 41. It started taking in patients in December 1915, with Olwen nursing there during the 1916/17 Christmas holidays. (illustrations 65, 66) His daughter Dorothy's husband, retired soldier Godfrey Drage, wrote to Mrs Lloyd George:

> I hear you were good enough to propose that my wife should be quartermaster of the Cricieth Branch of the Red X, and I am letting them have the use of the Drill Hall. I shall be only too glad to lend the Drill Hall to your Liberal Association for any cause not connected with politics, which I am glad to think are all in abeyance at this time of grave national crisis.[3]

The VADs represented yet another volunteer dimension of support for the war, the nurses being unpaid, often funding their own uniforms. Those volunteering to serve in the Women's Auxiliary Army Corps (the WAACs), were paid.[4]

Women in the Red Cross and the VAD

In a 1915 interview with MP and social reformer Percy Alden, Mrs Lloyd George praised the women in the Red Cross and the VAD.

> 'The story of what the Red Cross has accomplished and of what women have done through the Red Cross is simply amazing. Let me give you two or three figures. Eighteen hundred trained nurses are working to-day in England and on the Continent in connection with the British Red Cross. That in itself is a tremendous achievement, and the RAMC [Royal Army

Medical Corps] would be the very first to acknowledge the wonderful devotion and skill that have been displayed by these nurses. In addition, the VAD has supplied 1,500 women to serve under trained nurses. They are posted at hospitals both in England and in France, and the effect of their aid is to set free fully trained women for higher posts. All these have obtained certificates in first-aid and home nursing, while many have certificates also in hygiene, sanitation, and cookery.

'They "call nothing common or unclean," they are just as willing to scrub a floor, or to wash crockery as they are to nurse the sick or act as orderlies. If you would like see some of the hospital work you can find it either at the large Red Cross hospitals for the British at places like La Touquet and Rouen, or you can go to Calais and see the Anglo-Belgian hospitals there, or the Queen Alexandra at Malo-les-Bains [a Dunkirk beach resort], or the Elisabeth at Poperinge [in Belgium, close to Ypres]. Many women are giving their services at the rest stations which have been established at various railway centres. They meet the men as they come back from the trenches and supply them with food and comforts and clothing and generally refit them for the next move forward.'

'Would you mind telling me what a Women's Voluntary Aid Detachment consists of? I don't think most people are really aware of how such a detachment is constituted?'

'Of course, you know that originally the idea was that they should act as temporary nurses to look after the wounded in improvised hospitals. The RAMC approved this work, and conducted examinations and inspections of the women volunteers. It was thought that they would fill the gap left by the War Office, since the War Office machinery made no arrangements for rest stations or sorting hospitals for dealing with wounded or sick coming back from the dressing stations.

'A detachment consists of a commandant, a quartermaster, and a superintendent nurse, with twenty nurses. The organisation was put to a severe test when, at the fall of Antwerp, in October, the wounded Belgians had to be evacuated from hospitals in Belgium and accommodated in England. Since then the War Office has mobilised the VAD and thrown more and more work upon their shoulders, and the women have responded in a very remarkable fashion. It was naturally found necessary to supplement the work of amateurs, and so trained nurses were called in to supervise, but the greater part of the work of the hospital, whether cooking or washing or scrubbing, is carried out by these women, who, without payment, and with wonderful self-abnegation, have accomplished a most valuable piece of public service.'

Mrs Lloyd George may well have been drawing on her daughter's reports, which Olwen later recalled:

I didn't see much of France because I was stuck at Boulogne, where part of the platform at the railway terminus was roped off as a reception area for the hospital trains. I was what they called a cooklet, and I also used to scrub the platforms. I used to say to my friends, 'If you see a patch which is cleaner than all the rest, that's my bit.'[5]

One reason for this extensive station cleaning was that ambulance and troop trains often stood there for a long time, during which the toilets drained straight to the tracks. VAD Commandant Katherine Furse would establish sanitary squads for all stations at French bases.[6]

Mrs Lloyd George's interviewer then enquired:

'Has the war discovered any Florence Nightingale or any other woman, who will stand by her as typical of the spirit of the present age? I see a very large number of names mentioned as serving abroad in one capacity or another.'

'I cannot say whether there will be any outstanding personality at the close of this war. I am rather inclined to think that Florence Nightingale was somewhat of an exception in her generation and quite unique. But the number of women who have emerged as real leaders is so astonishing that it is extremely difficult to mention names at all without doing injustice. Still I ought not to forget Lady Paget's work in Serbia, Mrs Clair Stobart's Hospital in Antwerp, which she followed by taking a unit to Serbia, and what shall we say of that heroine, Nurse Cavell!'[7]

The interview took place on 5 November 1915, less than a month after Edith Cavell had been executed by the German army in Belgium, on 12 October.

NUWSS Scottish Women's Hospitals

In May 1915, Mrs Lloyd George and other leading Welsh women were supporting a Welsh unit for the NUWSS Scottish Women's Hospitals, founded in 1914 by Dr Elsie Inglis, secretary of the Scottish Federation of Women Suffrage Societies. *The Common Cause* reported:

NUWSS Scottish Women's Hospital: WELSH UNIT FOR SERBIA: As a result of Dr Inglis' visit to Newport and Cardiff, on March 24th (when she spoke of the urgent need for help in Serbia), it was decided to try to raise enough money to equip a Welsh Unit, £1,500. A letter signed by Mrs Lloyd George, the Lady Mayoress of Cardiff, Mayoress of Newport, the Hon. Violet Douglas-Pennant, Mrs Lewis (President of the S. Wales and Monmouth Federation of Women's Suffrage Societies), and Mrs James Robinson, ex-Lady Mayoress of Cardiff, appealing for money, was sent to all the leading Welsh newspapers. A very warm response to this appeal has already been received, and many gifts in kind have been sent.

In N. Wales much zeal and enthusiasm is shown, Bangor alone having already sent in a contribution of £250. We were very glad to welcome the second contingent for Serbia which passed through Cardiff on Monday, April 19th. The smart nurses, wearing uniforms with the Gordon tartan, attracted much attention and sympathy when their mission was known.[8]

The Scottish Women's Hospitals provided nurses, doctors, ambulance drivers, cooks and orderlies. By the end of the war 14 medical units had been outfitted, serving in Corsica, France, Malta, Romania, Russia, Salonika and Serbia. Referred to as 'The Woman with the Torch', a tribute echoing Florence Nightingale's 'The Lady of the Lamp', Dr Inglis is still commemorated in Serbia, on Scottish banknotes, and her funeral was possibly the largest ever held in Scotland.

In her interview with Percy Alden, Mrs Lloyd George paid tribute to the women of such hospitals:

> The Scottish women's hospitals have done splendid work both in Serbia and France, and I am sorry to say some lives were lost in Serbia as result of typhus. Among the women who have sacrificed their lives are Dr Ross and Mrs Dearmer, who was well known in London.[9] [10] Then you remember how splendid was the work accomplished by the Women's First-Aid Nursing Yeomanry at Antwerp, Ghent, and Calais in the early days, a work which is being continued with redoubled vigour today in connection with the Belgian Military Field Service.
>
> Miss Fyfe, who has received the Order of Leopold II for her services, took out a convoy to Furnes and Dunkirk last year.[11] She remained on in Flanders to care for the refugees who are still in their ruined villages behind the firing lines. Splendid work is being accomplished there by the

Hospitals and Healthcare (1914 to 1918)

Aide Civile Belge, at the head of which are the Comtesse d'Ursel and the Comtesse den Steen de Jehay. Helping the Belgians also are Mrs Wynne, who took out her ambulance to Flanders,[12] and Mrs Knocker and Miss Chisholm, 'the Women of Pervyse'.[13] The two latter are now attached to a division of the Belgian Army and very near the line of fire. They are sacrificing everything in their desire to help the Belgian soldiers, nursing them, dressing their wounds, and supplying them with the most necessary things in the shape of clothing and boots.

These are only a few among many. There are many heroines whose names will never be known, but who deserve that we should hold them in remembrance.[14]

The Welsh Hospital at Netley

While Olwen scrubbed France's railway platforms, on 17 September 1915, her mother and sister Megan accompanied Lady Mond to Netley, near Southampton, where a moveable Welsh hospital had been built in October 1914, alongside the country's largest military hospital, the Victoria National Military Hospital, begun in 1856 during the Crimean War. As the wounded returned from the Front, campaigns financed new wings and beds and various English counties established wards. (illustrations 59 to 62)

Lady Mond and her husband Sir Alfred had recently acquired Melchet Court nearby, which they turned into a 60-bed hospital for the recuperation of Netley patients, a gesture made in another 700 country houses.[15] Lady Mond also opened her London home to Belgian refugees.

The Hospital described the Netley project and its rapid construction.

THE WELSH WAR HOSPITAL, NETLEY: The Movable Hospital. This is a temporary hospital and has been specially designed so that it can, if necessary, be removed to France or elsewhere. The architects were only given instructions about a fortnight before the hospital was started, and it is estimated that the time occupied between the commencement of the construction to the date of readiness for occupation will not have been more than six weeks.

The Welsh Hospital, Netley, is the gift of the Principality of Wales to HRH the Prince. Its four wards provide accommodation for 104 patients, and provision is made for adding four other wards if necessary. The buildings are disposed on both sides of a central covered way. They are constructed externally of iron with felted roofs, and internally of asbestos sheets. The plumbing and sanitary fittings are of course as complete as for a permanent hospital. The buildings will be lighted by electricity throughout, and heated generally by gas radiators. The hot-water supplies throughout are by califonts. The drainage is connected to the general drainage of Netley Hospital. The site is to the north-east of the Netley Hospital property. The total cost of the hospital will be between £6,500 and £7,000, exclusive of furniture and fittings.[16]

The ever supportive *Brecon & Radnor Express* reported Mrs Lloyd George's September visit. The final assault in the fated Dardanelles campaign had begun on 6 August.

The hospital was full, there being 204 men and 8 officer patients, a large number having been admitted from the Dardanelles on the previous evening.

It was a beautiful day, and the hospital was looking its best. All the wards were visited, and Mrs Lloyd George took the greatest interest in conversing with the patients, particularly those from Welsh regiments, of whom there were a number recently admitted. The majority of the wounded are from the Dardanelles, comprising members of many British Territorial Regiments, besides Australians, New Zealanders and Canadians – 'all sorts and conditions of men'.

The 'Lloyd George' bed was occupied by an Irishman, who said it was 'a very good bed to sleep on,' and others of the endowed beds which excited interest were the 'Women's Suffrage' and the 'Welsh Dogs' beds. The occupant of one of the former expressed his sympathy with the suffrage cause, although he did not approve of 'window smashing' methods. The Welsh Dogs bed represents £450 collected by dogs throughout Wales, and a photograph album of the dogs in their collecting costumes, which is placed near the bed, much interested Miss Megan.

The visitors lunched with the staff, after which further wards were visited, also the operating theatre, X-Ray, domestic and other departments. During the eleven months it has been at Netley, the Welsh Hospital has thoroughly established itself, and, with its open corridors surrounded by shrubs, bright, cheerful, country surroundings, and spacious wards, it presents a most attractive appearance, and drew the warmest praises from the visitors.

A packet of letters which saved a man's life caused Mrs Lloyd George

Hospitals and Healthcare (1914 to 1918)

to voice her approval of 'armour'. The tales of the wounded, particularly dramatic incidents connected with the landing and fighting in the Dardanelles, excited much interest. Gifts of cigarettes for the patients and flowers for the wards from the visitors were greatly appreciated. The visitors were shown around by the Commanding Officer, Col. A. W. Sheen, the matron, Miss E. G. Evans, A.N.S.R., and other officers of the hospital, and spent between three and four hours on their visit.

Before leaving, Mrs Lloyd George expressed her great admiration of the hospital and the worth it is doing, and said she hoped to bring her husband on another occasion when he had time to spare.[17]

In his book on wartime Ceredigion, Gwyn Jenkins writes, 'the most formidable nurse from the county was Emilie G. Evans, who was the Matron of the Aberystwyth Infirmary', recruited to Netley in October 1914. He notes one commentator's observation:

But how do know it is Welsh? There can never be any doubt. One only has to pass the sisters on the corridor, to hear the orderlies. Welsh faces, Welsh eyes and Welsh voices stamp the Hospital as Welsh.[18]

One month into war, Mrs Robinson, Mayoress of Cardiff (and a co-signatory of the plan for a Welsh unit for the Scottish Women's Hospitals), had written to Mrs Lloyd George:

Dear Madame, City Hall, Cardiff, September 8th 1914
I think it would be very nice for suffragists to be represented in the Welsh Hospital by endowing a bed, cost £25.0, to be named the 'Women Suffrage Bed' – if all who have the cause at heart in Wales and Monmouthshire were to help, I think there should be no great difficulty in getting up that sum. I should be glad to know what you think of the idea. As soon as possible, as I am anxious to get this done at once.
Yours sincerely, Agnes Robinson (Lady Mayoress)[19]

Agnes Robinson, whose husband was a medical practitioner, was the granddaughter of a noted Welsh litterateur, Caradoc o'r Fenni.[20]

A further visit by the Lloyd Georges in March 1916 had to be cancelled, Lloyd George having to attend a conference with M. Thomas, his French opposite number. They were to have spent the weekend with the Monds at Melchet Court.[21] In July 1917, Mrs Lloyd

343

George would take advantage of a promised visit to Bournemouth to spend the weekend with Lady Mond, enabling a follow-up visit to the hospital to open several new verandas that had been financed by Lady Mond and other donors.[22]

Of course, Welsh casualties did not have to rely solely upon Welsh nursing, as this letter, reproduced in the Bury St Edmunds press in January 1917, bears witness:

> Following the departure from Cross Hospital, Northgate Street, Bury St Edmunds, of some wounded Welsh soldiers, who were there for a period of nursing, care and attention, the Sister Fitzgerald has received the following letter from Mrs Lloyd George, wife of the Prime Minister, 10. Downing Street, Whitehall, W., Jan. 25th 1917.
>
> Dear Sister Fitzgerald, I have had a letter from a number of Welsh soldiers who have been patients in your hospital, and they tell me, to use their own words, that 'the treatment meted to them was simply magnificent,' and they go on to say, 'Sister Fitzgerald, who is in charge, and also her staff, seemed to anticipate our wishes and, if possible, immediately gratified them. We as Welsh boys (some of us have not very good English) wish to testify that we were treated as guests, and we are now quite fit again.'
>
> I feel that I cannot do less than express on behalf of these men, and of Welsh people generally, my gratitude to you and your staff for all that you did for them, and I'm sure that you in turn will be glad to see that these boys thoroughly appreciate the kindness which they received at your hands.
>
> Yours faithfully, M. Lloyd George[23]

One reason put forward by Lloyd George for raising a Welsh Army was that many soldiers would only have spoken Welsh – while Kitchener wasn't in favour of his troops speaking anything but English. The Welsh language was banned in troops' letters until a Welsh censor was appointed to censor letters, as Dewi David of the 53rd Welsh explained in closing a letter home from Gallipoli in October 1915: 'Yr eiddot yn gariadus (Yours lovingly). P.S. I put Yours lovingly in brackets in case the censor deletes the Welsh translation of that phrase.'[24]

During the 1919 Paris Peace talks, Lloyd George and his team would use Welsh to add an extra layer of confidentiality to their communications.

TB hospital Caernarfon

Mrs Lloyd George, and her husband, were great promoters of fresh air, no doubt a concern linked to the much greater prevalence of tuberculosis than today. At Eastertime 1914, accompanied by Olwen and Megan, they had visited the Four Crosses Council School, an 'open-air' school some three miles north of Pwllheli, not only with well-ventilated classrooms but also giving training in carpentry, gardening, and cookery.[25]

On 26 April 1916, accompanied by Olwen, Mrs Lloyd George opened a new TB hospital in Caernarfon, hoping that preventative care and healthy housing would one day make such facilities redundant.

> The new tuberculosis hospital at Bryn Seiont, Caernarfon, under the auspices of the Welsh Memorial Association, was opened on Wednesday by Mrs Lloyd George. The hospital occupies a healthy and pleasant site. It stands in its own grounds of about two acres, i.e. well sheltered from the easterly and north-easterly winds by a screen of pine trees, and has neatly laid out grounds for recreation, as well as a commodious kitchen garden.
>
> After undergoing extensive alterations, the residence provides accommodation for 24 patients, together with dining-rooms for patients and staff, ward kitchens, nurses, and servants' quarters. A powerful hot water and disinfecting apparatus is provided in an annex, and the outbuildings have been converted into an electric power-house and for other purposes. There are also detached wards providing accommodation for 15 more patients, together with the necessary duty rooms, etc. In front of these wards is a spacious verandah, so arranged that the patients' beds can be wheeled out upon it.
>
> The detached wards are of the patent construction of the contractors, Messrs Humphreys and Co., of Knightsbridge, being framed of timber, and lined externally with corrugated sheeting, lathed and finished with cement pebble dashing, while the internal lining is of patent plaster slabs, covered with patent plaster. The plans were those of Mr Joseph Owen, county architect of Anglesey, who also had the supervision of the work.
>
> The proceedings were presided over by the Mayor (Mr Charles A. Jones), who was supported by the Mayoress, Miss Olwen Lloyd George, the Hon. Violet Douglas-Pennant, and Dr Meredith Richards (Commissioner under the Insurance Act), Mr D. W. Evans (director of the Welsh Memorial Association), members of the Caernarfon Town Council, members and

clerk of the Caernarfonshire Insurance Committee, Mr J. R. Hughes (chairman of the House Committee), Sir Thomas Roberts, etc.

Mrs Lloyd George was a great believer in prevention:

Addressing the gathering, Mrs Lloyd George said excellent work, both of a preventative and curative character, was being effected through the agency of the public health authorities and the Welsh Memorial Association. To eradicate consumption however, she thought there must be better housing and improved conditions provided for the people upon their return from the hospitals, while the feeding and care of the children must receive much more attention. (cheers)

She regarded the tuberculosis campaign much as she did the war. When she saw the large number of wooden huts put up all over the country, it made her think the war would be over some day. And so with regard to consumption. She was not very keen upon seeing substantial buildings being provided as hospitals. She preferred to see temporary structures as affording a hope that we should overcome consumption as surely as we were going to win the war. (cheers)

Dr Meredith Richards, deputy-chairman, Insurance Commission, commented upon the unnecessary waste of human life in Wales, and especially waste due to deaths of women at childbirth, and to diseases of infancy and to tuberculosis. Expectant mothers, he said, ran greater risks in the countryside of Wales than in the slums of London. The lack in many parts of Wales of proper provision for maternity was leading to a loss of life which was not only deplorable, but was a form of extravagance which the nation must no longer tolerate if we wish to recover from the effects of the war.[26]

The conversion of houses into hospitals was frequent, often the first step in establishing new facilities.

The incidence of TB in the UK did fall steadily and significantly up until the late 1980s, after which it rose before falling again. The first vaccine was tested in France in 1921 but was not used significantly until after the Second World War. Nonetheless, Mrs Lloyd George's hope that such facilities would prove to be a temporary need was not fulfilled, Bryn Seiont being extended in the 1970s–80s. It was later demolished and the site replaced by a new dementia care centre built in 2015.[27] TB remains a threat today.

Presiding at the Caernarfonshire Nursing Association's annual meeting, in Pwllheli on 23 January 1918, she advised her compatriots not to be afraid of fresh air:

> The death rate from tuberculosis was higher in Caernarfonshire than in any other county in the Principality, although it was generally admitted that Caernarfonshire was the healthiest county in Wales. Much could be done to protect children from tuberculosis by teaching the mothers how to prepare healthy food and keep healthy homes. Welsh people were afraid of fresh air and to keep their windows open. She appreciated very much all the establishments for the cure of tuberculosis, but prevention was better than cure.[28]

The Prince of Wales Hospital for the Limbless and Disabled, Cardiff

The Lynn-Thomas Hospital, a reference to the Prince of Wales Hospital for the Limbless and Disabled in Cardiff, was fourth on Mrs Lloyd George's list of 'Movements in which I have been interested / mostly active' in JTR's Notes for her putative autobiography.[29]

Dr John Lynn-Thomas, the driving force behind the hospital, was the former senior surgeon to the Welsh Military Hospital in South Africa during the Boer War.[30] A colonel in the army, he was knighted in 1919. In 1916, the shortage of medical facilities at Roehampton Hospital, London, for Welsh casualties, prompted him to assist the Lord Mayor of Cardiff in purchasing a house, then on loan to the British Red Cross, to enable the treatment of the limbless and disabled. The hospital opened in 1917 and specialised in the provision of prosthetic limbs and related medical treatment and rehabilitation, initially serving as an annexe to the Welsh Metropolitan War Hospital at the time in premises provided by Cardiff Council in Whitchurch Hospital. From 1917, the hospital also occupied two nearby premises to expand capacity.[31] (illustration 64)

In May 1917, *en route* to Criccieth, Mrs Lloyd George stayed with Dr John and Mary Rosina Lynn-Thomas in Cardiff and attended the first council meeting of the hospital. Mary Rosina had joined the Troops Fund committee in November 1915. Mrs Lloyd George would later chair the hospital council as the project grew during and after the war.

MRS LLOYD GEORGE'S TOUR: WAR INSTITUTIONS VISITED AT CARDIFF: At Mrs Lloyd George's express wish, her visit to Cardiff on Thursday was kept as private and as quiet as possible. She travelled alone from Swansea, arriving at Cardiff by the 12.35 p.m. train, and was met at the station by Colonel Lynn-Thomas, C.B., C.M.G., and Mrs Lynn-Thomas, at whose residence, Greenlawn, she stayed overnight. This was her first visit to Cardiff since Mr Lloyd George became Prime Minister.

It will be remembered that when she was to have opened the Girls' Club, in Duke street, the illness of Mr Richard Lloyd George prevented her visit.

The party motored at once to the Prince of Wales Hospital, and were entertained by Mr J. P. Cadogan and Mr Percy Miles to luncheon, given to the council of the hospital, together with the Lord Mayor, the Lady Mayoress, Mrs Gwynne Holford, of Buckland (one of the founders of the Roehampton Hospital), Surgeon-general Russell, C.B., Deputy-Director-General of the Army Medical Service; Mrs J. P. Cadogan and her daughter, and Mrs Jones.

After luncheon Mrs Lloyd George made a tour of the hospital, which was opened three weeks ago for the treatment of limbless soldiers and sailors, of whom there are at present eighteen under treatment. Mrs Lloyd George took part in the first council meeting held at the hospital, which was also private, but the *Western Mail* understands the main business was to decide the date of the formal opening.

To-day (Friday) Mrs Lloyd George and Surgeon-general Russell, with their host, Colonel Lynn-Thomas, will visit the Welsh Metropolitan War Hospital, Whitchurch [Cardiff].[32]

In July, she chaired a hospital council meeting at No. 10, at which they would be briefed on the laying out of a portion of the hospital garden:

… in order to assist the men fitted with artificial legs in the art of walking and down variable gradients and on different sloping paths. It is evident that this special training ground, with its miniature hills and dales, will enable Welshmen to return to their homes with a greater confidence in the artificial limbs to tread their native mountains and valleys.[33]

In February 1918, an endowment plan was launched to fund the hospital permanently. Becoming a charity in 1926, it would remain reliant on voluntary support until the advent of the NHS. The *Western Mail* published a letter from Mrs Lloyd George and the Lord Mayor of Cardiff, appealing for support:

> It has been decided to raise £100,000 to endow permanently the Prince of Wales Hospital for Limbless Sailors and Soldiers as a memorial of the war and to enable its benefits to be extended to civilian limbless cases throughout the Principality and Monmouthshire as soon as the demands arising from the war permit.[34]

This specialist hospital was by no means unique around the country, war leaving so many disabled soldiers and sailors requiring artificial limbs to make their way in life.[35]

Furthermore, broken limbs were not the only life-changing legacy for survivors. On 7 May 1917, after handing over an initial cheque at the BFSS (British and Foreign Sailors' Society) AGM, it was off to the Albert Hall for the opening day of the bazaar in aid of St Dunstan's Hostel for Blinded Soldiers, Sailors and Airmen, established in 1915 by Arthur Pearson (a newspaperman blinded by glaucoma). Mustard gas attacks alone led to many casualties. First set up in Bayswater, the hostel had soon moved to Regent's Park. This first day was opened by Queen Alexandra, and Mrs Lloyd George and many other ladies were in attendance to run the stalls, she and Olwen doing a good trade in dolls and toys.[36]

She returned the next day to re-open proceedings, remarking:

> All our soldiers and sailors are heroes. These men who are blinded must continue their heroism day after day and year after year always. At the Hostel at St Dunstan's sunshine is brought into their darkened lives, and to keep this sunshine about them always is the object we have in view.
>
> The after-care of the blind who have been taught, who, with splendid courage have learned again to become self-reliant, cannot be left to chance. Already some 600 men have passed through St Dunstan's or are there now. They are proud of their self-reliance in the face of a handicap that make the bravest among us hopeless and helpless. To help them maintain this spirit of self-reliance is the object for which your liberal support of this bazaar will not be asked in vain.[37]

The charity is another of the organisations established during this war that continues around the country today, as Blind Veterans UK, with two wellbeing centres, one in north Wales and one on the south coast.[38]

In August 1917, one hospital visit, where recuperating patients were learning to flex their muscles again, might have been scuppered if the Welsh inclement weather, which the day before had blown down a marquee and disrupted a fete in Holyhead, had persisted a little longer. (see p.100) But the gods were kinder and, accompanied by Red Cross VAD Olwen, she was able to open a sale at a Red Cross Hospital near Bangor. Works made by the soldiers were sold and Private Loud, Nurse Jones *et al* competed in the races.

> SALE OF WORK AT BODLONDEB HOSPITAL: GIFTS FROM PRINCESS VICTORIA: Mrs Lloyd George opened a sale of work done by wounded soldiers at the Bodlondeb Red Cross Hospital, near Bangor, on Wednesday. Dull and foreboding in the morning, the weather improved for the opening ceremony, which was conducted in front of the hospital in the presence of a large gathering.
>
> Since the hospital was opened, nearly 800 men had passed through it, greatly benefitted by the invigorating air, the pleasant surroundings, and the assiduous attention of Dr Thomas, the medical officer, and the nurses of the VAD, who staffed the hospital under the Matron (Miss Dickenson). The hospital had been very fortunate in its friends, who included Princess Victoria. The Hon. Violet Vivian had also helped them, and the Treborth family had proved loyal friends, while now they had the good fortune to have Mrs Lloyd George interesting herself in their work.
>
> LUCKY WOUNDED SOLDIERS: Mrs Lloyd George, who was accompanied by her eldest daughter, Mrs Carey Evans, congratulated the staff of the hospital on the way it was being conducted. 'I have great admiration for and sympathy with Red Cross work,' added Mrs Lloyd George. 'These hospitals throughout the country are carrying on a beneficent work, but I do not know what they would have done without the services of the bands of young ladies who work in them. I congratulate also the wounded soldiers who have been so lucky as to be sent here, a peaceful spot after their strenuous days in France. I see the soldiers here have been busy, and that the result of their work is being offered for sale to-day. I have seen a good deal of the beautiful work done by wounded soldiers, but I am sure that what is done here is equal to anything I have yet seen.'

Hospitals and Healthcare (1914 to 1918)

THE SALE: A brisk sale was carried on in one of the large green houses. A number of articles, including cushion covers, postcard covers, blotters, etc. made by the soldiers, were sold. The artistry shown by the men in making these articles evoked much favourable comment.

In the collection of flowers offered for sale were a number of exquisite carnations sent by Princess Victoria. The Hon. Violet Vivian had charge of the fruit and flower stall, and Miss Bayne, Corfandy, sold the men's handiwork; while Sir Michael Duff, of Vaynol, was busy selling apples, unusually large in size.

Concerts were given in the Hut, those taking part being Mrs Hughes Williams, Gaerwen; Mr Mulliner, Rifleman South, Lance-Corpl. Farmary, and Private Bramwell. The 'Clio' Band, conducted by Mr Bates, played selections, and dances were given by Miss Doris Bayne.

THE SPORTS: The day's programme concluded with sports featuring the nurses and the soldiers competing in a blindfold race; flower-pot race; egg and spoon race; cigarette race; costume race; apple race; potato race; and a tug o' war.[39]

The Troops Fund had been sending comforts to the hospital, albeit sharing their supply with the Welsh Hospital at Netley.[40]

After the fun and games in Wales, in the final week of November it was again acceptable to be both frivolous and serious in a London exhibition for the Surgical Requisites Association. Olivia Maitland-Davidson of *The Sphere* explained the distinction between the serious and frivolous:

From November 20 to 29 the Surgical Requisites Association, a branch of Queen Mary's Needlework Guild, is holding a Frivolous Fair and Serious Exhibition at the Grafton Galleries for the benefit of their funds. It will be opened on Tuesday, the 20th, by Princess Patricia of Connaught, on the 21st by Princess Alice, Countess of Athlone, and on the following days by Mrs Lloyd George and Lady Lloyd [who had joined the Troops Fund committee in December].

The serious part of it will consist of a most interesting exhibition of the surgical appliances made by the voluntary workers at 17, Mulberry Walk, Chelsea, during this war, and of the many new inventions carried out by them.

The 'frivolous' part will be a fair, at which all kinds of pretty things, lingerie and laces, antiques, cushions, bags, and boudoir caps, china and glass, pictures, etc. will be sold, and at which the most charming Christmas presents may be bought.

There will also be all kinds of musical and theatrical entertainments, teas, and the cinematograph each day, and such artists as Mlle Astafieva, Miss Ethel Levey, Miss Lee White, and Violet Loraine are kindly giving their services. Admission on the first two days will be 5s. from twelve to 3.30, and 2s. 6d. from 3.30 onwards. Olivia.[41]

Russian ballet dancer and teacher Serafina Astafieva had been running her Russian Dancing Academy at The Pheasantry, King's Road, Chelsea, since 1916, pupils including Margot Fonteyn and Alicia Markova. Singers Ethel Levey, Lee White, and Violet Loraine were all performing in London that year.

Mrs Lloyd George would pay further tribute to the Red Cross on 15 May 1918 when opening a bazaar in their aid, in Hanley, one of the six Pottery towns of Stoke-on-Trent, thirty miles from the Welsh border. The first day had a royal opening, by Princess Arthur of Connaught, then a full-time nurse at St Mary's Paddington (later qualifying as a State Registered Nurse in 1919).[42]

Mrs Lloyd George's speech was a typical performance, warm words on the location, making links with Wales, giving her tribute to their fighting men, and compliments to those working hard to make the returning wounded men comfortable. As on other occasions it was her first time in the town.

> Mrs Lloyd George, who was accorded a very cordial reception, said 'Mr Chairman, Mr Mayor, Ladies and Gentlemen, I am very pleased to visit your busy town and to take a small part in the big effort you are making for the Red Cross Society. I have heard a great deal about the Potteries and have seen your beautiful work, but I have never been here before. I remember years ago Mr Lloyd George came here and brought home with him two specimens of your pottery – a Chamberlain coffee pot and a Lord Salisbury tea pot. (Laughter)
>
> 'I believe you are like the people of Wales, very musical, and I fancy you have come over the border to our musical festival and several times run away with the prizes. You have also, like Wales, done splendidly in sending men out to fight. The men of north Staffordshire and the Welshmen are now fighting side by side for our homes, and they have done splendid service for Britain, and we are justly proud of them.

Hospitals and Healthcare (1914 to 1918)

They have gone out to defend our land for us to live at home in safety.

'The least we can do, therefore, is to make them as comfortable as possible under very trying circumstances when wounded, and to see that they and their families shall not suffer on their return. In no war have the arrangements for the wounded been so perfect. No one can say how many brave lives have been saved by the Red Cross. No one can calculate the amount of suffering of those gallant men who have been saved by this noble institution, and we ought to support it in every possible way so that they can carry on the work to the end. I hear that already you have in hand more money than you expected at the end of the week. It is a great comfort to the organisers and workers to see that their labour has not been in vain. I very much hope the following days will be as successful as the first, if not more successful. I have great pleasure in declaring the Bazaar open.' (Cheers)

Upon the conclusion of her address, Mrs Lloyd George was presented with a lovely bouquet of cream tea roses by Miss Mary Butler Henderson, the little daughter of Capt. the Hon. Eric B. Butler Henderson and the Hon. Mrs Butler Henderson. The presentation formed a charming incident in the proceedings and much applause was evoked when Mrs Lloyd George lifted the little lady and kissed her by way of thanks.[43]

The three-year-old Miss Mary Butler Henderson was one of many children (often related to the organisers) who, over the years, presented bouquets to the flower-loving Mrs Lloyd George.

The Prime Minister's wife was greeted in Welsh by the local Welsh community, she inspected a guard of honour made up of around 100 discharged soldiers and sailors, and was presented with a pair of Wedgwood blue jasper vases which she said she would treasure to the end of her days.

A week or so earlier the presence of the wife of the Prime Minister in Hanley was in jeopardy, as Lloyd George, in one of his more serious battles with the military hierarchy, had to survive a serious vote of no-confidence in the House of Commons. He won the so-called 'Maurice debate', despite Asquith and his followers voting against him or abstaining. Even in wartime, domestic party politics were never far away. (see p.123)

353

'It is more dangerous to be a baby in England than a soldier in France'

High child mortality alongside the long casualty lists from the Front made the outlook even more stark. The opening words of a full-column leader of *The Croydon Times* on 13 June 1917 had read:

> It was not long since Mrs Lloyd George emphatically declared, 'What we want is a mobilisation of motherhood.' The cause which prompted the remark is one of vast importance to the British race. Mrs Lloyd George was speaking of the great loss sustained each year in preventable infantile mortality, and serious as this subject has been in the past, the present war, with its terrible drain on the virile manhood of the country, has now invested it with a grave import which the nation can no longer afford to overlook. We must remember that while, for years past, the birth-rate of Germany has been continually mounting higher, that for Great Britain has just as insistently inclined to the opposite direction. The limitation of families in Great Britain may, or may not, have been justified by the then existing conditions. It is a question on which much may be said on each side, but for the object which we have in mind – the saving of the baby life of this country – there can be only one strong, determined, clear-cut opinion. We must save the babies.[44]

In January 1918, she made the stark comparison that 'It is more dangerous to be a baby in England than a soldier in France'.[45]

Wartime introduced a further childcare need – crèches to look after the children of working mothers, and not just in the daytime but in support of mothers working at night with their husbands absent at war. On 3 May 1917, she had been in Woolwich with the munitionettes, visiting Lady Julia Henry's crèche. (illustration 27)

> 'DAY AND NIGHT' CRÈCHE. SUBSIDY FROM THE MINISTRY OF MUNITIONS. The Woolwich Nursery for the Children of Munition Workers, at 57, St. Mary's-street, Woolwich, was opened yesterday by the Duchess of Marlborough, who spoke of the urgent need for such crèches. Earlier in the day, Mrs Lloyd George, with her daughter, went over to the nursery and expressed admiration of its many features. Those present in the afternoon included Lady Henry (chairman of the Committee), Lord Henry Bentinck (Hon. Treasurer), Lady Henry Bentinck, Lady Kathleen

Hospitals and Healthcare (1914 to 1918)

Lindsay, Lady (Francis) Lloyd, Dr Sloan Chesser, Mr W. Crooks, M.P., and Mrs Holman.

The most interesting event of the afternoon was the arrival of Miss Baker, the lady superintendent of the Arsenal, with 18 women representatives of the different workshops and a taxicab full of gifts from the women sufficient to afford supplies for a month. It was arranged to hold the day as 'pound' day, and this was their method of showing their appreciation of the new crèche. Later in the afternoon hundreds of women from the Arsenal went in parties through the building.

The Ministry of Munitions is paying part of the expenses, and the charge to the mothers will be 8d., and where the children are kept for day and night 1s. The crèche will be open day and night for 50 children, and in certain cases the babies will be allowed to remain for a fortnight.[46]

As noted earlier, Lady Henry's 22-year-old son Cyril was killed in September 1915 at the Battle of Loos. (see p.25)

Child mortality and wartime losses

In July 1918, the juxtaposition of child mortality and wartime losses was very much in the minds of her near neighbours in Surrey, when, during the nationwide Babies' Week, on Wednesday 24, she opened a two-day Baby Show in Guildford, not that far from the Lloyd George home at Walton Heath. This was more than just another visit of a mothering person to admire babies, as the *Surrey Advertiser* made clear in its front-page column:

WEEKLY GOSSIP: MRS LLOYD GEORGE'S VISIT: Mrs Lloyd George is to visit Guildford to-day (Wednesday) to open the two-day Baby Show and Child Welfare Exhibition which is to be held in the town. In these days we know no party politics, but Mrs Lloyd George comes on what is a matter of the highest Imperial politics, the safeguarding of the health and well-being of those upon whose shoulders will, in due course, rest the burden of maintaining all we are fighting for in the present war. We do not think the people of England realise even yet the fearful toll which has been taken of the young manhood of the nation. They see lists of names in the papers from day to day – the full lists are never published now in any paper – but they do not appreciate to what gigantic totals these daily losses are mounting up. If we were to publish the list just for the area in which the *Surrey Advertiser* circulates, readers would stand appalled at its length – it would include thousands of names – the very flower of the manhood of Surrey.

THE NATION'S BEST ASSET
Contemplation of such lists – we have been glancing down one as we write – brings home as nothing else can the importance the nation has of its child life. The birth-rate has fallen and is still falling, and we are not yet at the end of the war or of our losses. If the British Empire is to remain great and virile and capable of fulfilling its high destiny in the world, the children of the nation must more than ever before be regarded its most valuable asset, and be treated as such. This does not mean an excess of fussy coddling and pampering; but sensible practical measures to see that every child shall, as far as possible, be afforded the chance to grow up into a healthy man and woman fit to fill his or her niche in the world. How this can best be done is a question which is engaging the close attention of local authorities and societies interested in child life all over the kingdom, and we can but wish success to these efforts.

BABY SHOWS: A MEANS TO AN END
Baby shows do not commend themselves to us as altogether desirable things themselves. We regard them rather a means to an end; that end being to focus attention, particularly the attention of the mothers, upon this most important question. Ignorance, poverty and bad housing are three of the greatest foes against which those who wish to protect child life have to contend. Ignorance is being dispelled by the spread of knowledge, and its effects combatted by school inspection, clinics and similar agencies. Of poverty there is less to-day than before the war, and it is to be hoped that never again will it be possible to say with truth that thirteen millions of our people are on the verge of starvation. Better housing is also receiving attention, but in this matter great progress is not possible till after the war. It is good, however, to know that the foes to be fought are now fully recognised, and that there is everywhere determination to deal drastically with them. Mrs Lloyd George's encouragement in the work will be welcomed, but we hope and believe that in anything she may have to say to-day in this matter at Guildford, she will be preaching to the converted.[47]

Diarist Samuell Pepys Junior identified possible risks in attending Babies' Week events: 'Up very betimes, my wife having the greatest possible business over the babies' week. I did give her 10s. to pay for taxi-coaches, charging her that she ride this week in no buss nor tube, for fear of the flue sickness.'[48]

The Lloyd George 'brand' was not necessarily welcome in Guildford, where his 1912 Insurance Act had met strong local resistance, especially from farmers. Mrs Lloyd George's visit (along with the PM's determination to win the war) seemed to be improving neighbourly relations:

> MRS LLOYD GEORGE'S VISIT: Mrs Lloyd George was obviously very pleased with the warmth of her reception at Guildford last week. She admitted as much more than once, and she may have carried back to the Prime Minister such a good impression of the county town that he may be disposed to pay it the compliment for which some of the speakers last week are clearly looking. If the right honourable gentleman had come to Guildford say six years ago he would have had a mixed reception. But times have changed, and, though it is impossible altogether to forget the past, the nation believes that today Mr Lloyd George embodies the indomitable and inflexible will and determination of the nation to see the war to a victorious end, and to bring about a real and not a patched-up peace. That Guildford people share to the full that will and determination we are assured, and if Mr Lloyd George should see fit to pay the county town a visit, he would receive abundant demonstration of it.
>
> A NEAR NEIGHBOUR
> The Prime Minister, as most of our readers are aware, is now a resident of Surrey and a not very distant neighbour of Guildford. His weekend residence, which, by the way, the playful suffragettes tried to burn to the ground, is at Walton Heath, where the Premier obtains by an occasional round of golf that recreation and respite from the business of State of which he must sometimes stand in sore need. Mr Lloyd George is not ignorant of Guildford and its beautiful surroundings. He has motored through the town on many occasions, and four or five years ago he stopped his car halfway down the High Street to buy an evening paper and stood on the pavement opposite Adsett's eagerly scanning the news, oblivious of the curious glances of passers by.[49]

Having proffered their olive branch to the Prime Minister, the paper then suggested that while 'there was little that was new in the speeches at the Child Welfare Exhibition which Mrs Lloyd George opened ... they and the exhibition itself should help to focus attention upon a subject which is of ever greater importance to us than ever before,' going on to report on progress being made locally with respect to the acquisition of new sites for housing. It would prove to be one of the most challenging post-war issues.

The *West Surrey Times* did however spot a particularly forthright turn of phrase by their visitor's 'particularly apposite address': 'Speaking of the child welfare movement [Mrs Lloyd George] said there may be a legal difference between actively killing a child and passively allowing it to die but there was not much moral difference. The point could hardly be more tersely and tellingly put.'[50]

CHAPTER 25

Temperance and Wartime Sobriety
(1914 to 1918)

*'The evil of drink had taken a very deep root
in the nation, but if they went about the work
in the right way, and with pluck, they would get rid of it.'*
Margaret Lloyd George, January 1914

TEMPERANCE WAS A lifelong campaign of Mrs Lloyd George, and of her private secretary, J. T. Rhys. In wartime it assumed new dimensions – the need to keep the troops sober, to keep the workforce, not least munitions workers, sober, and to prioritise the use of foodstuffs such as barley. The imposition of alcohol prohibition in the USA and in Canada encouraged prohibitionists to believe their cause could be won, reducing their willingness to support anything less. Mrs Lloyd George attended and hosted several temperance conferences, though temperance probably occupied less of her time than other campaigns. Adding restrictions to one of life's recreational escapes was not to be imposed lightly in a period of increasing austerity and controls.

The dangers of drink in wartime

On St David's Day eve, Sunday, 28 February 1915, in Bangor, Lloyd George gave short shrift to anyone who thought he shouldn't talk about the war on the Sabbath; anyone who complained, didn't realise how serious things were. He also declared, 'Drink is doing us more damage in the war than all the German submarines put together,'[1] elaborating later to the Shipbuilding Employers Federation that Britain was 'fighting Germany, Austria and Drink, and as far as I can see the greatest of these three deadly foes is Drink.'[2] The drinks lobby, and others, thought he was overdoing it.

On Thursday, 24 March, Mrs Lloyd George was in Camberwell, south London, opening the Patriotic Club for the women relatives of soldiers and sailors, a project led by Mrs Frances Parker, temperance campaigner and sister of Lord Kitchener. Other such clubs included those run by the Tipperary League, under Lady Jellicoe, and the Women's War Clubs, under Lady Henry Somerset. (illustration 32) Local MP Tom Macnamara, a Lloyd George ally for whom she would campaign in 1920, occupied the chair.[3]

> Mrs Lloyd George, in opening a patriotic club for female relatives of soldiers and sailors at Waterloo-road, Camberwell Green, on Thursday, said the absence of the bread-winner threw a very great responsibility upon the women left at home, and the social intercourse which such clubs provided would help them to feel that responsibility to live good lives, look after the welfare of their children, and make the best use of the money at their disposal. The clubs would have valuable results upon the country in the future.
>
> They removed the temptation of strong drink. Drinking could not be denounced unless some other institutions were found for women to take the place of the public house. Drink was the great enemy of England, and had done much harm throughout the country.[4]

Her husband persuaded the King to take the pledge; on 30 March, the King's private secretary wrote to the Chancellor:

> ... if it be deemed advisable, the King will be prepared to set the example by giving up all alcoholic liquor himself and issuing orders against its consumption in the Royal Household, so that no difference shall be made so far as his Majesty is concerned between the treatment of rich and poor in this question.

A week later, on Tuesday, 6 April, the Royal pledge was confirmed.[5] It is said the King later regretted being persuaded by Lloyd George

Temperance and Wartime Sobriety (1914 to 1918)

to make such a comprehensive commitment,[6] 'which the King was virtually alone in taking seriously'.[7]

The wartime August 1914 Defence of the Realm Act (DORA) covered a range of measures to support the Allied war effort, and restricted opening hours for licensed premises to lunchtime (12:00 to 14:00) and later to supper (18:30 to 21:30).[8] Licensing hours were restricted in Scotland, and in 1915, in Wales, Gladstone's 1881 Sunday Closing Act was extended to include Monmouthshire. In 1916, Carlisle, home to many munitions factories, adopted the 'Carlisle Experiment', whereby the government's Central Control Board (Liquor Traffic), took local pubs into state ownership to allow more direct control. In some cases the premises became food taverns. However in her article a year later in the publication *Great Thoughts – A Weekly Paper for People who Think*, Mrs Lloyd George was cautious:

> I am not sure that restriction of hours of sale will do much to solve the problem. I am told by good authorities such a course only means that those who want drink will buy it in bottles, so as to have it when the 'pubs' are closed. I am more inclined to support lessening by far the number of licensed houses. A man or woman will not generally walk miles just to get a drink.[9]

To get something effective through Parliament, past the powerful drinks lobby, Lloyd George, when Prime Minister, would propose a compromise – State Purchase with Local Option – a form of nationalisation of the trade, with the ability to close pubs, and the opportunity for local communities to decide how stringent the curbs should be to suit local conditions. Temperance campaigners JTR and Mrs Lloyd George, though both preferring prohibition, backed this pragmatic approach.

In contrast, diehard prohibitionists, encouraged by American progress, felt the war offered the ideal conditions to achieve their ultimate goal. Others, wary of the wartime social and economic pressures, conscription and compulsory rationing, were willing to take it step by step. Lloyd George, already 'the bloke that's put a penny on our beer' in the words of one passer-by in Northampton back in November (see p.271), would also be watering it down as barley supplies tightened.

At a temperance military concert on 3 June in Cricieth, Mrs Lloyd

George encouraged the soldiers, and Parliament, to follow the Royal example.

> MRS LLOYD GEORGE CONDEMNS THE DRINK EVIL: Mrs Lloyd George, when presiding at a temperance military concert at Cricieth on Thursday night (at which several Swansea Valley boys were present), congratulated those soldiers of the Welsh Royal Field Artillery billeted in the district who had recently taken the temperance pledge to the number of 2,000. Russia, France and our King, she stated, had banned the drink, but the House of Commons had not yet had the strength to abolish it from its own table.
>
> John Bull, however, was slow to move, but the day was not far off when he would deal effectively with this evil, for he was already showing signs of anger at the havoc it created.
>
> Mr Lloyd George recently asked the Russian Finance Minister how they fared there after abolishing the drink, and he replied, 'If anybody attempted to reintroduce drink into the country there would be a revolution.' That revolution would come from people who were prone to drink, and who had awakened to a sense of its extreme peril to their nation. (Applause)[10]

In August, the King's cousin, the Tsar of Russia, had outlawed the production and sale of vodka. With or without drink, in 1917 the Russians got their revolution.

Not to leave a stone unturned, on 10 June Mrs Lloyd George also hosted an 'At Home' at No. 11 for members of the Nurses League of Total Abstinence. The Bishop of Willesden said that, 'the nursing profession was one of the hardest, and the demonstration that nurses could keep going without the use of stimulants was almost as valuable an object lesson as was their constant patience, tenderness, and skill'.[11]

Supply constraints: food first

As the war drew on, curbing the consumption of sugar and barley for beer (so those staples could be consumed in other ways) was perhaps more important than reducing beer consumption simply on grounds of sobriety. In December, she hosted another temperance demonstration in Cricieth, alongside the globe-trotting campaigner Agnes Slack, Lloyd George's brother, William George, and Mrs Greaves, wife of the Lord-Lieutenant of Caernarfonshire. The latter, in opening the meeting, stressed that 'it was not right that the brewer's dray should block the way of the ammunition waggon and the baker's cart'.

> Mrs Greaves urged the Government to take steps to stop the waste of 30,000 tons of barley every week, by the distillery, at a time of food shortage and scarcity of labour. Men and railways were required for the production and transit of munitions to-day, and it was not right that the brewer's dray should block the way of the ammunition waggon and the baker's cart. They could not fight a foe like Germany with one hand, at the same time holding a glass of beer in the other. To-day was the day for 'down glasses' and to abstain, entirely, not only as individuals but as whole communities. She called upon Cricieth to follow the example of the King and touch no alcohol for the period of the war at least, and theirs would be the glory of setting this fine and patriotic example to other towns and villages of north Wales.

Mrs Lloyd George called for unity.

> Mrs Lloyd George, who received a hearty welcome in proposing a resolution demanding the abolition of grocers' licences [introduced by Gladstone in 1861, the forerunner of off-licences], said that they were far more dangerous to women than the public-house. Many women owed their downfall and the destruction of their homes to this insidious way of procuring alcohol. These, she said, were earnest times, and she besought temperance people to be earnest, to work for all they were worth to free the land from the terrible curse of drink. The Germans were fighting as one man against the common enemy, but we in Britain were still not as united as we might be – there were too many small differences and divisions for such critical days.
>
> She saw a great need for some method by which women could be persuaded to save. Now, when money was coming in plentifully, some form of investment for small sums was much needed for women, where they could get a good rate of interest. The lean years would follow this war, and people needed to lay by for the rainy days that were sure to follow. She was glad to say she knew of countless women, thrifty and careful, who were doing this. The resolution was seconded by the Rev. J. Owen, M.A., and carried.
>
> Agnes Slack proposed a resolution in favour of the extension of the

areas for the closing of drinking bars throughout the country. She said that organisation was needed. Mrs Greaves had referred to the waste of the food stuffs. It had taken the most deadly, cruel war of all times to see the dangers of drink.

Lord Wolseley, years ago, had experimented with a whisky squad, a beer squad, and a water squad, and in the test marches he had given them to do, he had found the water squad always won.

Admiral Jellicoe, that lonely man in the mists of the North Sea, had told his men, 'Abstain from drink if you want to be able seamen.'

Mrs Lloyd George had had the courage to tell the nation that drink was a greater enemy than Germany. Last month she was visiting a large munitions factory. She asked the foreman whether drink was affecting the output there, and this was his reply 'Yes, drink is affecting us: we could turn out a third more work but for drink.' Teetotalism, she said, is a great munition of war, and every man and woman to-day who takes the pledge is helping the victory which is sure to come.

Mr W. George seconded the resolution, which was carried.[12]

Agnes Slack, Secretary of the World Women's Christian Temperance Union (WWCTU) was the first woman to preach at John Wesley's Chapel in London. Much travelled, her 1926 biography was subtitled, *Two Hundred Thousand Miles for Temperance in Four Continents*.[13]

1916

The February return of Richard from the Front for health reasons would prevent Mrs Lloyd George from attending back-to-back meetings of the British Women's Temperance Association, with Agnes Slack, at Barry Dock, on 28 March, and at the English Congregational Church, Bridgend, the next day.[14]

In September, she hosted the annual conference of the Lleyn and Eifionydd Temperance Society, at Brynawelon, her Criccieth home.[15]

The Minister of Munitions was doing his bit for temperance, if we believe diarist Samuell Pepys Junior's 14 February St Valentine's Day entry:

'Tis given out that Ll. George hath decreed a sequestration of divers great distilleries in Scotland, to the end of making powder and shott therein;

but many I hear say that he does it as much of his hatred of all drinking of strong waters as of his desire that we kill more Germans.[16]

With *Merched y De*

On 10 October, she and Agnes Slack were again together, in Swansea, with *Merched y De*, the south Wales women's temperance association. The event was 'attended by almost all the local ministers', almost certainly including JTR (yet to leave his Swansea parish) and probably my grandmother Jane Annie Rhys, a member of *Merched y De*, and onetime Honorary Secretary of the Garw branch. Mrs Lloyd George was a member of *Merched y Gogledd* (Women of the North).

At the meeting Mrs Lloyd George was presented with a framed portrait of the late Cranogwen, the founder of the movement.[17] 'Cranogwen' was the bardic name of Sarah Jane Rees, a Welsh teacher, poet, editor and temperance campaigner, who had died recently, aged 70, on 27 June.[18] Unusually, she was also a qualified master mariner. (illustration 81)

The Cambria Daily Leader's T. Awstin Davies,[19] a notable south Wales journalist, a son of a Pontypridd Baptist minister, and long associated with the Eisteddfod and Welsh cultural revival, covered the event at length:

MRS LLOYD GEORGE: STIRRING ADDRESS ON THE DRINK TRAFFIC
GREAT GATHERING AT MORRISTON
(By AWSTIN)
A public meeting organised by the South Wales Women's Temperance Union ('Merched y De') was held on Tuesday evening at the Tabernacle, Morriston, Mrs Lloyd George presiding. The audience, which filled the spacious chapel and over-flowed lobbies, vestries, and entrances, was estimated to number considerably over 2,000 people, and the proceedings were marked by great enthusiasm. With Mrs Lloyd George was her hostess, Mrs T. J. Williams, Maesygwernen, and among those who supported were: Mrs J. D. Evans (president of 'Merched y De'), Dowlais; Mrs Tydfil Thomas, B.A., Cardiff; Mrs Thomas, Newcastle Emlyn (treasurer); Miss Rosina Davies, Ferryside (the secretary); Mrs E. H. Davies, Pentre, Rhondda; Mrs Owen, Llwynypia; Mrs Morgan, Pentre; Miss Williams, London; Mrs Hope Evans, Rhondda; Miss Agnes Slack (secretary of the World Women's Temperance Union); and practically all the leading local ministers, and others.

Although announced for 6.30 p.m., the building was crowded long before six, and a powerful choir of local singers, under the leadership of Madame Kate Morgan-Williams, Brynamman, contributed much to the success of the gathering, the rendering of Welsh hymns being a magnificent feature of the proceedings.

THE WOMEN'S BATTLECRY
When the devotional part of the work of the evening had been concluded – and it was all carried out by women – Miss Rosina Davies, the new secretary, on whom it is felt Cranogwen's mantle has fallen, said the battle cry of 'Merched y De' was 'Temperance and Purity'. She asked permission to add to it 'Thrift'. It was possible to be temperate and pure without being thrifty, but it was not possible to be thrifty without being temperate. She asked for a show of hands from the members of 'Merched y De' as to whether she had their permission to add 'thrift' to the battlecry. The response was seemingly a unanimous one, and the audience cheered heartily.

MRS LLOYD GEORGE SPEAKS IN WELSH
Mrs Lloyd George, as chairman, then delivered an address in Welsh, and the cheers, which had been very cordial when she rose, were re-doubled when it was noticed that she was speaking her native tongue. She first of all expressed regret at being somewhat late in arriving, and explained that the reason was, she and the ladies who were with her had been for some time unable to enter the building because it was so densely crowded. She was very pleased to be there to preside over the annual public meeting of 'Merched y De', but she hoped the audience would bear with her, as she was not accustomed to the task of presiding over such a great assembly as she now saw before her. (Applause)

She had promised their late leader 'Cranogwen', whose death they all deeply lamented, that she would come to preside over one of the meetings of the Union, but until now had not been able to do so. Although 'Cranogwen' was not with them that day in the flesh, she was with them in spirit. (Applause) She remembered the first time she heard Cranogwen was when that lady lectured at Cricieth, and she (Mrs Lloyd George) was then only a little girl, prompted by curiosity to see and hear a woman lecturer, for to hear a woman speaking in public was not then so frequent as it was to-day – as they could see. (Laughter and applause) Her father told her that he regarded Cranogwen as a very manly, determined woman,

Temperance and Wartime Sobriety (1914 to 1918)

and she had since seen Cranogwen's determined attitude in carrying on her life's work. (Applause) She had also since then had the pleasure of taking the chair for Cranogwen, and subsequently they became great friends. She and others were at first a little afraid of Cranogwen, but when she came to knew her she found she was a tender and loveable woman. (Applause)

CRANOGWEN'S MANTLE

She did a great work, and in connection with this movement it was to be hoped that her mantle would fall upon one of the daughters of the South. (Applause) The drink traffic was one which was the subject of much anxiety in this country. It was felt that the present time was opportune for dealing with it, and some of them had thought that with the beginning of this great war had come the time for putting an end to the traffic. They were disappointed. They had had improvements and amendments in regard to regulating it, and they were thankful for small mercies. It was a traffic which caused poverty and discomfort in homes, and it was a traffic which marred the efficiency of the nation.

They heard much in these days of war economy, and of proposals for meatless days. Well, she would like to see a drinkless day – one day in every week without the drink and the money so saved to be spent in helping the war. (Applause) She had heard from a prominent gentleman connected with one of the Welsh seaside resorts that the restriction of hours had done good – that the streets were as quiet now at half-past eight as they were at midnight before the restrictions were put in force. (Applause)

A VISION OF VICTORY

There was anxiety among the women of Wales and the women of Great Britain concerning their sons who were in the trenches. But among the women of the Colonies, whose sons had come forth to fight for the Motherland, there was also deep anxiety lest their brothers and their sons should be led astray when in this country by the temptations of the drink traffic, and towards relieving that anxiety they, as 'Merched y De', were doing, and needed to do, all they could to secure further improvements and to help in attaining what they all looked forward to – victory in the end. (Great cheering)

Miss Agnes Slack was pleased to have responded to the invitation of Mrs Lloyd George to come here to help 'Merched y De' in their great Welsh movement for temperance. Mrs Lloyd George, like herself, was a life-long teetotaller. She stood before them to-night for prohibition. She reviewed the steps taken by Russia in regard to the drink traffic, and declared that it was Russia's teetotal army that had saved France and England, and probably Wales, from the fulfilment of the plans of the Kaiser. (Applause)

HOW TO BEAT THE GERMANS
'If you want to beat the Germans,' emphasised Miss Slack, 'you must send out a teetotal army,' and she went on to point out that drink was the British nation's greatest enemy. In the first year of war 85,000 men were killed by the Germans, while in the same period more children died at home through drink than that total. And that enormous loss, when a child's life was more sacred than ever before! She referred to the temptations which beset soldiers from the other countries when they came to Britain, and made a strong plea for the abolition of the liquor traffic.

Rev. Barrow Williams, Llandudno, delivered an address in Welsh, and remarkably effective solos were sung by Madame Kate Williams and Miss Rosina Davies, the great meeting being brought to a close with votes of thanks to Mrs Lloyd George and the principal speakers for their assistance, and to the chapel authorities and the Morriston people for receiving the visitors as honoured guests. Pledges were then signed by a large number of women. It was stated that the 'Merched y De' now number over 12,000 members, who were represented at Morriston by about 80 delegates. As emphasising the vision of the people on the work of the organisation and the movement it carries on, the vast audience sang, and several times repeated the triumphant Welsh hymn, 'O Fryniau Caersalem'.[20]

If JTR had renewed acquaintance with Mrs Lloyd George during the meeting, he may have told her about his impending move to London.

On 3 December, with her son Richard still in hospital with dysentery, she excused herself from a Caernarfon meeting supporting State purchase and control of the drink traffic. Lloyd George, seeking to restrict the amount of barley and agricultural products used for drink, sent his own message to the meeting: 'Now that the food problem is becoming every day more and more urgent, the liquor problem has assumed a new aspect, and the nation must be prepared to see agricultural products put to their most urgent uses.'[21]

1917

Deadly enemy or imaginary foe?

Just before Christmas 1916, she penned a top-billing cheery 'Message to the lads' in a popular Christmas magazine, *Answers*. On 13 January, the *Faringdon Advertiser and Vale of the White Horse Gazette* responded positively to her call for restraint:

> In a special article in *Answers*, Mrs Lloyd George deals with the liquor problem, under the title, 'Our Most Deadly Enemy'. The question of how to deal with the trouble the nation has, she says, becomes more and more important and insistent, and she does not profess to say how far the endeavours and schemes to deal with it have been successful.
>
> 'But I do think that the diminution of the sale and consumption of alcoholic liquors is neither so great nor so universal as we have every right to expect, seeing the strain and tension of the nation, and remembering all the warnings and sound advice which have been given by competent and influential counsellors in this matter. Parliament can do a great deal towards helping forward the solution of this problem. (It has done much since the war began, but could do very much more and will, later on, when the war is over, have to tackle the thing thoroughly!) But we men and women, as individuals, also can do far more than we imagine by our example, by our advice, by our help, by our determined resolve that all excessive drinking, if not all the drink traffic itself – shall be put down. And I trust all women will be ready and resolved to do their part. Let us see to it that we grasp this opportunity, and that we set our faces towards the "Vision Splendid" right from the start.'[22]

In contrast, on the same day, the *Burton Daily Mail*, from Burton-on-Trent, home of many breweries, attacked the idea that drink was the country's worst enemy, indeed the war on drink, 'this imaginary foe', was an unnecessary diversion from the real wartime enemy, and was 'libelling the masses':

> Mrs Lloyd George describes drink as England's greatest and most terrible enemy, and adds that 'we shall have an unique opportunity – the chances of a lifetime – when this war is over and our land has to begin a new life conquering it.'
>
> If England has no greater enemy than the supposed tendency of her

people towards drinking, she is, indeed, fortunate, and Mrs Lloyd George herself admits that the people are growing in sobriety.

We suggest that, under all the circumstances, this contest with an imaginary foe should be postponed until the 'unique opportunity' occurs in that happy time to which Mrs Lloyd George, like all us, looks forward, 'when the war is over'. In the meantime, we have a very real enemy to fight, and the efforts to force prohibition and State purchase upon the nation, by libelling the masses, is likely to divert our energies from that important business, and to cause dissension when united effort and goodwill are demanded.[23]

The *Faringdon Advertiser*, of 20 January, published a letter from a local vicarage (though not the vicar) reacting against Mrs Lloyd George's point of view:

To the Editor: The Premier's wife seems to have taken up the cry of the total abstainers on the matter of total prohibition, as she expresses the wish that 'all excessive drinking, not all the drink traffic itself, shall be put down.'

Now, Sir, if this revolutionary and drastic method were adopted, it would not in any way finally solve the problem. The real solution lies in the hands of the people, and that solution is the complete reformation of the public houses and the silly laws and regulations edging them all round. As the public houses are at present, they are simply drink shops, instead of what they should be, namely, places of entertainment as well as refreshment.

If they were 'run' after the Continental Café style, and made places where not only men, but women and children could call and obtain social intercourse, the person who indulged to excess would soon be a thing of the past, as he would not be tolerated by the other customers. Thanking you in anticipation for inserting my letter. I am, Sir, Yours obediently. G. HEMMING. 16th January, 1917. Uffington Vicarage, Faringdon, Berks, 15th Jan., 1917.[24]

It was at Uffington Vicarage that Thomas Hughes penned the novel *Tom Brown's School Days*, sixty years earlier.

In July, G. Hemming sought the latest scientific support, in this instance coming from the increasingly voluble eugenics movement, when writing to the *Banbury Advertiser*:

Temperance and Wartime Sobriety (1914 to 1918)

A first study of the influence of parental alcoholism on the physique and ability of the offspring, issued from 'The Francis Galton Laboratory for National Eugenics' shows throughout that offspring of temperate or moderate drinkers are healthier than those of total abstaining parents, and its publication caused a great wave of anger to pass over the teetotal camp. Yours obediently. 9th, July, 1917. G. HEMMING.[25]

In 1916, JTR, no fan of continental cafés, noting the higher levels of alcohol consumption in France, had disputed their advisability with G. Hemming – but the latter was convinced France had solved its problem with its ban on absinthe.

Horatio Bottomley's *John Bull* newspaper also was unimpressed with the logic of the PM's wife:

To Mrs Lloyd George, 10, Downing Street, S.W. DEAR MRS LLOYD GEORGE, Do you think it wise, now that you are in perhaps the most honoured position any woman can hold, to allow your Welsh enthusiasm to overcome discretion? That you are sincere in your temperance zeal I should be the last to deny, but exaggeration never helped any cause – good or bad – and when you declare in the columns of a weekly contemporary that drink is 'England's greatest and most terrible enemy', you make me wonder whether after all it is worthwhile going on with the war. I thought the Hun was our greatest enemy, and I seem to remember that someone who, in a burst of rhetoric a few months ago, told us that we were fighting three enemies and the greatest was drink, was very soon sorry for what he had said. Really, do let us preserve a sense of proportion and try to avoid wild exaggeration. If drink is our most terrible enemy, then let us make terms with the Hun forthwith, and all join the Band of Hope. JOHN BULL.[26]

A powerful drinks lobby in Parliament was a strong adversary, and division in the temperance ranks was a major handicap. Threatening people's favourite tipple was hardly popular, as this gossip on Mrs Lloyd George's recent conversations show:

A friend who was with Mrs Lloyd George during her visit to Cardiff tells me of an amusing incident. A local doctor, who, like the Premier's wife, is an enthusiastic collector of old pewter, was presented to Mrs Lloyd George, and they fell to discussing recent 'finds'. The doctor enumerated his possessions, adding, 'and then I have "Big Lloyd George" and "Little Lloyd George".' 'Good gracious,' exclaimed the Premier's wife, 'whatever do you mean?' Then the doctor explained that they were two noggins, one representing the size in vogue before the increased taxation instigated by the Premier, and the little one the minute portion of beverage supplied for similar payment at present.[27]

In Ireland, the licensed traders in Dungarvan also were ready to take the Lloyd Georges down a peg or two, as the *Waterford Star* reported on 26 May. Mr James Hayes, seconding a motion, was clear:

> Lloyd George got his education from his uncle, who was a cobbler by day and a preacher by night, and he was not much good at either. He was educated in the school of Henry George and Michael Davitt [Irish 19th-century land reformers] but when he got into the Cabinet he got a swelled head, and Mrs Lloyd George wanted to rub her skirts with lady this and lady that, and he is forgetting the poor man from whom he got his strength. He wants now to substitute weak beer that was little better than water. And he wants to do this for the English people. He has interfered with the poor man's tobacco, and now he must deny him his pint of stout.[28]

Letting the cat out the bag

Mrs Lloyd George then offered the liquor lobby a little more ammunition in an interview with Judge Neil of Chicago (a US campaigner for 'Mother's Pensions'), published on 30 June 1917, during National Baby Week. After reflecting on suffrage, and calling for the closure of pubs, she recognised that a substitute for beer would be needed to make headway on temperance – an idea which the drinks lobby were happy to exploit:

The interview was given wide coverage, as here in *The Pall Mall Gazette*:

> WOMEN THROWN MORE INTO PUBLIC LIFE: Mrs Lloyd George has recently had a conference with Judge Neil, of Chicago, on the subject of the great festival of National Baby Week, the success of which both are actively interested. During the interview, says the *Exchange*, Mrs Lloyd George pointed out how, in her opinion, the newly won right of suffrage for women might directly affect the baby saving campaign. Repression of

the drink evil and a greater interest on the part of women in the national aspects of social questions and child welfare work were among the results she predicted.

'Our first great hope is that women will use the vote now they have it,' Mrs Lloyd George said. 'Experience has shown that in some municipal elections women have been laggard in using the suffrage which was already theirs. But the effect of the war has been to throw women into much closer relations with public life and national activities than were formerly theirs. I fully believe they will now be keen to use their new rights of suffrage.'

Men Who May Want Beer
'And to what purpose do you think they will use it?' Judge Neil asked.

'Toward the solution of social problems,' Mrs Lloyd George replied. 'And perhaps first of all,' she added, 'their influence with the vote will show in the handling of the drink problem. I think ultimately the women voters will secure the abolition of public-houses and of the liquor traffic, just as they have done in some regions of the United States. By a system of local option, probably this effect would be greatly hastened, as one community, in abolishing the public house, becomes at once an influential example to others.

'But it is true that in England, and especially during their great sacrifices in war work, the men employed in hot munition factories and around the great furnaces with their terrific heat, will continue to want their beer, and medical opinion backs them in their statement that they must have a plentiful supply of beverages of some sort.'

A Substitute Wanted
'I often tell temperance workers that they must find a really satisfactory substitute for beer before they can make great headway. But if women's influence with the vote finally does away with the drink evil, as I think it will,' Mrs Lloyd George continued, 'many of the other great social problems will likewise be solved by this one fact.'

'My experience in the United States has been that drink is one of the great causes of poverty,' said Judge Neil, 'and that a high death rate among babies always accompanies conditions of poverty. Do you believe the women of Great Britain in the use of their suffrage will help remedy these conditions?'

'It seems reasonable, does it not?' answered Mrs Lloyd George. 'If women rid the land of the drink evil, I believe a great forward step will be taken in the baby saving campaign. We may expect that the little ones will then be raised in happier and more healthful homes. Mothers will be stronger and more reliable, and fathers more fit for the care of their families.'[29]

A reader in Belfast, possibly a hotel manager, suggested that she had 'let the cat out of the bag'.

MRS LLOYD GEORGE ON DRINK: TO THE EDITOR OF *THE NORTHERN WHIG*
Sir, Mrs Lloyd George has surely 'let the cat out of the bag' in asserting that 'ultimately the women will secure the abolition of public-houses and of the liquor traffic'.
 The idea pervading the minds of certain advocates of woman suffrage is evidently not that women should be given the vote because they have become part of the 'industrial army at home' during the war, but because it imagined that votes would 'secure the abolition of public-houses'.
 Mrs Lloyd George, however, not only 'let the cat out of the bag', but has proved the inconsistency of her suggestion by (at the same time) pointing out that the hard workers 'will continue to want their beer and medical opinion backs them in their statement'. She also said, 'I often tell temperance workers that they must find a really satisfactory substitute for beer before they can make great headway.'
 Mrs Lloyd George does not shine brilliantly as a logician as a result of her interview with a Chicago judge on 'National Baby Week'. A very large number of women do not want the vote, and if it is forced upon them they may turn the tables on their teetotal 'friends' by the recollection of the uncalled for and unwarranted charges of excessive drinking which they brought against women generally. There are many women who have no desire for 'the abolition of public-houses' and no desire to deprive workers of their beer, which medical opinion agrees is necessary for them. Yours, &c. George Sanderson, Prince of Wales Hotel, Belfast.[30]

Her comment concerning some women being 'laggard in using the suffrage which was already theirs' is a reminder that although women did not have the vote for Parliamentary elections, women ratepayers had had the vote in various local elections since 1867. Her later active electioneering included urging women to vote and not ignore the hard-

Temperance and Wartime Sobriety (1914 to 1918)

won opportunity. Not all women gained the vote in 1918, and it was important to show they would use it, supporting the ongoing campaign for universal suffrage.

Mrs Lloyd George knew very well what the temperance movement was up against, as the Scottish *Campbeltown Courier* related back in May:

> Addressing a women's welfare meeting Mrs Lloyd George painted a moral with a quaintly pathetic little story. It concerned a Yorkshire collier's wife who each Saturday made a practice of calling at the pit where her husband worked, with a view to getting him safely home, and, by persuasions and tact, preventing him getting too much to drink en route. The poor woman, however, was fain to confess that she seldom succeeded, and asked why, she replied as follows: 'Aw, yer see, lady, Ah might get Bill all reight past t' White Hoss, but, don't yer see, lady, theer's t' King's Heead, an' t' Brahn Coo, an' t' Blue Pig – seven other White Hosses, so to speyke, – afore Bill gets dohn that hawf-mile to ahr haase.'[31]

Intemperance in Carmarthen

On 22 October 1917, Mrs Lloyd George was again with *Merched y De*, in Carmarthen. As she pleaded for the movement to unite, things got lively.

> Mrs Lloyd George was accorded a rousing reception at Lammas-street Independent Chapel, Carmarthen, on Monday night, when she presided over a crowded public meeting in conjunction with Merched y De Temperance Union, who are holding their annual meetings in the town.
>
> Alluding to the recent discussion as to the best policy for Wales in regard to the licensing question, Mrs Lloyd George said they did not want the temperance party to be divided into two camps, and suggested that what they wanted was for temperance reformers in Wales, men and women, to come together to a conference to try and adopt a plan as to the best course to take. Both must respect each other's views, for if they had bad blood they might put temperance reform back for many years to come.
>
> Referring to the housing question with relation to temperance, she said they hoped to get better houses after the war. Prof. J. Oliver Stephens, B.A., B.D., as President of the Carmarthen Free Church Council and the Cymmrodorion Society, extended an official welcome to the 'Merched y

De'. Miss Rosina Davies, Ferryside (secretary of the Union), Mrs Tydfil Thomas. B.A., Cardiff, Miss Ellen Williams, London, also spoke, and pointed out that the Union stood for Prohibition.[32]

The full meaning of 'a rousing reception' emerges in the front-page gossip column entitled 'The Talk Is' of the local Tory, Church of England supporting paper, *The Carmarthen Journal*:

> The Talk Is:
> That Mrs Lloyd George has a very soft voice and could scarcely be heard. That the same could not be said of some of the 'Merched y De', especially when they shouted Prohibition.
> That certain ardent members of the 'Merched y De' are grieved because they were not among those selected for introduction to the Premier's wife.
> That it was not quite discreet for 'Merched y De' to shout 'Prohibition for ever' in the presence of Mrs Lloyd George.
> That the 'merched' will have nothing to do with Mrs Lloyd George's suggestion at Lammas-street Chapel that the State Purchasers and Prohibitionists of Wales should meet in conference.[33]

In the February 1921 Cardiganshire by-election, JTR was speaking alongside Mrs Lloyd George in support of Lloyd George's pragmatic temperance proposals, in direct opposition to Rosina Davies, who was sticking to prohibition and supporting the Asquithian candidate Llewelyn Williams. The Cardigan branch of *Merched y De* voted against the *Merched y De* party line, leading Miss Davies to deny there was a branch in Cardigan. The temperance movement was as divided as the Liberal Party.[34]

JTR promotes the PM's temperance proposals

In late 1917, JTR engaged in a lively exchange of views with prohibitionists in *The Welsh Outlook* journal, following his two-page article in October calling for support for the PM's proposals for State purchase and local option, rather than prohibition. In November the anonymous 'Doubter' disputed JTR's assertion that 'no other adequate proposal stands the slightest chance of being realised at present or for many years to come,' by citing the success in America and Canada and a recent plebiscite on the Clyde, and referencing the views of Lord Northcliffe.

JTR responded in December that the conditions between North America and Wales were completely different:

> Public sentiment in this country is far behind that of either the United States or Canada. It is certain that in Wales the activity of the temperance organisations does not stand comparison with those of America or the Colonies. In elections, either imperial or local, temperance plays a quite insignificant part. If anyone thinks temperance has been a living subject in Wales in recent years, let him study the election addresses of recent elections and the political speeches of Parliamentary representatives in the last ten years. Are there any public meetings so badly attended in Wales as temperance meetings?
>
> As for Lord Northcliffe, what has he done, I ask, through his powerful Press to help prohibition or any measure of temperance reform? Has he not always been on the side of the tempter rather than on the side of the tempted?

And concluding a debate over the cost of State purchase, JTR observed:

> Nothing amazes one more than to find men praising sobriety as an inestimable boon, yet refusing to pay the price of it. Any money spent in ridding the land of the drink traffic would be well and profitably spent.[35]

In the same December issue, the Rev. Lewis Williams of Bangor questioned whether what JTR claimed to be the PM's proposals were actually what the PM was proposing, and indeed whether they represented temperance proposals at all. The Rev. Williams offered no alternative approach but was wary of a huge State-owned liquor business being created, involving 'a vast number of lawyers and bankers' and along with it 'safe government positions and work'.[36]

Little would get past the liquor lobby.

1918

In April 1918, the arrival of granddaughter Margaret Carey Evans didn't stop Mrs Lloyd George from slipping out to chair another Cricieth temperance meeting. It was probably congratulations all round too.

A public meeting was held on Wednesday under the auspices of the Women's Temperance Association. Mrs Lloyd George, who presided, said the drink question was a difficult problem to settle in an old country like Great Britain where the people were inclined to move slowly. Since the war, drink had caused greater destruction than people realised, but now women had got the vote she looked for brighter days, trusting that they would use the vote properly and that good social work, especially better housing, would be the result. (Cheers)

A presentation followed by Professor Nichol, of Boston, Massachusetts, USA, on prohibition.[37]

A trip to Scotland with Lloyd George in May prevented her from chairing the ladies' conference at the annual congress of the Kent County Temperance Federation, held in Tunbridge Wells.[38]

In September, the interestingly named Vineyard Brotherhood Congregational Church group kept JTR and his prohibitionist opponent, in this case a JP, well apart, their presentations being on successive Sundays:

> Do you believe in (1) State Purchase of the Liquor Traffic, or in (2) Total Prohibition, as a solution of the Drink Problem. On Sunday, Sept. 8th, at 3.15 p.m. the Rev. J. T. Rhys (Sydenham) will speak on No. 1. On Sunday, Sept. 15th, at 3.15 p.m. Capt. Walter Cunningham, J.P. (Kensington) will speak on No. 2.
>
> Men and Women come and make up your mind as to which is the better solution![39]

In November, while Mrs Lloyd George accompanied the Prime Minister to Wolverhampton to launch the election campaign, JTR was in Hastings, making the case for Lloyd George's proposals and for putting temperance issues on the school syllabus. The local paper reported: 'He spoke out very strongly on the chaotic state of temperance parties upon this great social question and the crying need of union upon some practical scheme. It was a sad and futile waste of our best forces to be thus divided on means and methods.'[40]

Though both JTR and Mrs Lloyd George would reflect on the long-term 'failure' of the temperance movement, alcohol consumption was markedly reduced during the First World War, and did not jump back up afterwards, nor rise significantly again until the 1960s.[41]

Temperance and Wartime Sobriety (1914 to 1918)

It was also noted that many troops, primed with Army rum, returned with an alcohol problem. However, a medical officer of the Black Watch put it bluntly to a post-war parliamentary enquiry: 'Had it not been for the rum ration, I do not think we should have won the war.'

The negative and positive legacies of war.

Postscript: from War to Peace campaigns

While temperance remained a lifelong campaign for Margaret Lloyd George, the advent of peace led to a change of focus. The Troops Fund campaign continued awhile, in the form of the Welsh Children's Fund, but her recruitment campaign for the armed forces had ended with the arrival of conscription. The communal food kitchens were rapidly closing and her fund-raising for the sailors was much reduced, though she continued to support the cause of seafarers. She remained active with respect to healthcare, not least the treatment of the wounded, as well as child and maternal health. But now peace brought politics back to the fore and, for the first time, the wife of a Prime Minister was an active campaigner around the country, promoting and defending her husband's government as it sought to rebuild the war-weary nation. My grandfather, the Rev. J. T. Rhys, continued to provide his support as her private secretary through this period.

The story continues in *The Campaigns of Margaret Lloyd George, The Wife of the Prime Minister, 1916–1922*.

Endnotes

Introduction
1. Margaret Lloyd George did not keep a diary as such, and a memoir, often said to be well in progress, never saw the light of day.
2. Bryce Evans, *Feeding the People in Wartime Britain* (Bloomsbury, 2022); and Bryce Evans, 'The British "National Kitchen" of the First World War', *Journal of War & Culture Studies*, 10 (2016), ISSN 1752-6272, https://drbryceevans.wordpress.com/2017/03/29/the-national-kitchens-of-ww1/ provides an excellent analysis of the kitchen phenomenon, through both world wars and up to today.
3. Sally White, *Ordinary Heroes: the Story of Civilian Volunteers in the First World War* (Amberley Publishing, 2018).
4. Vivien Newman, *We Also Served, The Forgotten Women of the First World War* (Pen and Sword History, 2014).
5. *The Sketch*, 14.8.1918, p.4.
6. Mrs C. S. Peel O.B.E., *How We Lived Then* (John Lane, 1929), p.20.
7. For an extremely clear review of Britain's welfare debate, see Pete Alcock, *Why we need welfare, Collective Action for the Common Good* (Policy Press, 2016).
8. Sally White, *Ordinary Heroes*, p.10.
9. Justin Davis Smith, *100 Years of NCVO and Voluntary Action: Idealist and Realists* (Palgrave Macmillan, 2019), p.17. This work offers a rich review and analysis of volunteering in the UK over the past century, 'through the lens of the NCVO', set up during the war.
10. Peter Grant, *Philanthropy and Voluntary Action in the First World War: Mobilizing Charity* (Routledge, 2014), p.1.
11. Ibid.
12. Ibid.
13. Sally White, *Ordinary Heroes*, p.204.
14. The contribution of Sir Edward Ward is lauded by Peter Grant, *Mobilizing Charity*.

Chapter 1 – Peacetime Prelude
1. The church was demolished in the late 1990s and replaced by housing. His first church, in Pontycymer, still stands, now used by a charity.
2. *The Swansea Free Church Magazine*, No. 9, Vol. 3, September 1914.
3. *The Cambria Daily Leader*, 5.7.1910, p.5.
4. *The Cambria Daily Leader*, 5.12.1913, p.8.
5. Ibid.
6. Ibid.
7. Eglwysi Annibynnol ABERTAWE A'R CYLCH 1860–1915 gan John Williams, Waunwen / Congregational Churches SWANSEA AND DISTRICT 1860–1915 by John Williams, Waunwen, published by Joseph Williams & Sons (Merthyr) Ltd., Office of *Y Tyst* (Merthyr Tydvil).
8. *The Cambria Daily Leader*, 5.12.1913, p.8.
9. *Huddersfield Daily Examiner*, 3.4.1914, p.3.
10. *Daily Telegraph*, 5.9.1917, p.4.
11. *The Cambria Daily Leader*, 2.5.1914, p.8.
12. *The Leeds Mercury*, 12.5.1914, p.5.
13. *The Western Gazette*, 15.5.1914, p.11.
14. *Liverpool Daily Post*, 21.5.1914, p.11.
15. *Nottingham Evening Post*, 8.6.1914, p.5.

16 *Stockton Herald*, 13.6.1914, p.3.
17 *The (Dundee) Courier*, 10.6.1914, p.6.
18 *The Common Cause*, 19.6.1914, p.5.
19 *The Cambria Daily Leader*, 1.7.1914, p.6.
20 *The Times*, 1.7.1914, p.5.
21 Olwen Carey Evans, *Lloyd George Was My Father* (Gomer Press, 1985), p.49.
22 *The Manchester Courier*, 2.7.1914, p.6.
23 *Birmingham Daily Gazette*, 13.7.1914, p.4.
24 Angela V. John, *Turning the Tide, The Life of Lady Rhondda* (Parthian, 2013).
25 *Nottingham Journal*, 14.7.1914, p.6.
26 Ibid.
27 *The Westminster Gazette*, 25.2.1914, p.6.
28 *The Times*, 26.2.1914, p.11. See also, Richard Rhys O'Brien, *The Campaigns of Margaret Lloyd George, The Wife of the Prime Minister 1916–1922* (Y Lolfa, 2022), p.49.
29 *Nottingham Evening Post*, 26.2.1914, p.3.
30 *Yorkshire Post*, 15.7.1914, p.6.
31 Margaret Lloyd George, 'How do you help your husband?', typed draft, A. J. Sylvester Papers C25, NLW.
32 *The Daily Mirror*, 13.1.1914, p.7.
33 *The Newcastle Daily Journal*, 5.2.1914, p.5.
34 *The Mail*, 20.7.1914, p.1.
35 *The Westminster Gazette*, 24.7.1914, p.10, and *Yorkshire Telegraph and Star*, 24.7.1914, p.4.

Chapter 2 – 1914: Onto a War Footing
1 *Y Dinesydd Cymreig*, 29.7.1914, p.4.
2 *Lincolnshire Echo*, 20.8.1914, p.2.
3 *The Cambrian News*, 28.8.1914, p.7.
4 Peter Grant, *Mobilizing Charity*, p.23.
5 Ibid., p.26.
6 *The Daily Citizen (Manchester)*, 1.10.1914, p.3.
7 *Sunday Pictorial*, 23.1.1916, p.5.
8 On 29 July the Cabinet had decided that the 1839 treaty that European powers signed to protect Belgium's neutrality did not formally commit Britain to war, but that Britain would go to war if Germany did invade. See also Chapter 20: 'Recruitment'.
9 Peter Grant, *Mobilizing Charity*, p.27, and Sally White, *Ordinary Heroes*, Chapter 1: '"Guest of the Nation:" Belgian Refugees in Britain'.
10 *Carnarvon and Denbigh Herald*, 15.1.2015, p.2.
11 *The Shoreditch Observer*, 6.11.1914, p.3.
12 *The Chester Chronicle*, 2.1.1915, p.8.

Chapter 3 – 1915: Campaigns Get Underway
1 *Aberdeen Press and Journal*, 22.1.1915, p.6.
2 *The Carmarthen Weekly Reporter*, 29.1.1915, p.4.
3 *Western Mail*, 25.1.1915, p.6.
4 Lloyd George to Mrs Lloyd George, 19.11.1895, cited in Kenneth O. Morgan, *Lloyd George Family Letters 1885–1936* (University of Wales Press and Oxford University Press, 1973), p.91; and in Ffion Hague, *The Pain and the Privilege* (Harper Perennial, 2009), p.270.
5 Bob Wyatt, 'The First Air Raid, Great Yarmouth', Western Front Association, accessed online 22.2.2023 www.westernfrontassociation.com
6 *Bolton Evening News*, 23.1.1915, p.4.
7 *Liverpool Daily Post*, 8.2.1915, p.10.
8 *Carnarvon and Denbigh Herald*, 12.2.1915, p.6.
9 *Liverpool Echo*, 20.10.1915, p.4.
10 *Marylebone Mercury*, 6.2.1915, p.6.
11 Ivor Nicholson, O.B.E., Trevor Lloyd Williams, M.A. (eds), preface Sir E. Vincent Evans, *Wales: Its Part in the War* (Hodder and Stoughton, 1920), p.118.

12 Owen Lloyd George, *A Tale of Two Grandfathers* (Bellew, 1999), p.6.
13 David Thomas, 'Robert Silyn Roberts' (Rhosyr; 1871–1930), Calvinistic Methodist minister, poet, social reformer, tutor', *Dictionary of Welsh Biography* (National Library of Wales, 1959).
14 *The Lloyd George American Relief Fund, Report and Accounts for 1923 and 1924*, Lord Davies of Llandinam Papers, C4/8, National Library of Wales.
15 *The (Dundee) Courier*, 4.2.1915, p.4.
16 *Stratford-upon-Avon Herald*, 13.8.1915, p.4.
17 *Cambrian News*, 18.8.1916, p.2. Also reported in *The Welsh Citizen*, 16.8.1916, p.8.
18 *North Wales Chronicle and Advertiser for the Principality*, 1.3.1918, p.2.
19 *The Cambrian News*, 28.6.1918, p.7.
20 The *Lloyd George American Relief Fund, Report and Accounts for 1923 and 1924*, Lord Davies of Llandinam Papers, C4/8, NLW.
21 *Linlithgowshire Gazette*, 9.4.1915, p.2.
22 *Western Mail*, 5.5.1915, p.4.
23 *The Daily Mirror*, 6.5.1915, p.5.
24 *The Daily Citizen (Manchester)*, 6.5.1915, p.3.
25 Samuell Pepys Junior, *A Diary of the Great Warr*, Vol. 1, 1915, pp.145–6.
26 The new statue of Margaret Rhondda, unveiled by the Monumental Welsh Women project in Newport, Monmouthsire, in 2024, sees her standing on the prow of the *Lusitania* looking defiantly over the River Usk.
27 See Richard Rhys O'Brien, *The Campaigns of Margaret Lloyd George*, Chapter 18, 'The Secret Missioner'.
28 Lloyd George to Margaret Lloyd George, 26.5.1915, as cited in Kenneth O. Morgan (ed.), *Lloyd George Family Letters, 1885–1936* (University of Wales Press & OUP, 1973), p.178.
29 Ffion Hague, *The Pain and the Privilege* (Harper Perennial, 2009 edition), p.293.
30 Richard Lloyd George/Viscount Gwynedd, *Dame Margaret, The Life Story of His Mother* (George Allen and Unwin, 1947), p.142.
31 *North Wales Chronicle and Advertiser for the Principality*, 28.5.1915, p.3.
32 Olwen Carey Evans, *Lloyd George Was My Father* (Gomer Press, 1985), p.82.
33 *Derby Daily Telegraph*, 1.6.1915, p.2.
34 *Western Mail*, 2.6.1915, p.5.
35 *Western Mail*, 21.6.1915, p.4.
36 *The Brecon and Radnor Express*, 24.6.1915, p.5.
37 *Hampstead Advertiser*, 1.7.1915, p.5.
38 *The Liverpool Daily Post*, 5.7.1915, p.3.
39 *Western Mail*, 3.7.1915, p.5.
40 Richard Lloyd George/Viscount Gwynedd, *Dame Margaret, The Life Story of His Mother*, p.211.
41 *Liverpool Daily Post*, 13.7.1915, p.2.
42 Samuell Pepys Junior, *A Diary of the Great Warr*, Vol. 1, p.210.
43 *The Warwick and Warwickshire Advertiser*, 17.7.1915, p.5. See also Chapter 14, 'Parcels for Prisoners, Flags for the French'.
44 *The Leeds Mercury*, 5.8.1915, p.4.
45 *The Leeds Mercury*, 7.8.1915, p.2.
46 *The Cambria Daily Leader*, 9.8.1915, p.5.
47 *Western Mail*, 30.8.1915, p.7.
48 *The Bicester Herald*, 6.8.1915, p.2.
49 *The Dalkeith Advertiser*, 12.8.1915, p.4.
50 *North Wales Chronicle*, 27.8.1915, p.6.
51 From Military Service card.
52 Rhys David, *Tell Mum Not to Worry, A Welsh Soldier's World War One in the Near East* (Deffro, 2014), p.35.
53 *Liverpool Echo*, 22.9.1915, p.8.
54 *Welsh Gazette*, 21.10.1915, p.5.
55 *Pictures and the Picturegoer*, 6.11.1915, p.6.

56 *North Eastern Daily Gazette (Middlesbrough)* [online access as the *Daily Gazette for Middlesbrough*], 5.11.1915, p.2.
57 *Western Mail*, 1.12.1915, p.4.
58 See Richard Rhys O'Brien, *The Campaigns of Margaret Lloyd George*, Chapter 10: 'Cardiganshire Decides'.
59 *Carnarvon and Denbigh Herald*, 24.12.1915, p.8.
60 *The Cambria Daily Leader*, 9.12.1915, p.1.
61 *North Wales Chronicle and Advertiser for the Principality*, 10.12.1915, p.8.
62 *The (Hull) Daily Mail*, 23.12.1915, p.4.

Chapter 4 – 1916: Last Year at No. 11
1 *North Wales Chronicle and Advertiser for the Principality*, 14.1.1916, p.6. See also Chapters 22 and 23, 'Food and Economy, 1917 and 1918'.
2 *The Daily Mirror*, 4.2.1916, p.2, and Sally White, *Ordinary Heroes*, p.180.
3 *The Western Daily Press*, 10.2.1916, p.7.
4 *North Wales Chronicle and Advertiser for the Principality*, 10.3.1916, p.5.
5 *The Daily Mirror*, 16.3.1916, p.10.
6 Samuell Pepys Junior, *A Second Diary of The Great Warr*, Vol. 2, 1917, p.54.
7 *Cambria Daily Leader*, 27.3.1916, p.4.
8 *Western Mail*, 13.4.1916, p.4.
9 *Yr Herald Cymraeg*, 11.4.1916, p.4.
10 *Cambria Daily Leader*, 1.6.1916, p.3.
11 *North Wales Chronicle and Advertiser for the Principality*, 9.6.1916, p.2.
12 *Holloway Press*, 2.6.1916, p.5.
13 Richard Lloyd George, Viscount Gwynedd, *Dame Margaret, The Life Story of His Mother* (George Allen and Unwin 1947), p.165.
14 Ibid., p.213.
15 Ffion Hague, *The Pain and the Pleasure* (Harper Perennial, 2008), p.357.
16 *The (Dundee) Courier*, 14.6.1916, p.3.
17 *Herald of Wales*, 17.6.1916, p.1.
18 *Cambria Daily Leader*, 11.12.1916, p.4.
19 *Western Mail*, 26.6.1916, p.4.
20 *The Brecon and Radnor Express*, 6.7.1916, p.3.
21 *Llais Lafur (Labour Voice)*, 15.7.1916, p.3.
22 The Children's Society, 'A Brief History of the Waifs and Strays' Society', online, accessed 3.11.2023 https://www.hiddenlives.org.uk/articles/history.html
23 *The (Dundee) Courier*, 15.7.1916, p.6.
24 David Lloyd George to Margaret Lloyd George, 7.7.1916 letter, 3130 in Letters Lloyd George, NLW MS 3127-3182, 20475C, cited in J. Graham Jones NLW MS 20478A.
25 *The (Hull) Daily Mail*, 22.7.1916, p.2.
26 *The Belfast News-Letter*, 24.7.1916, p.6.
27 The Badsey Society, May 1st 1917, Letter from Mela Brown Constable to her fiancé, Major Cyril E Sladden, accessed online 26.5.2023 https://www.badseysociety.uk/sladden-archive/letters/aabc19190329
28 The Badsey Society, June 12th 1917, Letter from Mela Brown Constable to her fiancé, Major Cyril E Sladden, accessed online 26.5.2023 https://www.badseysociety.uk/sladden-archive/letters/aabc19190329
29 *The Cambrian News and Welsh Farmers' Gazette*, 11.8.1916, p.5.
30 *Daily Record*, 3.1.1916, p.4.
31 W. J. Lewis, *Born on a Perilous Rock* (Cambrian News, 1980), p.234.
32 *Liverpool Echo*, 22.6.1917, p.5.
33 *Liverpool Daily Post and Mercury*, 19.8.1916, p.6.
34 *Llais Llafur (Labour Voice)*, 26.8.1916, p.7.
35 *South Wales Weekly Post*, 26.8.1916, p.5.
36 *Y Genedl, The Welsh Nation*, 22.8.1916, p.7.
37 *Gwyliedydd Newydd*, 19.9.1916, p.4.
38 *Llais Llafur (Labour Voice)*, 2.9.1916, p.5.

39 *The Rhondda Leader*, 21.10.1916, p.1.
40 Marie Corelli to Margaret Lloyd George, 18.5.1919, letter 112, JTR Private Collection.
41 *The Scotsman*, 16.10.1916, p.4.
42 *Western Mail*, 18.10.1916, p.5.
43 Richard Lloyd to David and Margaret Lloyd George, December 1916, letter 142, Translation J. Graham Jones, JTR Private Collection.
44 *The Glamorgan Gazette*, 1.12.1916, p.3.
45 *The Mail (London)*, 8.12.1916, p.8.
46 *North Wales Chronicle*, 15.12.1916, p.7.
47 *The Daily Mirror*, 15.12.1916, p.2.
48 *Lancashire Evening Post*, 15.12.1916, p.2
49 *The Daily Mirror*, 8.12.1916, p.9.
50 *Cambria Daily Leader*, 11.12.1916, p.1.
51 *The Daily Mirror*, 12.12.1916, p.10.
52 *The Belfast News-Letter*, 11.12.1916, p.10.
53 *The Daily Record*, 14.12.1916, p.2.
54 *The Sunday Mirror*, 17.12.1916, p.6.
55 *The Bystander*, 20.12.1916, p.642.
56 *Sheffield Daily Telegraph*, 27.12.1916, p.6.
57 *The Pall Mall Gazette*, 15.1.1917, p.5.

Chapter 5 – 1917: First Lady, with Celtic Commitments

1 *The Times*, 3.1.1917, p.11.
2 *The Western Times*, 30.1.1917, p.5.
3 Michael Brock and Eleanor Brock, *Margot Asquith's Great War Diary, 1914–1916, The View from Downing Street* (Oxford University Press, 2014), n.2, p.312, citing Frances Stevenson, *The Years that are Past* (Hutchinson, 1967), p.99.
4 *The Liverpool Post* as cited in *The Liverpool Echo*, 27.1.1917, p.3.
5 *The Graphic*, 20.1.1917, p.5.
6 A fully digitally restored copy of the film has recently been released https://www.laurarossi.com/live-music-to-silent-film/ancre/
7 *The Pall Mall Gazette*, 23.1.1917, p.5, *Sunderland Daily Echo and Shipping Gazette*, 24.1.1917, p.2.
8 *(Dundee) Evening Telegraph*, 23.1.1917, p.3.
9 *The Times*, 26.1.1917, pp.10–11.
10 *Liverpool Echo*, 2.2.1917, p.6.
11 *The Globe*, 2.2.1917, p.5.
12 Ibid.
13 Peter T. Marsh, 'Chamberlain, Beatrice Mary (1862–1918)', *Oxford Dictionary of National Biography* (OUP 2014).
14 David Lloyd George to Mrs Lloyd George, 20.2.1917, JTR Private Collection.
15 David Lloyd George to Mrs Lloyd George, 22.2.1917, JTR Private Collection.
16 David Lloyd George to Mrs Lloyd George, 23.2.1917, JTR Private Collection.
17 David Lloyd George to Mrs Lloyd George, undated, JTR Private Collection.
18 David Lloyd George to Mrs Lloyd George, Tuesday 1917 (postmark shows only time and year), JTR Private Collection.
19 *The Leeds Mercury*, 24.3.1917, p.8.
20 *The Times*, 9.3.1917, p.11.
21 *The Leeds Mercury*, 24.3.1917, p.8.
22 *The Leeds Mercury*, 31.3.1917, p.2.
23 *The Southern Reporter*, 5.4.1917, p.4.
24 *The (Dundee) Courier*, 30.3.1917, p.3.
25 Ibid.
26 *Daily Record*, 23.3.1917, p.4.
27 JTR Lantern Lecture Notes for *Lloyd George as I Knew Him*, JTR Private Collection.
28 John Grigg, *Lloyd George War Leader, 1916–1918* (Allen Lane, 2002), pp.68–9.
29 *Sheffield Daily Telegraph*, 7.4.1917, p.4.

30 *Daily Record*, 13.4.1917, p.4.
31 *The Scotsman*, 13.4.1917, p.17.
32 *Western Mail*, 25.8.1919, p.8.
33 *The Daily Mirror*, 18.4.1917 p.10.
34 *(Dundee) Evening Telegraph*, 27.4.1917, p.1.
35 *The Scotsman*, 2.5.1917, p.4.
36 *Sussex Daily News*, 3.5.1917, p.4.
37 *The Leeds Mercury*, 12.5.1917, p.4.
38 *Ealing Gazette and West Middlesex Observer*, 19.5.1917, p.2.
39 *The Mail*, 18.5.1917, p.8.
40 Sally White, *Ordinary Heroes*, p.74.
41 *The Mail*, 18.5.1917, p.8.
42 *Liverpool Post and Mercury*, 17.5.1917, p.4. See also Chapter 18: 'Treatment and Retraining'.
43 *Liverpool Post and Mercury*, 23.5.1917, p.6.
44 *The Westminster Gazette*, 23.5.1917, p.6.
45 *Western Mail*, 25.5.1917, p.2. See also Chapter 24: 'Hospitals and Healthcare'.
46 *Liverpool Daily Post*, 30.5.1917, p.4.
47 *The Pall Mall Gazette*, 25.5.1917, p.8.
48 *Hampstead News*, 31.5.1917, p.7.

Chapter 6 – 1917: The Uncrowned Queen of Wales
1 *Carnarvon and Denbigh Herald*, 8.6.1917, p.8.
2 Sally White, *Ordinary Heroes*, p.206.
3 *Ealing Gazette and West Middlesex Observer*, 9.6.1917, p.6.
4 T. Cazalet-Keir, *From the Wings* (Bodley Head, 1967), p.48. Thelma Cazalet, later MP for Islington, was a close friend of Megan Lloyd George, and would address Mrs Lloyd George as Aunt Margaret.
5 *The Hanwell Gazette*, 16.6.1917, p.2.
6 *Bournemouth Guardian*, 9.6.1917, p.8.
7 *The Daily Mirror*, 20.6.1917, p.2.
8 John Grigg, *Lloyd George, War Leader* (Allen Lane, 2002), p.165, citing the diary of Maurice Hankey.
9 *Cambridge Daily News*, 22.6.1917, p.2.
10 Olwen Carey Evans, *Lloyd George Was My Father* (Gomer Press, 1985), p.96.
11 *The Illustrated War News*, 20.6.1917, p.39.
12 *Evening Despatch*, 25.6.1917, p.3.
13 *The West Ham and South Essex Mail*, 29.6.1917, p.5.
14 *The West Ham and South Essex Mail*, 22.2.1924, p.4.
15 *The Daily Mirror*, 20.6.1917, p.2.
16 *The Birmingham Daily Post*, 20.6.1917, p.4.
17 *Western Mail*, 27.6.1917, p.6.
18 *The Mail*, 29.6.1917, p.4.
19 *Britannia*, 6.7.1917, p.1.
20 *Dundee People's Journal*, 7.7.1917, p.7.
21 *The Bournemouth Graphic*, 6.7.1917, p.7.
22 *Western Mail*, 12.7.1917, p.5.
23 *The Daily News (London)*, 9.7.1917, p.1.
24 Winston Churchill to Margaret Lloyd Geoprge; 19.7.1917, Letter 2, JTR Private Collection.
25 Richard Lloyd George, *Lloyd George* (Frederick Muller, 1960), p.185.
26 *Norwood News*, 20.7.1917, p.4.
27 *Sussex Daily News*, 23.7.1917, p.4.
28 *Hendon & Finchley Times*, 27.7.1917, p.7
29 *Liverpool Post and Mercury*, 22.8.1917, p.6.
30 *The Common Cause*, 25.5.1917, p.2.
31 *Cambria Daily Leader*, 13.8.1917, p.2.

32 Mari Takayanagi, 'Gone Grille: The removal of the Ladies' Gallery Grilles', 23.8.2017, accessed 7.8.2023 https://ukvote100.org/2017/08/23/the-ladies-gallery-grilles/
33 Charles T. King, *The Asquith Parliament* (Hutchinson, 1910), p.319. See also Richard Rhys O'Brien, *The Campaigns of Margaret Lloyd George*.
34 *North Wales Chronicle and Advertiser for the Principality*, 24.8.1917, p.6.
35 *Liverpool Post and Mercury*, 30.8.1917, p.6.
36 Reverend Gomer Morgan Roberts, 'Williams, William (1717–1791), Methodist cleric, author, and hymn-writer', in *Dictionary of Welsh Biography*, 1959.
37 Richard Lloyd George, Viscount Gwynedd, *Dame Margaret, The Life Story of His Mother*, p.204.

Chapter 7 – 1917: Keeping Going
1 William M. Hughes to Margaret Lloyd George, Letter 53, JTR Private Collection.
2 *The Tamworth Herald*, 15.9.1917, p.3.
3 *Sunday Pictorial*, 10.6.1917, p.13.
4 *Liverpool Daily Post*, 7.9.1917, p.7.
5 John Grigg, Lloyd George, *War Leader, 1916–1918* (Allen Lane, 2002) p.230, citing Hankey diary, 21 and 23 September 1917.
6 *Newcastle Daily Journal*, 10.9.1917, p.4.
7 *The Chester Chronicle*, 15.9.1917, p.6.
8 'Who Was Olive Edis', Olive Edis Project online accessed 22.6.2020, https://oliveedisproject.wordpress.com/
9 *North Wales Chronicle and Advertiser for the Principality*, 26.10.1917, p.2. and also Chapter 18: 'Treatment and Retraining'.
10 *Liverpool Post & Mercury*, 26.10.1917, p.4.
11 *Edinburgh Evening News*, 27.10.1917, p.4.
12 Ibid.
13 *Sunday Pictorial*, 18.11.1917, p.9.
14 Samuell Pepys Junior, *A Diary of the Great Warr*, Vol. 1, 1915, p.50.
15 *Liverpool Echo*, 24.11.1917, p.3.
16 *The Westminster Gazette*, 19.11.1917, p.8.
17 *The Pall Mall Gazette*, 23.11.1917, p.5.
18 *Sunday Pictorial*, 25.11.1917, p.10.
19 *Manchester Evening News*, 30.11.1917, p.5.
20 *The Pall Mall Gazette*, 28.11.1917, p.2.
21 Laurence Alma Tadema to Margaret Lloyd George, 28.11.1917, Letter 93, JTR Private Collection.
22 Laurence Alma Tadema to Margaret Lloyd George, 30.11.1917, Letter 92, JTR Private Collection.
23 A. J. P. Taylor (ed.), *Frances Stevenson, Lloyd George. A Diary* (Hutchinson, 1971), p.38 (uncorrected proof).
24 For a clear review of the complexities involved in re-establishing the country of Poland for the first time since the 1790s, including Lloyd George's role, see Margaret Macmillan, *Paris 1919, Poland Reborn*, Chapter 17 (John Murray, 2002).
25 Peter Grant, *Mobilizing Charity*, p.48.
26 *The Tatler*, 5.12.1917, p.6.
27 Margaret Lloyd George to Olwen, 9.12.1917, Lloyd George Family Letters, NLW MS 22827 C.
28 *The Stirling Observer*, 15.12.1917, p.3.
29 *The Sketch*, 26.12.1917, pp.8–9.
30 *The Pall Mall Gazette*, 20.12.1917, p.4.
31 Olwen Carey Evans, *Lloyd George was My Father* (Gomer Press, 1985), p.99.
32 *The Illustrated Sporting and Dramatic News*, 29.12.1917, p.17.

Chapter 8 – 1918: Saving Money, Saving Lives
1 *Llangollen Advertiser*, 18.1.1918, p.5.
2 *Berks and Oxon Advertiser*, 25.1.1918, p.7. The painting today hangs in the offices of the Law Society in London.

Endnotes

3. *Liverpool Echo*, 18.1.1918, p.6.
4. *Huddersfield Daily Examiner*, 17.1.1918, p.2.
5. *Y Herald Cymraeg* (The Welsh Herald), 22.1.1918, p.2, translated from the Welsh.
6. *Western Mail*, 24.1.1918, p.2.
7. Owen Lloyd George, *A Tale of Two Grandfathers* (Bellew, 1999), p.3.
8. *Sheffield Daily Telegraph*, 27.2.1918, p.2.
9. *The Ladies' Field*, 23.2.1918, Supplement, Vol LXXXI, No. 1041.
10. *North Wales Chronicle and Advertiser for the Principality*, 1.3.1918, p.2.
11. See Richard Rhys O'Brien, *The Campaigns of Margaret Lloyd George*, pp.199–204.
12. *The Westminster Gazette*, 2.3.1918, p.3.
13. *The Leicester Daily Post*, 8.3.1918, p.1.
14. School Log Book, EM6/2 Blaengarw Mixed, Bridgend School Logbooks, Glamorgan Archives, accessed online 30.9.2023 https://glamarchives.gov.uk/wp-content/uploads/2016/04/Mid-Glamorgan-Bridgend-WWI-Log-Book-Summaries1.pdf
15. Ibid.
16. *Liverpool Post and Mercury*, 6.3.1918, p.4.
17. UK Parliament, *Education Act 1918*, online, accessed 28.10.2023 https://www.parliament.uk/about/living-heritage/transformingsociety/parliament-and-the-first-world-war/legislation-and-acts-of-war/education-act-1918/
18. *Western Mail*, 13.3.1918, p.4.
19. See Richard Lloyd George, p.195.
20. JTR MLG SP1 Free Church Council women, on Social Rescue, Rev. J. T. Rhys (Margaret Lloyd George) Papers, NLW.
21. *Sunday News*, 4.9.1927, p.10.
22. *Cambria Daily Leader*, 9.3.1918, p.1.
23. *Western Mail*, 8.3.1918, p.3, and *North Wales Chronicle*, 15.3.1918, p.2.
24. *Baner ac Amserau Cymru* (The Banner and Times of Wales), 30.3.1918, p.4.
25. Olwen Carey Evans, *Lloyd George Was My Father* (Gomer, 1985), p.101.
26. George Rees, *Gwersi Mewn Llysieueg* (Cambrian News, 1896), p.88.

Chapter 9 – 1918: Sustaining the Effort

1. David Lloyd George to Margaret Lloyd George, Letter 3, JTR Private Collection.
2. David Lloyd George to Margaret Lloyd George, Letter 4, JTR Private Collection.
3. See Richard Rhys O'Brien, *The Campaigns of Margaret Lloyd George*, Chapter 2, 'Peace and Coupon Election'.
4. *The (Sunday) Post (Glasgow)*, 26.5.1918, p.3.
5. *The Pall Mall Gazette*, 24.5.1918, pp.1–2.
6. MeganLG2, JTR Private Collection.
7. *Kent and Sussex Courier*, 31.5.1918, p.6, and Chapter 24, 'Temperance and Wartime Sobriety'.
8. *Westminster Gazette*, 30.5.1918, p.3, and *The Birmingham Post*, 30.5.1918, p.9.
9. *(Dundee) Evening Telegraph*, 31.5.1918, p.5.
10. *Newcastle Journal*, 31.5.1918, p.4.
11. *Derby Daily Telegraph*, 31.5.1918, p.2.
12. *South Wales Weekly Post*, 1.6.1918, p.1.
13. *Carmarthen Journal*, 7.6.1918, p.1.
14. *Cambria Daily Leader*, 19.6.1918, p.1.
15. *The Sketch*, 19.6.1918, p.5.
16. *Western Mail*, 24.6.1918, p.6.
17. *The Pall Mall Gazette*, 24.6.1918, p.5.
18. *Leeds Mercury*, 28.6.1918, p.8.
19. *Llais Llafur (Labour Voice)*, 29.6.1918, p.7.
20. *Llangollen Advertiser and Merionethshire Journal*, 28.6.1918, p.4.
21. *Norwood News*, 28.6.1918, p.4.
22. *The Daily Mirror*, 1.7.1918, pp.4–5.
23. *Sheffield Daily Telegraph*, 3.7.1918, p.2.
24. *The Globe*, 7.10.1918, p.4.

25 *The Sketch*, 6.2.1918, p.5.
26 *The Daily Mirror*, 3.7.1918, p.6.
27 *The Daily Mirror*, 5.7.1918, p.6.
28 *Western Mail*, 6.7.1918, p.5.
29 *The Graphic*, 13.7.1918, p. 52.
30 *Hendon and Finchley Times*, 12.7.1918, p.5.
31 *The Times*, 15.7.1918, p.9; *The Daily Mirror*, 15.7.1918, p.1.
32 *The Pall Mall Gazette*, 17.7.1918, p.2.
33 *The Daily Mirror*, 18.7.1918, p.2.
34 *West London Press, Chelsea News*, 16.8.1918, p.3.
35 *North Wales Chronicle and Advertiser for the Principality*, 19.7.1918, p.3.
36 See also Richard Rhys O'Brien, 'Margaret Lloyd George, Opening Up New Opportunities in 1919' / 'Yn Agor Cyfleon Newydd yn 1919', *Memories of Menai Bridge*, Volume 16 / *Atgofion Porthaethwy*, Cyfrol 17 (Menai Bridge and District Civic Society / Cymdeithas Ddinesig Bro Porthaethwy, 2019).

Chapter 10 – 1918: War Begins to Turn
1 *Llangollen Advertiser*, 9.8.1918, p.5.
2 *Baner ac Amserau Cymru (The Banner and Times of Wales)*, 10.8.1918, p.5.
3 *The Herald of Wales*, 3.8.1918, p.1.
4 *The Herald of Wales*, 17.8.1918, p.4.
5 *The Sketch*, 14.8.1918 p.4.
6 *The Cambrian News and Merionethshire Standard*, 30.8.1918, p.5.
7 *Llangollen Advertiser and Merionethshire Journal*, 30.8.1918, p.6.
8 *Dundee Evening Telegraph*, 8.4.1918, p.3
9 *The Times Educational Supplement*, 29.8.1918, p.364.
10 Ivor Nicholson, O.B.E., Trevor Lloyd Williams, M.A. (eds), preface Sir E. Vincent Evans, *Wales: Its Part in the War* (Hodder and Stoughton, 1920) pp.158–9.
11 *Manchester Evening News*, 6.9.1918, p.2.
12 *The Sketch*, 18.9.1918, p.42.
13 *Manchester Evening News*, 12.9.1918, p.3.
14 *Sunday Mirror*, 15.9.1918, p.9.
15 *Aberdeen Daily Journal*, 23.9.1918, p.4.
16 John Grigg, *Lloyd George, Warleader* (Penguin Allen Lane, 2002) p.594, n.32.
17 *Liverpool Echo*, 14.9.1918, p.3. https://en.wikipedia.org/wiki/The_Life_Story_of_David_Lloyd_George
18 Samuell Pepys Junior, *The Last Diary of the Great Warr*, Vol. 3, 1919, p.217.
19 *The Leeds Mercury*, 20.9.1918, p.4.
20 *Western Mail*, 24.9.1918, p.2.
21 *The Ealing Gazette and West Middlesex Observer*, 14.9.1918, p.7.
22 *Evening Despatch (Birmingham)*, 15.10.1918, p.2.
23 *Western Gazette*, 2.4.1926, p.14.
24 *Hendon and Finchley Times*, 11.10.1918, p.8.
25 *Sheffield Evening Telegraph*, 18.10.1918, p.3.
26 *Sunday Pictorial*, 20.10.1918, p.14.
27 *The Leeds Mercury*, 24.10.1918, p.8.
28 *The Scotsman*, 21.10.1918, p.2.
29 *The Daily Mirror*, 1.11.1918, p.4.
30 *The Scotsman*, 29.10.1918, p.3.

Chapter 11 – 1918: Peace at Last
1 *The Birmingham Daily Post*, 5.11.1918, p.8.
2 *The Daily Mirror*, 7.11.1918. p.4.
3 *Derby Daily Telegraph*, 7.11.1918, p.2.
4 Margaret Lloyd George, Speech (handwritten) to the Welsh Temperance Union, 20472C, 3019, NLW. Translation by J. Graham Jones.
5 *The Daily Mirror*, 7.11.1918, p.2.

Endnotes

6 *The People*, 10.11 1918, p.3.
7 Mrs J. Williams to Margaret Lloyd George, Letter 31, JTR Private Collection.
8 *Shepton Mallet Journal*, 19.1.1980, p.4, and online BMD records.
9 *The Western Daily Press*, 9.11.1918, p.7.
10 *The Scotsman*, 11.11.1918, p.6.
11 *The (Evening) Mail* (published by *The Times*), 20.7.1914, p.1.
12 *The (Dundee) Courier*, 11.11.1918, p.3.
13 Margaret Lloyd George, 'How do you help your husband?', typed draft, A. J. Sylvester Papers, C25, NLW.
14 JTR Notes for a possible autobiography by Dame Margaret Lloyd George GBE, JP, JTR Private Collection.
15 *The Times*, 12.11.1918, p.5.
16 *The Westminster Gazette*, 8.11.1918, p.7.
17 Lord Reading to David Lloyd George, Letter DLG1, JTR Private Collection.
18 *Yorkshire Telegraph and Star / Sheffield Evening Telegraph*, 12.11.1918, p.4.
19 *Richmond Herald*, 16.11.1918, p.1.
20 *The Westminster Gazette*, 16.11.1918, p.7.
21 *The Derby Daily Telegraph*, 18.11.1918, p.2.
22 Samuell Pepys Junior, *The Last Diary of the Great Warr*, Vol. 3, 1919, p.276.
23 *The Yorkshire Evening Post*, 15.11.1918, p.4.
24 *Newcastle Daily Journal*, 16.11.1918, p.4.
25 *The Sketch*, 27.11.1918, p.10.
26 *Liverpool Echo*, 6.12.1918, p.6.
27 NLW MS 22823C, f.73, David Lloyd George, 10 Downing Street, to Margaret Lloyd George, 'Wednesday, 18 August 1920', cited in J. Graham Jones, 'Dame Margaret in Cardiganshire', *Ceredigion, Journal of the Cardiganshire Historical Society*, 2004 (Vol XIV, No 4).

Chapter 12 – Establishing the Fund and Reactions

1 *Welsh Gazette*, 17.12.1914, p.4.
2 For the in-depth story of the Boer War Welsh Hospital see David Jones, *Gallant Little Wales: The Welsh Hospital* (Y Lolfa, 2023).
3 *The Western Daily Press*, 19.12.1914, p.5.
4 Sally White, *Ordinary Heroes*, p.68. The St Fagans estate, given to the nation in 1948, now houses the St Fagans National Museum of History, including Troops Fund flags and mementos.
5 Troops Fund Minutes, 27.3.1919, Minute Book 4, Mân Adnau / Minor Deposit 18A, Papers of E. Vincent Evans, NLW ex2145, National Library of Wales.
6 *The [Flintshire] County Herald*, 15.1.1915, p.7.
7 *The Brecon & Radnor Express*, 8.1.1914, p.5.
8 *Dundee Courier,*, 20.6.1912, p.6.
9 Gwyn Jenkins, *A Welsh County at War* (Y Lolfa, 2021), p.17.
10 Troops Fund Minutes, 5.1.1915, Minute Book 1, Mân Adnau/Minor Deposit 15A, Papers of E. Vincent Evans, NLW, ex2145, National Library of Wales.
11 *Western Mail*, 6.1.1915, p.6.
12 The Alexandra Rose Charity and annual June Rose Day continue today under the presidency of Queen Alexandra's great-granddaughter, Princess Alexandra, Lady Ogilvy. https://www.alexandrarose.org.uk/
13 *The [Dublin] Daily Express*, 27.6.1912, p.4.
14 'The Origin of Flag Days', Voluntary Action History Society paper, 12.11.2005 online, sourced 9.3.2023. https://www.vahs.org.uk/vahs/papers/vahs3.pdf
15 *The Cambrian News*, 1.1.1915, p.4.
16 Troops Fund Minutes, 11.1.1915, Book 1, 15A, NLW.
17 Ibid.
18 *Western Mail*, 15.2.1915, p.6.
19 Troops Fund Minutes, 18.1.1915, Book 1, 15A, NLW.
20 *Western Mail*, 21.1.1915, p.7.

389

21 Ibid.
22 *Llangollen Advertiser and North Wales Journal*, 22.1.1915, p.8.
23 *Western Mail*, 26.1.1915, p.6.
24 Troops Fund Minutes, 25.1.1915, Book 1, 15A, NLW.
25 See Wartime Diary, Chapter 3: 'Campaigns Get Underway'.
26 *Western Mail*, 29.1.1915, p.6.
27 *Porthcawl News*, 4.2.1915, p.7.
28 Troops Fund Minutes, 2.2.1915, Book 1, 15A, NLW.
29 *The Pioneer*, 30.1.1915, p.3
30 Detailed in Introduction: 'Wartime Welfare', p.7.
31 *Liverpool Daily Post and Mercury*, 4.2.1915, p.8.
32 *Brecon County Times*, 25.2.1915, p.5.
33 *The Aberdare Leader*, 27.2.1915, p.2.
34 *Northampton Chronicle and Echo*, 27.1.1915, p.3.
35 Sally White, *Ordinary Heroes*, pp.199–200. And BBC News Online, 'Cigarette case that "stopped WW1 bullet" to be auctioned', published 5.11.2019 https://www.bbc.co.uk/news/uk-england-derbyshire-50302592. Also, 'Cigarette Case Saves Soldier's Life at Gallipoli', porthcawlmuseum/2015-2019.html
36 *The War Pictures and London Illustrated Weekly*, 21.1.1915, p.9.
37 *Western Mail*, 26.1.1915, p.6.
38 *Western Mail*, 9.2.1915, p.6.
39 Troops Fund Minutes, 2.2.1915, Book 1, 15A, NLW.
40 *Western Mail*, 11.2.1915, p.6.
41 *North Wales Weekly News*, 4.2.1915, p.5.
42 Ibid., p.8.

Chapter 13 – The Fund Settles In
1 Troops Fund Minutes, 8.2.1915, Book 1, 15A, NLW.
2 Troops Fund Minutes, 22.2.1915, Book 1, 15A, NLW.
3 See also Richard O'Brien, 'The Missing Mahogany WW1 Memorial, Mrs Lloyd George and the Royal Dental Hospital twenty-nine, 1916 to 1926', *Dental Historian*, Volume 67 (2), July 2022, and Richard Rhys O'Brien, *The Campaigns of Margaret Lloyd George*, pp.82–83 and p.208.
4 Troops Fund Minutes, 22.2.1915, Book 1, 15A.
5 *The Daily Mirror*, 2.3.1915, p.16.
6 *Porthcawl News* 27.5.1915, p.3.
7 *Western Mail*, 16.3.1915, p.9.
8 Troops Fund Minutes, 8.3.1915, Book 1, 15A, NLW.
9 Troops Fund Minutes, 15.3.1915, Book 1, 15A, NLW.
10 Samuell Pepys Junior, *A Diary of the Great War*, Vol. 1, p.107.
11 *Western Mail*, 12.4.1915, p.8.
12 Troops Fund Minutes, 12.4.1915, Book 1,15A, NLW.
13 Ibid.
14 *Llais Llafur (Labour Voice)*, 22.4.1916, p.3.
15 National Army Museum, 'First World War, Salonika Campaign', online, accessed 30.10.2023. https://www.nam.ac.uk/explore/salonika-campaign
16 Troops Fund Minutes, 3.5.1915, Book 1, 15A, NLW.
17 *Western Mail*, 4.5.1915, p.6.
18 *Western Mail*, 13.5.1915, p.7.

Chapter 14 – Parcels for Prisoners, Flags for the French
1 Troops Fund Minutes, 7.6.1915, Book 1, 15A, NLW.
2 *Western Mail*, 11.6.1915, p.8.
3 *The Graphic*, 13.5.1916, p.18.
4 *Western Mail*, 16.7.1915, p.6.
5 'Duty and Democracy, Parliament and the First World War', Houses of Parliament online, accessed May 2023, https://www.parliament.uk/globalassets/documents/WW1/duty-and-democracy-parliament-and-the-first-world-war.pdf

6 *Western Mail*, 10.11.1915, p.6.
7 'The tragic coincidence linking the deaths of the De Guélis siblings', online article, Roath Local History Society, 20.7.2024.
8 *Western Mail*, 16.7.1915, p.6.
9 'Wales Day by Day', *Western Mail*, 17.7.1915, p.4.
10 *The Daily News (London)*, 26.6.1915, p.6.
11 *Western Mail*, 7.7 1915 p.4.
12 *The Cambrian News*, 16.7.1915, p.8.
13 Samuell Pepys Junior, *A Diary of the Great Warr*, Vol. 1, p.210.
14 *The Manchester Courier*, 25.9.1915, p.7.
15 Peter Grant, *Mobilizing Charity*, pp.104–8.
16 *Western Mail*, 30.7.1915 p.7.
17 *The Cambrian News*, 16.7.1915, p.8.
18 Peter Grant, *Mobilizing Charity*, p.97.
19 Troops Fund Minutes, 5.7.1915, Book 1, 15A, NLW.
20 Troops Fund Minutes, 12.7.1915, Book 1 15A, NLW.
21 Ibid.
22 *Liverpool Echo*, 21.7.1915, p.6.
23 Troops Fund Minutes, 6.9.1915, Book 1, 15A, NLW.
24 *The Times*, 21.9.1915, p.8, and cited in Peter Grant, *Mobilizing Charity*, p.61.

Chapter 15 – The War Office Steps In
1 *The Brecon & Radnor Express*, 7.10.1915, p.7.
2 *The Brecon & Radnor Express*, 14.10.1915, p.5
3 Troops Fund Minutes, 11.10.1915, Book 1, 15A, NLW.
4 *Annual Register*, 1915 proquest/clarivate.
5 *The Scotsman*, 9.10.1915, p.8.
6 *The Times*, 12.10.1915, p.11, cited in Peter Grant, *Mobilizing Charity*, p.74.
7 *101 Scheme for Co-ordinating and Regulating Voluntary Work Organisations throughout the United Kingdom*, 2nd ed. (HMSO, 1.12.1915) cited in Peter Grant, *Mobilizing Charity*, p.74.
8 *102 Report of the Director General of Voluntary Organisations, 4*, cited in Peter Grant, *Mobilizing Charity*, p.74.
9 Peter Grant, *Mobilizing Charity*, p.74.
10 Troops Fund Minutes, 4.10.1915, Book 1, 15A, NLW.
11 *The Llangollen Advertiser*, 22.10.1915, p.3.
12 Troops Fund Minutes, 18.10.1915, Book 1, 15A, NLW.
13 *Cambria Daily Leader*, 29.10.1915, p.6.
14 *The Brecon & Radnor Express*, 20.1.1916, p.7.
15 *The Brecon & Radnor Express*, 18.11.1915, p.2.
16 St Marylebone Parish Church website, 'Margherita Howard de Walden', accessed 19.8.2023. https://stmarylebone.org/about-us/heritage/people-of-st-marylebone/changing-faces-of-st-marylebone/margherita-baroness-howard-de-walden-1890-1974/ and Museums Victoria Collections, 'Lady de Walden Hospital, Alexandria, 1915–1918', accessed 19.8.2023. https://collections.museumsvictoria.com.au/items/1774155
17 See David Jones, *Gallant Little Wales: The Welsh Hospital* (Y Lolfa, 2023).
18 Troops Fund Minutes, 27.7.1916, Book 2, 16A, NLW.
19 'Epson and Ewell History Explorer', accessed 15.8.2023 https://eehe.org.uk/?p=40915/#HopkinsonHJP
20 Troops Fund Minutes, 15.11.1915, Book 1, 15A, NLW.
21 See Chapter 19: 'From Comforts to Care and Children'.
22 Not to be confused with Gwendoline Davies, Llandinam, the philanthropist.
23 Troops Fund Minutes, 6.12.1915, Minute Book 2, Mân Adnau/Minor Deposit 16A, Papers of E. Vincent Evans, NLW, ex2145, National Library of Wales.
24 *Flintshire Observer and News*, 26.11.1914, p.4.
25 *Y Cymro*, 7.4.1915, p.4.
26 Troops Fund Minutes, 8.11.1915, Book 1, 15A, NLW.

27 Troops Fund Minutes, 29.11.1915, Book 1, 15A, NLW.
28 Ibid. Also see *Wartime Diary*, Chapter 3: '1915: Campaigns Get Underway (January–December 1915)'
29 Troops Fund Minutes, 15.11.1915, Book 1, 15A, NLW. See Chapter 3: '1915: Campaigns Get Underway (January–December 1915)'.
30 Troops Fund Minutes, 6.12.1915, Book 2, 16A, NLW.
31 *Carnarvon & Denbigh Herald*, 24.12.1915, p.2.
32 *The Cambria Daily Leader*, 15.12.1915, p.1.
33 *The Brecon & Radnor Express*, 2.12.1915, p.5
34 *The Cambria Daily Leader*, 9.12.1915, p.8.
35 Rhys David, *Tell Mum Not to Worry* (Deffro, 2014), p.36.
36 Troops Fund Minutes, 20.12.1915, Book 2, 16A, NLW.
37 Troops Fund Minutes, various, 1915–1916, Books 1 and 2, 15A, 16A, NLW.
38 *The Carmarthen Journal and South West Weekly Advertiser*, 17.12.1915, p.3.
39 *The North Wales Weekly News*, 16.12.1915, p.10.
40 *The Cambrian News*, 24.12.1915, p.5.
41 For a thorough discussion, see Gwyn Jenkins, *A Welsh County at War*, Chapter V, 'Unpatriotic Farmers?' (Y Lolfa, 2021).
42 *The Brecon & Radnor Express*, 23.12.1915, p.2.
43 Troops Fund Minutes, 13.12.1915, Book 2, 16A, NLW.
44 Olwen Carey Evans, *Lloyd George Was My Father* (Gomer Press, 1985), pp.73–5.

Chapter 16 – Coordinating with Wales
1 *The Herald of Wales and Mid Glamorgan Herald and Neath Gazette*, 22.1.1916, p.10.
2 Troops Fund Minutes, 20.12.1915, Book 2, 16A, NLW.
3 *Sheffield Daily Telegraph*, 5.1.1914, p.9.
4 *South Wales Weekly Post*, 22.1.1916, p.7.
5 Ibid.
6 For more on what Swansea did for the Swansea boys, see the online posting: 'Ystalyfera Ystradgynlais and District 1914–1918', that compiles many views from the Front. http://www.ystradgynlais-history.co.uk/ystalyfera-ystradgynlais-ww1-full.pdf
7 *The Cambrian News and Welsh Farmers' Gazette*, 28.1.1916, p.7.
8 *Carmarthen Journal*, 4.2.1916, p.2.
9 *Herald of Wales and Mid-Glamorgan Herald and Neath Gazette*, 22.1.1916, p.10.
10 *North Wales Chronicle and Advertiser for the Principality*, 28.1.1916, p.4.
11 *The Brecon & Radnor Express*, 20.1.1916, p.7
12 *The Cambria Daily Leader*, 18.5.1915, p.6.
13 *Y Drych*, 13.1.1916, p.8.
14 *Dundee Evening Telegraph*, 25.1.1916, p.4.
15 Sally White, *Ordinary Heroes*, p.172.
16 *West London Observer*, 25.2.1916, p.5.
17 Troops Fund Minutes, 14.2.1916, Book 2, 16A, NLW.
18 *Carmarthen Weekly Reporter*, 25.2.1916, p.4, and also in the *Herald of Wales* of the same date.
19 *The Brecon & Radnor Express*, 2.3.1916, p.5.
20 *North Wales Chronicle and Advertiser for the Principality*, 10.3.1916, p.5.
21 Troops Fund Minutes, 15.11.1915, 15A; 22.11.1915, 15A; 17.1.1916, 16A; 14.2.1916, 16A, NLW.
22 Peter Bird, *The First Food Empire: A History of J Lyons and Co* (Phillimore, 2000), p.50.
23 *The Globe*, 1.3.1916, p.5.
24 'Epson and Ewell History Explorer', accessed 17.1.2021 https://eehe.org.uk/?p=25581
25 Troops Fund Minutes, Sub-Committee, 20.1.1916, Book 2, 16A, NLW.
26 *Haverfordwest and Milford Haven Telegraph*, 15.3.1916, p.3.
27 *The Streatham News*, 3.3.1916, p.4
28 *The Cambrian News and Welsh Farmers' Gazette*, 10.3.1916, p.3.
29 Comparisons of value over time have been made using the Bank of Inflation

calculator, based on retail prices. With prices more than doubling during the war, the multiplier to a value today varies according to the year in question, but in general First World War prices can be multiplied by between 100 to 50 as the war progresses.
30 *Llanelly Star*, 4.3.1916, p.1.
31 *Llangollen Advertiser*, 10.3.1916, p.5.
32 *The Carmarthen Weekly Reporter*, 17.3.1916, p.4.
33 Troops Fund Minutes, 9.10.1918, Book 4, 18A, NLW.
34 *Western Mail*, 12.5.1916, p.4, and *Evening Mail*, 22.5.1916, p.8.
35 *Western Mail*, 19.5.1916, p.4.
36 Troops Fund Minutes, 6.7.1916, Book 2, 16A, NLW.
37 Troops Fund Minutes, 11.10.1917, Minute Book 3, Mân Adnau / Minor Deposit 17A, Papers of E. Vincent Evans, NLW, ex2145, National Library of Wales.
38 *The Brecon & Radnor Express*, 25.5.1916, p.7.
39 Troops Fund Minutes, 17.7.1916 and 27.7.1916, Book 2, 16A, NLW.
40 Troops Fund Minutes, 11.10.1917, Book 3, 17A, NLW.
41 Troops Fund Minutes, 17.7.1916, Book 2, 16A, NLW.
42 Troops Fund Minutes, 27.7.1916, Book 2, 16A, NLW.
43 Troops Fund Minutes, 21.9.1916, Book 3, 17A, NLW.
44 Troops Fund Minutes, 11.10.1917, Book 3, 17A, NLW.
45 *The People*, 16.7.1916, p.4.
46 *The Chester Chronicle*, 29.7.1916, p.8.
47 *The Cambrian News and Welsh Farmers' Gazette*, 11.8.1916, p.7.
48 Troops Fund Minutes, 12.10.1916, Book 3, 17A, NLW.
49 Troops Fund Minutes, 9.11.1916, Book 3, 17A, NLW.
50 Troops Fund Minutes, 23.11.1916, Book 3, 17A, NLW.
51 *The Scotsman*, 22.2.1917, p.10.
52 *Richmond Herald*, 24.2.1917, p.8.
53 *The Globe*, 26.2.1917, p.5.
54 Samuell Pepys Junior, *A Second Diary of the Great Warr*, Vol. 2, pp.167–8.

Chapter 17 – Olwen Flies the Flag
1 Troops Fund Minutes, 12.1.1917. Book 3, 17A, NLW.
2 Troops Fund Minutes, 5.12.1916. Book 3, 17A, NLW.
3 *The Globe*, 16.1.1917, p.1.
4 The firm Robert Lewis was acquired in 1992 by the 1881 Dublin-founded firm of James J Fox, now trading as J. J. Fox (St James's) Ltd.
5 Troops Fund Minutes, 18.1.1917, Book 3, 17A, NLW.
6 George Robey to Margaret Lloyd George, letter 29.1.1917, Letters to Margaret Lloyd George, NLW MS 22826 C.
7 *The Ealing Gazette and West Middlesex Observer*, 17.2.1917, p.2.
8 Troops Fund Minutes, 15.2.1917, Book 3, 17A, NLW.
9 *The Pall Mall Gazette*, 1.3.1917, p.7.
10 Sally White, *Ordinary Heroes*, p.84.
11 *The Pall Mall Gazette*, 1.3.1917, p.7.
12 Ibid., p.12.
13 *Western Mail*, 1.3.1917, p.3.
14 *Western Mail*, 16.1.1917, p.2.
15 Samir Rafat, *Egyptian Mail*, 27.5.1995, 'Davies Bryan & Co. of Elmad El Din St.', accessed 30.10.2023 from http://www.egy.com/landmarks/95-05-27.php
16 *The Daily Graphic*, 14.4.1917, p.3.
17 *Liverpool Post & Mercury*, 24.4.1917, p.8.

Chapter 18 – Treatment and Retraining
1 Letter William Lewis to David Davies, 16.3.1917, Lord Davies of Llandinam Papers C4/8 1917, National Library of Wales.
2 Letter William Lewis to David Davies, 17.3.1917, Lord Davies of Llandinam Papers C4/8 1917, NLW.

3   Ibid.
4   Letter William Lewis to David Davies, 20.3.1917, Lord Davies of Llandinam Papers C4/8 1917, NLW.
5   Letter William Lewis to David Davies, 27.3.1917, Lord Davies of Llandinam Papers C4/8 1917, NLW.
6   Letter William Lewis to David Davies, 17.3.1917, Lord Davies of Llandinam Papers C4/8 1917, NLW.
7   Marlay Samson letter to William Lewis, 15.6.1917, Lord Davies of Llandinam Papers, C4/7, Welsh Disabled Soldiers, NLW.
8   Letter William Lewis to David Davies, 3.4.1917, Lord Davies of Llandinam Papers, C4/8 1917, NLW.
9   William Lewis, unpublished, Lord Davies of Llandinam Papers, C4/7, Welsh Disabled Soldiers.
10 William Lewis to David Davies , 13.4.1917, Lord Davies of Llandinam Papers, C4/8, 1917, NLW.
11 *Western Mail*, 11.4.1917, p.4.
12 *Manchester Guardian*, clipping in NLW David Davies archive indicated as 21 May, though it does not appear in available online editions.
13 William Lewis to David Davies, 21.6.1917, Lord Davies of Llandinam Papers, C4/8, 1917, NLW.
14 William Lewis to David Davies, 1.5.1917, Lord Davies of Llandinam Papers, C4/8, 1917, NLW.
15 William Lewis to David Davies, 29.6.1917, Lord Davies of Llandinam Papers, C4/8, 1917, NLW.
16 Troops Fund Minutes, 7.6.1917, Book 2, 16A, NLW.
17 *Newcastle Daily Chronicle*, 1.6.1917, p.3.
18 *The Daily Mirror*, 17.7.1917, p.6.
19 Troops Fund Minutes, 4.7.1917, Book 2, 16A, NLW.
20 *North Wales Chronicle and Advertiser for the Principality*, 7.12.1917, p.6.
21 Troops Fund Minutes, 10.1.1918, Book 4, 18A, NLW.
22 *The Ealing Gazette and West Middlesex Observer*, 22.12.1917, p.5.
23 *Sunday Mirror*, 4.11.1917, p 12.

Chapter 19 – From Comforts to Care and Children
1   *Manchester Evening News*, 18.1.1918, p.3.
2   *Liverpool Echo*, 19.1.1918, p.3.
3   *The Chester Chronicle*, 26.1.1918, p.2.
4   *The Cambrian News, Merionethshire Standard and Welsh Farmers Gazette*, 1.3.1918, p.8.
5   *North Wales Chronicle and Advertiser for the Principality*, 1.3.1918, p.2.
6   *Cambria Daily Leader*, 1.3.1918, p.1.
7   *The Times*, 2.3.1918, p.3.
8   *The Illustrated London News*, 13.4.1918, p.19.
9   *Cambria Daily Leader*, 2.3.1918, p.3.
10 *North Wales Chronicle*, 15.3.1918, p.3.
11 *North Wales Chronicle and Advertiser for the Principality*, 26.4.1918, p.3.
12 *Western Mail*, 11.6.1918, p.3.
13 *The Cambrian News, Merionethshire Standard and Welsh Farmers Gazette*, 28.6.1918, p.5.
14 *The Cambrian News*, 10.1.1919, p.5.
15 *Western Mail*, 24.6.1918, p.8.
16 Troops Fund Minutes, 26.6.1918, Book 4, 18A, NLW.
17 Troops Fund Minutes, 30.7.1918, Book 4, 18A, NLW.
18 Ibid.
19 Ibid.
20 Troops Fund Minutes, 9.10.1918, Book 4, 18A, NLW.
21 Troops Fund Minutes, 24.3.1920, Book 4, 18A, NLW.

22 Samuell Pepys Junior, *A Second Book of the Great Warr*, Vol. 3, pp.281–2.
23 Troops Fund Minutes, 9.12.1919, Book 4, 18A, NLW.
24 *The Times*, 1.6.1934, p.11.

Chapter 20 – Recruitment
1 Viscount Gwynedd, *Dame Margaret: The Life Story of His Mother* (Allen & Unwin, 1947), pp.201, 203.
2 Gwyn Jenkins, *A Welsh County at War* (Y Lolfa, 2021) p.17.
3 *North Wales Chronicle and Advertiser for the Principality*, 18.9.1914, p.7.
4 John Grigg, *Lloyd George, From Peace to War, 1912–16* (University of California Press), p.161.
5 *The Times*, 30.9.1914, p.4.
6 John Grigg, *Lloyd George, From Peace to War, 1912–16* (University of California Press), p.178n.
7 *The Cambrian News*, 2.10.1914, p.6.
8 *Northampton Mercury*, 20.11.1914, p.6.
9 Ibid.
10 *The Cambrian News and Welsh Farmers' Gazette*, 27.11.1914, p.8.
11 Frederick James Hodges, *Men of 18 in 1918* (Arthur H. Stockwell, 1988), p.14.
12 *Mercury and Herald (Northampton)*, 24.12.1947.p.7.
13 *Northampton Chronicle and Echo*, 24.12.1914, p.2.
14 *Llangollen Advertiser and North Wales Journal*, 5.2.1915, p.7.
15 *Llangollen Advertiser and North Wales Journal*, 12.2.1915, p.6.
16 *Liverpool Daily Post and Mercury*, 23.2.1915, p.8.
17 *Liverpool Daily Post and Mercury*, 26.2.1915, p.6
18 *Reading Mercury, Oxford Gazette*, 8.5.1915, p.8.
19 *Western Mail*, 21.6.1915, p.7.
20 *The Brecon and Radnor Express*, 24.6.1915, p.7.
21 *The Brecon and Radnor Express*, 24.6.1915, p.7. This version is slightly abridged.
22 The National Archives, archived blog 'Spotlights on History: The First World War'. https://webarchive.nationalarchives.gov.uk/ukgwa/+/https://www.nationalarchives.gov.uk/pathways/firstworldwar/spotlights/antiwar.htm
23 *The Streatham News*, 3.3.1916, p.4.
24 *North Wales Chronicle and Advertiser for the Principality*, 12.5.1916, p.3.
25 *The Globe*, 2.2.1917, p.5.
26 Richard Lloyd George, Viscount Gwynedd, *Dame Margaret, The Life Story of His Mother* (George Allen and Unwin, 1947), pp.159–160.

Chapter 21 – Safe Havens for Sailors
1 Margaret Lloyd George: 'What it means to be the wife of the Prime Minister of England', Sixth Instalment, 20472C, Lloyd George Papers 1, published in *Sunday News*, 4.9.1927, Document 3044, NLW.
2 *The Glamorgan Gazette*, 1.12.1916, p.3.
3 *The Cambrian News and Merionethshire Standard*, 6.12.1918, p.4.
4 *Southall-Norwood Gazette*, 22.3.1917, p.2.
5 *The Birmingham Daily Post*, 8.5.1917, p.4.
6 *Chart and Compass*, June 1917, the magazine of the British & Foreign Sailors' Society. With thanks to the Society's archivists.
7 See also Richard Rhys O'Brien, 'Margaret Lloyd George, Opening Up New Opportunities in 1919' / 'Yn Agor Cyfleon Newydd yn 1919', *Memories of Menai Bridge*, Volume 16 / *Atgofion Porthaethwy*, Cyfrol 17 (Menai Bridge and District Civic Society / Cymdeithas Ddinesig Bro Porthaethwy, 2019).
8 Kenneth O. Morgan (ed.), *Lloyd George Family Letters 1885–1936* (University of Wales Press, Oxford University Press, 1973), p.194.
9 *The Scotsman*, 11.1.1918, p.3.
10 *Forest Hill & Sydenham and Penge Examiner*, 29.3.1918, p.2.
11 *Sydenham, Forest Hill, & Penge Gazette*, 10.5.1918, p.6.

12 *Western Mail*, 8.6.1918, p.4.
13 *Western Mail*, 24.10.1918, p.3. A full report was also published in the BFSS publication, *Chart and Compass*.
14 *Western Mail*, 22.10.1918, p.2.
15 *The Pall Mall Gazette*, 4.11.1918, p.5. It may explain why the JTR collection includes a copy of *The Times* for 7 November 1805.
16 *West London Observer*, 13.9.1918, p.4.
17 *Middlesex Chronicle*, 26.10.1918, p.3.
18 *The Cambrian News and Merionethshire Standard*, 6.12.1918, p.4.
19 *Ealing Gazette*, 14.12.1918, p.4.

Chapter 22 – Food and Economy, 1917

1 Alan G. V. Simmonds, *Britain and World War One* (Routledge, 2003), p.205, quoted in Bryce Evans, 'The British "National Kitchen" of the First World War', *Journal of War & Culture Studies*, 10 (2016), ISSN 1752-6272.
2 *The Times*, 6.3.1917, p.9.
3 Bryce Evans, 'The British "National Kitchen" of the First World War', *Journal of War & Culture Studies*, 10 (2016), ISSN 1752-6272.
4 Sally White, *Ordinary Heroes*, p.175ff.
5 *North Eastern Daily Gazette (Middlesbrough)*, 5.11.1915, p.2.
6 *The Pall Mall Gazette*, 4.4.1917, p.7.
7 Richard Lloyd George, Viscount Gwynedd, *Dame Margaret, The Life Story of His Mother* (George Allen and Unwin, 1947), pp.166–7.
8 *The Westminster Gazette*, 4.4.1917, p.6.
9 *Liverpool Post and Mercury*, 19.5.1917, p.5.
10 *The Scotsman*, 22.5.1917, p.4; *Bradford Daily Telegraph*, 22.5.1917, p.4.
11 Mrs C. S. Peel, O.B.E., *The Way We Lived Then* (John Lane, 1929), pp.83–4.
12 *The Common Cause*, 25.5.1917, p.7 (79).
13 Bryce Evans, 'The British "National Kitchen" of the First World War', *Journal of War & Culture Studies*, 10 (2016), ISSN 1752-6272, citing the public kitchens handbook at that time: Hippisley Cox, R, Bradley H. J. and Miles E., *Public Kitchens* (Stationary Office, 1917).
14 Samuell Pepys Junior, *A Second Book of the Great Warr*, Vol. 2, p.293.
15 Sir William Beveridge, 'The Ministry of Food under Lord Rhondda', Chapter XV in *D. A. Thomas, Viscount Rhondda – by his Daughter and Others* (Longmans, Green & Co., 1921).
16 *Liverpool Daily Post*, 31.5.1917, p.6.
17 Ibid.
18 *Staffordshire Sentinel*, 11.7.1917, p.6.
19 *Kenilworth Advertiser*, 4.8.1917, p.4.
20 *The Pall Mall Gazette*, 12.7.1917, p.5.
21 *Cambridge Daily News*, 12.7.1917, p.3.
22 *Annual Register*, 16.7.1917, Proquest / Clarivate.
23 *Daily Telegraph*, 5.9.1917, p.4.
24 Bryce Evans, 'The British "National Kitchen" of the First World War', *Journal of War & Culture Studies*, 10 (2016), ISSN 1752-6272, citing the 1918 National Kitchens Order.
25 *The Kerry Evening Post*, 8.9.1917, p.3.
26 *The Hendon and Finchley Times*, 14.9.1917, p.2.
27 *Derby Daily Telegraph*, 28.9.1917, p.3.
28 *Gloucestershire Echo*, 4.10.1917, p.1.
29 *The Daily Mirror*, 14.9.1917, p.10.
30 *Folkestone, Hythe, Sandgate & Cheriton Herald*, 22.9.1917, p.6.
31 Sally Roberts Jones, Neape (née Bellis), 'Mary Edith (1876–1960), novelist', *Dictionary of Welsh Biography*, 2001.
32 *The Lichfield Mercury*, 9.11.1917, p.4.
33 *The Leeds Mercury*, 10.11.1917, p.6.

Endnotes

34 *West London Observer*, 30.11.1917, p.6.
35 *Illustrated War News*, 28.11.1917, p.8.
36 *The Tatler*, 5.12.1917, p.4.

Chapter 23 – Food and Economy, 1918

1   *Nottingham Evening Post*, 26.1.1918, p.2.
2   *The Tatler*, 6.2.1918, pp.5–6.
3   Mrs C. S. Peel, O.B.E., *How We Lived Then* (John Lane, 1929), p.67.
4   Bryce Evans, 'The British "National Kitchen" of the First World War', *Journal of War & Culture Studies*, 10 (2016), ISSN 1752-6272.
5   *Y Brython (The Briton)*, 14.3.1918, p.4.
6   Bryce Evans, 'The British "National Kitchen" of the First World War', *Journal of War & Culture Studies*, 10 (2016), ISSN 1752-6272.
7   *The Graphic*, 17.8.1918, p.14.
8   *Western Mail*, 14.3.1918, p.3.
9   Bryce Evans, 'The British "National Kitchen" of the First World War', *Journal of War & Culture Studies*, 10 (2016), ISSN 1752-6272.
10 J. T. Rhys, from 'Lady Rhondda's Maiden Speech', unpublished typescript, written between 1925 and 1938. JTR Private Collection.
11 *Islington News and Hornsey Gazette*, 31.5.1918, p.4.
12 *The Pall Mall Gazette*, 30.5.1918, p.2.
13 Bryce Evans, 'The British "National Kitchen" of the First World War', *Journal of War & Culture Studies*, 10 (2016), ISSN 1752-6272.
14 *Sunday Pictorial*, 30.6.1918, p.9.
15 *The Pall Mall Gazette*, 16.7.1918, p.5.
16 T. Farrell, 'Hospitality: Fortune's Buffets and Rewards: Spiers & Pond', 30 June 2015, retrieved online 6.5.2023. http://letslookagain.com/2015/06/a-history-of-spiers-pond/
17 Ibid.
18 *The Pall Mall Gazette*, 16.7.1918, p.5.
19 Samuell Pepys Junior, *The Last Diary of the Great Warr*, Vol. 3, p.168.
20 *The Herald*, 5.10.1918, p.7.
21 *Sunday Pictorial*, 30.6.1918, p.9.
22 *The Streatham News*, 3.3.1916, p.4.
23 Bryce Evans, 'The British "National Kitchen" of the First World War', *Journal of War & Culture Studies*, 10 (2016), ISSN 1752-6272, Citing Ministry of Food Kitchens Advisory Committee Minutes, 3.3.1919, TNA MAF 60/329.
24 T. Farrell, 'Hospitality: Fortune's Buffets and Rewards: Spiers & Pond', 30 June 2015, retrieved online 6.5.2023. http://letslookagain.com/2015/06/a-history-of-spiers-pond/
25 Sidney Webb, 'British Labor Under War Pressure', *The North American Review*, June 1917, Vol. 25, No. 739 (June 1917), pp.874–85, University of South Iowa.
26 *The Globe*, 26.7.1918, p.3.
27 *Evening Mail*, 26.7.1918, p 8.
28 Bryce Evans, 'The British "National Kitchen" of the First World War', *Journal of War & Culture Studies*, 10 (2016), ISSN 1752-6272.
29 Mrs C. S. Peel, O.B.E., *The Way We Lived Then* (John Lane, 1929), p.85.
30 Bryce Evans, 'The British "National Kitchen" of the First World War', *Journal of War & Culture Studies*, 10 (2016), ISSN 1752-6272, citing the public kitchens handbook at that time: Hippisley Cox, R, Bradley H. J. and Miles E., *Public Kitchens* (Stationery Office, 1917).
31 *Sheffield Daily Telegraph*, 18.9.1918, p.2.
32 *Reading Mercury and Oxford Gazette*, 5.10.1918, p.8.
33 *Newcastle Daily Journal*, 15.10.1918, p.4.
34 Samuell Pepys Junior, *The Last Diary of the Great Warr*, Vol. 3, p.209.
35 Ffion Hague, *The Pain and the Privilege* (Harper Perennial, 2008), p.360.
36 JTR Margaret Lloyd George SP2, National Federation of Women's Institutes Exhibition, Caxton Hall, November 1918, copy in Rev. J. T. Rhys (Margaret Lloyd

George) Papers, National Library of Wales. In her own hand on First Lord of the Treasury embossed notepaper, 10 Downing Street, Whitehall, S.W.1.
37 Emmeline Pankhurst, *My Own Story* (Eveleigh Nash, 1914), p.50.
38 *Suffolk and Essex Free Press*, 6.11.1918, p.6.
39 *Western Mail*, 31.10.1918, p.2.

Chapter 24 – Hospitals and Healthcare
1 Sally White, *Ordinary Heroes*, pp.50–1.
2 *Carnarvon and Denbigh Herald*, 14.8.1914, p.8.
3 Godfrey Drage to Margaret Lloyd George, 12.8.1914, NLW MS 20469c, no. 2829.
4 Sally White, *Ordinary Heroes*, p.59.
5 Olwen Carey Evans, *Lloyd George Was My Father* (Gomer Press, 1985), p.82.
6 For an excellent analysis of the many layers of nursing support in the war, see Sally White, *Ordinary Heroes*, Chapter 2, 'Caring for the Sick and Wounded on the Home Front', and Chapter 3, 'Medical and Supporting Volunteers on the Western Front'.
7 *North Eastern Daily Gazette (Middlesbrough)*, 5.11.1915, p.2.
8 *The Common Cause*, 7.5.1915, p.12.
9 'Dr Ross – Commemorated in Serbia', Ross and Cromarty Heritage Society, accessed online 6.10.2023.
10 'Mabel Dearmer, novelist, playwright, translator and illustrator', *London Remembers*, online, accessed 6.10.2023.
11 See 'Women's History Month: Miss Georgiana Fyfe', *Women's History Network*, 1 March 2010, accessed online, 6.10.2023.
12 'Mrs Hilda Wynne, 1884–1923, Female Poets, Inspirational Women and Fascinating Facts of the First World War', online blog accessed 6.10.2023.
13 See also Diane Atkinson, *Elsie and Mairi Go to War: Two Extraordinary Women on the Western Front* (Cornerstone, 2010).
14 *North Eastern Daily Gazette (Middlesbrough)*, 5.11.1915, p.2.
15 Peter Grant, *Mobilizing Charity*, p.36.
16 *The Hospital*, 24.10.1914, p.95.
17 *The Brecon & Radnor Express*, 23.9.1915, p.7.
18 Gwyn Jenkins, *A Welsh County at War* (Y Lolfa, 2021), pp.108–9.
19 Agnes Robinson (Lady Mayoress) to Margaret Lloyd George, 8.9.1914, NLW MS 20470c, no. 2917.
20 *The Portadown News*, 9.8.1913, p.8.
21 *Cambria Daily Leader*, 27.3.1916, p.4.
22 *Taunton Courier*, 18.7.1917, p.6.
23 *The Bury Free Press*, 3.2.1917, p.8.
24 Rhys David, *Tell Mum Not to Worry* (Deffro, 1914), p.29.
25 *The Cambrian News and Welsh Farmers' Gazette*, 17.4.1914, p.7.
26 *North Wales Chronicle and Advertiser for the Principality*, 28.4.1916, p.3.
27 'Historic Hospitals, An Architectural Gazetteer', www.historic-hospitals.com
28 *The Shields Daily News*, 24.1.1918, p.3.
29 JTR Notes, JTR Private Collection.
30 Described in David Jones, *Gallant Little Wales: The Welsh Hospital* (Y Lolfa, 2023).
31 'DHPW Prince of Wales Orthopaedic Hospital, Cardiff, Records – 1917–1997', Online description accessed 1.8.2023.
32 *Western Mail*, 25.5.1917, p.2.
33 *Western Mail*, 25.7.1917, p.4.
34 *Western Mail*, 18.2.1918, p.4.
35 See Sally White, *Ordinary Heroes*, pp.316–17.
36 *The Grantham Journal*, 12.5.1917, p.7.
37 *Liverpool Post & Mercury*, 9.5.1917, p.6.
38 Blind Veterans UK www.blindveterans.org.uk
39 *North Wales Chronicle and Advertiser for the Principality*, 31.8.1917, p.6.
40 Troops Fund Minutes, 11.10.1915, Book 1, 15A, NLW.
41 *The Sphere*, 'Women's Sphere in Wartime', p.iv., 17.11.1917, p.28.

42 *Leek Times*, 18.5.1918, p.2.
43 *The Staffordshire Sentinel*, 15.5.1918, p.3.
44 *Croydon Times*, 13.6.1917, p.2.
45 *Middlesex & Buckinghamshire Advertiser and the Uxbridge Gazette*, 11.1.1918, p.5.
46 *Evening Mail*, 4.5.1917, p.8.
47 *The Surrey Advertiser*, 24.7.1918, p.1.
48 Samuell Pepys Junior, *The Last Diary of the Great Warr*, Vol. 3, p.158.
49 *The Surrey Advertiser*, 31.7.1918, p.1.
50 *West Surrey Times*, 26.7.1918, p.4.

Chapter 25 – Temperance and Wartime Sobriety
1 *The Manchester Guardian*, 1.3.1915, p.10.
2 *The Manchester Guardian*, 30.3.1915, p.7.
3 *Westminster Gazette*, 24.3.1915, p.7.
4 *Western Mail*, 26.3.1915, p.5. Waterloo Road / Street, is now Elmington Road.
5 *The Manchester Guardian*, 28.4.1915, p.12.
6 David Freeman, 'George V, King of Great Britain', *International Encyclopaedia of the First World War*, online 4.8.2017.
7 Kenneth O. Morgan, *Lloyd George Family Letters*, p.176n.
8 Roger Kershaw, 'The Carlisle Experiment – limiting alcohol in wartime', 15.1 2015, The National Archives Blog, accessed 1.12.2022.
9 *Kilmarnock Herald and North Ayrshire Gazette*, 30.4.1915, p.4.
10 *Llais Llafur (Labour Voice)*, 5.6.1915, p.1.
11 *Western Daily Press*, 10.6.1915, p.8.
12 *North Wales Chronicle and Advertiser for the Principality*, 31.12.1915, p.7.
13 See also 'Eve Colpus, Slack (married name Saunders) Agnes Elizabeth', *Oxford Dictionary of National Biography*.
14 *Barry Dock News*, 31.3.1916, p.3, and *The Glamorgan Gazette*, 31.3.1916, p.6.
15 *Gwyliedydd Newydd*, 19.9.1916, p.4.
16 Samuell Pepys Junior, *A Second Diary of the Great Warr*, Vol. 2, p.20.
17 *The Cambrian News and Welsh Farmers' Gazette*, 20.10.1916, p.3.
18 Cranogwen's statue now stands at her coastal birthplace, Llangrannog, erected in 2023 by the Monumental Welsh Women campaign.
19 *Western Mail*, 19.5.1934, p.6.
20 *The Cambria Daily Leader*, 11.10.1916, p.4.
21 *Liverpool Post and Mercury*, 4.12.1916, p.6.
22 *Faringdon Advertiser and Vale of the White Horse Gazette*, 13.1.1917, p.2.
23 *Burton Daily Mail*, 13.1.1917, p.3.
24 *Faringdon Advertiser and Vale of the White Horse Gazette*, 20.1.1917, p.2.
25 *Banbury Advertiser*, 19.7.1917, p.8.
26 *John Bull*, 20.1.1917, p.8.
27 *The Daily Mirror*, 5.6.1917, p.10.
28 *The Waterford Star*, 26.5.1917, p.17.
29 *The Pall Mall Gazette*, 30.6.1917, p.5.
30 *The Northern Whig*, 26.7.1917, p.6.
31 *Campbeltown Courier*, 5.5.1917, p.4.
32 *Cambria Daily Leader*, 23.10.1917, p.3.
33 *The Carmarthen Journal*, 26.10.1917, p.1.
34 Richard Rhys O'Brien, *The Campaigns of Margaret Lloyd George*, p.155.
35 *The Welsh Outlook*, November 1917.
36 *The Welsh Outlook*, December 1917.
37 *The Cambrian News and Welsh Farmers' Gazette*, 26.4.1918, p.7.
38 *Kent and Sussex Courier*, 31.5.1918, p.6.
39 *Richmond Herald*, 7.9.1918, p.4.
40 *The Hastings and St Leonard's Observer*, 30.11.1918, p.2.
41 Dr James Nicholls, 'The highs and lows of drinking in Britain', History and Policy Blog, 30.4.2014, Institute of Historical Research, University of London.

Bibliography

Documents and Archives

National Library of Wales (NLW)
Lloyd George papers; with thanks to the National Library of Wales and the Lloyd George family.
The Rev. J. T. Rhys (Margaret Lloyd George) Papers, copies from the JTR Collection. With thanks to the Lloyd George family.
Papers of E. Vincent Evans – The Welsh National Fund (NLW ex 2145).
Welsh Disabled Soldiers, 1917 – Correspondence between William Lewis and David Davies (NLW: Lord Davies of Llandinam Papers C4/7).
Disabled Soldiers, 1917 – The Treatment and Training of Disabled and Discharged Soldiers in France (NLW: Lord Davies of Llandinam Papers C4/7).
The Lloyd George American Relief Fund, Report and Accounts for 1923 and 1924, Lord Davies of Llandinam Papers, C4/8 NLW.
National Fund for Welsh Troops Minute Books, 1915–1920 (NLW: Minor Deposits 15A-18A).
Margaret Lloyd George: 'What it means to be the wife of the Prime Minister of England', Sixth Instalment, 20472C LG Papers 1, published in *Sunday News*, 4.9.1927, Document 3044.
Margaret Lloyd George, interview, 'How do you help your husband?', typed draft, A. J. Sylvester Papers, AJS C25.
Margaret Lloyd George, 'Petticoats behind Politics', typescript for release in the *Sunday Herald*, 12.6.1927.
J. Graham Jones, *Lloyd George papers at the National Library of Wales and Other Repositories* (NLW, Aberystwyth, 2001).
Welsh Newspapers Online; and the *Welsh Gazette*.

Other Archives
Online: British Newspaper Archive; *The Manchester Guardian*.
The British Library: *The Times, Daily Telegraph, Welsh Gazette, Daily Sketch, Daily Mail, Evening Standard*.
The JTR Private Collection: speeches and correspondence of Margaret Lloyd George.

Books
Pete Alcock, *Why we need welfare, Collective Action for the Common Good* (Policy Press, 2016).
Diane Atkinson, *Elsie and Mairi Go to War: Two Extraordinary Women on the Western Front* (Cornerstone, 2010).
Michael Brock and Eleanor Brock, *Margot Asquith's Great War Diary, 1914–1916, The View from Downing Street* (Oxford University Press, 2014).
Olwen Carey Evans, *Lloyd George Was My Father* (Gomer Press, 1985).
Thelma Cazalet-Keir, *From the Wings* (Bodley Head, 1967).

Bibliography

Rhys David, *Tell Mum Not to Worry, A Welsh Soldier's World War One in the Near East* (Deffro, 2014).
Bryce Evans, *Feeding the People in Wartime Britain* (Bloomsbury, 2022).
Peter Grant, *Philanthropy and Voluntary Action in the First World War: Mobilizing Charity* (Routledge, 2014).
Viscount Gwynedd (Richard Lloyd George), *Dame Margaret, The Life Story of His Mother* (George Allen and Unwin, 1947).
Ffion Hague, *The Pain and the Privilege, The Women Who Loved Lloyd George* (Harper Perennial, 2008).
Owen Lloyd George, *A Tale of Two Grandfathers* (Bellew, 1999).
David Jones, *Gallant Little Wales: The Welsh Hospital* (Y Lolfa, 2023).
W. J. Lewis, *Born on a Perilous Rock* (Cambrian News, 1980).
John Grigg, *Lloyd George, War Leader* (Allen Lane, 2002).
Gwyn Jenkins, *A Welsh County at War*, Chapter V, 'Unpatriotic Farmers?' (Y Lolfa, 2021).
J. Graham Jones, *David Lloyd George and Welsh Liberalism* (The Welsh Political Archive, NLW, 2010).
Charles T. King, *The Asquith Parliament (1906–1909)* (Hutchinson, 1910).
Kenneth O. Morgan Ed., *Lloyd George, Family Letters 1885–1936* (University of Wales Press and Oxford University Press, 1973).
Vivien Newman, *We Also Served, The Forgotten Women of the First World War* (Pen and Sword History, 2014).
Ivor Nicholson, O.B.E., Trevor Lloyd Williams, M.A. (eds), preface Sir E. Vincent Evans, *Wales: Its Part in the War* (Hodder and Stoughton, 1920).
Richard Rhys O'Brien, *The Campaigns of Margaret Lloyd George, The Wife of the Prime Minister, 1916–1922* (Y Lolfa, 2022).
Mrs C. S. Peel, O.B.E., *How We Lived Then* (John Lane, 1929).
Samuell Pepys Junior, *A Diary of the Great Warr*, Vol. 1; *A Second Diary of the Great Warr*, Vol. 2; *The Last Diary of the Great Warr*, Vol. 3, (John Lane, The Bodley Head, 1916, 1917 and 1919).
George Rees, *Gwersi Mewn Llysieueg* (Cambrian News, 1896).
Justin Davis Smith, *100 Years of NCVO and Voluntary Action: Idealist and Realists* (Palgrave Macmillan, 2019).
Frances Stevenson, *The Years that are Past* (Hutchinson, 1967).
A. J. P. Taylor (ed.), *Lloyd George, A Diary by Frances Stevenson* (Hutchinson, 1971).
Sally White, *Ordinary Heroes, The Story of Civilian Volunteers during the First World War* (Amberley, 2018).

Articles

The Badsey Society, 'May 1st 1917 – Letter from Mela Brown Constable to her fiancé, Major Cyril E Sladden', accessed online 26.5.2023.
BBC News Online, 'Cigarette case that "stopped WW1 bullet" to be auctioned', published 5.11.2019 https://www.bbc.co.uk/news/uk-england-derbyshire-50302592
Eve Colpus, 'Slack (married name Saunders) Agnes Elizabeth', *Oxford Dictionary of National Biography*, online 4.10.2012, accessed 26.12.2020.
'Duty and Democracy, Parliament and the First World War', Houses of Parliament online, accessed May 2023. https://www.parliament.uk/globalassets/documents/WW1/duty-and-democracy-parliament-and-the-first-world-war.pdf
Bryce Evans, 'The British "National Kitchen" of the First World War', *Journal of War & Culture Studies*, 10 (2016).
T. Farrell, 'Hospitality: Fortune's Buffets and Rewards: Spiers & Pond', 30 June 2015, retrieved online 6.5.2023, http://letslookagain.com/2015/06/a-history-of-spiers-pond/
David Freeman, 'George V, King of Great Britain', *International Encyclopedia of the First World War*, online 4.8.2017. https://encyclopedia.1914-1918-online.net/article/george_v_king_of_great_britain
Carol Harris, '1914–1918: How Charities helped to win WW1', Third Sector, online 27.6.2014, Haymarket Media Group.

J. Graham Jones, 'Dame Margaret in Cardiganshire', *Ceredigion: Journal of the Cardiganshire Historical Society*, 2004, Vol. XIV, No. 4.

Roger Kershaw, 'The Carlisle Experiment – limiting alcohol in wartime', 15.1.2015, The National Archives Blog, https://blog.nationalarchives.gov.uk/pubs-vs-first-world-war/ accessed 1.12.2022.

Lucy London, www.inspirationalwomenofww1.blogspot.co.uk, July 2018, 'Mrs Hilda Wynne, 1884–1923, Female Poets, Inspirational Women and Fascinating Facts of the First World War', online blog, accessed 6.10.2023.

St Marylebone Parish Church website, 'Margherita Howard de Walden', accessed 19.8.2023. https://stmarylebone.org/about-us/heritage/people-of-st-marylebone/changing-faces-of-st-marylebone/margherita-baroness-howard-de-walden-1890-1974/

Museums Victoria Collections, 'Lady de Walden Hospital, Alexandria, 1915–1918', accessed 19.8.2023. https://collections.museumsvictoria.com.au/items/1774155

National Army Museum, 'First World War, Salonika Campaign', online, accessed 30.10.2023. https://www.nam.ac.uk/explore/salonika-campaign

Dr James Nicholls, 'The highs and lows of drinking in Britain', History and Policy blog, 30.4.2014, based at the Institute of Historical Research, Senate House, University of London, https://www.historyandpolicy.org/opinion-articles/articles/the-highs-and-lows-of-drinking-in-britain

Richard O'Brien, 'Mrs Lloyd George and the first Women Students at the Royal School of Dentists, 1916 to 1926', *Dental Historian*, Vol. 65 (1), January 2020.

Richard O'Brien, 'The Missing Mahogany WW1 Memorial, Mrs Lloyd George and the Royal Dental Hospital twenty-nine, 1916 to 1926', *Dental Historian*, Vol. 67 (2), July 2022.

Samir Rafat, 'Egyptian Mail', 27.5.1995, 'Davies Bryan & Co. of Elmad El Din St', accessed 30.10.2023, http://www.egy.com/landmarks/95-05-27.php

Rev. Gomer Morgan Roberts, 'Williams, William (1717–1791), Methodist cleric, author, and hymn-writer', in *Dictionary of Welsh Biography*, 1959.

David Thomas, 'Robert Silyn Roberts' (Rhosyr; 1871–1930), Calvinistic Methodist minister, poet, social reformer, tutor', *Dictionary of Welsh Biography*, 1959.

David Thomas, 'The National Egg Collection for Wounded Soldiers and Sailors 1914–1919'.

Mari Takayanagi, 'Gone Grille: The removal of the Ladies' Gallery Grilles', 23.8.2017, accessed 7.8.2023. https://ukvote100.org/2017/08/23/the-ladies-gallery-grilles/

Sidney Webb, 'British Labor Under War Pressure', *The North American Review*, June 1917, Vol. 25, No. 739, University of South Iowa.

Bob Wyatt, 'The First Air Raid, Great Yarmouth', Western Front Association, accessed online 22.2.2023 www.westernfrontassociation.com

***

All images from British Newspaper Archive created courtesy of the British Library Board.

Place names have generally been given their modern Welsh spelling, except in the quoted newspaper extracts, speeches and correspondence, where the original spelling, and other conventions, e.g. Downing-street, have been retained. Cricieth has been given its current Welsh spelling throughout.

Newspaper titles (which change over time) are given as of the date quoted, albeit omitting subtitles which some papers added as a result of acquisitions.

Index

A

Aberaeron 162, 204, 211
Aberystwyth 60–1, 103, 172, 175, 190–1, 250, 261, 276, 343
Active Service Club for Women, Eaton Square 131, 142
Admiralty 30, 83, 151, 289, 292, 300
Agricultural Organisation Society (AOS) 53, 294
Air raids 110, *see also* Zeppelins
Alden, Percy (MP, social reformer) 49, 297, 337, 340
Aldershot 58, *see* Percy Illingworth Soldiers' Institute
Alma Tadema, Laurence; Lawrence 108–9
America/United States/USA 24, 36, 40, 52, 61, 128, 150, 225, 287, 298; American Troops 82, 101, 298; prohibition 359, 361, 372–3, 376–8; *see also* Lloyd George American Relief Fund
American Ambassador, *see* Walter H. Page 297–9
American Express Agency 186
American Women's War Relief Fund 140
Angell, Norman 27
Anglesey 53, 75, 158, 171, 200, 250, 266, 270, 289, 345
Anglo-French conference, Paris 77
Arsenal (Woolwich) 25, 50, 106, 128, 355
Askwith, Lady 297
Asquith, Elizabeth (daughter of H. H. and Margot) 128; Asquith, H. H. (PM 1908–16) 14, 26–8, 41, 51, 65, 123–4, 130, 151–2, 189, 306, 353, 376; Asquith, Margot, Mrs H. H. 21, 26–7, 67, 69, 73, 126, 130, 151–2, 314; Asquith (Bonham Carter), Violet (daughter of H. H. Asquith) 51, 53
Astor, Mrs Waldorf 307
Australia 55, 101, 126–7, 134, 144, 149, 151, 286, 332
Austria-Hungary 27–8, 147, 360

B

Baby Show and Child Welfare Exhibition, Guildford 132, 355; Rhostryfan 22; *Baby Week* 93, 96, 102, 129, 309, 372, 374
Balfour, Arthur 77; Lady Frances 143
Bangor 24, 41–2, 46, 52, 75, 84, 86, 100, 103, 107, 114, 154, 160, 167–8; War Memorial 241, 250; 263, 259, 289; War Economy Exhibition 302–3, 340, 350, 359, 377, War Savings Association 302; Women's Patriotic Guild 86, 167, 259, 304–5
Baptists 47, 365; Sustenation Fund 22; Catford Hill 55; Welsh Chapel, Castle St 57, 90–1, 126, 290; Baptist Union 58; Baptist College, Cardiff 121; Llandudno 275
Barbier / Vailliant de Guélis 34–5, 186–8, 191
Barlow, Lady 27
Barnes, George N., Minister of Pensions 245–8, 260
Bastille Day, 58, 186, 189–90, *see also* French Flag Day *and* Cardiff
Bath 75, 81–2, 214, 285
Battle for the Ancre, The (film) 74
Bayley, W. A. (London Welsh Stage Society) 214–15
Bazaar/sale of work 20–2, 30–1; 42, 56, 66–7, 79, 83, 93, 104, 124, 142, 152, 160, 250, 290–2, 349, 350–3
Beatty, Lady 289, 316
Bective, Alice, Countess of 184–6
Belgium Flag days 221; Independence Day 96; journalists 24; neutrality 47; refugees 31–2, 42, 50, 96, 103, 341; Military Field Service 340; Repatriation Fund 44; Soldiers Fund 191; Wounded Fund 60, 226; Carnarvon Belgian Relief Fund 32; soldiers 270, 338; Belgium 28, 31–2, 47, 221, 261, 268, 270, 275, 277; Anglo-Belgian hospitals 338–9; Aide Civile Belge 341; *La Brabançonne* 96

403

Benn/Wedgwood Benn family 93, 292–9
Berlin 21, 28, 64
Bethesda sock workrooms 38, 115
Bible, The 91, 191, 313
Black Chair, The, Birkenhead Eisteddfod 102–3
Blackpool 138–9
Blaenau Ffestiniog 38–9, 115, 201, 335
Boer War 47, 58, 157, 159, 198, 267–8, 278, 347
Bolland, Mrs, Commandant, Criccieth VAD 337
Bonar Law, Andrew 74, 129, 190; Isabel 74
Bond St 257, New Bond St 144, Old Bond St 55, 223
Boot, Sir Jesse and Lady Florence 25, 89; Boots Cash Chemists 224
Boulogne 43, 48, 88, 339
Bournemouth 89, 94, 120, 344
Braid, James (golfer) 193
Brangwyn, Frank 223, 237
Breconshire/Brecon 158, 161, 197, 201–2, 224, 228
Bridgend 63, 175, 364
British and American Tobacco Company 169
British and Foreign Bible Society 191
British and Foreign Sailors' Society (BFSS), *see* Sailors
British Legion, The 16
British Women's Hospital Star and Garter Fund 54
Bromley Cripples' Parlour 93
Bryan Bros, Cairo 237
Bryce, Viscount and Viscountess 85
Bryn Seiont, TB hospital, Caernarfon 345–6
Brynawelon, Criccieth 31, 61–3, 82, 100, 122, 124, 136, 267, 364
Brynmor Jones, Florence, Lady 157, 177, 201
Buckingham Palace 91, 128, 216, 277, 283
Buckingham Palace Road 257, 321–2
Builth Wells 168

C
Caernarfon 22, 24, 34, 36, 55, 63, 75, 100, 106, 139, 198, 211, 237–8, 345, 368; Carnarvon 32, 34, 75, 269; Carnarvon Belgian Relief Fund 32; Carnarvon Boroughs 103, 139, 167, 170, 175
Caernarfonshire 41, 121, 259, 337, 346–7 362 **Carnarvonshire** 36, 97,197, 270, 304
Calais 78, 338, 340
Calvinistic Methodist 19–20, 22, 37, 40, 42–3, 104, 175, 212, 242, 267, 281
Camberwell 22, 83, 300, 360
Cambridge 175
Canada 53, 261, 359, 376
Cardiff 35–6, 38, 45–4, 54, 61, 64, 82, 85–6, 118, 120–2, 127, 129, 158–9, 163–6, 174–5, 181; Prisoners of War Fund 183–6; French Flag Day (Cardiff) 35, 186–90, 198, 209, 219, 241, 260–1, 263, 268, 270, 274, 290–2, 334, 336, 340, 343, 347–9, 365, 371, 376
Cardigan House Club, Richmond, Surrey 151
Cardiganshire 51, 162, 197, 248, 376; Ceredigion 118, 267, 343
Carey Evans, Olwen, née Lloyd George 24, 26–7, 30, 43, 48, 55–6, 58–60, 63, 65–9, 73, 76, 78, 82–4, 90, 100, 106–7, 110, 112, 122–3, 129, 136, 138, 193, 205, 217, 223, 226, 230, 233–5; 237, 255, 313, 336–7, 339, 341, 345, 349–50, 377
Carey Evans, Tom (husband of Olwen) 26, 58–60, 90
Carey Evans, Margaret 122, 377
Carlisle Experiment 361
Carmarthen 104, 175, 375–6; Soldiers' Welfare Fund 220–2; Carmarthenshire 96–7, 157, 182, 197, 199
Cave, Sir George and Lady 117 257
Cavell, Edith 339
Caxton Hall 144, 160, 294, 331–5
Cazalet, Mrs 236, 248; Thelma 89
Chailey, Heritage Craft School 117, 233–4, 255
Chamberlain, Austen 76, 322; Ivy, Mrs Austen 322; Miss Beatrice 76, 316; coffee pot 352
Chancery Lane Safe Deposit Company 230, 258
Charing Cross Road, Welsh Calvinistic Church 40, 44
Charity fatigue 117, 189, 255, 259
Chelsea 34, 351; Chelsea china 226
China 38, 250
Church Army 107, 120
Churchill, Clementine, Mrs Winston 53, 59, 129, 324
Churchill, Lady Randolph 144
Churchill, Winston 26, 81, 87, 95–6, 129, 149, 190, 331
Cinema Day 49

Index

City Girls Club, London 145
Clapham 43, 152, 263, 292
Clifford, Dr John (Baptist preacher) 47
Clynes J. R., Food Controller, Leader of the Labour Party; Clynes, Mrs 324
Clwyd, Vale of (toy making) 37–8, 137, 207, 262, 302
Coalition Liberal / Government 11, 41, 124, 127, 224, 261, 289
Colwyn Bay 169, 172, 175, 261
Commons, House of 19, 39, 68, 97–8, 105, 110, 114, 123, 150, 219, 333, 353, 362
Concerts 32, 43, 45, 59–60, 64, 83, 92, 121, 124, 127, 137, 141, 163, 215, 225–6, 231, 255, 271, 289, 361–2
Connaught, Princess Patricia of 352
Conscientious objectors 222, 285
Conscription 12, 30, 35, 44, 47, 57, 266, 271, 276, 278–9, 284–6, 361, 379
Constable, Miss Mela Brown 59
Conway 171–2; Conwy 24, 55, 170, 207, 286
Corelli, Marie 64–5, 103, 289
Corfe Mullen, Dorset 141
Covent Garden 21, 230, 234–5
Cowdray, Lady 59, 225
Cranogwen (Sarah Jane Rees) 365–7
Crewe 36, 75, 190,
Criccieth 22, 26, 30–3, 43, 47–8, 52–3, 61–3, 71, 73, 75–8, 86, 99, 103, 112, 115, 121–6, 133–4, 136, 141, 210, 226, 233, 253, 269, 294, 318, 333, 336–7, 347, 361–4, 366, 377
Crimean War 83, 282, 341
Crooks, Will (Labour MP) 75, 94–5, 355
Cymmrodorion 64, 141, 156, 163, 375,
Cymru Fydd 272, 317

D

Dardanelles 95, 178, 342–3
Dartford 130
Davies, Alfred (Tory MP) 127
Davies, Sir Alfred T., Board of Education 166
Davies, T. Awstin (journalist) 365
Davies, Rev. Ceitho 175
Davies, J. T. (PPS to David Lloyd George) 127, 139
Davies, Joseph, Cardiff 36–9
Davies, Miss Rosina, *Merched y De* 365–6, 368, 376
Davies, Elizabeth, Mrs Timothy 157

Defence of the Realm Act (DORA) 361
Denbigh 137, 190, 197; Denbigh Boroughs 158; Denbighshire 37, 137, 197, 207, 241, 248
Denmark 21, 64, 162
d'Estournelles de Constant, M. 18, 24
Devonport 203, 299; Lord 169, 295, 301; Lady 294
Dickins & Jones department store 46, 130
Director General of Voluntary Organisations (DGVO) 194–200, *see also* Sir Edward Ward
Domestic economy and science 12, 16, 296, 304; MLG article 101, 307–13; 321–2, 330
Dr Williams' School, Dolgellau 48
Drage, Godfrey 335; Mrs Dorothy 335, 337
Dunfermline College of Hygiene and PE 124

E

Edinburgh 73, 79–81, 94, 124
Edis, Miss Olive, FRPS 104
Edwards, J. Hugh (Liberal MP) 141
Edwards, Mrs Principal, Cardiff Baptist College 120
Edwards, Sir Francis (Liberal MP) 159, 224
Eggs 87–8, 334, 351
Egypt 158, 198, 203, 224–5, 237, 247, 305
Eisteddfod 37, 156, 207, 277, 365; (Bangor) 46, 102–3; (Aberystwyth) 60–1, 103, 276; (Birkenhead) 97, 103; (Neath) 133–6
Ellis Griffith, Sir Ellis (Liberal MP for Anglesey) 75, 270
Ellis, Tom and Mrs 271–2
Empire 46, 69, 85, 86, 101, 116–17, 140, 147, 153, 156, 162, 212, 215, 267–8, 271, 277, 291, 292, 356
Emsley Carr, William and Mrs 64–5
Enmore Road Church, South Norwood 152, 292
Eryri (Snowdonia) 99, 270
Euston 50, 94, 139, 253, 306
Evans, Beriah 121, 317
Evans, Dr (father of Tom Carey Evans) 58
Evans, J. Owain 36–8, 115
Evans, Matron Emilie. G., Aberystwyth, and Netley 343
Evans, Laura and Constance (musicians) 64–5

405

F

Fashion 316
Fawcett, Millicent, Mrs Henry 98, 116
Ffestiniog 58, 99, 201, 335
Fitzgerald, Sister, Bury St Edmunds 344
Flag Days
Aberdare 168, 174; Armenian Flag Day 85–6; Bangor 167, 304–5; Belgian Flag Day 221; Cardiff 164–6, *see also* Cardiff, French Flag Day 174; Carmarthen 221; Italian Flag Day 67; Llangollen 220; Manchester 114, 254; Liverpool/Merseyside 114, 232; Machynlleth 117, 255; Porthcawl 166–7; Russian 221; Salford 232, 254; Serbian Flag Day 48–9; Streatham 218; Swansea 170, 258; St David's Day Flag Day (esp. London) 37, 39, 54, 76, 111, 117, 125, 163, 165, 170, 174, 212–13, 215–21, 227–8, 230–7, 251, 255–8, 276–7, 359
Flag Day returns in Welsh towns 174–5
Flag selling 'Ladies in Waiting', London 1918 257
Flintshire 133, 197, 237
Flower Festival, Welsh Chapel, London 57, 91
FOOD AND WAR ECONOMY, CHs 22–23 (293–335)
Campaign Launch 76, 293–6
Food and War Economy Exhibitions: County Hall, London 94, 306–7; Bangor 302–4
Food Kitchens (communal, canteens, National)
NK National Restaurant, Blackfriars 130, 323–9
Camberwell, Kempshead Hall 83, 300
Holborn Baths 130, 329–30
Lambeth, 'Kitchen for All' 301
London Bridge, Lady Limerick's Hostel 106, 176, 313,
Lycett Chapel, Mile End Road 297–8
National Training School of Cookery 321
Paddy's Goose, Shadwell High St 298
Salvation Army, Whitecross St 298–9
South Norwood 127
Tottenham, Down Lane 125, 323
White City canteen 107, 313
WRAF canteen and club for women, Fulham 151
YWCA, Tolmer's Institute, Euston 306–7
Food Controller 169, 293, 296, 301, 313, 317, 319, 321, 324

'Nationalise the Caterers' – *The Herald* 324–9
Rationing (MLG interview) 121, 169, 293, 295, 297, MLG interview 317–320, 330, 361
France 24, 32, 35, 43, 48–9, 56, 58, 77–8, 100, 104, 106, 109, 120, 129, 147, 149–51, 158, 179, 217, 227–8, 237, 247, 253, 261, 270, 272, 294, 297, 305, 336, 338–341, 346, 350, 354, 362, 368, 371
Free Church Council 89, 94, 118–21, 375
Freedom of Birkenhead 102; Blackpool 139; Edinburgh 124; Glasgow 93; London, City of 82; Manchester 138; Neath 133–4; Salford 139
Freeman, Mrs Emma Kate 34–5, 186, 188, 190
French Flag Day, National Relief Fund (Secours National) and Relief Fund 35, 46, 186–191
French Red Cross 189–91
French Wounded Emergency Fund 55, 76
Furse, Katherine 339

G

Gallipoli 199, 203, 216, 344
Gandhi, Mahatma 47
Garreglwyd 100, 103, 122, 132, 289
Garthcelyn, Criccieth 76
Geddes, Sir Eric 151, 292; Sir Auckland 142
George, Mrs William 30, 61, 99, 335–7
George, William 61, 77, 269, 362
Girl Guides 89, 130; Guildry, Elthorne Park 87–9
Gladstone, H. N., Lord-Lieutenant of Flintshire 133
Gladstone, Mr and Mrs W. E. 67, 363
Glamorganshire 197, 208, 216
Glanusk, Lord 158, 197
Glasgow 82, 93, 162, 245
Grafton Galleries 351
Greaves, John 337; Marianne 337, 362–4
Greece 151, 177
Greenway Manor 278–84, 240; Greenway, J. L. 278
Griffith Boscawen, Sir Arthur, MP 247–8, 260–1
Guildhall, London 82, 148, 257; Swansea 208

Index

H
Hackney Reform Club 25
Haig, Field Marshal 78, 174; Haig, Lady 316
Hampstead 44, 53, 56, 212, 255–7
Hanwell, Middlesex, St Ann's School 87–9
Harlech, Lady 236; Lord 84, 158, 219
Harris, Nugent (Agricultural Org. Soc.) 99, 333
Hassall, John (writer and illustrator) 37
Heaton, Miss Mary 38, 137–8
Henry, Lady Julia 25, 354–5; Lieut. Cyril 25, 355
Herald, The, 'The Nat. Labour Weekly' 246, 324–9
Hersee, A. W. 255–6
Highland Bazaar (Fèill) 79
Hilton, Constance (Mrs J. S. Franklin) 222–3, 227, 235, 252
Hither Green PSA 290
Hodges, Frederick James 273
Holborn, Mayor, Mayoress 130, 329
Holyhead 100, 103, 122, 132, 175, 289, 350
Hopkinson, F. T. 223; Hugh 199, 216; Mrs F. T., *see* Troops Fund

HOSPITALS & HEALTHCARE
Healthcare 14, 16, 20, 33, 153, **CH 24** *336–58*
Hospitals
Aberystwyth: Infirmary 343; Red Cross 61
Alexandria, Lady de Walden Hospital 198
Anglo-Russian Hospital 59
Bodlondeb Red Cross Hospital 100, 350–1
British Women's Hospital Star and Garter Fund 54
Brondesbury Park Hospital 253
Bryn Seiont TB Hospital, Caernarfon 345–6
Bryndyffryn Hospital, Trefnant 137
Bury St Edmunds, Cross Hospital 344
Caerderwen Hospital, Neath 263
Colwyn Bay Convalescent Hospital 261
Countess of Dundonald Hospital, Eaton Square 207
Croesnewydd Military 54
Highgate Hospital War Supply Depot 146
Hospitals in Belgium, France 338
Hospital trains 43, 339
John Leigh Memorial Hospitals, Manchester 138
Kensington War Hospital Supply Depot 83
King Edward VII Hospital, Cardiff 189
Lochee Red Cross Hospital 93–4

Melchet Court convalescent hospital 296, 341
Middlesex War Hospital Depots 131
Millbank Hospital 90
Mumbles, Victoria Red Cross Hospital 86
Northwood VAD Hospital 65
NUWSS Scottish Women's Hospitals 339–40
Prince of Wales Hospital for the Limbless and Disabled, Cardiff 61, 198, 336, 347–9
Runcorn Vicarage Hospital 253
St Fagans convalescent hospital 158
Swansea General Hospital 262
War Hospital Supply Exhibition 65
Welsh Hospitals: Boer War 157, 198, 347; Bombay 199, 225
Welsh Hospital, Netley 48, 54, 61, 94, 228, 296, 336, 341–4, 351
Wern Military Hospital, Porthmadog 73, 337
Whitchurch, Cardiff 347–8
Wrexham Hospital 137; Plas Acton, Plas Darland 263
Hughes, William M., PM of Australia 55, 101, 126–7, 134, 144, 286, 332; Mary Hughes 127, 144

I
Illingworth, Percy, MP 58, Mrs Percy 290
India 26, 59, 122, 197; Indian troops 272
Influenza 76, 110, 138–9, 145, 251, 277, 330
Inglis, Dr Elsie 339
Ireland 27, 39–40, 121, 186, 209, 212, 227, 253, 268, 309, 372
Institutional Committee for Wales 260
Inter-Allied Exhibition, Cardiff 127, 261
Ipswich by-election 22
Islington 55–6; 66–7, 170
Italy 67, 151, 261

J
Jellicoe, Admiral 364; Jellicoe, Lady 316, 360
Jewel Fund 55, 125, 140, 143–4
John, Sir William Goscombe (sculptor) 223
Jones, Edna Gwenfron (Mrs Gwilym Lloyd George) 34
Jones, Col. Sir Robert, Inspector, Military Orthopedics 219, 248
Jones, Dr Gladstone 337
Jones, Haydn MP 219
Jones, J.R., of Ammanford, sock supplier 177
Jones, Private Tom, Salonica 177–8
Jones, Professor Lewis, Bangor 46

407

Jones, Towyn, MP 35
Jones, Rev., Richmond Hill, Bournemouth 89

K
Kensington 257; Palace 234; War Supply Depot 83
King George V 43, 46, 90–1, 139, 151, 153, 360–3
King's Cross Welsh Chapel 146, 288
Kingsway Hall, Holborn 41
Kitchener, Lord 57, 128, 190, 268, 344, 360

L
Labour Party 14–15, 37, 63, 75, 167, 245–6, 267, 270, 299, 324, 329
Ladies' Empress Club 90
Ladies' Gallery / Grille 68, 97–8
Lady Mayoress of London 148
Lady Thomas Convalescent Home, Holyhead 132
Lamp Day 83
Land of My Fathers, The (gift book) 46, 122, 178, 182, 194, 202, 216
Lewis, Herbert Rt. Hon, MP 271
Lewis, Herbert, of Cardiff, St John's Ambulance 175
Lewis, Mrs (Henry) 340
Lewis, William, Hon. Sec. Troops Fund
DIARY 12–13, 20, 53, 63, 81, 121, 132, 153
FUND, CH 13 156–8, early career 160–2, 164–6, 168; *CH 14* 173, 192; *CH 15* 193, 197–8, 201–6; *CH 16* 207–11, 214, 223–8; *CH 17* 230–3, 237–8; *CH 18* 239 ('Our Debt to Wales') 241–50; *CH 19* 253–4, 259–64; *RECRUITMENT, CH 20* 278–9, 281–4 (Rallying call), 289
Liberal meetings: Women's Liberal Federation 23; Croydon 26, 141; Nottingham 25–6; Central Hackney 25; Tottenham 26
Liberal Party 14, 34, 51, 53, 123–4, 151–2, 266, 376
Lichnowsky, Prince, Ambassador of Germany 28
Lifeboat Day 82
Life Story of David Lloyd George, The (film) 115
Limerick, Lady 176, 313
Lisburne, Lord 219, 248

Liverpool 4, 84, 114, 118, 160, 194, 225, 231–2
Llandrindod Wells 44–5, 186, 193
Llandudno 34, 39, 121, 157, 162, 169, 172, 174–5, 192, 204, 255, 259, 275–7, 313, 368
Llanwnda 22, 63
Llanystumdwy 103, 318
Llewelyn, Col. and Mrs Venables 278
Lleyn and Eifionydd Temperance Society 63, 364
Lloyd George American Relief Fund 36–8, 115
Lloyd George, David
In DIARY As *Chancellor of the Exchequer* 14, 16, 18, 21–2, 24, 27, 34–5, 39, 41; As *Minister of Munitions* 41, 43, 45–6, 52; As *Minister of War* 57–8, 60–1; As Prime Minister 71, 73, 75–8, 81–2, 90, 93, 95–6, 98, 102–3, 105, 109–10, 122–4 (Maurice Debate), 125–6, 134–6 (Neath), 138–9 (Manchester flu), 148–53
In Campaign chapters 157, 159–60, 186, 190, 194, 196, 216, 219, 227, 233–6, 247, 267–71 (call for a Welsh Army), 277, 288–9, 293, 299, 305, 313, 318, 343–4, 352–3, 357, 359–62, 368, 372, 376–8
Lloyd George, Margaret (selected)
Swansea with JTR 18; Recruiting nurses and troops 30; Housing refugees 31; **1915** Establishing Troops Fund 33, 156; final recruitment rally 278; Welsh Hospital, Netley 341; Negotiations with Regulator 48, 193; **1916** Criccieth WI 53; BFSS Appeal 66; Into No. 10 66; **1917** Scotland 79, 93, 124; War Economy Campaign launch 294; First Council Prince of Wales Hospital 347; East End kitchens with Lady Rhondda 297; Domestic Science training 307; **1918** Savings and Lending Campaign 'Women's Manifesto' 315; London Flag Day 255; President Free Church Women's Council 118; Scotland 124; Blackfriars Kitchen 323; Manchester with LlG 138; WI Exhibition Caxton Hall 332; Armistice 147
Lloyd George, Gwilym (son of Margaret and David Lloyd George) 32, 34, 58, 75–6, 175, 268, 271
Lloyd George, Megan 27–8, 43–7, 61, 63, 67, 73, 78–9, 82–3, 91, 99, 124–5, 134, 138–9,

Index

145, 151, 186, 236–7, 269, 289, 300, 312, 314, 319, 341–2, 345
Lloyd George, Richard (son of Margaret and David LlG) 34, 37, 60, 91, 95, 100, 115, 157, 267–8, 275, 286, 299, 318, 348, 364, 368
Lloyd George, Roberta, *see* McAlpine
Lloyd, Sir Francis 84, 219, 230
Lloyd, Richard (LlG uncle) 41, 63, 65–6, 76–8, 223, 233, 372
London Opera House 54, 215, 218–9
London Palladium 115, 125
London Underground 67, 82, 106, 128, 301
London Welsh Stage Society 54, 214
London Welsh Women's Temperance Union 146
Lord Mayor of Cardiff 82, 164–6, 187, 347–9
Lord Mayor of London 74, 111, 117, 142, 148, 194, 215, 231, 236, 251, 256–7
Ludendorff, General 134
Lusitania 40, 283
Lynn-Thomas, Col. Sir John 13, 61, 65, 198, 219, 347–8
Lyons, Joseph, Co. 215, 324–9

M

Machynlleth Rural Council 117, 255
Macnamara, Tom, MP 83, 300, 360
Maitland-Davison, Olivia of *The Tatler* 109, 351
Majority and Minority Reports (on welfare) 14
Malta 340
Manchester 84, 114, 118, 138–9, 217, 231–2, 246, 254
Mansion House (London) 27, 32, 74, 111, 142, 148, 231, 236, 251, 256–7, 289
Mappin & Webb 252, 256
Marconi 26, 95, 161
Markham, Lady 112; Miss Lucy 131
Marlborough, Duchess of 102, 117, 140, 144, 354
McAlpine family: Mr and Mrs David 137; Robert 81; Thomas 91; Roberta Lloyd George, née McAlpine 34, 37, 81, 90–1, 115, 137
McKenna, Reginald 41, 48, 158, 190
Melchet Court 94, 296, 341, 343
Memorial College, Brecon 288
Menai Bridge 170, 267, 304

Mendoza Art Gallery, Old Bond St 55, 223
Merionethshire 36, 99, 197
Merthyr 167, 174; Merthyr, Lady 236
Mesopotamia 59, 224, 237
Military Service Act 79, 285
Milligan, Sir William 139
Milner, Lord 142–3
Mond, Sir Alfred 18, 20, 74, 97–8, 159, 210, 341; daughters Eva 21, and Mary 26; *see also* Lady Mond, Fund Committee
Monmouthshire 158, 165, 175, 182, 197, 260, 343, 349, 361
Monnet, M. Raphael, Consul of France 186, 188, 191
Montgomeryshire 197, 223, 248
Morris-Jones, Professor John, Bangor 46
Motherhood 60, 284, 336, 354; *Motherhood*, film 102; Mothers and Babies Welcome, Swansea 20, 57, 86
Mountain Ash 168, 175
Munitions 33, 36, 74, 263, 361, 363–4
Munition workers/Munitionettes 25, 50, 53, 93, 106, 127, 138, 148, 224, 228, 237, 336, 354, 359; crèche 25, 354
Munitions, Minister of 11, 41, 43, 45–7, 53–4, 65, 95, 129, 182, 364
Munitions, Ministry of 46, 91, 127, 199, 216, 354–5

N

National Institute for Blind Soldiers 61
National Registration Act (the Derby Scheme) 284
National Relief Fund (NRF) 30–1
National War Savings' Committee 76
Nationalisation (catering) 324–9; (drink) 361
Neath 133–6, 141, 263,
Nepean, Mary Edith (writer) 312–3
Nesbit, Edith (children's writer) 37
New County Hall, South Bank 94, 306
New Zealand Fund 222
Newport 159, 174, 273, 340
Nichol, Professor, Boston, Mass., USA 378
Nightingale, Florence 52, 83, 339
Nivelle, General 78
Northampton 32, 175, 271–4, 361
Northcliffe, Lord 376–7
Nottingham 25–6, 89, 232

409

O

Overseas Club (Royal Over-seas League), London 85

P

Paddington 49, 118, 352
Paderewski, Jan 109
Page, Walter H., US Ambassador, and Mrs Page 297–9
Paget, Lady Louise 339
Palestine 39, 106, 223, 247
Pankhurst, Miss Christabel 93, 116
Parker, Mrs Frances 128, 360
Parker, Viscountess (Carine, née Loveden) 157
Pearson, Arthur 349, Lady Arthur 223
Pearson, the Hon. Mrs Geoffrey 236
Peel, Mrs C. S., Food Ministry 14, 295–6, 301, 306, 330
Pembrokeshire 163, 248, 197–8
Penrhiwceiber Sewing Guild 168
Penrhyndeudraeth Women's Institute hall 99, 335
Penygroes wool workrooms 38, 115
Percy Illingworth Soldiers' Institute, Aldershot 58
Pervyse, The Women of (Elsie Knocker, Mairi Chisholm) 341
Pétain, Marshal 78
Philipps, Owen, MP 198–9; Philipps, Major General Ivor 58, 199–200, 237, 268; Philipps, John Wynford, Lord St Davids 199, 218, 223
Plashet Park Congregational Church 91
'Pleasant Sunday Afternoon' PSA Brotherhoods 290–1
Plymouth, Earl of 158, 258
Poincaré, Henri, President of France 190
Poland 108–9; Polish Victims Relief Fund 109
Porthcawl 166–7, 174–5, 181
Portland, Duchess of 316
Porthmadog 73
Preston 138
Prichard-Jones Hall, Bangor 302–3
Prichard-Jones, Sir John 46, 130; Lady 130, 235
Prince of Wales 31, 218 (postcard), 233, 251; patron
Prince of Wales Fund 36, 221; Prince of Wales National Relief Fund 165, *see also* Hospitals (Prince of Wales)
Princess Christian 36, 189
Princess Royal 56
Prisoners of War, *see* Welsh Prisoners of War Fund
Prizes 43, 57, 87, 94, 96, 111, 302, 335, 352
Prohibition 80, 359, 361, 368, 370, 376–8
Pryce-Jones, Edward, MP, woollen goods trader 159
Pwllheli 24, 60, 226, 267, 269, 345, 347

Q

Queen Alexandra 31, 39, 56, 59, 88, 126, 143–4, 162, 214–5, 218, 224, 256, 349
Queen Alexandra's Field Force Fund 170, 173, 203
Queen Mary 142, 301, 332
Queen Mary's Needlework Guild 146, 195, 351
Queen Mary's Army Auxiliary Corps 131, 137, *see* WAACs
Queen's Hall, London 83–4, 96, 268

R

Radnorshire 44, 158–60, 194, 197, 201, 224, 246–7, 278–84
Railway Executive Committee 203
RAMC (Royal Army Medical Corps) 275, 337–8
Ray, Ted, golfer 193
Reading, Lord (Rufus Isaacs) 26, 150–1; Lady 26, 173, 236, 294; Gerald 26
Anglo-French Commission 150–1
RECRUITMENT 12, 30, 44, 55, 142, 242 CH 20, 266–286 Pwllheli and Cricieth meetings 267–70; Northampton 271–4; MLG article on Recruitment 274–5, Llandudno 275–7; Great Patriotic Rally, Greenway, Radnorshire 278–84; Conscription 284–5; with Billy Hughes of Australia 286
Red Cross 30, 43, 48–9, 61, 67, 86, 90–1, 93–4, 100, 109, 124, 126, 162, 180, 186, 189–92, 195, 199, 220–1, 248, 260–1, 336–8, 347, 350, 352–3, *see also* Hospitals
Red Dragon 59, 166, 216, 218, 233, 255
Rees, Lady Milsom 107, 235, 257
Regiments
Household Guards: Coldstream 268;

Index

Grenadier 268; Irish 268; Scots 268; Welsh 84, 92, 106, 175, 188, 216, 219, 236, 247–8, 268, 277
Welsh Army 12, 30, 34, 39, 59, 153, 157–8, 169, 174, 176, 180, 199, 211, 214, 242, 266, 268, 270, 274–6, 293, 344; 38th Batt./ Welsh Division 59, 97, 103, 199, 200, 237, 247, 262, 268
15th (Carmarthenshire) Batt. 222; Glamorgan Yeomanry 224–5, 278; Bantam Batt., Porthcawl 166–7
Royal Welch Fusiliers 17th Batt. 103; 18th Batt (2nd London Welsh) 176–7; 3rd Batt. 199; London Welsh Battalion 157, 191, 201;
South Wales Borderers 165; 6th Batt. 177; (Brecknockshire) Volunteer Batt. 197; 18th Welch 253; 2nd Batt. Welch 177;
Territorials 161, 165, 268, 273, 290
Irish regiments 209, 212, 227, 268
King's Royal Rifle Corps 12th Batt. 177
Royal Defence Corps 225
Royal Engineers 269, 275
Regulator (War Office) 48
Representation of the People Act 116
Retail food prices 307
Reville, Alma 139
Rhondda 174, 365
Rhondda, Lord, Viscount / Thomas, D. A. 40, 129, 159, 218, 293, 301–2, 317–19, 321–4, 329
Rhondda, Margaret, Lady 40
Rhondda, Sybil, Lady 78, 83, 102, 117, 125, 140, 218, 236, 257, 288, 293–4, 297–301, 316, 321–2
Rhyddings Congregational Church, Swansea 18
Rhyl 133, 169
Rhys, Rev. J. T.
Private Secretary 11, 230, 359, 379; Swansea 18–20; BFSS (British and Foreign Sailors' Society) Org. Sec. 287–92, 321; Temperance campaigning 13, 64; 81, 361, 365, 368, 371, 376–8; Campaigning for LlG 41; Speechwriting 120–1; Food campaigns with Lady Rhondda 288, 321–2; JTR family members 20, 118, 365
Richards, Dr Meredith, Insurance Commission 345
Richards, Alderman J. T. Mayor of Cardiff 164, 166

Richards, Mrs J. T., Lady Mayoress of Cardiff 165–6, 183–5, 187, 189, 241, 340
Riddell, Lady 64, 314; Sir George 64–5, 103, 314
Ridge, Pett, (writer) 37
Roberts, Ellis (artist) 65
Roberts, Mrs Cornelius, Mayoress of Pwllheli 60
Roberts, Mrs William, Lady Mayoress of Cardiff 348
Roberts, Field Marshal Lord 272
Roberts, R. Silyn 36–7
Robertson, Sir William, County of Fife 124
Robey, George 100, 106, 125, 231
Robinson, Agnes Mrs James, Lady Mayoress of Cardiff (former Lady Mayoress) 340, 343
Royal National Lifeboat Institution (RNLI) 66
RNVR Welsh Choir, Crystal Palace 127, 290
Royal Normal College and Academy of Music for the Blind, Norwood 96, 127
Royal Silver Wedding 128, 130
Russell, Surgeon-General C. B., Army Medical Service 348
Russia 24, 32, 35, 42, 59, 70, 221, 270, 280, 340, 352, 362, 368; Russian Revolution 82, 108, 362; Tsar of Russia 57, 127

S

SAILORS
DIARY 11–12, 15–16, 20, 31, 60, 63, 66, 69, 78, 80, 84, 108, 118, 127, 137, 144, 153
CHs 12–20 162, 167, 181, 198, 210, 221, 230, 236, 239, 249–51, 253, 258–60, 266, 284
CH 21: SAFE HAVENS FOR SAILORS, 287–92,
CHs 23–25 321, 348, 349, 353, 360, 379
British and Foreign Sailors' Society (BFSS) 12, 66–7, 69, 175; ***CH 21*** 287–92, 349
Sailors' Rest and Hostel, London 291–2
Salford 138–9, 232, 254
Salisbury 21
Salonica / Salonika 177–8, 202–3, 224–5, 340
Salvation Army 120, 183, 189, 297–9
Samson, E. Marlay 241, 248, 258, 260, 263
Save the Children 16
Sawyer, G. A. 251, 256, 258, 314; Miss Mildred 256
Sclater, Mrs, QAFFF 173

411

Scotland 79–80, 82, 90, 93, 124–5, 248, 260, 270, 340, 361, 364, 378
Scottish MPs 93; Scottish people 73, 79; Scottish troops 79–80
Selfridge, Gordon / Selfridges 24, 111–12
Serbia 28, 31, 42; Flag Day 48–9; Relief Fund 221; 261, 339–40
Shackleton, Ernest 24
Shipbuilding Employers Federation 360
Shrewsbury conference 104, 108, 214, 249–51
Slack, Agnes 52, 362–5, 367–8
Slate 37–8, 337
Smithfield Market 234–5
Smoking 106, 169, 175; Cigarettes 53, 156–7, 164, 168–9, 175, 178, 180, 212, 224–5, 228, 231, 262, 343; Virginian cigarettes 224; Tobacco 106, 157, 164, 169, 180, 224, 228, 262, 372
Smuts, General 149
Socialism / Socialist 15, 167, 329
Soldiers' and Sailors' Families Association (SSFA) 31
Somerset, Duchess of 189
Somerset, Lady Henry 129, 131, 144, 360
South Africa 151, 251, 261, 282, 347
Southall 288
Southampton 48, 61, 203, 217, 336, 341
South Wales Women's Temperance Union *Merched y De* 64, 365–8, 375–6; *Merched y Gogledd* 365
Spencer, Charles, and Mrs Charles 321, 323–4
St Asaph, Bishop of, and Mrs Edwards 133
St David's Day Flag Day, *see* Flag Days
St Davids, Lord, *see* John Wynford Philipps
St Dunstan's for the Blind 16, 130, 349
St Fagans Castle 158
St George's Day 237
St Margaret's, Westminster 39, 51, 54
Staffordshire 189, 313, 352
Staines 291
Star Wars 74
Stepney, East London 93, 297
Stobart, Mrs Clair 339
Stoll, Oswald 64, 219
Suffrage 21–3, 26, 28, 49, 65, 92–3, 98, 116, 128, 160, 186, 257, 301, 311–12, 333, 339–40, 342–3, 372–5
Sunday school 21–2, 44, 121, 165

Surgical Requisites Association 61, 107, 351
Swansea 12, 18, 20, 34–5, 49, 53, 57, 62, 64, 86, 159, 170, 177, 188, 207–10, 213, 223, 232, 258, 260, 262, 288, 321, 348, 362, 365

T
Talybont Council School, Ceredigion 172
TEMPERANCE DIARY 13, 18, 22–3, 43, 52, 54, 63–4, 78, 81, 93, 104, 122, 125, 129, 146, 153; **CH 16** 212; **CH 19** 263; **CH 20** 272; **CH 25, TEMPERANCE AND WARTIME SOBRIETY** Camberwell Patriot Club 360; Royal Pledge 360; State Purchase with Local Option 361; Criccieth military concert 361; Criccieth meeting, curbing supplies 362–4; with *Merched y De*, Swansea, recollections of Cranogwen 364–8; MLG article in 'Answers', and reactions 369–72; MLG lets 'cat out of the bag', and reactions 372–4; intemperance in Carmarthen 375–6; JTR promotes PM's proposals 376–7; Criccieth meeting 378; JTR debates 378; Agnes Slack, campaigner 52, 362–7, *see also* Prohibition
Tennant, Violet (niece, Margot Asquith) 65
Thomas, M. Albert, War Ministry, France 54, 73, 343
Thomas, Dr, Medical Officer, Caernarfon 350
Thomas, Edith and Leah 253
Thomas, Leason 216
Thomas, Brigadier / Major General Sir Owen 34, 60, 84, 103–4, 108, 118, 199, 214, 226, 232, 249–51, 258, 260, 266, 269–70
Thomas, Sir Robert J. 84, 100, 110, 132, 137, 241, 289
Thomas, Lady Robert 132
Tippett, Mrs, Food Control Campaign 303
Tobacco, *see* Smoking
Tottenham 26, 125, 323
Toys and Toy making 37–8, 302, 331, 334, 349, *see also* Trefnant
Trafalgar Square 217; flower show 127; bazaar 291
Treaty negotiations 147
Tree, Sir Herbert 40
Trefnant, Vale of Clwyd, Denbighshire 137, 176, 262

412

Index

Trocadero restaurant 215, 257

TROOPS FUND COMMITTEE MEMBERS

Bankes, Lord Justice Sir Eldon 65, 114, 219, 223, 226, 237, 251, 253

Crichton-Stuart, Lady Ninian / the Hon. Mrs A Maule-Ramsay 158, 164, 188

Davies, David, of Llandinam 58, 61, 64–5, 81, 227, 237, 239, 241, 245–6, 248, 260, 290

de Walden, Lady Howard 198

Douglas-Pennant, Hon. Violet 55, 65, 84, 121, 158–9, 164–5

Dundonald, Countess of 207, 236

Edwards, Catherine, Lady Francis 158, 224

Ellis Griffith, Mary, Mrs 23, 157–8

Evans, Sir Vincent (Treasurer) 46, 64–5, 132, 141, 156, 159–60, 163, 197, 214, 224, 226, 230, 237, 248, 261–3, 324

Glanusk, Lady 33, 44, 55, 104, 158, 170, 173, 175, 191, 194, 197, 249

Gwynne-Hughes, Beatrice, Mrs 198–9, 213, 222

Herbert, Albertina, Lady Ivor (later Lady Treowen) 158–9, 175, 223

Hinds, Mrs John 126, 157

Hopkinson, Mrs F. T. (Lilian) 198–9, 216–18, 223, 227–8, 237, 263

Lewis, Mrs Herbert 159, 194, 226

Lisburne, Countess of 248

Lewis, William, Hon. Secretary, see separate entry

Lloyd, Lady Francis (Mary) 219, 230, 355

Lynn-Thomas, Mary Rosina, Lady 198, 347–8

McKenna, Pamela, Mrs Reginald 158–9, 161, 163

Mond, Lady Violet 18–21, 26–7, 48, 57, 59, 68, 210, 225, 294, 296, 341, 344

Mostyn, Lady 199, 257

Ormsby-Gore, Beatrice, the Hon. Mrs 158–9

Philipps, Lady Owen 198, 228, 237, 256, 262–3

Plymouth, Lady, President of the Fund 59, 157–8, 165, 204, 208, 225, 262

Pryce-Jones, Beatrice, Mrs Edward 159

St Davids, Lady 223, 257

U

U-Boats, submarine warfare 12, 40, 66, 79–80, 237, 287–8, 300, 360

V

Vaillant de Guélis, see Barbier

Versailles 109, 147, 263

Victoria Cross 127

Victoria Station 48, 321; Victoria Street 85, 257, 331

Victoria Working Men's Club, Kew Gardens 117

Voluntary Aid Detachment (VAD) 126, 158, 336–9, 350

W

Waifs and Strays (The Children's Society) 58

Walton Heath 64, 124, 132, 149, 193, 318, 355, 357

War bonds 110–11, 117, 315–16, 327

War Charities Act (1916) 226

War Economy Exhibition, Bangor 86, 302

War Emergency: Workers' National Committee 14

War Hospital Supply Exhibition, Muswell Hill 65

War Office 149, 161, 168, 171–2, 178, 191–8, see also DGVO

Ward, Sir Edward 48, 192–7, 201, 203, 211, 213

Waring & Gillow 216, 252, 313–14

Waring, Mr and Mrs S. J. 252, 314

Watt, Mrs Madge 53, 332–3

Weddings: Primrose/Derby 39, 106; Bonham Carter/Asquith 51; Lloyd George/McAlpine 81–2; Carey Evans/Lloyd George 90; Hinds 126

Welsh Calvinistic Methodist 19–20, 37, 40, 43, 298

Welsh communities: Bethnal Green 52; Croydon 141; Ealing 231; Hanley, Shropshire 353; Liverpool 84, 114, 160, 194, 231–2, 254; London 20–1, 34, 54, 57, 83, 126, 146, 157, 176–7, 191, 201, 214, 218–19, 225; Manchester 84, 114, 118, 138, 217, 231–2, 254; Rosyth 124; Salford 138–9, 232, 254

Welsh Heroes Memorial 100, 107, 109, 241, 289

Welsh Housing and Development Association 97

Welsh Industries Association (WIA) 92, 166, 181, 199, 203, 207, 209

Welsh Memorial Association 345–6

413

Welsh National Bazaar (London), 1912 20, 160
Welsh National Fund for the Welfare of the Sailors and Soldiers of Wales (the combined fund) 249
Welsh National Society, Liverpool 194
Welsh National War Memorial 85
Welsh Pageant, London 106, 111
Welsh Prisoners of War Help Fund 43, 55, 115, 125–6, 131, 166, 175–6, 183–7, 192, 209, 221, 237, 241, 290
Welsh Temperance Society 78, 146
Western Front
Flanders 59, 97, 103, 275, 340–1; Loos 25, 355; Mons 158, 167, 269, Passchendaele 59, 97, 103; Pilckem Ridge 97; Ypres 97, 223, 338
Somme 58–9, 74, 82, 134, 188, 223, 273; Mametz 58–9, 65, 97; Verdun 59, 78; Vimy Ridge 82
Westminster Bridge, London 162, 217, 301, 322, 329
Whinney, Smith and Whinney, auditors 224
White City 107, 313
Whitehall, London 34–5, 46–8, 129, 149, 158, 189, 217–19, 257, 309, 344
Williams and Davies, drapers 161
Williams, Alice (WI) 99–100, 331–4
Williams, Christopher (artist) 223
Williams, Mrs J., Dulcote Wells, Somerset 147
Williams, Margaret Lindsay (artist) 122, 223
Williams, O. T., JP, Chairman, Criccieth Council 269
Williams, Percival, Mayor (Northampton) 273
Williams, Philip (Adviser Troops Fund), draper 37, 65, 161, 219, 228
Williams, R. J., Mayor of Bangor 303; Mayoress 305
Williams, Rev. John, Brynsiencyn 61, 267–9
Williams, Sergeant, Carnarvon 269
Williams, Rev. T. C. of Menai Bridge 267
Williams, T. J, Mr & Mrs, MP, Maesygwernen 134–5, 365
Williams, W. Llewelyn, MP 34–5, 46–7, 57, 376
Wilson, Woodrow, President USA 114, 298
Women's Army Auxiliary Corps (WAAC)/ Queen Mary's Army Auxiliary Corps 128, 131, 137–8, 337

Women's Auxiliary Force 128
Women's Institute (WI) 16, 53, 99, 144, 294, 331–4
Women's Land Army 332
Women's Manifesto to Women 115, 293, 315–16
Women's Royal Air Force (WRAF) 131, 151, 159
Women's Royal Naval Service (WRENs) 131
Women's First-Aid Nursing Yeomanry 340
Women's Social and Political Union (WSPU) 333
Wool 37, 38, 115, 200, 203, 223, 249,
Woolwich 25, 50, 75, 106, 128, 354
Wrexham 37, 54, 137, 175–6, 211, 232, 241, 250, 261, 263, 289

Y
YMCA 51, 53, 61, 104, 163, 203, 254, 271, 287, 304–6
Young Wales Society 160
YWCA 94, 142–3, 147–8, 224, 228–9, 306–7, 316

Z
Zeppelins 35, 43, 95, 106, 230

Praise for *The Campaigns of Margaret Lloyd George*

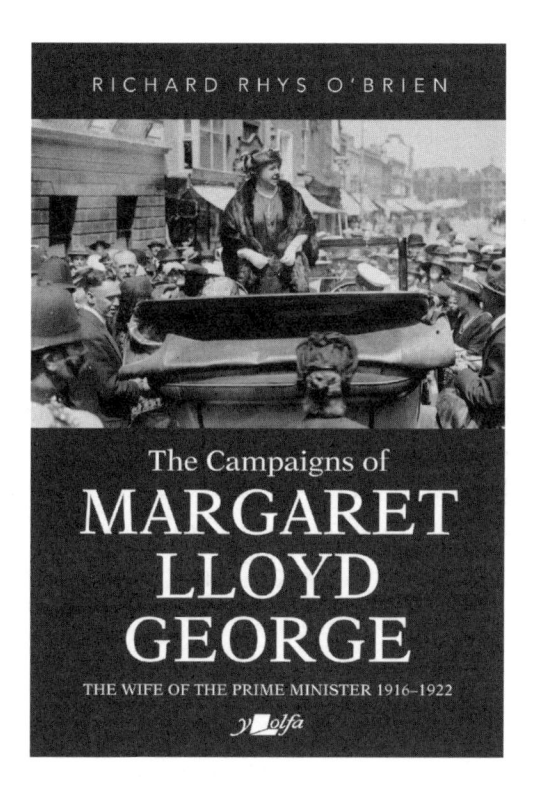

'For those studying the politics of the period, this is a gem of a book. We can learn much more about the role played within both the Liberal party and politics as a whole. It illustrates how political spin and "false news" have been around for well over a century. [Margaret Lloyd George] was certainly the most political of the prime ministers' wives in the UK in the twentieth century. Those seeking a more balanced view of history will find this a fascinating and detailed read.'

Professor Russell Deacon, visiting professor and lecturer at the University of South Wales, Chair of the Lloyd George Society, author of *The Welsh Liberals: The history of the Liberal and Liberal Democrat parties in Wales* (Welsh Academic Press, 2014)

Reviewed in *Journal of Liberal History*, Autumn 2023

'*The Campaigns of Margaret Lloyd George* encapsulates a brief, pivotal moment in modern British political history. O'Brien's account of a family his grandfather knew also offers a distinctive insight into generational change for political women and party politics over the course of the twentieth century.'

Samuel Rutherford, Lecturer in LGBTQ+ History/
History of Sexuality at the University of Glasgow.

Reviewed in *The Pelican Record*,
Corpus Christi College, Oxford, December 2023

'This fascinating book gives [Margaret Lloyd George] a far more substantial role in history. It was indeed a remarkable life for any woman in high politics then, only a year after women first gained the vote. Dame Margaret is shown as an indefatigable campaigner in national and by-elections across England and Wales. This book is an important contribution to Welsh history as well as to the story of party politics in general after the First World War.'

Kenneth O. Morgan, House of Lords

'The authentic voice of Dame Margaret Lloyd George comes through loud and clear.'

Dr J. Graham Jones, Director Emeritus,
National Library of Wales

'A meticulous and valuable contribution to our understanding of the admirable Margaret Lloyd George.'

Ffion Hague, Biographer of Margaret Lloyd George
in *The Pain and the Privilege: The Women in Lloyd George's Life*

'Thanks to the archive of the Rev. J. T. Rhys we can now understand rather better the remarkable work and words of this indefatigable woman whose influence has previously been underplayed.'

Angela V. John, President of Llafur,
the Welsh People's History Society